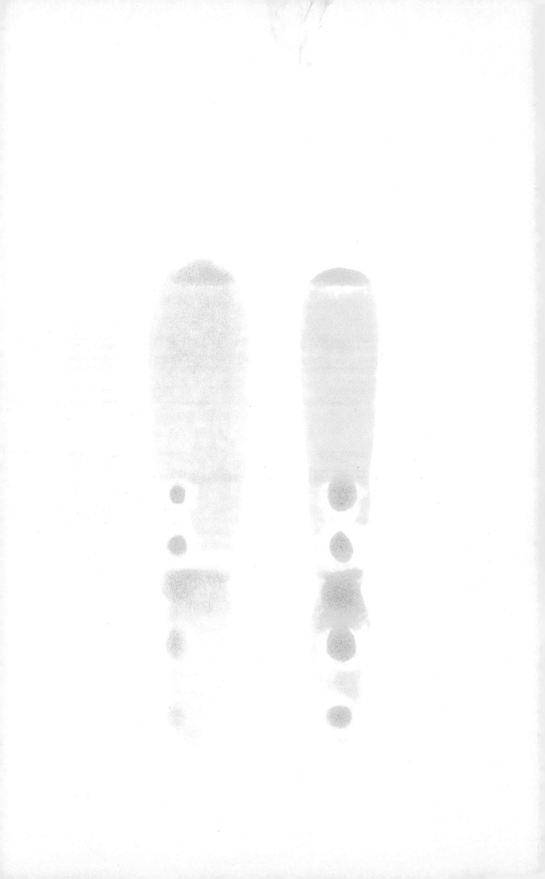

CLASS CONFLICT AND THE CRISIS OF FEUDALISM

CLASS CONFLICT AND
THE CRISIS OF FEUDALISM

ESSAYS IN
MEDIEVAL SOCIAL HISTORY

RODNEY HILTON

THE HAMBLEDON
PRESS

Published by The Hambledon Press, 1985

35 Gloucester Avenue, London NW1 7AX (U.K.)

309 Greenbrier Avenue, Ronceverte,
West Virginia 24970 (U.S.A.)

ISBN 0 907628 36 2

History Series 28

British Library Cataloguing in Publication Data

Hilton, R.H.
    Class conflict and the crisis of feudalism.
    — (History series; 28)
    1. Feudalism — England 2. England — Social
    conditions — Medieval period, 1066-1485
    I. Title
    321. 3'0942   HD604

Library of Congress Cataloging-in-Publication Data

Hilton, R.H. (Rodney Howard), 1916-
    Class conflict and the crisis of feudalism.
    Includes index.
    1. Peasantry — England — History — Addresses, essays,
    lectures. 2. Feudalism — England — History — Addresses,
    essays, lectures. 3. England — Social conditions —
    Medieval period, 1066-1485, Addresses, essays, lectures.
    I. Title
    HD604.H48   1986   305.5'0942   85-21855

Printed and bound in Great Britain by
Robert Hartnoll (1985) Ltd, Bodmin, Cornwall

29442

CONTENTS

ACKNOWLEDGEMENTS

The articles reprinted here first appeared in the following places and are reprinted by the kind permission of the original publishers.

1   *Studies in Leicestershire Agrarian History*, ed. W.G. Hoskins (Leicester, 1949), pp. 17-40.

2   *University of Birmingham Historical Journal*, ii (1949-50), pp. 31-52.

3   *Annales de l'Est*, mémoire xxi (Nancy, 1959), pp. 272-83.

4   Introduction to *Ministers' Accounts of the Warwickshire Estates of the Duke of Clarence, 1479-80*, Dugdale Society, xxi (1952).

5   Introduction to *The Stoneleigh Leger Book*, Dugdale Society, xxiv (1960).

6   *Vale of Evesham Research Papers*, II (1969), pp. 5-10.

7   *English Historical Review*, lvi (1941), pp. 90-7.

8   *Economic History Review*, 2nd series, ii (1949), pp. 117-36.

9   *Journal of Peasant Studies*, I (1974), pp. 207-19.

10   *Journal of Peasant Studies*, V (1978), pp. 271-83.

11   *Il Tumulto dei Ciompi* (Olschki, Florence, 1981), pp. 223-40.

12   *Socialism, Capitalism and Economic Growth*, ed. C.H. Feinstein (Cambridge, 1967), pp. 326-37.

13   *Urban History Yearbook* (1982), pp. 7-13.

14   *Midland History* (1982), p. 1-8.

15   *Past and Present*, no. 97 (November, 1982, pp. 3-15. World Copyright: The Past and Present Society, Corpus Christi College, Oxford, England.

16   Published here for the first time.

17   *Revolte und Revolution in Europa* , ed. P. Blickle *(Historische Zeitschrift*, Beiheft iv, Munich, 1975), pp. 31-46. Originally published in German under the title, 'Soziale Programme in Englische Aufstand von 1381'.

18   *Britain and France: Ten Centuries* (Dawson, Folkestone, 1979), pp. 39-50.

19   *Annales E.S.C.* (1951), pp. 23-30. Originally published in French under title, 'Y-eut-il une crise générale de la féodalité?'.

20   *Georges Duby. L'Arc*, 72 (1978), pp. 32-7. Originally published in French under title, 'Idéologie et Order Social'.

21   *Społeczeństwo, Gospodarka, Kultura: Studies Offered to Marian Małowist*, ed. S. Herost (Panstwowe Wydawnictwo Naukowe, Warsaw, 1974), pp. 111-28.

22   *Past and Present*, no. 1 (1952), pp. 32-43. World Copyright: The Past and Present Society, Corpus Christi College, Cambridge. Oxford, England.

23   *Past and Present*, no. 1 (1952), pp. 32-43. World Copyright: The Past and Present Society, Corpus Christi College, Oxford, England.

Introduction

The title of this collection of articles reflects a theme in my historical research which is illustrated by the earliest published piece in the collection. ('A Thirteenth Century Poem on Disputed Villein Services'). My view has been that conflict between landlords and peasants, however muted or however intense, over the appropriation of the surplus product of the peasant holding, was a prime mover in the evolution of medieval society. I also think that the social and political crises of the late medieval feudal order cannot be understood if what Marc Bloch called 'the crisis of seigneurial fortunes' is not seen as the consequence of a failure by the ruling aristocracies to keep up the level of appropriation. It will be noticed, however, that a substantial proportion of the articles here printed is concerned with the economic context within which conflicts over the level of appropriation took place. From the outset, I have tried to understand and to explain the considerable variations in the size, composition and management of landed estates. I have also (and paticularly recently) attempted to investigate the nature of medieval urbanisation, a consequence of the development of both simple, local commodity production and long distance trade in — especially — luxury goods. This has been associated, of course, with an interest in the vexed problem of the medieval origins of capitalism.

I make these points in order to emphasise that, crucial though I consider the relationships of the two main classes of medieval society to have been, these relationships can only be understood within the broad economic context - the nature of the peasant economy as well as that of the landlord, the consequences of the commercialisation (however limited) of peasant production. But this no more implies a crude economic determinism than the opposite error of a crude class-struggle reductionism. Hence, I also emphasise the positive role of ideologies — for both the rulers and the ruled.★

In spite of these over-arching themes, the reader may think that this is rather a haphazard collection of articles and introductions to texts. The principal reason for the exclusion of articles which might be thought worthwhile including in the collection is that they have been (or are about to be) re-printed elsewhere in reasonably accessible publications. This applies, for instance, to those already re-printed in my *English Peasantry in the Later Middle Ages*; in *Peasants, Knights and Heretics* (Past and Present publications); and in Volume II of *Essays in Economic History*, edited by E. Carus-Wilson. Likewise, I have not included 'A Crisis of Feudalism' which will appear in the collection of pieces which were sparked off by Robert Brenner's *Agrarian Class Structure and Economic Development* (Past and Present publications, forthcoming).

On the other hand, 'Women Traders in Medieval England' appears here almost simultaneously with its appearance in the American journal *Womens Studies* on the grounds that the journal is not familiar to most English readers. Other studies have not been re-printed on the grounds of overlap with material which appears here or elsewhere (e.g. 'Peasant Society, Peasant Movements and Feudalism in Medieval Europe', in H.A. Landsberger (ed.) *Rural Protest: Peasant Movements and Social Change* and 'A Crisis in England 1376-99', *Medievalia Bohemica* iii).

Some studies, however, which have already been re-printed, appear again. They complete the presentation of a theme (e.g. 'Capitalism, What's in a Name?' and 'Feudalism and the Origins of Capitalism').

R.H.H.

★ - For consideration of these issues, see my article 'Feudalism in Europe: Problems for Historical Materialists' in *New Left Review, No.147, 1984.*

Kibworth Harcourt—A Merton College Manor in the Thirteenth and Fourteenth Centuries

I

A great French historian has stated a view of local and economic history which all engaged in such studies should take to heart. 'Local history', he says, 'can be nothing more than the diversion of the dilettante, material for simple curiosity, if it brings nothing new to general history, by which I mean the interpretation of political and social movement. The pursuit of economic history, if it does not aim at social conclusions, if it does not enlarge or deepen the usual explanations, is equally vain'.[1] When we study, therefore, with as meticulous attention to detail as we can achieve, the social and economic movement in one manor in an English county over a short period of time, we only do so in the hope that, on the basis of this necessary detail, a wider understanding may be reached of movements only so far imperfectly explained.

The social and political changes from feudal to capitalist England have been the subject of a variety of generalisations, but we are still very much in the dark as to what sort of re-grouping in the elements of agrarian society between the 14th and 17th centuries formed the basis for the swift and radical social and political changes at the end of the period. It seems clear that the crux of the matter lies in the nature of the economic and social relationships between the producing class of rural England, the peasantry, and the class whose members (whatever their position in the tenurial hierarchy) had an enforceable claim to some portion of the peasants' surplus product. This has been recognised for many years, though the change from labour to money rents, as the expression of those changing relationships, does not have the same exclusive stress placed on it by the modern as by the older historians. We are still, however, working over the same sort of documents as were the basis for the conclusions of economic historians such as Thorold Rogers. And because these documents are the by-product of manorial administration, the manor remains our starting-point. It is right that it should be so, for the manor court was the instrument by which the peasant surplus was transferred to the lord, the focus where the balance was struck between the conflicting interests of the two sides, and where the form that the surplus took was registered. Yet the great danger remains that the actual variety of village life may be concealed by the rigid categories of the manorial formulary.

The great pioneers in the scientific study of medieval agrarian history, such as F. Seebohm and P. Vinogradoff, have, unintentionally left us with a too-simplified and unvaried picture of the manor, the village, and the estate. They were attempting to find out and describe the essential features of medieval serfdom, and consequently, in searching through documents from different regions, they were concerned to pick out the like rather than the unlike. So that, in spite of the considerable number of the regional studies that have subsequently diversified our picture of the medieval social structure, most of us still have a mental picture of the 'typical' unit of English rural life as being a norm from which we admit a number of interesting though perhaps not vital variations. Our norm for the central period of the middle ages (say the twelfth and thirteenth centuries) is the village which coincides with the manor. This 'normal' manor is one amongst anything from, say, five to thirty which make up the estate of the abbot, bishop, baron, or knight, who is the lord. In it there is a manor-house, a lord's demesne, and peasant tenements.[2] The demesne and tenements are mostly scattered over two or three arable fields, though there are some small enclosures around the houses of the nucleated village. The needs of mixed farming are met by the existence of common rights over wood, waste, and stubble. The peasants are divided into a minority of freeholders and cottagers and a majority of villeins, who each hold fifteen to thirty acres, and owe predial services as well as rents in money and kind.

Of course every historian nowadays says that this typical manor only existed as an exception. Nevertheless it has been a useful model by whose help we can understand the nature of the lord-serf relationship. The original constructors of the model hardly wished to do more than to demonstrate this. Now, having progressed a stage further, we must make an effort to understand the historical significance of the exceptions, while still bearing in mind the equally important historical significance of the norm. For the defect of the 'typical' manor as a model was that the social structure that was demonstrated in it did not reveal any factors making for change. There was no apparent reason (apart from agencies like money and plague, incorrectly considered as impacts from without) why the typical manor should not have gone on indefinitely without serious change. The problem has been to explain the phenomena which heralded the disintegration of those economic and social relations which we have regarded as typical of feudal society: phenomena such as peasant accumulation of property and class differentiation on the one hand, and the lord's withdrawal from economic activity on the other. The answer seems to lie in the investigation of those manifold variations which make possible the generation, within one system, of the elements of its successor. The most modest local investigation, such as is attempted in this paper, can perhaps help us along the way.

The Hundred Rolls of 1279 are evidence which allow us to see something of the real life of the thirteenth century village beneath the manorial pattern.[3] The answers which village jurors gave to the royal commissioners did not of course ignore the manor and its lord, for they dominated the jurors' lives. What those answers enable us to do is to see how and where village and manor fit together. We are shown villages dominated not by one, but by a variety of lords. We see manors within the village which bear no resemblance to our preconceived ideas of what a manor should be like. We see groups of tenants in one village who are part of a manorial organisation centred in another village. The complexities of the social relationships revealed are much greater than we would have gathered by confining ourselves to manorial material alone. But unfortunately these rolls are almost unique, so that we may, through the intensity of our interest in them, be misled into assuming too great a permanency for the social and tenurial structure which they mirror.

Unfortunately, the Rolls of 1279 survive for only a few of the English counties, and not all of these are printed.[4] There are no surviving Rolls for Leicestershire. All that we have is a transcript of a document made by William Burton, the early 17th-century antiquary.[5] There is much less detail in Burton's transcription than there is in the printed Rolls, or in such unprinted contemporary transcripts as that which records the answers of the jurors of two hundreds in Warwickshire.[6] Only the two hundreds of Guthlaxton and Gartree are covered, and even here there are some omissions. Yet there is sufficient evidence in these transcripts to give us some idea of the complexity of the manorial structure of the county. Such in fact is the complexity, that considerable difficulty is experienced in reducing the information to a statistical form. The reduction itself inevitably conceals many of those details which could hardly be expressed in a simpler manner than in the original itself.

The first point of interest which can be illustrated in figures concerns the coincidence of village and manor. There are in all 134 villages for which information is given concerning the number of lords owning land and tenants. Only 37 of these 134 villages, or about 28 per cent., have one manorial lord only over them. Not all of these 37 are 'normal' in the sense of containing both demesne and tenant land. Twenty-eight contain both, but in eight villages there was no demesne land, and in one there was apparently no tenant land. In a further 34 villages there were two ruling lords, though only in eleven were there two manors, both comprising demesne and tenant land. In the remaining 63 villages the tenants owed their rents and services to three or more lords. The number of lords varied considerably, but there were few villages with more than two manorial demesnes. In most cases those lords, beyond the two or three who owned demesnes with tenants attached, merely had groups of tenants owing suit of court, rent, and service, but no demesne land. However, the prominence of these groups of tenants emphasizes the complexity of the tenurial situation at the time, a complexity not without its social and economic significance.

One of the most interesting villages from the point of view of the complexity of manorial structure was Kibworth Harcourt in Gartree

Hundred. I will give a full transcript of the entry, since it is not printed in Nichols' *History of Leicestershire,* and since it is a good sample of the type of entry to be found in these transcripts.[7]

> Dicunt quod sunt in eadem quinque carucatas terre de quibus Scholares domus Walteri de Merton in Oxon' habent tertiam partem ville cum toto dominico unde tenent in dominico duas virgatas terre, in villenagio duas virgatas. Thomas de Wortinges tenet in dominico unam virgatam, in villenagio unam virgatam. Alanus de Portesmue in dominico unam virgatam, in villenagio unam virgatam. Magister Robertus de Pwelle[8] in dominico unam virgatam, in villenagio unam virgatam. Thomas Tayllard in dominico unam virgatam, in villenagio unam virgatam. Hubertus de Told duas carucatas & dimidiam que tenentur in villenagio. Henricus Person dimidiam virgate & quartam partem unius virgate. Nicholas Sab[9] dimidiam virgate. Willelmus de Reynes dimidiam virgate. Robertus Polle dimidiam virgate. Robertus Harin dimidiam virgate. Ricardus filius Rogeri dimidiam virgate. Mathildis filia Fabri unam virgatam. Johannes Boton dimidiam virgate. Johannes Sibile dimidiam virgate & tenetur de Ricardo de Harecurt & Ricardo de Comite de Warewike & Comes de rege in capite & dat eidem scutagium pro dimidio feodi.

Here we have six lords, five of whom have manors consisting of both demesne and tenant land, and a group of small freeholders. The tenurial relation between the largest lord, Merton College, and the rest is a little vague, since the phrase 'cum toto dominico' does not lend itself to precise interpretation, but taken as it stands the passage would suggest the sort of social structure which Professor Stenton has taught us to expect in this very part of the world,[10] and which is also to be found in parts of eastern England.[11] When we examine the history of this village more closely, however, we find that this state of affairs had only just come into being and was soon to change again.

Not many years before the evidence contained in the Hundred Rolls was collected, another royal enquiry had been made into the affairs of Kibworth Harcourt. This was in 1265, when an extent was made of the confiscated lands of Saer de Harcourt, the King's enemy. Kibworth Harcourt was one of Saer's manors, having been made over to him as provision for a younger son, by his father Richard in 1258, together with the manor of Newton Harcourt, also in Leicestershire.[12] In 1265 Saer was clearly the immediate lord of the greater part if not the whole of the village. He had a manorial demesne of nine virgates (probably about 200 acres of arable) and a dependent peasantry consisting of villeins holding 18 virgates, together with free tenants and cottars about whose land no details are given, and a miller. The King's rancour towards Saer was remitted in 1267, and the land was officially restored by Saer's immediate lord, represented in this case by Alice, widow of William Mauduit, Earl of Warwick.[13] But the events of the civil war had apparently involved Saer in financial difficulties, so that he was obliged to sell his manor of Kibworth. It was as a result of this sale that the curious situation recorded in the Hundred Rolls came about.

II

Kibworth Harcourt in 1270 became part of the *Vetus Fundatio* of the scheme for the maintenance of scholars at Oxford, begun as early as 1262 by Walter of Merton, King Henry III's Chancellor. This enterprise evolved quickly from a trust vested in the Priory of Merton, Surrey, for the support of the scholars at the university, to the establishment of England's first University collegiate body, whose members lived together, were governed according to statutes drawn up by the founder, and were, by the date of the definitive statute of 1274, supported by an estate including land in fourteen villages scattered through six counties.[14] Merton College has been more fortunate in the historians concerned with its scholastic importance than in those interested in it as an estate owner. J.E. Thorold Rogers in his *History of Agriculture and Prices* drew very considerably on the estate records of Merton College for his evidence as to prices, and his second chapter entitled 'Medieval Agriculture' is based largely on the conclusions he drew from studying those records.[15] But Rogers did not intend to make a systematic study of the estate as an economic enterprise, and this still remains to be done. Mrs. E. C. Lowry has gone part of the way in an excellent study of the College's Cambridgeshire manors during the 14th century.[16] This work, unfortunately still unpublished, begins with a survey of the administration as a whole, before going on to a detailed study of the Cambridgeshire estates. Beyond these two works little seems to have been done, although the manuscript material available for a detailed study of the College estates is immense. For Kibworth Harcourt alone, there are almost unbroken series of reeves' accounts and court rolls from the late 13th to the 17th centuries,[17] rentals of the late 13th and early 14th centuries,[18] and a large number of deeds excellently catalogued and described by the late W. H. Stevenson.[19] Of this abundance of material for one manor alone, I claim only to have touched a fragment for the purpose of elucidating some of the problems under discussion.

Walter of Merton gave Saer de Harcourt £400 for Kibworth Harcourt.[20] If the price of the land at this time was normally ten times its annual value,[21] this would appear to have been a not abnormal transaction. The *inquisition post mortem* on Richard de Harcourt in 1258 had given the annual value of the manor as £30, and such inquisitions must often have underestimated in the interests of the heir. Saer appears to have been anxious to raise money, for he had already transferred, possibly as security for debt, the whole manor, less the advowson, to John le Ferron (Farrier) citizen of London.[22] Hence, as part of the transaction with Walter of Merton in 1270, John le Ferron also made a grant to Walter of the manor, and this time the advowson, of Kibworth Harcourt.[22a] This was probably a necessary measure by which Walter protected himself against claims on the manor. Another such safeguard has survived among the college records in the form of a copy of an enrolment of a deed of acquittance dated 1270. This was given by a Jew named Cok, son of Cresse, for any claim he might have on the manor on account of Saer's debts to him.[23]

Although Kibworth Harcourt is counted among the manors of the Old Foundation of Merton College, the college did not acquire complete control for some time. As the 1279 Hundred Rolls transcript makes clear, Walter made over to the College only one third of the manor, keeping the rest in his own hands. Walter was a man of strong family feeling, as early details of his scholastic foundation show. The first eight scholars to be supported at Oxford under this scheme were his own nephews and the founder's kin were subsequently to have rights of priority.[24] Similarly in 1276/7 he gave his sister Edith, wife of Thomas Tayllard, 8 marks of rent for life chargeable against 11 specified tenements in the manor.[25] The nephews who were provided for at Oxford in 1262/4 were not the only progeny of his prolific sisters who benefited from his generosity. Walter died in 1278 and his heirs were found to be: Christiana de Wortynges (wife of Thomas of Worting near Basingstoke), Agnes de Ewelle (wife of Gilbert of Ewell), Edith (wife of Thomas Tayllard), being three of his sisters; Peter de la Clyve, son of Walter's sister Alicia, Alan de Portemuwe (Portsmouth), son of his sister Mathilda, and Richard Olyver, another nephew. Seisin was granted, to be divided between the heirs, saving the right of Merton College in the manor, and the chief messuage and chattels to Saer de Harcourt.[26] The lords of four of the small manors in Kibworth Harcourt, described in the Hundred Rolls a year or so after Walter's death, had clearly become so established as his heirs,[27] and it took time and money before the College could get rid of them.

Between 1278 and 1280 the rights of Richard Oliver, Peter de la Clive, Agnes of Ewell and her sons Robert and William, Alan of Portsmouth, and Thomas of Worting had been transferred. The College paid 66 marks for Oliver's share, 13 marks and the education of his sons at Oxford for de la Clive's share, and 60 marks for Worting's share.[28] How much was paid for other shares is not known. The policy of achieving complete control was carried on after this initial brief sweep. A man who had received a couple of bovates with their servile tenants from Saer de Harcourt in 1263 was bought out for £5 in 1284,[29] but there were still complicated negotiations ahead before the complete unification of the manor came about.

The earliest extant reeve's account roll of Kibworth Harcourt is for 1283-4,[30] and the entries under the heading *Assize Rent* show traces of the divided possession of the village. The rents from the parts that had belonged to Thomas Tayllard, Alan of Portsmouth, and Robert of Ewelle are accounted for separately from the rents from the original scholars' part. There is no mention of rent from Thomas of Worting's part, but he and his tenants are entered as paying chevage. This suggests that the transfer of his part, though recorded in two deeds of 1280,[31] had that the transfer of his part, though recorded in two deeds of 1280,[31] had not yet taken place. Possibly the reason for this is that the College did not pay the 60 marks for his part until 1283 or 1284.[32] At this date too, although the College reeve was collecting the rent from Thomas Tayllard's part of the village, amounting to £5 8s. 1½d., he had to pay out again 'ad opus Tayllard' nearly the same amount, possibly in acquittance of the 8 marks charge on the manor granted by Walter of Merton to his sister, Edith Tayllard.[33]

Edith and her husband Thomas Tayllard were unwilling to abandon their interest in Kibworth Harcourt. In 1290, when Edith's son Robert renounced by deed his own claim as an heir to Walter of Merton,[34] his parents were engaged in a suit with the College for two messuages, a fraction of another messuage, one and a half virgates, and a mill as Edith's inheritance.[35] This estate was one which Agnes, widow of Saer de Harcourt, had obtained after 1283 as dower.[36] We do not know whether the Tayllards were successful in their suit, but this land as a separate estate was not renounced in favour of the College until 1309. This was done by William Seneschal of Evesham, and in the deed the estate is described as having been Agnes' dower.[37] The extent of this renunciation is not however clear, for as late as 1324 the College reeves were accounting for rents from the demesne *less* William of Evesham's part. Indeed, a rental of about this period gives details of the lands that William of Evesham had once had, consisting of 3½ virgates held by three tenants, a mill, and part of the manor house, the total value being £2 15s. 8d. a year.[38]

Apart from this late survival of two somewhat confused claims, the College appears to have successfully liquidated most of the separate interests of the heirs of its founder with fair speed—mostly by the end of the 1280's. There was, however, an estate mentioned in the 1279 evidence which has not yet been discussed—the two and a half carucates held in villeinage under Hubert de Told. The name of Hubert de Told does not appear again in the Kibworth documents, but so considerable a holding can hardly escape mention amongst such a wealth of material as exists for this village. We find that, as late as the second half of the 14th century, the Kibworth Harcourt reeves were still accounting separately for the rents of free and villein tenants once belonging to a certain Laurence of Apetoft, amounting in all to £8 15s. 4d.[39] The separate identity of this small estate must have been much more strongly established than that of the ephemeral manors of Merton's nephews, for otherwise it could hardly have remained even as a name for so long. There is a document dated 1288 in the possession of the College which records a recognition by an inquest into the services owed from the tenants of Laurence of Apetoft.[40] This recognition goes back to the days of William de Harcourt (d. 1230) in order to establish the form of the services, and the implication appears to be that this Laurence was William's contemporary.[41] Whether this was so or not, the jury goes on the tenement on farm for a term of years from Saer. He was followed by another farmer for a term, and then first John le Ferron (Fferun), and afterwards Walter of Merton held the lands in fee. The recognition finishes by saying that these customs were used until the scholars of Merton leased the tenement to farm again.

The date on which this property was fully taken over by the College is not at first apparent. The recognition quoted is vague about the matter, since that was not one of the things about which the jury had to speak. There is, however, a deed which records the transfer to two Fellows of the College[42] of a property in Kibworth Harcourt from a certain William of Ingwardby (Ingarsby) and his wife, in or about the year 1295. It was then transferred to the College by the two Fellows, under licence, and confirmed by a final concord of June 1301.[43] The property consisted of eight messuages, six virgates and two acres in villeinage, and four virgates in free tenure. The rents of the villein tenements are not given in the conveyances, but the information is given in a letter close of 1326.[44] This letter was an instruction to the escheator to leave these lands in the College's possession. In 1299, it seems, when the two Fellows were transferring the property to the College, the Earl of Warwick (d. 1315) had seized it on pretext of the Statute of Mortmain, though he was not the immediate lord of the fee.[45] He held it until five days before his death and then restored it to the College. The most interesting part of this letter is that which describes this property as a *manor* held at half a knight's fee, and having an annual value of £8 15s. 4d. This cleariy identifies it as the tenement *quondam Laurence de Apetoft,* and although the holding of Hubert de Told in 1279 was described as being held in villeinage, the coincidence of its size (2½ carucates equals 10 virgates) with that of the Apetoft tenement makes it likely that in fact they were identical.

The object of recounting the somewhat tedious process by which Merton College gradually bought up the owners of small manors and estates in Kibworth Harcourt, has been to show how the purpose of a determined landlord was able to transform the social structure of a village in which at first he only had a minority holding. Professor Stenton has already indicated that this process of consolidation and levelling was carried out by the new Norman lords in the Northern Danelaw soon after the Conquest.[46] It was a policy which would naturally be continued during the thirteenth century, the age par excellence of the improving feudal landlord. But once the whole village was placed under single control, economic trends of a different character started off a contrary process of disintegration. Before showing some of the features of this disintegration, we may draw on our documents to show something of what these small manors that the College was swallowing up consisted.

One of the by-products of this process of absorption was a spate of rentals, drawn up between 1280 and about 1340, with the apparent purpose of showing to the administrators of the College estates exactly what the facts of a complicated tenurial situation were. Nine out of ten of the extant Kibworth Harcourt rentals fall within this period, the tenth being a rental of the year 1527. It is from these rentals that we are able to see what went to make up the manor of a Portsmouth, an Apetoft, a Ewelle, or a Tayllard.

One of a bundle of small membranes[47] contains a rental and demesne terrier of the *Pars quondam Alan de Partismowe.* There is no date, but it must belong to the decade or so after the release by Alan of Portsmouth of his claim, for the names of the tenants occur in various deeds of the period.[48] According to this document Alan had four free and five villein tenants. The holdings of the free tenants were half a virgate; a virgate; a piece *(placea)*; another piece. Judging by contemporary rentals covering the whole village, these tenants held land only of Alan. The five villein tenants held half a virgate each. In addition Alan had a dovecote, a mill part of the perquisites of the court,[49] and the chevage of his tenants.

Most interesting, however, is the terrier of his demesne land estimated elsewhere at one and a half virgates, but here described down to the last selion. This demesne was distributed over three fields, being East field, Hore field, and West field. In the East field Alan had 36 selions, three roods, and a complete furlong *(cultura).* The selions and roods were distributed in twelve blocks, varying in size between one and five selions, the blocks being in ten different cultures, furlongs, or wongs, whose names are given. In Hore field, he had 45 selions and one-third of a culture, distributed in 16 blocks of a similar size to those in East field, over fifteen named furlongs. In West field there were 32 selions, three butts, and a complete culture, the selions and butts being distributed in 13 blocks over 11 named furlongs. Meadow and pasture is not described except as appurtenant to the land in each of the three fields. This is the only terrier of its kind in all the Kibworth Harcourt documents, except for one deed of 1270 conveying eight acres, whose location in the fields is described in similar detail.[50] Both show that the consolidation of strips was little advanced at the time.

The uncertainty that was apparently felt by the College authorities at the time as to the tenurlal arrangements and that prompted them to draw up six almost contemporary rentals (roughly 1280-1290) is illustrated by variations of detail in another rental[51] showing Alan of Portsmouth's part. This rental is shorter than the first, for there is no demesne terrier. According to this, there were in Alan's part only three free tenants. The five villein tenants of the first rental are present, but in addition to them there is a reeve's widow holding a whole virgate. Alan is also credited now with ten shillings' worth of pasture and a rent of two shillings.

Information about the other little manors is less detailed than that about Alan of Portsmouth's part. We know that Laurence of Apetoft had ten virgates, four of which were free and six villein,[52] but neither in the rentals nor in the manorial accounts is there any trace of demesne land. However, the enquiry of 1288 into the works owed[53] from Laurence's tenants showed that at one time they had to plough thrice a year on the demesne and do reaping services. But Walter of Merton's other heirs, as we know from the Hundred Rolls, had demesne as well as tenant land, and the rentals give us details of some of these.

That part of Kibworth once in the possession of the Ewelle family can also be reconstructed. It is mentioned in only one of the rentals of this period, which is in bad condition and scarcely decipherable.[54] It appears that this share, like that of Alan of Portsmouth, had its virgate and a half of demesne, its ox pasture, valued at 10 shillings, its share of dovecote, mill, and perquisites of the view of frankpledge. The tenants were five villeins, each holding half a virgate, and three cottages. It was charged, as was Portsmouth's part, with a portion of the rent due to the Tayllard family. Then there are two rentals that include a description of the remaining two little manors, those of Worting and Tayllard.[55] The demesne land of each was one virgate; Worting had four tenants, holding two and a half virgates; and Tayllard had five, holding two and a half virgates and a cottage.

There are no further details of interest about these last manors, apart from the curious fact that one half of the demesne and half of the tenants of each is described on one of the rentals and the other half of each on the other rental. What one would have expected would have been a full description of one manor on each membrane. A proper explanation of this division might lead us back into pre-conquest folklore; for on the one membrane one half of the demesne of each manor is described as being *ex parte umbre*, on the other membrane the other halves as *ex parte solis*. An attempt has been made to explain these terms by derivation from the Scandinavian *solskift*.[56] It is suggested that the order of the strips in the furiongs was not only determined by the position of the owners' tofts in the village, but that they were counted in a clockwise direction round the fields in imitation of the sun's course. Hence the strips in each furlong, according to their conventional proximity to a sun travelling clock-wise round the fields, would be described as being 'on the sunny side' or 'on the shady side'. That there was some strong convention in Kibworth is indicated by the curious splitting of the rental, the reflection, no doubt, of the order in which a local jury recited the tenements as it knew them. It is obvious that merely to translate *ex parte umbre* and *ex parte solis* as 'North' and 'South' in a three-field village would not meet the case, but neither is the evidence sufficient to justify the tentative *solskift* hypothesis.

III

This consideration of the composition of the small manors gradually bought up by Merton College brings us to ask what sort of a manor that institution had achieved as a result of these negotiations. It may well be that the two curious complementary rentals described above mirrored the penultimate phase of the College's achievement of manorial unity. For these two rentals do not merely contain an account of the sunny and shady sides respectively of the manorial demesnes late of Worting and Tayllard, and of the tenants under the lords of those demesnes. There are, in addition, the names of other tenants, some of which occur in rentals of Portsmouth's and other parts. Each of these two rentals ends its lists of tenants' names with a valuation of one third of each of the appurtenances of the demesne, such as one third of the dovecote, one third of the mill, one third of the perquisites of the court, and three virgates of demesne land valued at 20/- a virgate. The two thirds which these two rentals together describe may then well be that part of Walter of Merton's inheritance which went to his sisters and nephews when the remaining third was reserved to the College. The total value of each third on each of the two rentals is identical, being £9 12s. 6¾d. If we turn next to a rental which appears to contain a list and valuation of all tenements and all parts of the demesne that stood outside the Apetoft manor, we find a grand clear total of £28 18s. 10d. almost exactly thrice the valuation of the separate thirds.[57] Having got all this down on parchment does not seem entirely to have satisfied the College administration, for there are three other rentals,[58] containing substantially the same information, except for a few variations in tenants' names, and which must therefore have been drawn up within comparatively few years of each other. The tenurial situation must have become clear before 1301,[59] for the next group of rentals seem to have been prepared with a different problem in view—the disintegration and regrouping of small tenements from about the second decade of the 14th century.

It might have been supposed that the object of the absorption of the whole village of Kibworth Harcourt into the College manor was to make possible a more profitable use of the manor's resources, according to the precepts of the Founder.[60] This might be best achieved, not only by adding to the rent-roll, but, following the contemporary practice of most big landlords, by extending the cultivation of the demesne so as to take advantage of the favourable state of the market for agricultural produce. We know from the 1279 Hundred Rolls that the College had then two virgates of its third of the village in demesne.[61] Yet as the manor was expanded, demesne cultivation was abandoned, though this was not the policy for the estate as a whole. Demesne production was not abandoned on the Cambridgeshire manors until the second half of the 14th century.[62] For some reason Leicestershire demesne farming was not profitable, and local market conditions may have been the reason for this.[63]

Very early on, then, Merton College became, and remained, a rentier as regards its Kibworth manor. The earliest account roll extant, that of 1283-4, shows that at this date no demesne was cultivated. It does not

not profitable, and local market conditions may have been the reason for this.[63]

Very early on, then, Merton College became, and remained, a rentier as regards its Kibworth manor. The earliest account roll extant, that of 1283-4, shows that at this date no demesne was cultivated. It does not give as much information about the other sources of income as the later accounts. The reeve is much more concerned to account for his expenditure, which he does in great detail. The rentals already mentioned, which are roughly contemporary with this account, give a good overall picture of the village, less, of course, the Apetoft manor.[64] The resources of the manor house and its immediate appurtenances were worth 16/- a year; the mill 42/- a year; and 8 virgates of demesne land, £9 12s. 0d. The majority of tenants were customary tenants, of whom 24 held half a virgate, 3 a whole virgate, and one a virgate and a half. The rents of half virgates varied between 6/- and 7/-, but the works were all valued at 3/4 from the half and 6/8 from the whole virgate. There was one large free tenant with three virgates, 5 holding one virgate each, and 3 holding half a virgate each. One toft holder was counted among the free tenants, but the other rentals make it clear that those who were entered under the 'cottager' rubric were also of free condition. There were 8 of them, each paying 2/- for a toft. Their surnames show their rôle in the economy of the village—a shepherd, a miller, two brokers, a laundress, a 'medicus', and a skinner. Together with £1 as the estimated profit of the view of frankpledge, the annual value of the manor is variously estimated between £31 and £32, with charges such as £2 5s. 0d. to the Tayllards and 6/5½ to William of Evesham to be offset. In practice the receipts of the College from its manor varied somewhat from the level set by the rental. By 1320 the actual money paid over in one year of account to the College Bursars (*depositarii*) was £44 14s. 8d.[65] The year of account on this occasion ran, not from Michaelmas to Michaelmas as on most estates, but from the Feast of St Kenelm (July 17) to that of the Translation of St Thomas the Martyr (July 7). A sum of £14 4s. 10d. was paid over against a tally to the Bursars after the rents due at the Michaelmas term were taken; £12 19s. 10d., also against a tally, after the taking of rents at the term of the Purification (February 2); and a further £17 10s. 0d. *super compotum* was paid over at the annual audit.[66] A good proportion of the increased yield was due of course to the increase of assize rents resulting from the acquisition of the Apetoft manor.[67] There was no significant increase in the rents from demesne, but there was a considerable increase over the amount allowed for in the rental in the yield of the courts. Eight courts and two views of frankpledge had been held during the course of the year of account, and the profits, swelled by an entry fine of 5 marks from a demesne lease, amounted to £7 2s. 11d.[68]

Manorial expenses were small, covering the needs of the steward at the courts and of the reeve bringing rents to Oxford, reclaiming stray beasts,

College estates that Kibworth Harcourt would provide a steady rent revenue, and that intervention in the affairs of the village could be limited to the steward's presidence over the courts for the purpose of regulating the succession to tenements and punishing minor transgressors. The reeve, chosen by the villeins from among themselves, was the responsible accountant, but would in practice be little more than a rent collector. But the abandonment of demesne farming had very important consequences which contemporaries may not have observed. It is true that during a period of stable or falling prices,[70] the payment by the average villein holding half a virgate, of a quarter of a mark as a commutation of labour services, may have pressed harder on him that the obligation to work on the manorial demesne.[71] If the rent, in whatever form it is rendered, is conceived as a portion of the peasant's surplus product, it is clear that the obligation to render it in money transfers the burden of marketing the product from the lord to the peasant. On the other hand the abandonment of demesne production had two results advantageous to, at any rate, some of the peasants. In the first place, since there was no longer any need for serf labour on the demesne, manorial labour discipline with many of its implications would disappear, to be replaced by the discipline of the rent-collector. In the second place it is no longer as necessary for the lord to maintain the integrity of the holding as the source of labour service. As long as a virgate or half virgate had to produce a number of men to work in the fields, it was necessary to keep it whole as the source of those men's subsistence. When it only had to yield money rent it could conveniently be divided, or frequently alienated, without the total rent of necessity diminishing. This tendency to disintegration always starts, as might be expected, with the free tenements, most of which, in Kibworth Harcourt as elsewhere, owed mainly money rent.[72] But it also affects the villein tenements, though these are thrown on to the land market after demesne land and the free tenements.

The relaxation in the immediate control over the manor by the lord, resulting from his becoming a rentier, produces a situation in which the circulation of land among the villagers becomes easier, tending therefore to be more rapid than previously. It is in a freer land market of this sort that the successful farmers are able to add still further to their holdings from both demesne and tenant land, and to form the source for later recruitment to the ranks of the gentry.[73] It is not proposed to illustrate this from the Kibworth Harcourt records, though clear cases of peasants thriving to gentry status exist,[74] but to end this paper some of the evidence for the swifter circulation of land in the first half of the 14th century will be described.

This rapid circulation of tenements is curiously illustrated by a rental of about the middle of the century.[75] It is a full rental of the village, including the tenants of the Apetoft manor. The top of the roll is badly decayed, so that the list of free tenants is almost entirely illegible. The customary tenants, all the Apetoft tenants, the cottagers, and the lessees of the demesne can easily be read. The rental shows tenements changing hands three or even four times, changes which are revealed by additions and interlinings on the original membrane. To give an example: the second entry in the list of customary tenants tells us that Alice Leye holds half a virgate, at one time in the tenure of Robert, son of Robert Nichol, paying 6/7½ rent and 40d. for works. The name Alice Leye is crossed out and two names are interlined. Boldly interlined is the name Hugh Thorp, and in a fainter ink the name John Carter, a name which seems to be that of an intermediate tenant between Alice Leye and Hugh Thorp.

There are 31 names of customary tenants holding tenements at the date of the original compilation of the rental. Of these 26 are half virgators, 4 hold one virgate each, and one holds a piece of land. In 11 cases the name of the previous tenant is given, but only 4 of the 11 have the same surnames as their successors. By the date of the boldly interlined alterations, all the tenements except one had changed hands.[76] The same number of tenements was now held by 24 instead of 31 tenants, for some men were now holding twice as much land as their predecessors. Of these 24, only 7 bear the same surnames as the previous tenants. The intermediate set of alterations only affects 14 tenements, and in only 4 cases have the new tenants the same surnames as those they have succeeded. Also only 4 tenements have 3 successive tenants with the same surname. Almost all the surnames in this rental are old-established village surnames, so that, in the great majority of cases a change of surname from generation to generation can be ruled out.

These facts suggest a remarkable interchange of tenements among the village population. In some cases these interchanges can be followed through. William Gilberd held half a virgate at the time of the original compilation of the rental, but his successor was John Nogge. In the meantime, William Gilberd had taken over another half virgate, once belonging to Alice Allot, and before her to William Allot. It was to this half virgate that Nicholas Gilberd, presumably William's heir, succeeded; and we find from a list of demesne lessees at the end of the rental[77] that both Nicholas Gilberd and John Nogge each had taken on some demesne land—three quarters and a quarter of a virgate respectively. It would be possible to produce many similar instances of changes of tenements, giving an impression of a much freer market in land than we usually think of at this time. Even more remarkable things can be seen from the same rental to have been happening to the tenements of the old Apetoft manor. Two of the free virgates of this property[78] had become completely disintegrated. By the time of the rental a virgate once held by Hugh Harcourt was divided among 15 tenants, the pieces varying in size between one rood and 6 acres. These 15 had had 13 predecessors as lessees, only in two cases bearing the same family name. The virgate once belonging to Robert Hokke was first split up among 9 lessees, the predecessors of 8 who were lessees at the time of the rental, but 5 of these pieces when changing hands kept in the same family. The virgate was split into ten parcels, one large one of 15 acres which kept in one family, and 9 small parcels varying in size between a quarter of a rood and one acre and a quarter of a rood.[79] No similar disintegration had happened to the other virgate and two half virgates in free tenure in the Apetoft manor, but none of the 7 tenants who at various times succeeded to these three holdings appear to have been related by blood. It may also be noted that the majority of the lessees of these free virgates, whether taking on lease small or large parcels, were villeins.

The customary virgates of the Apetoft manor did not become divided as did the free virgates. But they were subject to the same process of circulation as the rest of the customary tenements of the village. Eight tenants were succeeded by six, who had no apparent relationship to their predecessors, nor had the five who succeeded the six. This lack of continuity is also characteristic of the succession to the tofts. Only one of eight descended within the family, and that family was not a cottager family of the earlier sort—village tradesman or smallholder—but one of the more prosperous villein families with considerable holdings in the open fields. These holdings, as they had descended to the latest representative of the family in the rental, William Polle, may illustrate the varying provenance of different parts of a 14th century villein's lands. This William succeeded to the half virgate of Roger his father—not an ancient hereditary virgate, for its tenant before Roger Polle had been Roger le Bonde, and Roger's father was called Hugh.[80] William also succeeded Roger in a small piece of land called a *Twodelrode,* lately belonging to that virgate in the Apetoft manor which Hugh Harcourt had held. From the other Apetoft virgate (Hokke's) he had an acre and a quarter of a rood. And since the manorial demesne too was part of the pool of available land,[81] he rounded off his holding with a quarter of a virgate from it.

There is no other fourteenth century rental of Kibworth Harcourt which gives as much detail as that described above. There are, however, a few small rentals which confirm the impression of a brisk market for land among the peasants.[82] A repetition in two of these small rentals of the information already contained in the bigger rental concerning the splitting up of the two free virgates of the Apetoft manor shows the concern of the estate administration with these developments. Two other disintegrated half virgates, one villein, the other free, also have two small rentals devoted to each of them. One of these rentals in each case not only shows how much land there was in each of the many parcels leased out, but precisely where these parcels were in the village fields. Since one of these half virgates was split up among thirteen and the other among fourteen lessees, this precision as to the location of parcels as small as half a rood was no doubt necessary. Other evidence suggests that without these precautions much land, and therefore much rent, was lost from the view of the manorial officials.[83] A small membrane which has found its way among these rentals has on it a list of sixteen small parcels of arable, leased out to tenants, from which, it is stated, the reeve cannot *(nescit)* get the rent.

This complaint of difficulty in getting in the rent is a presage of a financial crisis which the accounts for the second half of the fourteenth century reflect very vividly. I do not propose to discuss these in detail, but a few indications of the nature of this crisis will point a contrast to the days of expansion with which we have primarily been concerned. As early as 1320 the Kibworth reeve entered the year of account with a considerable sum of arrears from the previous year—12 per cent. in fact of the total on the receipt side of the account.[84] Although the manorial account was not a document which even purported to present a profit and loss statement of the year's activities, it is possible to see the steadily rising of arrears in the Kibworth Harcourt accounts as a symptom of a downward economic trend. By 1361 the accumulated arrears of previous reeves amounted to 22 per cent. of the receipt total of the year of account.[85] In this year there is a symptomatic item, common to late medieval manorial accounts but seldom found in accounts of the late thirteenth or early fourteenth centuries—Defects of Rent. It consists of reductions of rent agreed to by the lord, and the rents of land for which no tenant can be found. At this date it amounted to 5 per cent. of the rent due.

These permanent defects of rent tended to increase, and this element of a declining rent income was perforce accepted by the estate administration. Nor does this appear to have been the most serious factor with which the College had to contend. In six years the defects only increased from 40 shillings to 70 shillings. But during the same period a much greater sum of money from rents was simply not collected from the tenants, although no reduction had been agreed to, as in the case of items under the heading Defects of Rents. In 1362 for instance the reeve who inherited £14 of previous reeves' arrears, attached to his account a small slip showing that that year there was owing 35 shillings from ten tenants.[86] This year's arrears have been added to the grand total of past arrears and handed on to the next reeve, who increased them in the following year by failing to collect nearly £14 from no less than 37 tenants.[87] This same reeve was in office the following year, and handed over to his successor arrears of about £39 consisting of £16 of arrears from his predecessors and £23 of his own for two years.

This curious story of debt could be traced further through the account rolls and would give an important insight into the causes of the collapse of seigneurial revenues, so important in the political and social history of late medieval England. The facts already quoted suggest that the decline was not simply a mechanical and impersonal process. The period was one of chronic agrarian unrest, of which only the most striking episode was that of 1381. These documents may be telling us of something like a rent strike, a counter-part on the manor of an absentee landlord to the withdrawal of services from the demesnes of those whose presence was closer. Here indeed is a great change in the lord-serf relationship. The College authorities, who worked so patiently at the end of the previous century to bring under their control the whole of this village, could hardly have imagined that their success would appear irrelevant in face of the new problems with which history presented them.

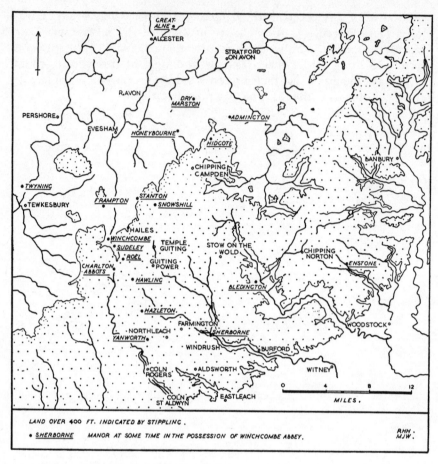

LAND OVER 400 FT. INDICATED BY STIPPLING.

• *SHERBORNE*   MANOR AT SOME TIME IN THE POSSESSION OF WINCHCOMBE ABBEY.

RHH.
MJW.

The Estates of Winchcombe Abbey

2

Winchcombe Abbey and the Manor of Sherborne[1]

I

It is not the purpose of this article to describe the economic development of Winchcombe Abbey, but rather to suggest possible lines of approach to such a history. For in spite of the early date of its foundation, its part in the expansion of the monastic economy in the tenth century[2] and its great wealth,[3] Winchcombe has been overshadowed by the other Benedictine houses of the Severn Valley, and its history is little known. The medieval buildings of St. Mary's Cathedral Priory, Worcester, of St. Peter's, Gloucester, of Tewkesbury, Pershore and Evesham have remained as significant monuments to the former glory of the religious communities which they housed, while hardly a stone of Winchcombe Abbey is now to be seen. Worcester Cathedral Priory's annals, its cartulary, its register and some of its estate accounts have been in print for many years, whilst, though scantier, the printed records of Gloucester, Tewkesbury and Evesham are equally well known.[4] Winchcombe Abbey's excellently edited *Landboc* or register has been in print for over half a century but seems to be little studied and none of the other materials for the abbey's history have been widely used.[5] Yet a study of the organisation and development of the estates of Winchcombe Abbey would undoubtedly throw considerable light on the mediaeval economy of the Cotswolds, as well as on the triumphs and tribulations of a great feudal landowner.

Winchcombe Abbey's manors were distributed over both wold and vale, and Winchcombe, on the frontier of wold and vale, was a conveniently placed centre from which to administer the estate. Winchcombe town, which was a royal manor, appears to have been of comparatively minor significance in the economy of the West Midlands. In the middle ages and later it never regained its remote and misty glory as the *villa regalis* at the centre of a *scir* of the Mercian kingdom. In spite of its burghal status in Domesday Book, it hardly seemed to compete in population and prosperity with many villages in the same county.[6] Its taxed population according to the unreliable assessment of 1381.[7] was 201, which may be compared with the figure of 303 at nearby Chipping Campden. An analysis of the occupations of the tax-payers shows an interesting variety of urban pursuits without indicating any form of specialisation.[8] Its economic function was simply to provide services for the monastery which was in its midst and to act as a regional market centre. A letter close of 1238 exempts the men of the nearby village of Hailes from the obligation to pay toll on entering Winchcombe, unless they were merchants exercising their trade for gain.[9] This suggests that the town was a recognised centre for local exchanges, mainly no doubt of agricultural produce.[10] There may have been a tendency for the town to specialise as a stock market, if we are to judge by evidence of royal purchases of 40 oxen for transfer to Windsor in 1254, and of 4 horses in 1256.[11] One of the medieval streets was called the Horsemarket.[12] But there are no other indications of any activity which one might not find in a market town of similar size anywhere in England. Even wool is inconspicuous, for reasons which will become clear later.

Although the abbey owned manors in the Severn and Avon valleys, the Cotswold part of the estate was economically predominant. A late indication of the special attention that was paid to this part of the property is in the list of expenses allowed in the survey contained in the *Valor Ecclesiasticus*. Amongst these is the fee paid to a steward *pro partibus de la Wolde*.[13] The principal reason for the importance of the Cotswold part of the estate was that here were the pastures for the abbey's sheep, about whose existence our information is scarce, though impressive. Winchcombe Abbey figures prominently in the list of estimated annual yields of wool from religious houses drawn up in the early 14th century by the Florentine Pegolotti.[14] Only 12 out of 202 English and Scottish monasteries on the list could be expected to provide 40 or more sacks a year, and Winchcombe, assessed at 40, was one of them. It is true that some of this wool might be from tithes, or collected from tenant farmers by the abbey acting as a middleman, but it has also been shown that Pegolotti's figures are likely to have been the minimum rather than the maximum.[15] It would not be rash therefore to suggest that these 40 sacks represent a flock of some 8,000 sheep and an income (at 13 marks a sack) of about £350 a year.[16]

The Cotswold possessions of the abbey, the balance of whose economy was by no means entirely pastoral, were, at the time of Domesday Book about equal to those in the valley and elsewhere. This numerical balance was preserved by subsequent acquisitions. In 1086 the Cotswold manors were Sherborne, Snowshill, Charlton Abbots, Hidcote and Bledington. Perhaps Stanton too, on the edge of rather than in the wolds, should be counted as a Cotswold manor, as should the possessions in or adjacent to Winchcombe itself. The remainder of the estate in 1086 consisted of a group of manors in the flat valleys north and west of the wolds, Twining, Frampton, Admington, and Honeybourne. There were also two important outlying properties, Enstone in Wychwood Forest and Great Alne in the Forest of Arden.

The essential framework of Winchcombe Abbey's estate was in existence in 1086, as was the case with the other ancient Benedictine foundations. There were, however, important subsequent acquisitions, additional to that constant piecemeal accumulation by gift, purchase and exchange characteristic of monastic property owners during the middle ages. The larger acquisitions were not, it is important to note, free gifts. The three almost contiguous Cotswold manors, Hawling, Hazleton and Yanworth, were bought of William of Béthune, a Flemish noble, in about the year 1200. A sum of £228 cash down was paid, and a rent of £20 (later reduced to £9) a year was reserved to the vendor and his heirs. The manor of Dry Marston was bought from the Benedictine monastery at Coventry before 1250 for 1,130 marks (£753. 6s. 8d.), with a rent of 20/- a year reserved to the vendor. The manor of Roel was added in 1318 as a link to the chain of properties running along the ridge of the wolds towards Northleach. It was bought from the Abbey of St. Evroul for £550, to be held at an annual rent of £20. In 1509 Abbot Kydderminster acquired for a short period the manor of Sudeley at a fee farm rent of £50 a year.[17]

In 1535 the gross spiritual income of the abbey was one-eighth of the gross general income. This spiritual income came largely from churches whose incomes had been appropriated by the abbey during the long and familiar process of attrition by which religious houses, having acquired the advowson of a parish church, forced the transfer to themselves of the revenues originally intended to support the incumbent, the church and the parish poor. In 1175 the Pope confirmed to the abbey the possession of 8 parish churches with their appurtenances, together with the right of advowson.[18] This in effect gave control of the ecclesiastical revenues in all but two of the parishes where the abbey had temporal possessions. This general confirmation by the Pope had to be strengthened subsequently in most cases by episcopal confirmations of the appropriation of individual churches, which laid down the division of the tithes between the abbey as rector and the vicar. Subsequent acquisitions of advowsons without appropriation sometimes led to bitter controversy. The abbey and the rector of Hazleton fiercely disputed the division of tithes, and in the final settlement the abbey managed to acquire as much of the spiritual income as if there had been a complete appropriation.[19] The importance of the spiritual income can be seen from the total figures quoted above. This is .borne out by some comparisons in detail. Enstone demesnes in 1535 were farmed for £9, the rectory for £15. 13s. 4d. ; Twining manor site and demesne for £18. 13s. 4d., the rectory for £17; Stanton demesne for £7. 6s. 8d., the rectory for £8.

II

Some of the materials for the history of Winchcombe have been used for the preceding sketch of the layout of the abbey property. The starting point for a detailed study of the economy of the abbey must necessarily be as precise a knowledge as possible of its resources at different periods of its existence. Domesday Book contains the earliest enumeration of the abbey's properties in which any confidence can be placed. The latest is the survey made by Henry VIII's commissioners of First Fruits and Tenths in 1535, contained in the *Valor Ecclesiasticus*.[20] This is more detailed than many other surveys in the *Valor*. For each manor a rough division of the sources of income is made, as between assize rents, farms of demesnes, tithes and several pasture and perquisites of courts. The allotment of sources of revenue amongst the different obedientiaries is shown, a fact that suggests that the centralised financial system controlled by the two Treasurers, whose existence is revealed in episcopal ordinances of 1329, may not have lasted.[21] The expenses on fees, alms and pensions which are entered in the *Valor* in some detail, give some information about administration and miscellaneous commitments, such as the payment of the wages of the masters of the grammar schools of Winchcombe and Cirencester.

Between 1086 and 1535 there are a number of other documents which establish the extent of the abbey property at different dates. Of these may be mentioned the Papal confirmation of 1175, a royal grant of free warren in all manorial demesnes of 1251,[22] the *Taxatio Ecclesiastica* of Pope Nicholas IV of 1291 and a manuscript rental of 1355-8.[23] The papal confirmation and the grant of free warren do no more than give a list of manors. The 1291 ecclesiastical taxation assessment purports to give for each manor the area in carucates and value of demesne, the values of demesne appurtenances such as mills and dovecots, the assize rents and the profits of stock. But these returns have been shown by various scholars to be no true record of the actual situation.[24] There is no doubt that there is a grave under-assessment, and that at most the return can only show where the abbey's properties lay and what were the main sources of income.

The rental of 1355-8 is a puzzling document whose apparent inconsistencies I do not propose to discuss in detail. The greater part of the manuscript is composed of manorial rentals, but the first entry is a statement of the main annual expenses of each manor, consisting of the rent allowance to the reeve and other officials, expenses incurred at harvesting and haymaking and some odd payments charged against the manorial revenues. The principal rubric of the document follows next, stating that the date of the rental is 1355, a date probably referring to the rentals of the individual manors. This rubric is, however, followed by a statement of the total of all the rents from the manors in the year 1358. After this there is an estimate of the central expenses each year *(communibus annis)*. These occur under the headings of rents paid out, pensions, robes and furs for officials, officials' wages, necessary purchases and purchases of corn. The total of these centrally incurred expenses is added to that of the manorial expenses and the sum deducted from the total receipts. The last item before the manorial rentals is what seems to be a casual list of grain sold and after the manorial rentals there is a small rental of the office of the infirmarer.

The information contained in these lists is of great value, especially in view of the lack of other types of evidence, but there are obviously many important omissions. The value of the demesne produce does not appear to be included in the estimates of income, wool sales being the most striking omission. There is no mention of ecclesiastical revenue. Revenues from Winchcombe town, from possessions in the neighbourhood of Winchcombe, from Great Alne, from Twining, and from Enstone do not appear in the body of the rental, and are presumably not included in the general statement of income at the beginning.[25] These omissions cannot have been accidental, and may be explained as resulting from expedients taken during a period of crisis six years earlier. The manor of Twining had, in 1352, been placed in the hands of trustees who were instructed to pay its issues to an ex-abbot who had resigned following a period of dissension between him and his monks.[26] In the following year a commission of four persons was appointed by letters patent to administer the abbey, which owing to misrule had fallen into debt.[27] The commission was to maintain the pious works and sustain the personnel of the abbey, but use the balance of the income to reduce the burden of the debt. Their activities may well have included the drawing up of a rental describing a purely temporary situation. The description of the rents and tenements in the individual manorial rentals is probably complete, the difference between the overall total in the rental and that accounted for by 15th century rent collectors being explained by the omission from the rental of some of the sources of rent. Much information of importance emerged from a study of the names of tenants, their holdings and their obligations. As one would expect in 1355, considerable evidence of the disintegration resulting from plague and economic crisis is to be found. This is to be seen in what appears to be a radical re-grouping of the customary tenements. At Bledington, for instance, we find that out of a total of 30 virgates, 12 (judging by the admittedly chancey evidence of personal names) are held by tenants not the direct heirs of their predecessors. Other virgates have lapsed into the lord's hands and are being let out again not whole, but piecemeal. Four persons hold composite holdings made up from portions of the holdings of three other tenants. At Hawling the same phenomena occur. Here there were 28 virgates, of which 6 were in free tenure, held by 15 tenants. Only 4 tenants were not holding land previously in the tenure of persons with different family names. An example of a composite holding in this village is that of William James. He held a virgate in free tenure which was probably his hereditary holding. In addition he had a messuage and a virgate once belonging to a certain Squier, and an enclosure and 24 acres from a two-virgate holding once belonging to John of Honeybourne. Similar conditions seem to have existed on the other manors.

In view of the importance of demesne farming in English medieval agriculture, evidence of the extent of the demesne and the character of the labour services performed on it will naturally be sought. The situation in 1355, so soon after the catastrophe of the Black Death, both as regards demesne farming and the use of labour cannot be expected to be normal. Rentals, however, often state the maximum number of services claimable long after commutation has become regular. We might therefore expect to find in this rental a statement of a greater number of labour services than would necessarily be claimed in any one year. The actual situation as regards labour services revealed by the rental is in fact somewhat surprising. There are no formal statements of the services owed from the regular unit of tenure, the virgate. All information about services is jotted down in the left-hand margin opposite each holding and obligations tend to vary from holding to holding. Since many of the holdings are of a composite character this is not surprising. The labour services that are noted are surprisingly light. Many customary tenants appear to owe only money rents and, sometimes, small produce rents. Apart from Sherborne, where there are some services of washing and shearing sheep, the virgator, whether in the Cotswolds or in the vale, appears to be burdened, in addition to his money rent, with, at the most, four boon services at harvesting and perhaps a day at the haymaking. Money rents vary widely and, on the face of it, inexplicably. They are often fairly heavy, say from 8/- to 10/- or more a virgate. This might be the result of a commutation of labour services. Others on the other hand are light, 1/- or 2/- a virgate, without apparently being supplemented by labour services.

The rentals contain no reference to manorial demesnes, apart from an occasional mention of small and insignificant portions of demesne leased out to tenants. This, together with the lightness of labour services, might be taken to suggest that the demesnes were no longer in existence on any significant scale. But the manorial expenses listed at the beginning of the rental show a heavy expenditure for harvesting and haymaking, most of which must have been made up of wages for labour hired for the demesne.[28] The average money expenditure per manor, out of 15 manors, was £3. 13s., the range being from £1 (at Honeybourne) to £10 (at Sherborne and Winchcombe). As we shall see, the mowing and harvesting costs at Sherborne in the first half of the 15th century came to about £10, when there was an arable demesne of possibly 400 acres. Consequently we cannot assume that in the middle of the 14th century labour services had been commuted because demesne farming had been contracted or abandoned.[29] Since figures for the expenditure of money on wages are given us, we may assume that labour services had been abandoned, in part at any rate, in favour of wage labour. If this was so, then the Winchcombe Abbey estate has a special interest. For the most common solution applied by the lords of great estates when faced by a shortage of labour and a fall in the profitability of demesne farming, was to reduce considerably or to abandon the direct cultivation of the demesne.

The evidence from the surveys and the rental should give us an overall picture of the structure of the estate. If there were in existence accounts of central officials of the house, such as the treasurers, the cellarer, or other obedientiaries, we might be able to see the economy of the estate as a whole in movement. Such accounts do not exist. We turn next therefore to examine such evidence as will enable us to fill in details left unexplained by the documents considered hitherto. Most important in this respect is the evidence of the Landboc or register of the abbey. There are two volumes, one written for the most part in the later years of Henry III's reign, with additions up to 1332, the other at the beginning of the 15th century. In the first volume there are about 300 charters and other deeds, and in the second volume a little over 500. The second volume does not merely reproduce documents issued at dates subsequent to the latest in Volume I, but contains many 12th and 13th century deeds not included in Volume I. The variety of documents is enormous. They include royal grants and confirmations, Papal privileges, private charters from all classes and describing all manner of transactions, whether of gift, sale, lease or exchange. Although the great majority of documents record land transactions of one sort or another, there are also, as is common in such cartularies, some miscellaneous documents containing details of significance about the abbey and its property. An example of this type of document is a list of the abbot's and the convent's servants and their wages, at the end of Volume I.[30]

To the student of agrarian history some of the most interesting charters in the Landboc are those which record the transfer of quite small pieces of land, often less than 10 acres. Such small quantities of land are often precisely described as to their location in the fields, so that from these descriptions we can catch a glimpse of the village field layout—the names and locations of the furlongs, the number of open fields, the existence and location of enclosures, woods, quarries and mills. For some villages, charters are much more abundant than for others. Winchcombe and its environs, Sherborne, Hawling, Hazleton, Yanworth. and Enstone are remarkably well documented, while there is a relative scarcity of descriptive charters for Charlton Abbots, Twining, Dry Marston, Honeybourne, Bledington and Admington. The Enstone charters are especially interesting in that they include a number of references to an extensive assarting movement in Wychwood Forest in the early 14th century. There are similar references in the documents of the Arden manor of Great Alne.[31]

The most useful records of economic and social life on the manors of a great estate are the annual accounts of the manorial officials and the rolls of the manor courts. Few of these documents have survived from the Winchcombe manors and are the more precious because of their rarity. All are now well preserved at Sherborne, and are calendared.[32] The manorial documents of the kind referred to here consist of a series of court rolls covering all the manors of the estate, and some account rolls of the reeves of Sherborne and Yanworth. The first court roll contains records of the courts of the various manors held at various times between May 1340 and January 1341, and written in succession on the one roll. The last is a roll of courts held in 1466. Intermediate in date are 16 other similar manor court rolls, and three rolls of the Hundred Courts of Kiftesgate, Holford and Greston.[33] The accounts of the reeves, farmers and rent collectors of the manor of Yanworth are 15 in number, ranging from 1406 to 1420. They are very short, and lack the sort of detail which might give a picture of manorial activity. The reeves', farmers' and rent collectors' accounts of Sherborne on the other hand, though later in date, are very full. It is primarily on the evidence they provide that the following remarks on some aspects of Sherborne manor are based.

III

The village of Sherborne lies along the bank of a tributary of the River Windrush called the Sherborne Brook. This stream runs part of the way along a deep valley parallel to, and a mile or two to the north of the main road between Oxford and Gloucester. The main road is 600 feet above sea level, while the village is built along the 400 feet contour line or thereabouts. The distance from the east to the west end of the village is more than a mile, and the two ends are in fact now, as in the middle ages, two separate groups of houses separated by the park and the hall. In the rental of 1355 the lands and tenements of the inhabitants of the 'Esteende' are listed separately from those of the inhabitants of the 'Westende:' Since their arable lands lay mingled in the same open fields, it is clear that, for the purposes of drawing up the rental, the messuage or cottage was the basis.[34]

The village fields stretched uphill on both sides of the Sherborne Brook, extending over the main road on the south side. The charters in the Landboc, particularly those of the 13th century, contain many field-names, the object having been to enable the land which was the subject of the charter to be precisely located. A comparison between these field-names and surviving modern field-names makes possible a rough reconstruction of the medieval field layout. In some cases the description of the situation of a piece of land in a charter is so detailed that it can be straightway placed on the map.[35] The charters make it clear that Sherborne, after the Cotswold fashion, was working on a two-field system.[36] This being so, given the topographical conditions, the field layout could hardly have been other than it was. North of the river was the North Field[37] and south of the river was the South Field, stretching over towards the fields of Aldsworth. There was meadow land along the Sherborne Brook and on the right bank of the River Windrush. The Cowham pasture and meadow which is still called by that name lies along the Windrush bank, north of the Sherborne Brook.

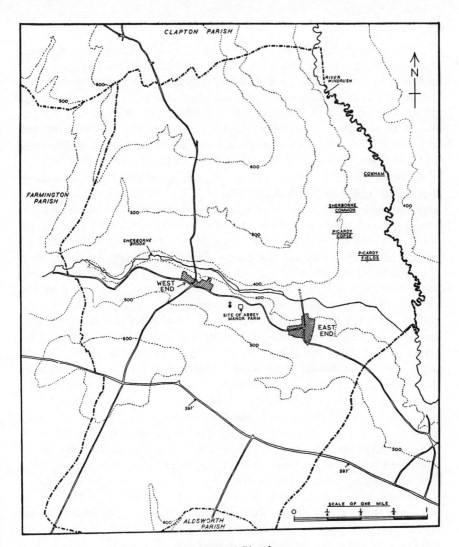

The Parish of Sherborne

It is referred to frequently in the 13th century charters as demesne meadow. In 1470 it was being farmed out as meadow land for £8 a year, and in 1535 it was being farmed out as pasture for half as much (£10) as the whole farm of manor site and demesne arable.[38] Part of the rough common pasture and woodland was probably at the east end of the North Field where the names 'Sherborne Common' and 'Picardy' are still found. 'Pycardy' was being enclosed by a ditch in 1448, though whether it was then woodland, as it is now, cannot be determined.[39]

A corn-mill was a normal feature of a medieval village. In 1086 there were four mills in Sherborne. Although the valuation of 1291 only mentions one mill, the rental of 1355 mentions 3 mills which must have been cornmills, and one fulling-mill. Two of the corn-mills were in the hands of abbey tenants and the rent for the third was paid by the lord of neighbouring Farmington. The fulling-mill, also held by a tenant, may have been the successor of one which is referred to in a charter issued some time between 1192 and 1224. Another charter, which may be ten years earlier in date records the transfer of one of the Sherborne corn-mills to the lord of Farmington with the proviso that he should not attempt to set up a fulling-mill without the abbot's licence. The implication is that the abbot already had a fulling-mill in Sherborne whose monopoly he did not wish to be infringed. Such a monopoly was still in existence in 1340 for at that date a number of tenants were fined in the manor court for taking their cloth to be fulled outside the manor.[40]

The rental of 1355 gives us our first impression of the people who lived in Sherborne. The east end of the village was apparently more populous than the west end, for there were 54 landholders in the east as compared with 7 in the west. However some names are common to both lists, so (leaving aside those persons dependent entirely on the manor house) we have a population of between 80 and 90 landholders. This implies a village population of about 300 persons. Sherborne, then, would be one of Gloucestershire's bigger villages.[41] Most of the holdings are expressed as virgates or fractions of virgates,[42] though in a large number of cases tenants have, in addition to their virgate holdings in the open fields, crofts, closes, and odd acres of land from the demesne, from glebeland or from lapsed tenements. A good example of such a composite holding is that of Thomas de Leye. This consisted of a messuage and its virgate; a piece of meadow from another virgate; a cottage with half a virgate and a piece of land attached; another cottage with an adjacent croft and half an acre in the fields; a piece of pasture; another messuage with half a virgate; the meadow once appurtenant to two other virgates; 4 acres of demesne land; and a piece of bracken land.

The extent to which social differentiation and its associated phenomenon, the disintegration and re-grouping of holdings, had developed, is illustrated well in the rental. It is clear that at a time not far back the majority of holdings had been single virgates. By 1355 there were one or two much bigger holdings. A man significantly named

Henry atte Halle held $5\frac{1}{2}$ virgates, and there were two tenants with 3 virgates each. As many as 23 tenants held two or more virgates, as compared with 33 whose basic holding was a virgate. There were 7 half-virgate holders and 21 smallholders of one sort or another. An appreciable quantity of tenant land had lapsed into the hands of the abbot, amounting to about 11 virgates, 4 cottages and a few odd acres. The abbot in some cases had managed to re-lease out portions of lapsed tenements, examples being the messuage, croft and 4 acres from a lapsed virgate and the messuage, close and meadow land from a lapsed half-virgate. But the separate identity of the 'parent' holding was preserved in this pool of surplus tenant land. An entry in a court roll of 1357 shows that it was not from choice that the abbey was leasing out portions rather than complete holdings. A man took on lease a croft and 4 acres of land for 12 years *vel quousque tenens advenerit ad integrum*.[43]

The rents which were paid varied, as in other Winchcombe manors, in a way which cannot be explained in terms of economic laws invented for a laissez-faire capitalist economy. Some small groups of virgates paid uniform rents. For example, 19 virgates in the east end paid 8/- a year each, and 6 virgates in the west end paid 4/- a year each. But apart from these, rents varied considerably between 3/- and 8/- a virgate, with corresponding variations for fractions and multiples of virgates. Cottagers' rents varied between 6d. and 2/-. As pointed out above, there is no evidence that variations in money rent were related to a correspondingly varied burden of labour rents. At the heaviest, labour services work out at a rate of 4 *bederippe* or boon reaps a virgate. Sherborne is distinguished from the other Winchcombe manors in the rental in the greater variety of services demanded. This is the only manor from which services for the washing and shearing of sheep were owed. These were performed principally by cottagers. From 14 cottages came $12\frac{1}{2}$ days' washing and $12\frac{1}{2}$ days' shearing service, and a further 3 days of each service from a half-virgator and a virgator. An annual total of 31 works clearly would not deal with many sheep, and as we shall see, the labour services could have only served as a supplement to hired labour—though the customary tenants owing the services may very well have had an important supervisory role.

The problem posed by the lightness of labour services has been mentioned. Were labour services equally light in the middle of the 13th century, when the general level of labour services in this region was high? A complete contrast with the manors of St. Peter's, Gloucester, would be unexpected. It must be remembered that on St. Peter's manors near to Sherborne—Guiting Power, Northleach, Aldsworth, Coln Rogers, Coln St. Aldwyn and Eastleach—the customary tenants were burdened with very heavy labour services.[44] There is no indication in the records of the surrender and re-issue of customary holdings after 1340 in the Sherborne court rolls, or of more labour rents being required than are recorded in the rental, and there is no 13th century evidence about labour services in the Landboc. Of great significance therefore is an entry in the first Sherborne court roll of 1340. A widow came to court and surrendered her holding of a messuage and a virgate, saving her dower. The holding was taken on lease by the vicar for 5 years, until the widow's son should be of age, at a rent of 8/- a year. As if in explanation of the amount of money charged as rent, the record goes on to say, 'because before it was *ad opera.*'[45] The distinction between tenements held *ad opus* or *ad opera,* and those held at a money rent was, of course, familiar on many medieval estates, and a change from a lease *ad opera* to one involving a payment of money rent meant the commutation of the labour services for money.[46] The decision one way or another in many cases might be a matter of policy from year to year, but in fact on the Winchcombe estates it seems to have been a permanent decision in favour of money rents a decade before the Black Death, with the exception of a small number of boon works at harvest time.

Before leaving the Sherborne tenants, something may be said about those holding in free tenure. In 1355 there appear to have been only two free tenants, each holding two virgates. But the large number of charters referring to Sherborne in the Landboc suggests the existence in the 12th and 13th centuries of a greater amount of free land than at the date of the rental. Some of the charters show that the abbey was probably deliberately buying up such small independent landowners as existed in its territory. The history of a man named John, son of John le Knyst (or Knyt) of Sherborne, illustrates this. John was granted by a charter of Abbot John of Yanworth (1247-82) a scale of rations and clothing equivalent to that of the *medii servientes* of the abbey.[47] In return John quitclaimed to the abbey all his lands and rights in Sherborne. Judging by other deeds this was the final act of a history of financial embarrassments of which the abbey, and others, had taken full advantage. There are 18 deeds altogether[48] in which we find John transferring pieces of land or portions of rent. The recipients are the abbey and another Sherborne free tenant, Elias of Foxcote. Elias was a man of some importance who was the abbey steward. He was granted in 1278 a much more lucrative corrody, with residence on the abbey premises, than John. This corrody was granted in return for all his Sherborne lands, as well as for services rendered in the past. It is for this reason that John of Sherborne's charters transferring land to Elias are in the Landboc.

According to the 18 charters mentioned, John handed over more than 80 acres of arable land, a hall called Burymilde Hall and many pieces of meadow, pasture and other land.[49] The lands were disposed of piecemeal, at first less than 10 acres at a time, then in greater quantities, the three largest transfers being to Elias of Foxcote, of 18, 19 and 25 acres. Some of the charters make no reference to anything given to John in return for the land, and sometimes even suggest that he transferred land to the abbey for the good of his soul. In others, however, the real motive for transfer appears. A piece of land in the village and 12 acres in the fields were sold to the abbot for 6 marks and a quarter of wheat *ad urgens negotium meum,* and references to similar transactions with this explanatory phrase, or as in one charter *ad magnam necessitatem meam,* occur several times[50]

The reeves' and rent collectors' accounts for Sherborne, unusually detailed for the period, illustrate the special function of the manor in the economy of the abbey in the middle of the 15th century. All our general surveys show that Sherborne was the most valuable of the abbey's manors as far as total revenue was concerned. This superiority in value was in the main due to a greater sum received in rent from the tenants, but the demesne resources of Sherborne were also high in value. In 1535 only the demesne farm of Honeybourne yielded a greater sum than that of Sherborne.[51] Since Sherborne lay equidistant between the two market towns of Burford and Northleach, and near a main highway, it might be expected that its economic arrangements would be directed towards production for the market. It was, as we shall see when we consider the part Sherborne played in the Cotswold wool trade, quite intimately connected with the commercial activity for which the Cotswolds were most famous. Otherwise its economy was almost self-subsistent—not manorially, but within the framework of the estate.

It would be a mistake to ignore the arable farming of the Cotswolds. At the end of the 18th century, Marshall (while still insisting on the importance of sheep) could say 'This is, in the strictest sense of the phrase, an *arable country*.'[52] The labour services of the customary tenants of Gloucester Abbey imply a considerable extent of arable demesne farming. In the upland manor of Temple Guiting, there were 250 acres of demesne under crop in 1335 of which 235 acres were sown with spring corn.[53] The arable demesne of Sherborne a century later was of similar size, and here too there was a predominance of spring corn.[54] It may be assumed that if there was still a two–course rotation of crops, the total demesne acreage must have been over 400.

SHERBORNE DEMESNE: ACREAGES UNDER CROP

Crop	1425-6	1435-6	1445-6	1452-3	1462-3
wheat	88	76	58	48	69
pulse	11	12	—	8	—
drage	90	112	160	160	140
oats	28	22	9	24	28
Total	217	222	227	240	237

This considerable grain production did not yield a cash revenue of any significance. Most of the wheat, the pulse and the oats was consumed internally either as a supplement to money wages or as provender for beasts or for the consumption of visitors. The drage, of which there was more, was used differently. Some of it was made into malt for beer for local consumption, but the bulk was sent to Winchcombe to the abbey brewery- 154 out of 270 quarters in 1426 and much the same quantity and proportion of the total product in other years. These transfers of corn (and some livestock) from Sherborne to Winchcombe appear as a cash transaction in the accounts of 1446 and 1453. The goods were valued, perhaps at the current market price,[55] and accounted for under corn and stock sales on the receipt side of the account. But the same money value also appears on the expenses side under foreign payments (that is from the manor to the abbey). In other words neither estate nor manor increased its cash income by this purely internal transaction, though of course indirectly the abbey would achieve the same result by not having to buy the grain on the market. The economic effect is not on the estate but on the marketing system outside it.

Other products of husbandry yielding a cash income are found under the heading *Exitus manerii*. These are miscellaneous items, such as the hides of oxen or the products of the dairy,[56] and do not raise more than £3 or £4. The most profitable item in terms of cash, according to all the surviving accounts, was the hay from the demesne meadows. This appears to have been sold each year after mowing to a number of persons, some of whom came from outside the manor. In 1426 hay sales brought in £12 15s. 4d. In some years it was a good deal less. In 1436 only £5 worth was sold, but that was largely because of bad weather and the use of 80 cartloads as winter feed for the abbey's sheep. But the chief source of cash revenue from Sherborne in the 15th century was the money rent paid by the tenants. Assize rents due were steady at between £43 and £45 from 1426 to 1469, but the total taken was reduced on account of various allowances and defects of rent varying from year to year between £2 and £10. These rents were accounted for separately by a rent collector, so that the reeve's account was concerned with husbandry only. In fact, that rare event, a medieval attempt to calculate the true profits of agriculture, appears at the end of the reeve's account of 1445-6 under the rubric *valor husbondrie ultra superplusagium*.[57] The *valor* is given as £22. 9s. 5d., but whatever the basis for its calculation, it should be noted that Sherborne did not conform to the Beaulieu Abbey class of those manors able to pay their expenses out of their own receipts. The always large item, 'foreign receipts' (ranging, 1425-63, from £8 to £20), mostly consisted of subventions from the abbey, either direct or by the diversion of other revenues, or from the Sherborne rent collector.

These subventions in cash were of course needed for cash expenditure. The principal item of cash expenditure was for wages of various categories. It is possible, from a well-preserved account to analyse in detail the composition of agricultural expenses, although a fully accurate classification cannot be obtained, owing to the payment of some wages in kind and to the confusion in some single items of prices of material and the wages of the workers using the material. Such an analysis of the agricultural expenses of Sherborne in 1435-6 shows that the proportion of wages in *cash* to total cash expenses was 88 per cent. Since the wages of the permanent farm servants (the *famuli*) were supplemented by issues of 35 quarters of wheat, 37 quarters of drage, together with the crop from an acre of each grain, the percentage of wages to total costs must be considered much higher.[58] This picture is only slightly complicated by the survival of customary services. The full-time servants were the ploughmen, the various types of herdsmen and the carters. They also winnowed the grain after threshing and of course helped in the harvest work. Part-time or casual labour hired *in grosso* (that is for a complete job) was used for building works. Men hired *ad tascam* (that is by the piece) were used for threshing, hoeing and the various haymaking operations. At the harvest, 161 acres of grain were reaped, bound and stacked by hired labour brought in for the purpose, while the only appearance of the customary tenants was in the reaping, etc., of 61 acres together with the *famuli*. This was the *metebederipp* which appears in the rental. Although the accountant calculates the cost per acre of the hired reapers it does not appear clear that they were paid by the acre, but possibly by the job or by the day.

This form of manorial organisation remained virtually unchanged until. 1464 when the manor was put into the hands of a farmer. The farmer held two separate farms, that of the manor with its arable, meadows and pastures, and that of the great Cowham meadow. He took on the first for £13. 16s. 8d. a year for 7 years in 1464, and the second on an 8-year lease in 1468 for £8 a year. The farmer also acted as rent collector and continued to be responsible to the abbey for the care of the sheep flocks when they visited Sherborne as they had been doing for many years past.

Knowing Winchcombe Abbey's leading role in the early 14th century Cotswold wool trade, we naturally turn to the manorial stock accounts for information about sheep. The stock accounts of the Sherborne reeve show that on this manor there were no great sheep flocks under his control. At the most he only accounts for 12 sheep killed at the *metebederipp* for the customary tenants.[59] It is clear that the abbey sheep flocks were centrally controlled. Those sheep that were issued to the Sherborne reeve for the *metebederipp* were issued by the Master Shepherd. This official is also mentioned in a list of those abbey servants entitled to robes at the abbey's expense. The list is part of the account which precedes the rental of 1355. The Master Shepherd was not in the top grade of officials with the steward and the attorney, but in the middle grade with the granger and the abbot's pantler and cook. The manorial accounts tell us no more about this man, but it is clear from them that there were two under-shepherds at Sherborne. These men were receiving liveries of grain with the other farm servants at least as early as 1436. Two sheepfolds are mentioned in the 1436 account as receiving pulse from Sherborne for feeding sheep. It is probable that they were in or near to Sherborne, victualled and maintained from Sherborne, without being a charge on Sherbourne's reeve.[60]

It is impossible to discover where all the abbey sheepfolds were. A shepherd at Frampton issued the sheep for slaughter at the harvesting in 1446, and he is described as being an accounting official.[61] He may have been the Master Shepherd himself. The *Valor Ecclesiasticus* mentions extensive sheep pastures in 1535 in the upland manors of Snowshill, Hawling, and Charlton Abbots.[62] Beyond this we know nothing of the location of the abbey flocks, and in fact they may (since they were administered centrally) have moved about from place to place during the year.

One of the most important ports of call of the abbey sheep flocks was certainly Sherborne. It has been mentioned that when the manorial demesne was leased to a farmer, he was still responsible for expenses connected with sheep. The 1468 account of the farmer tells us that in that year 1,900 sheep were washed and shorn and the wool folded up with hired labour. Also some wool from the previous year's crop had been sown into sacks during the period of account. The same number of sheep were washed and shorn in 1483 and in 1485 there were 2,900. The accountant for this year was no longer the farmer, but a monk made responsible for collecting the rents and the farms.[63] The operation took four days and the wool was packed into 14 sacks of wool, making just over 200 fleeces to the sack[64]

The reeves' accounts for the earlier years do not contain any similar details of expenditure on the washing and shearing of the sheep and the weighing and packing of the wool. For this, unlike the farmers, they had no responsibility. But much of the expenditure incidental to the washing, shearing and packing was their responsibility, and the details of the accounts give some information indirectly about the way the operation was organised. Most of this information is contained in the grange accounts where the reeve has to show how much bread and beer, corn and other victuals were consumed by those attending the shearing.

It seems that after Easter every year the abbot and his servants moved from Winchcombe to Sherborne for the shearing period. It was they who were the principal consumers of the manorial produce—the beer, the bread, the pottage, the meat, the poultry and the cheese. Sometimes the cellarer and the steward came, in addition to their normal visits twice a year to hold the manor court. The abbot and his entourage did not come simply to enjoy an annual outing, although in this sheep country the shearing must have had the same festive aspects as the harvest. Business also was done in Sherborne at this time. The account of 1436 speaks of the expenditure of provender for Bernard Lumbard at the weighing of the wool. This man was probably one of those Italian exporters whose competition in the Cotswolds the Celys were obliged to note.[65] Very likely he had come from Southampton to Northleach to contact local graziers.

But the abbot was not only doing business with the big exporters, but also as a middleman with the local peasant wool-producers. Some of the cash that the Sherborne rent collector had in hand was used in 1446, not only to pay the wages of those washing the sheep, but also to buy up wool from the tenants. The value of the wool so bought was £5. 13s., which at £8 per sack of 200 fleeces would represent the product of 137 sheep.[66] In 1453 also the abbot was using the local rent collector's cash receipts for the expenses of the shearing. On this occasion 32 tods of wool were bought from three individuals at 10/- a tod. In 1463 the rent collector's receipts were used for wool purchases from local men (including the vicar of Sherborne), this time to the value of £2. 14s. 2d. It should not, of course, be assumed that the peasant producers in Sherborne were the only men on the estate who were using the abbot as a middleman for the disposal of their wool. If the tenants in each of the Winchcombe Abbey manors where sheepgrazing was an important occupation sold no less to the abbot than the Sherborne tenants, the *collecta* of which he disposed would still be a significant amount.

It might be thought that the absence of manorial accounts for the other Winchcombe Abbey manors precludes any assumption that there were or were not similar shearings of the flocks at other places besides Sherborne. But some positive conclusions are permissible. It will be remembered that Sherborne was the only manor on the estate in 1355 where services (however few) of washing and shearing the sheep were owed. The significance of this fact on an estate which contained areas more suitable for the grazing of flocks can only be explained with reference to Sherborne's geographical situation. In the first place it was near to the main road to London. It was also near to the principal wool-mart of the central Cotswolds, Northleach. It was fully capable, because of its size, of providing the extra victuals, fodder and labour necessary at the shearing. The Sherborne Brook, wide and shallow, would provide the water for washing 2,000 or 3,000 sheep. The broad, flat-bottomed valley through which it runs would provide the space for marshalling the sheep and shearing them. The evidence certainly seems to support the conclusion that once a year the Master Shepherd and his men collected the scattered flocks together and drove them over the wolds to Sherborne for the shearing, packing and disposal of the wool, where they were met by the abbot and his advisers, come there as the responsible heads of an organisation concerned in one of the few productive activities with which feudal landowners were still concerned. But if this conclusion is correct, the figures of 1468, 1483 and 1485 show a great decline from the scale of grazing since the days when Pegolotti compiled his list.[67]

3

Old Enclosure in the West Midlands:
a hypothesis about their late medieval development

I propose to discuss the agrarian system of a part of England which is well enough known in general, but about whose economic and social life not much has been written. I am not concerned with the whole of what is known as the West Midlands—this includes the counties bordering Wales as well as those of which Birmingham is the modern centre. I confine myself to certain parts of two river valleys and their drainage areas, that is the Warwickshire and Worcestershire Avon and the middle Severn. The region offers a good example of an aspect of agrarian history with which we are in general all familiar—uneven development, and consequently contrasting types of agrarian structure within a small distance of each other.

Although the whole of the region with which I am concerned lies in the so-called Midland Triangle, that densely wooded part of the country which was not seriously attacked by cultivators until after the Anglo-Saxon settlement, there were in fact some very early settlements, even Neolithic, in the Avon and Severn valleys, especially around Evesham. This place is of course only a few miles north of the northern edge of the Cotswold Hills, a dense area of prehistoric and Roman settlement. But going a few miles still further north, on the other side of the River Avon from the Cotswolds, we find ourselves in a well wooded region stretching from Worcester in the West to Coventry in the East. Part of this region was a Royal Forest, the Forest of Feckenham in Worcestershire. The other part, though not legally forest land, was nevertheless heavily wooded, and traditionally known as the Forest of Arden. This was Shakespeare's Arden, arbitrarily transported in his play *As You Like It* from England to some other country, just as the story itself, based on the *Tale of Gamelyn,* a poem of outlaw bands in the woodland, was transposed from an English to an imaginary foreign setting.

By the later middle ages—indeed, probably by the twelfth century—the contrast in field systems which you would expect to find already existed. In the valleys, but particularly in the lower Avon and the middle Severn, and to the south of Avon, the characteristic settlement was the large nucleated village with an open-field system of the traditional English type, two or three fields containing quarter-acre ridges, lands or selions grouped in units known as furlongs *(culturae).* In many cases these systems persisted until the Parliamentary enclosures of the eighteenth and nineteenth centuries. The Worcester Cathedral estates, first established between the eighth and tenth centuries, contained many of these traditional villages. Maps were made of them in the immediate pre-enclosure period, in the eighteenth century, showing intermixed holdings in open fields which could have changed little in essence in a thousand years.[1]

In the forests of Arden and Feckenham there were different settlements and different field systems. The settlements tended to be dispersed, hamlets and individual farms, and the field systems contrasted with those of the nucleated villages. They seemed to have a less coherent and regular organisation, to have, quite early on, a high proportion of land held in severalty, whether enclosed or not, and consequently to confine common of pasture to the woods and wastes.

The problems to be studied are these. What differences in natural environment, social organisation or economic activity caused the existence of contrasting systems so near to each other ? What chronology of development can we establish ? What more can be said of the enclosed systems than simply that they were different from the more familiar open field systems ? The answers to these questions depend of course on the evidence and this is not evenly distributed. The best medieval evidence comes from the ecclesiastical estates, most abundant where the monastic house was old and rich. The Severn and Avon valleys had several of these estates — famous ones such as those of Worcester Cathedral Priory, Worcester Bishopric, Pershore, Evesham, Gloucester and Winchcombe. The main structure of their landed properties had been established by the tenth century at the latest. But precisely because they were old and rich their estates consisted of anciently established agricultural settlements in the earliest cleared land in the valleys. These tended to be openfield villages, and this fact of documentation already establishes a fact of chronology. Other ecclesiastical estates of later foundation were in the enclosed country. It is no surprise that these were Cistercian houses, founded in less well cultivated parts of the region. However some of the best evidence of medieval enclosure comes from a Benedictine foundation of the eleventh century, the Cathedral Priory of Coventry, and this evidence warns us against a too simple correlation of enclosure with late woodland settlement.

The documents which provide the most detailed information about irregular field layouts come from a small Cistercian house in the upper Avon valley in Warwickshire, that of Stoneleigh in Arden near to the royal, later Lancastrian, castle of Kenilworth. Stoneleigh parish was also known as Stoneleigh soke (or area of jurisdiction) and had been a royal manor in 1066. In about 1154 it was given to some Cistercians for whom Cannock Chase in Staffordshire, and its inhabitants, had proved too wild. It was not the only land owned by the Abbey but it was the most important and the best documented. Our information comes from a register containing, in addition to documents illustrating the abbey's history, a late fourteenth century rental; and from a series of charters mostly of the late thirteenth and early fourteenth centuries.[2] The soke of Stoneleigh was about 10,000 acres (about 4000 ha) in area and contained ten separate nuclei of settlement referred to as hamlets, eight of which already existed by the end of the twelfth century and seven abbey granges. Three of the centres of settlement with their associated field systems were in the valleys of Avon and its tributary the Sowe, the others were in the middle of woodland and waste, parts of the Forest of Arden.

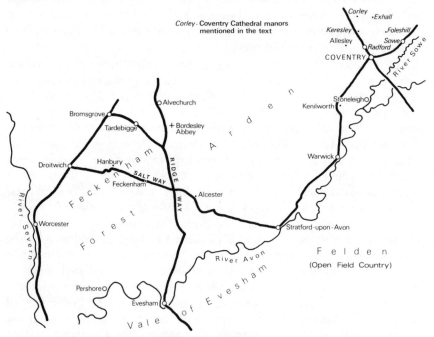

Fig. 1. The areas of medieval enclosure in the Warwickshire
and Worcestershire woodland.

By the end of the fourteenth century this estate had a curious appearance as far as its field system was concerned. At the centre was the village of Stoneleigh which gave its name to the whole soke. Its fields and those of two other riverside hamlets lay partly in divided ownership and open to the pasture rights of the villagers. These open fields lay for the most part along the valleys of the river Avon and its tributary. But immediately south of the Avon bank, where two woods had existed at the time of the Abbey's foundation, was an area of fields in severalty, for the most part belonging to the Home Grange of the Abbey, to a lesser extent to peasants of Stoneleigh and the nearby hamlet of Stareton. To the northwest had been a small nucleus of open land surrounded by the woods of Crackley, Westwood, Dalle and Armley, which as late as the end of the thirteenth century were still extensive.[3] The nucleus of open field land was now engulfed in a sea of separate fields in individual ownership, some still Abbey grange property, but mostly in the hands of tenants. Their names show their origin — they were still called assarts, wastes and moors even a century after they had been put under the plough.

Enclosure was either by ditch and earth bank or by hedge. Tenants had the right to take thorns and alders from the common wood *(sepes de spinis* and *de alnis)*[4] every two or three years for making their enclosures. Terms of fourteenth century leases actually embodied safeguards against the neglect of hedges. Live hedges were the natural forms of enclosure when arable was taken from the woodland, but by the fourteenth century, at any rate, hedges were also being set up in the old open land. In furlongs in which some tenants had open and intermixed parcels we suddenly come across a reference to a holding consisting of so many acres or ridges enclosed by hedges. A single acre for instance lies *inter sepes;* eight *selions* (ridges or lands) lie between two hedges; a croft in an open furlong consists of 23 ridges and two headlands lying *inter quatuor sepes.* Since one of the chief advantages of enclosure was to prevent access to other men's beasts, usually following the buying off of their rights of common, it is odd to find that some of these crofts, even those with hedges, were still subject to common rights. The last one quoted for instance *est commune et seminandum cum Starhulle* — its tenant could not even control the crop to be sown. But as sixteenth century advocates of this old type of enclosure (such as Tusser) have shown, there were other advantages, such as the protection of the crop from wandering animals before the harvest. If other men than the tenant were entitled to graze an enclosure after the harvest, at any rate he had the advantage of the dung.

The spread of hedged enclosure from the woodland assarts to the older core of open and commonable arable was made possible by the consolidation of parcels, a process made familiar to English agrarian historians at least as early as 1912 by R. H. Tawney in his *Agrarian Problem of the Sixteenth Century.* In the Warwickshire Arden country it was associated with another phenemenon not so generally appreciated. In each village the open-field core became less significant in comparison with the assarted enclosures — as the Stoneleigh register put it, *in quolibet hamletto manerii... sunt octo virgate terre et non amplius. Et si quod amplius habent hoc utique habent de approwacione et assartacione vastorum.* But if the openfield core had ever been organised as a two or three field system, this was no longer the case in the later middle ages. Holdings in Stoneleigh were not evenly distributed over two or three main fields as in the classic instances used by H. L. Gray in his *English Field Systems.* They tended to be concentrated in one part of the arable, so that it occurred that two of the biggest open field holdings in Stoneleigh did not have a single ridge of land in the same field. This Stoneleigh phenomenon was not unique, as I have shown elsewhere.[5] It is found in several other Arden villages.

There is no evidence for Stoneleigh of the way in which cropping was arranged. References to common rights in the arable and to the fact that certain crofts had to be sown at the same time as certain open furlongs show that a fallow, subject to common pasture was a feature of the scheme, and in fact the usual sequence, fallow — winter corn — spring corn, was no doubt followed. But in view of the tendency for holdings to be concentrated in one part of the fields, no simple arrangements, as in the two and three field systems, could have been made.

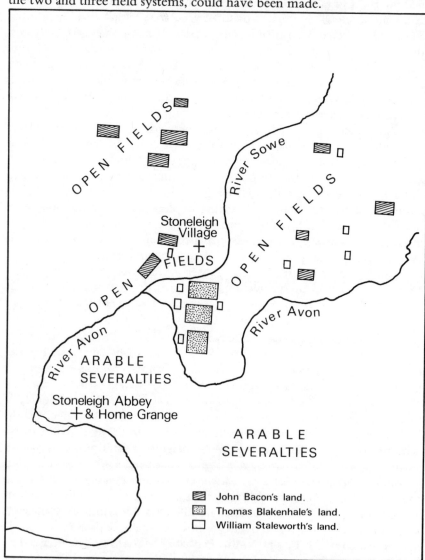

Fig. 2. Distribution of three holdings in Stoneleigh open fields
(each rectangle represents scattered parcels within one
furlong).

The question we must now ask is, are we taking all factors into consideration, when, in sketching the evolution of this estate, we refer simply, as the monk did who compiled the register, to the expansion of cultivation from an original core of open arable into woodland and waste, with as a consequence the creation of arable severalties? Obviously the making of assarts from the twelfth century onwards was the work of lords and individual peasants, not of communities. This is now a truism. It must also be stressed, in the case of Stoneleigh, that the newly approved land, still referred to as waste and moor when under crop, was about the best arable land in the county, certainly no worse than the older settled land in the valley. Perhaps the most important aspect that I have not yet stressed was that Stoneleigh was only four miles from the cloth manufacturing town of Coventry, hardly existing as a town at all in the eleventh century, but by the fourteeth century rivalling Bristol and Norwich as a centre of production, and therefore as a consuming centre as well. It seems not unlikely that the *bocage* of Midland England may have developed as much as a result of the stimulus of the market as from other more familiar causes, especially if we accept as a fact the superior efficiency of enclosed severalties.

The field system in the Stoneleigh soke was matched by that of other villages in the Coventry area, the most detailed documentary evidence for which is in a survey and rental of the lands of Coventry Cathedral Priory, drawn up in 1411, nineteen years after the compilation of the Stoneleigh Register.[6]

Holdings in five of these village are described in sufficient detail to give us some insight into their field organisation. The impression one gets is that they resemble the northernmost hamlets of the Stoneleigh soke very closely in the predominance of enclosed severalties. Out of 168 holdings in these villages which were held of the Priory, less than a quarter of them had any land which could possibly be open-field arable, though no doubt some of the intakes from the waste were commonable. As in Stoneleigh, the descriptions of holdings imply a small, vestigial core of old common field, engulfed in a great variety of holdings in severalty variously described as curtilages, crofts, wastes, fields, moors, or parroks. One of the difficulties about both the Stoneleigh and the Coventry Priory surveys is that these separate pieces are usually described without the area being given. This makes reliable comparisons of magnitude difficult. Some approvements from the waste, especially those in the hands of the lord or granted to other lords were very considerable: 64 acres assarted from Westwood in Stoneleigh manor and granted to the lord of the neighbouring manor of Allesley; 40 acres assarted from Dalle wood by the Abbots of Stoneleigh and leased out to a tenant; 50 acres granted to the same lord of Allesley by the Prior of Coventry; 400 acres recently approved by the Prior in Whitmore manor in Radford. But most of the tenants' holdings in severalty were quite small: ten acres was a big croft or field, most were between one and five acres. This sharply differentiates the medieval arable enclosures from the big enclosures for sheep pasture, often of several hundred acres, which were made at the end of the fifteenth and in the sixteenth century.

Although in Stoneleigh some enclosures were still affected by the exercise of common rights over them, the pointed way in which attention was drawn to these cases shows that they were exceptional. It was the object of enclosing landlords then, as both earlier and later, to buy off claimants to rights of common pasture, so that they might enjoy their severalties without hindrance. The lord of Allesley's considerable holdings of waste, just referred to, had been given to him by the Abbot of Stoneleigh in quittance of pasture rights. In so important a document as the Tripartite Indenture of 1355, by which the citizens of Coventry established their burgess rights as against their feudal lords, (the Queen Dowager and the Prior of Coventry), the Prior included a list of those pastures and other enclosures in the suburban hamlets which he claimed to hold in severalty the whole year round.[7] According to the survey of 1411 he made arrangements, as far as he could, with all neighbouring lords and freeholders in his various manors, that any claim they might have of common in any woods, wastes, moors, groves, meadows, pastures, ways, paths and approvements already made or to be made should be relaxed, often in exchange for considerable grants of land. The aim of those holding enclosed severalties, in other words, was to cut off these lands from all forms of communal obligation with which the medieval agrarian system was so closely bound up. Tenants as well as lords must have aimed at this. Common pasture rights in the end would be restricted to the diminishing area of the woods and wastes. It was this encroachment of arable severalties which precipitated sharp social struggles in Coventry itself at the end of the fifteenth century, in which enclosures favoured by the city authorities were resisted by those citizens who claimed common pasture rights for their beasts on the city lands. What must have been the typical grievances of the peasants in the surrounding villages were taken up by the citizens and lesser traders of a great urban community, as concerned about their pasture rights as if they had made their whole living from the soil.[8]

The villages[9] whose field systems I have been discussing all lie within a six or seven mile radius of the city of Coventry. Were their agrarian systems purely suburban, then? Were their enclosed fields simply extensions of the gardens and curtilages behind the homestead? That, I think, is not the case, for we find the same sort of system in other parts of the Arden-Feckenham woodland region which were clearly not suburban. Such enclosures were commented on in the sixteenth century by observers as being characteristic of Arden as a whole. We may add that the observation held good for the country across the county boundary. Perhaps the most striking evidence is that of a late sixteenth century map[10] of the fields of Feckenham, the village which gave its name to the royal forest. Here we see that diminished core of open-field arable surrounded by small hedged enclosures which we have envisaged from the documents in the Coventry area.

Unhappily this interesting map cannot be supported by other types of documentary evidence showing the growth of the Feckenham field system. It is true that two brief government surveys *(inquisitiones post mortem)* of the middle and the end of the thirteenth century, of the possessions of a family of noble foresters show an eccentric type of small landowner's holding consisting partly of scattered assarts, fields and crofts, but only in sufficient detail to hint that it must have been based on an agrarian system of an unusual type.[11] To the immediate west of Feckenham were a number of forest villages which belonged to the Bishop and to the Cathedral Priory of Worcester. As old settlements these had more open-field land than the other places we have so far discussed. Even so, thirteenth century surveys, which are not detailed enough to give us insight into the field lay-out, emphasise the large number of severalties and pieces of assarted land — for example, 33 and 64 assarts in the forest villages of Hanbury and Alvechurch as compared with only two or three in the villages of the valleys.[12] A few surviving charters of the early fourteenth century, transferring land in the parish adjacent to Feckenham, concern land in severalty only, a croft for instance *cum haytiis et fossatis*.[13] These are not enough to prove the universality or even predominance of arable enclosures, but the conjuncture of different sorts of evidence suggests that the sixteenth century map records an agrarian system several centuries old.

Another parish bordering on Feckenham was that of Tardebigge, in which lay the Cistercian house of Bordesley, mother to the Stoneleigh abbey that we have discussed. Bordesley records are scanty. Until recently all that were known were a number of twelfth and thirteenth century charters. One group was printed to illustrate diplomatic by the eighteenth century English antiquary Thomas Madox and a few extra charters are contained in another early diplomatic collection, Sir Christopher Hatton's Book of Seals.[14] These show that lands granted to this abbey, scattered from Holloway near Droitwich in Feckenham Forest, through the Forest of Arden to Oxhill in the south of Warwickshire, were for the most part in the form of assarts, crofts and fields, not intermingled with other men's lands as in open-field country. For example, land in Alvechurch (Worcestershire) was given with freedom of making hedges;[15] demesne lands granted elsewhere consisted of consolidated blocks of twenty and more acres; a number of crofts were included, sometimes described *sicut fossato clauditur*. But these were early contributions to the landed property to be worked by the monks themselves, and one would expect Cistercian grange land to be held in severalty. What about peasants in Feckenham Forest? Another document has come to light in recent months which illustrates the transfer of tenant land in Tardebigge during a century and a half.

By the end of the thirteenth century Bordesley abbey, like many other Cistercian houses, had forgotten the original rules of the order and was the lord not only of cultivated land but of men. The records of the abbot's court for the manor or Hundred of Tardebigge, preserved for intermittent periods between 1303 and 1471, yields some significant statistics of land transactions.[16] Tardebigge was somewhat larger even than the soke of Stoneleigh, and has subsequently been divided into three parishes. In the fourteenth and fifteenth centuries, like the Stoneleigh soke, it was an area of dispersed rather than nucleated settlement, there being six main hamlets besides other scattered farms. The whole area of jurisdiction was within the original bounds of the royal forest and was subject therefore to the Forest Law. But none of this, naturally, appears in the records of the Abbey's courts.

Records of 61 court sessions have survived, and contain transactions concerning 182 tenants' holdings. In most cases the lands composing the holding are described in sufficient detail to allow one to guess whether it consisted of ridges, mingled with those of other tenants, in the open fields, or of individual and separate pieces of land which, whatever the rights of common to which they might, or might not, be subjected, would not be part of an ordinary open-field system. One difficulty should be mentioned here. Some of the holdings were described as yardlands, or parts of yardlands. This unit of landholding was one quarter of a hide, the rough equivalent of the continental *mansus*. Originally the terms were used for land in open fields, but towards the end of the middle ages one suspects that a yardland need not necessarily mean 24 or 30 acres in the open fields but simply that number of acres of arable land in whatever form of field system. For instance, one and a half yardlands at Stoneleigh lay contained in two enclosures. However, in the Tardebigge records only 15 out of 182 holdings are described as yardlands, so the doubt is not of great weight statistically. Furthermore, only 11 holdings consisted entirely or partly of those ridges and butts which are usually taken to suggest the intermingled parcels of the open fields—one or two references do make clear that a few portions of common field lingered on. But no less than 142 holdings are so described that no suspicion of open field land appears in connection with them. Many of them are cottages or messuages by themselves but the majority consist of the tofts, crofts, gardens and separate fields already familiar to us in the Forest of Arden. The field system of the hamlets of Tardebigge must in fact have closely resembled that depicted on the map of Feckenham.

If the villages of Arden which were close to the great manufacturing centre of Coventry resembled in their agrarian system the villages of Feckenham Forest, must we then conclude that the development of the market played little part in encouraging the growth of arable severalties? I do not think that this conclusion is in any way justified. There are various means of gauging the commercialisation of peasant agriculture.

One of the surest is to measure the extent to which rents, services and terms of tenure have evolved as a result of the development of the market in land. This market was not negligible. According to the Tardebigge court rolls, only 34 out of 161 land transactions recorded resulted from the death of the tenant. Though it would be rash to conclude that the rest were all open or concealed sales or new leases, the proportion nevertheless gives some impression of commercial alienation. Rents were overwhelmingly money rents, with very occasionally a reference to a single boon work during the harvest. As far as tenure was concerned the tendency seemed to be, as years went on, for tenures which might either be hereditary or at the lord's will to be replaced by long leases for life, lives or long terms of years.

It is interesting to compare this situation with that in the villages near Coventry. Stoneleigh rents also were almost entirely in money with the exception of occasional autumn boon works; and in any case by the fifteenth century these boon works were hardly ever performed.[17] The tendency here too was for the replacement of hereditary or customary tenures by life leases or leases for long terms. By 1392 only 83 out of 218 holdings in the Stoneleigh Abbey rental were held hereditarily. Of the rest, 28 were at will and 107 were life or other long-term leases. The tenurial situation was in fact very similar to that in Tardebigge. On the Coventry Priory manors money rents were universal, there was no customary rent in the traditional sense and tenures were roughly in the proportion 24 per cent at will, 36 per cent for life and 40 per cent in fee. One suspects that these last were not so much ancient free tenures but free holdings of a more modern type bought for a premium by tenants who were often Coventry citizens. One has the impression that commercialisation had gone furthest in the nearest villages to Coventry, as one would expect with some investment of merchant capital there. But the tenurial structure was by no means radically different in Tardebigge in Feckenham Forest.

The explanation is of course partly that land newly colonised from the twelfth century onwards, whether in England, France or Germany, tended to be held in free or non-customary tenure for other reasons than commercial convenience. It was a bait to colonisers, and seigneurial pressure being relaxed, allowed some freedom of alienation. But the point is that these tenurial forms easily evolved with subsequent market conditions just as enclosed arable could be more easily adapted to such conditions than the land which was bound down by collective responsibilities. New market conditions encouraged the development of what already in part existed. The market in land, bringing about consolidation and further hedging, speeded up the liquidation of the open field core. This could happen in Feckenham Forest as well as in Arden near Coventry. Although Worcestershire's cloth industry was insignificant compared with that of the great Warwickshire town, it nevertheless existed and its product was marketed in the towns on the

THE FOREST OF
FECKENHAM
(from eighteenth-
century copy of
late sixteenth-
century map)

periphery of the forest—Worcester, Kidderminster, Evesham, Droitwich and Pershore.[18] Worcester, Evesham and Pershore were riverside markets on the way down from the central Midlands to the great port of Bristol. And Droitwich, on the northern edge of the forest, was the oldest and most important salt manufactury of the interior, the centre of a network of saltways, many of which went through the forest. These non-agricultural activities provided a market, and hence we must regard the cultivators of the forest enclosures as perhaps more advanced socially and economically than their fellows in the big old-established open-field villages of the valleys.

4

Ministers' Accounts of the Warwickshire Estates of the Duke of Clarence, 1479-80

INTRODUCTION

The Ministers' Accounts[1] here discussed are concerned with the greater part of the Warwickshire possessions of George Plantagenet, Duke of Clarence. Clarence's lands came into the hands of the Crown as a result of his attainder in January 1478, and were thenceforward administered by representatives of the Crown, accounts being rendered to the Exchequer. These are the first extant accounts after the attainder. However, as will be seen from the heading of the account, the estates were not treated as escheats, but as being in the King's hands on account of the minority of the son and heir of Clarence, Edward Plantagenet. The estates had come to Clarence after the death of Richard Neville, Earl of Warwick, because of his marriage to Isabel, Richard's elder daughter. Their son, Edward Plantagenet (executed 1499), was not allowed to succeed to his inheritance, and although the Clarence lands were in 1487 granted back to Anne, widow of Richard Neville and Edward's grandmother, she immediately reconveyed them back to the Crown.

The principal interest of these accounts is not, however, in the brief connexion of the lands for which they were rendered with the Duke of Clarence. It is rather in the fact that they are the fullest extant accounts of the Warwickshire lands of the Earls of Warwick, Beauchamp as well as Neville. The value of fifteenth-century manorial accounts to the economic and social historian is, it is true, considerably less than that of accounts dating from the hey-day of demesne farming in the thirteenth and early fourteenth centuries, as we shall show. Yet in the absence of earlier material for the Warwickshire estates of the earldom, these accounts have a unique value.[2]

It was common in the Middle Ages for estates which had an economic and tenurial unity to remain as administrative units over considerable periods in spite of political and family changes. Even permanent escheat into the hands of the Crown did not end the separate identity of such feudal estate organizations as the Honour of Wallingford, the Duchy of Cornwall, and the Duchy of Lancaster. The Warwickshire lands of the earldom were almost identical in 1480 not merely with the estates which Richard Neville acquired in 1449 through his wife, the last surviving heiress of the Beauchamp Earls of Warwick, but with the Beauchamp possessions at the beginning of the fourteenth century. According to his inquisition *post mortem* in 1316,[3] Guy Beauchamp had in demesne in Warwickshire the following possessions: Warwick borough, suburb and castle together with some escheated lands of the Templars in Warwick; and the manors of Sutton Coldfield, Haseley and Beausale, Lighthorne, Berkeswell, Brailes, Tanworth, Sherbourne, and Claverdon. By 1480 there were, it is true, some changes. Sherbourne was only temporarily in the Earl's hands in 1316, since it had been granted at an earlier date to the Templars. In 1308 it had escheated to the Earl as chief lord, but was subsequently regranted to the Hospitallers. On the other hand, the non-appearance of the manors of Claverdon, Haseley, and Beausale in the accounts does not signify that all had left the Warwick estate. Claverdon reappears in subsequent accounts.[4] Then, after the death of Guy Beauchamp, three manors were acquired and added to the earldom. They figure in the 1480 account. They were the manors of Budbrook, Erdington, and Morton. Budbrook and Grove (now Grove Park) were given to Thomas Beauchamp in Edward III's reign by John, Lord Hastings, in exchange for lands in Worcestershire. There were two manors at Erdington. One, known as the manor of Pipe, was bought by Thomas Beauchamp, Earl of Warwick (d. 1401), from the Abbey of Stoneleigh. Throughout the fifteenth century, therefore, it was part of the estates of the earldom. The other manor of Erdington passed from the Erdington family into the hands of the Duke of Clarence, according to Dugdale, not later than 1471. When the Warwick estates came to Clarence the two manors would probably be combined. At any rate the account of 1480 is presented as if for one manor only. Morton Morrell was sold by John Trimenell to Thomas Beauchamp in 1346.[5]

The manorial accounts printed here conform to the general type which had been in use on English estates since the beginning of the thirteenth century. The structure of the account changed remarkably little during the whole of this period, though there might be considerable variations between individual items of the account. The standardization of type was not only due to the fact that in spite of regional variations all manors were, from the point of view of the lord, organizations for the collection of rent and services from the tenants and of produce from the demesnes where such existed; it was also the consequence of the great elaboration of the technique of estate management in the thirteenth century. This produced an extensive literature of treatises on estate management and of formularies which set out how manorial accounts should be drawn up.[6] This literature was of great practical significance. The multiplication of copies shows that both the treatises and the formularies were widely diffused. It was this wide diffusion which caused the standardization of type on estates which were widely separated geographically and in different ownership. Furthermore, there is reason to believe that a class of professional manorial bailiffs was coming into existence versed in the techniques of estate management, and therefore in this most important aspect of management—accounting.

Manorial accounts, like the accounts of receivers, rent collectors, bailiffs of fees, and the like, were rendered annually, usually at Michaelmas (29 September). On some estates a halfyearly check was made by means of a document similar to a manorial account, known as a 'view of account'. The accountant for a manor could be either a professional bailiff, placed in charge of one or more manors by the central administration of the estate, or a peasant reeve chosen from among the customary tenants of the manor.[7] Sometimes bailiff and reeve might account jointly. Other manorial officials sometimes rendered separate accounts. It will be noticed that in 1480 the Warwick hayward *(messor)* rendered a separate account. Shepherds, woodwards, and dairymaids could also render accounts for the possessions under their charge.

The general purpose of the account was to enable the higher officials of the estate to know whether the lord's lands and rights were yielding him the maximum income. More particularly their purpose was to allot responsibility for income and expenditure as precisely as possible. Hence the sum total at the end of the income side of the account was sometimes referred to as the *total charge* rather than the *total receipt*. This total charge consisted of the arrears owing from the previous year's account, and various expected items of income, such as rents, sale of produce, profits from or lease of mills and fisheries, perquisites of manorial courts, and view of frankpledge. Some of these items, such as sales of produce and perquisites of courts, naturally varied from year to year. But other items were charged to the bailiff on the receipt side whether or not he received them. Most important among such items were rents. The central estate administration would have in its possession rentals which would give the details of rents due from a given manor. The bailiff or reeve would be charged with the collection of these rents and the total charged would go on the receipt side of the account whether or not the accountant managed to collect them.

The expense side of the account was not only a list of the actual sums spent on repairs, purchases of grain and stock, and the like during the course of the year. It also included entries by which the accountant attempted to reduce the burden of his charge. Most important was the item named 'Decay of Rent' *(Decasus Redditus)*. Under this heading were entered the sums by which the actual rent paid for various tenements fell short of the rent stated in the rental and charged up on the account. It also included sums of rent once paid from lands lapsed into the lord's hands through lack of tenants. Even when such items appeared among the expenses it often happened that the total receipt on the account considerably exceeded the total expenditure. This was not a happy state of affairs for the bailiff, as he had to produce the balance. By the end of the year he usually had very little cash, as the estate receiver or his agents came at intervals to take away the bailiff's spare cash, for which payments he accounted on the expenses side under the heading 'Payment of Moneys' *(Liberatio Denariorum).* After the expenses total therefore we find a series of entries described as allowances *(allocaciones)* or respites *(respecta),*[8] which include items such as payments to the lord's agents other than the official receiver (Tanworth), rents not acknowledged as decayed but uncollectable (Berkeswell), and other expenses of an extraordinary nature. If the accountant was lucky, the total of expenses and allowances would equal the total of arrears and receipts. He was then quit of his account *(Et quietus est).* If the receipt was greater than the expense side he was in debt and, if unable to pay, the debt appeared at the beginning of the next year's account as arrears. If the expenses added up to more than the receipts, the estate was in debt to the bailiff, and the sum would be paid to him or carried over as an allowance on the account of the following year (Wedgnock and Budbrook).

The account, which was strictly audited by expert, even professional, auditors, was the main method by which control was exercised over accountants. A subordinate form of check was by tally-stick or paper or parchment receipt. All of these performed the same function, that is, to provide for the accountant evidence which he could produce before the auditors of a transaction (usually the handing over of money). The thirteenth-century instructions for officials and reeves of St. Peter's Abbey, Gloucester, stipulated that accountants should obtain tallies for all manner of transactions including purchases and sales, even the handing over of winnowed grain by the winnower to the reeve.[9] In the 1480 accounts reference is made to tallies and paper or parchment receipts *(billae),* but only with reference to the handing over of money by the bailiff to the receiver.

Accounts which purport to give details of all manorial receipts and expenses during the course of one year are of course of great value to the economic and social historian. But their value varies according to the part played by the manorial organization in economic life. When the lord's bailiff was responsible for the running of a demesne consisting of arable, meadow land, and pasture, with livestock of all varieties, the account reflected the seasonal conduct of medieval agriculture. Let us take a typical example. A bailiff's account of the Catesby manor of Ladbroke in south Warwickshire for the year 1387-81 gives a most detailed picture of the resources of the demesne, though none about rents, which were accounted for by a separate rent-collector. The receipt side of the account includes details of sales of manorial produce, the most important of which was grain. The amounts of wheat and drage sold on different occasions are noted, together with the price at which the grain was sold per quarter. More revealing is the expenses side of the account. Details about spare parts and repairs of ploughs and carts tell us about the equipment of the demesne farm. The account of wages paid for autumn work tells us that there were in demesne 103 acres under crop. This figure can be checked from the grange account, on the back of the roll which, under the heading for each type of grain, tells how much was used and on how many acres. A considerable part of the expenses went on wages. The permanent staff consisted of the bailiff, a carter, two ploughmen, a dairymaid, and a shepherd. Fifty customary tenants owed labour services, but in addition to their work hired men and women were taken on for the threshing, for hay-making, harvesting, sheep-shearing, and building repairs.[11]

With its arrears and receipts, expenses and allowances, the cash side of the Ladbroke account is in structure similar to the accounts of 1480, whatever the contrast in the various items under these main headings. But the associated grange and stock account is of equal importance and greater length. This does not account in terms of cash. Various types of grain are listed—wheat, drage, peas, rye, and malt. The sources of the grain received during the course of the year are given, whether from the barns or from other manors on the estate. The use to which the grain was put is also set down, for seed, as payment in kind to farm servants or as fodder. As with grain, so with livestock. The turnover of stock during the year included six horses and two foals; seventeen oxen, a bull, and five cows; three steers and a calf; two boars, two sows, thirteen young pigs, and twenty-seven piglets. Then there were different types of poultry—geese, hens, capons, and doves. The sheep for whose washing and shearing women's wages were entered under the expenses of the sheepfold *(custus falde)* do not appear in the stock account. But a summary list of the manorial resources of the Catesby estate *(Status Maneriorum)*[12] drawn up at the annual audit two years previously shows that the estate sheep flock was concentrated at Radbourne. Perhaps they were brought over from there to the neighbouring village of Ladbroke because for some reason (perhaps a better water-supply) it was more convenient to wash and shear there.

The Ladbroke account is typical of the era of demesne farming, which indeed was nearly over in most parts of the country by the end of the fourteenth century. The great age of this type of seigneurial economic activity was the thirteenth and early fourteenth century, and it is therefore from this earlier period that most accounts of this type survive. Although Guy Beauchamp's inquisition *post mortem* of 1316 indicates that the Warwickshire manors of the earldom were then being run on these lines,[13] by the fifteenth century the earls had ceased to engage in agricultural production, and the manorial accounts of 1480 reflect the change.

By this time very few of the demesne resources were kept in hand. All the mills which were still in working order were leased out. Arable, pasture, and the bulk of the meadow were in the hands of lessees, as were the fishponds and river fisheries. The only sales of produce from possessions which were not leased out were of hay and wood, as at Warwick, Wedgnock, and Budbrook. But in other places where the bailiff still had parks and woodland on his charge, as at Tanworth and Brailes, there were no sales during the course of the year. Hence the historical significance of these accounts is very different from accounts such as that of Ladbroke. The stock and grange account has disappeared. Rents of various types are the principal items. Since the emphasis has shifted to rents, there is much more detail about them than is usually found in the earlier accounts where details about production predominate. Rents and the tenements for which they were paid are the economic features therefore which can be most usefully studied from these accounts.

The accounts do not merely illustrate a change in the nature of the manorial economy. They are a warning to all those who would use them and others of the same period uncritically as documents reflecting contemporary conditions. Each of the accounts here printed gives a long list of various types of tenement and rent under various headings on both the receipt and expense side of the account. The student, on first examining the accounts, naturally assumes that the information relates to the date of the account. This is true of some items. When we are told that no hay or wood was sold in the year of account, or that the demesne lands were on lease for a certain term of years at a given rent, or that a certain sum was spent on repairs to buildings, we have no reason to believe that these statements were not true. The situation is different, however, for items under the rent and decay of rent headings. The full summaries of rent-paying tenements under these headings in some of the 1480 accounts are identical in whole or in part with the entries in accounts half a century or more earlier. This must mean that the bailiffs were being charged with rents, or allowed money for decay of rent, on the basis of rentals drawn up at a date considerably earlier than the date of the account. Instead of being completely renewed, new rents and

Place	Arable	Meadow	Pasture	Woodland
Warwick	342 a.	93 a.	Various in severalty and common	Wedgnock Park
Do.(Templars)	160 a.	24 a.	Common	
Sutton Coldfield	120 a.	14 a.	In the woods	Sutton Park and another wood
Haseley	183 a.	5 a.	Unmeasured piece	An enclosed wood
Beausale	30 a.	3 a.	..	An enclosed wood
Lighthorne	250 a.	12 a.	12 a.	Enclosed spinney
Berkswell park	282 a.	24 a.	A pasture in severalty	3 woods and a park
Brailes	596 a.	208 a.	139a. and an unmeasured piece	A 36a. wood
Tanworth	217 a.	27 a.	6 pieces	A wood and a park
Sherbourne	204 a.	16 a.	Severalty and common	..
Claverdon	160 a.	12 a.	Severalty	Enclosed park

increases in rent were simply added to the old rentals.[14] Instead of reductions in rent being accepted as permanent and subtracted from the rents considered due, the separate item, decay of rents, was kept and added to as further rent reductions occurred.[15] In one sense this conservatism is an advantage to the student, for had rentals been constantly renewed and simplified, details of rents in the accounts could be kept to a minimum, and rent reductions would not have been noted. In the absence of a long series of annual accounts, single accounts in which newer items are superimposed on the old, like a series of rock strata, have their uses. But the dangers are obvious. To derive any information of historical value from out-of-date entries, we must know how out of date they are in fact.

A number of earlier accounts of some of the Earl of Warwick's manors have survived. They illustrate the points made above and assist the interpretation of the accounts of 1480. A short reeve's account of the large manor of Brailes, running from April to September 1401, gives but scanty details about rents. The change-over from demesne farming to leasing seems to have just begun, in such a way that the estate owner still maintained an interest in production. The demesne was sown *ad cambi partem,* that is, to use a term more familiar in France at this period, at *champart.* This was a form of lease by which the lessee paid a rent in the form of a proportion of the crop instead of money. It is not possible to tell from the account how many lessees there were on these terms, but it is possible that, in contrast with the later policy of leasing to one lessee, there were a number of local peasant lessees. Since it was to the lord's interest to improve production with this type of lease, we find that the lord's sheep were folded on the demesne. By 1414 the *champart* leases were abandoned. The whole demesne was leased to the reeve, and considerable detail about rents appears in the account. The two items under the heading *Incrementum Redditus* are virtually identical, including personal names, with the first two items of the 1480 account. The six items under the heading *Novus Redditus* are also identical with the first six items in 1480. There is less resemblance between the items under *Decasus Redditus,* though five items in the 1414 account are repeated almost word for word in 1480. By 1460 it seems that a process of ossification had set in. All the various rent items charged up on the receipt side of the account are entirely identical with those of 1480. Under the heading 'decay of rent', the twenty items of the 1460 account correspond to the first twenty of the 1480 account, the remaining eighteen items presumably representing rent reductions subsequent to 1460.[16]

According to an account of Tanworth of the year 1381, the manorial demesne was then already leased out for a money rent. There is already considerable detail about increments to rents of assize and about pasture rents. By 1430 the list of increments of rent is longer. The first four items under this heading are the same as those of 1381 as regards tenements, rents, and even the names of the tenants. The pasture leases have also increased in number from sixteen to eighteen items. The first sixteen pieces of pasture leased in 1430 are identical with those of the 1381 account, except that names of lessees are not given in the earlier account. In most cases rents in 1430 are lower than in 1381. Pasture leases are described in the accounts as sales *(venditio pasture),* so that there would not be a fixed charge on the bailiff as in the case of tenements with rents entered in a rental. They would be treated by the auditors as variable from year to year. In the 1381 account there are no decays of rent, but by 1430 a considerable number appear. The 1480 account repeats all the rent and rent reduction items of the previous accounts, with some added. The list of rent increases under the heading *Redditus Assise* repeats identically (except for some changes in the spelling of names) the twenty items of the 1430 account, and six extra items of rent increase are added. Pasture sales are now described as leases *(firma pasture).* They are the same as those of half a century before, except for a few reductions in rent. The rent reductions in 1480 also largely repeat those of 1430, with four additional items.[17]

What has been said of the accounts of Brailes and Tanworth also applies to four fifteenth-century accounts[18] of Erdington, where there appears to have been no manorial demesne. The first account, completed in 1408, is very short. It is a rent collector's account and gives no details of tenements. A rent collector's account of 1424 is fuller, chiefly as regards the entry of assize rents and decay of rents. A bailiff's account of 1438 repeats in their entirety the items of increases to rents of assize. The repetition here is not mechanical, for all of the tenements held by increased rent were held for terms of twenty years, and the account of 1438 states accurately how far each lease had run. Rent reductions by 1438 had increased by five items additional to the three of 1424. An account of 1461 shows practically no change in the items of rent increase, but there are fifteen additional items of decay of rent. So far the Erdington accounts show the same tendencies to accumulate and repeat detail as the others. The 1480 account, however, shows a break in continuity. This is probably because the Erdington bailiff at that date was accounting for the combined manors of Erdington, the earlier accounts having been rendered for the manor bought by Thomas Beauchamp. It is natural that when manors combined an administrative reorganization should take place. Hence there is no coincidence between rent or decay of rent items in the Erdington accounts of 1461 and 1480.[19]

In spite of the limitations to the usefulness and reliability of the Warwick accounts, they are of considerable importance to the social and economic historian as well as to the student of local history. While we would value records of agricultural management which would tell us about the activities of those who had taken over from the big estate owners—the lessees, often of peasant origin—we must recognize that in the nature of things this is impossible. Estate agriculture on a large scale needed its accounting system. Small lessees needed no such document-ation. We must therefore make the most of what exists.

The plainest message of the 1480 accounts is of the decline of the traditional seigneurial economy. We have reason to suppose that in certain sectors the medieval economy was recovering from its prolonged depression, and we must therefore treat this evidence strictly in its context. We would not be justified in assuming that the financial difficulties of the estate owners, revealed in their accounts, were paralleled among the active producers—the lesser gentry, the rich peasants, the merchants, or the manufacturers of cloth. But since the estate owners were the rulers of English society, their economic embarrassment is all the more significant. The fact that by 1480 these estates were in the hands of the Crown (as were many similar escheated properties) in no way diminishes the interest of the document. The behaviour of the Crown as a landowner is of as great general importance at the end as well as at earlier periods of the Middle Ages.

The basis of seigneurial incomes was rent. By this time rent was almost entirely money rent. There are references in the accounts to a few rents in kind—always expressed as if sold, and probably in fact commuted. All labour services were by 1480 commuted for a money rent. Judging by the earlier accounts for Brailes and Tanworth this commutation goes back at least to the beginning of the century. But money rents, whether old-established rents of assize or newer leasehold rents, show a universal, though uneven, tendency to fall. This can be seen by examining the *Decasus Redditus* items in the accounts and balancing them against increments of rent. It will be found that nowhere, during the period since the compilation of unknown date of the rental on which the accounts were based, were rent increases greater than rent releases. Taking decay of rent as a proportion of assize rent, increments and new rents together there is some unevenness of development from manor to manor. This unevenness is of course only significant if we know the period during which fall and increase in rent took place. A partial answer can be given for the manors for which we have earlier accounts.[20] The 1480 total of decayed rents at Brailes began to accumulate at least fifty years, and at Tanworth sixty-seven years earlier. At Tanworth the percentage of rent reductions by 1480 was only 9 per cent. of the original assize rents plus subsequent increments. At Brailes the reductions were 40 per cent. of the rent totals. On the manors where no date from which rent decays can be dated a similar percentage to that of Brailes is found at Morton (40 per cent.), Lighthorne (42 per cent.), and Warwick (39 per cent.). Smaller reductions had taken place at Erdington (20 per cent.), Berkeswell (14 per cent.), and Sutton Coldfield (8 per cent.). It should be remarked that the rents at Warwick were mostly urban rents. The decline there may perhaps be related to a fall of 60 per cent. in the farm of the market toll at Brailes between 1414 and 1460.[21]

The fall in those rents which had a less fixed character than assize rents was more consistent. The rents paid by demesne lessees at Warwick and Morton had by 1480 been reduced, as compared with some unknown previous date, by 36 per cent. Rents from pasture leases at Tanworth were reduced by 20 per cent., at Warwick by 32 per cent., and at Berkeswell by 38 per cent. The rents for the River Avon fisheries at Warwick were reduced by as much as 74 per cent. There was a complete loss of rent from the demesne at Sutton Coldfield, for no farmer would take it on. Nor could any lessee be found for the rabbits in the warren, for a demesne coppice, or for the weir fishery. There is even more concrete evidence of decay at this manor, for the dovecot was destroyed and the fulling-mill was in ruins.

It will be noticed that competitive rents had not, by 1480, made noticeably great inroads into the rent structure of the Warwick estates, at least as far as can be judged from these accounts. It is true that the terms of tenure of many holdings are not described, and that the phrase *ad consuetudinem manerii* makes only an occasional appearance, as at Sutton Coldfield. Although the terms of tenure of many holdings are not described we should not expect the same detail in an account as we should in a rental. The accounts do not list all holdings separately. The old rents of assize are given as a lump sum, and separate account is given only of new tenements, of those for which increases of rent have been obtained, and of those for which a rent reduction has been allowed. The old rents of assize were due from land held freely or by customary tenure, and we cannot assume that tenements mentioned separately without description of terms of tenure were not on similar tenures. Those few tenements which were certainly not held on customary terms were terminable leases of various types, but there are not more than thirty of these in the twelve accounts. Two-thirds are leases for life, and the rest for terms varying between twenty and a hundred years. The terms of tenure for demesne leases, where new forms of landlord-tenant relationships are often found, are not described apart from some piecemeal demesne leases for life at Brailes. The chief symptoms of the new forms of economic life of the period are occasional references to enclosure, of which the most interesting are in the Brailes account. Here, under new rents, account is given of three licences given to tenants to enclose land to be held in severalty. Brailes was a village whose fields lay open in the traditional Midland pattern. It was reported by the commission of inquiry of 1517 and 1518 as having suffered enclosure and depopulation on two occasions, once in 1496 and again sometime before 1518.[22] This earlier evidence of smaller scale enclosure in the same village is of some interest, for it indicates that small-scale enclosure might have been a factor preparing the way for the complete overthrow of the old agricultural system.

The economic historian will find in these accounts some useful indications of the field systems of Warwickshire. Most of the manors covered by the accounts were in north Warwickshire, where agrarian

conditions were somewhat exceptional.[23] The traditional type of open-
field agriculture was seldom found in the Arden forest, although some
sort of irregular openfield system probably existed. Owing to the extent
of individual assarting from the woodland there was a marked
predominance of holdings in severalty, whether of arable, meadow, or
pasture. It is true, of course, that even in 'normal' open-field areas there
was a tendency for the development of cultivation in severalty in the
later Middle Ages, but in the Arden forest area, as in Kent and Essex,
severalty and enclosure seem to have been prominent from a more
ancient date. Of this type of holding there is ample evidence in the
accounts. They contain a large number of field names, which, as the
editors of the English Place Name Society volumes have shown, are in
themselves a valuable source of information of early agrarian forms.[24]

The accounts contain information of use to the historian interested in
the internal administration of estates and in the administrative consequences of their appropriation by the Crown. It is true that the
references in the accounts themselves do not enable us to obtain a very
detailed picture of the workings of the estate. Yet enough will be found
to confirm the impression of an essentially conservative institution.

There are some dangers in trying to build up (from incidental notices
in the accounts) a complete picture of the estate administrative apparatus,
since for lack of evidence we are obliged to combine references to
persons and events when the estate was in private hands with those
contemporary with the accounts. Furthermore, we must remember that
the Warwickshire lands formed only a small proportion of the total
estates of the Beauchamp and Neville Earls of Warwick. There is no
reason, however, to suppose that there was any strictly separate
administration of the possessions in the county of Warwick. Officials of
the central administration would be responsible for all component parts
of the Earl's and later the Duke's estates. This is clear from the way in
which a receiver's account of 1395 is arranged.[25] No distinction is made
between the component parts of the widely scattered possessions.

By the fourteenth and fifteenth centuries the administration of a noble
household had become separated from the administration of the landed
property.[26] The household officials of the Duke of Clarence who are
described in his household ordinances of 1469 have nothing to do with
the running of the estate which is our concern.[27] The estate administration was simple enough and seems to have changed little, if at all,
between the end of the fourteenth century and 1480. There were two
principal officers of the estate in the days of the Beauchamp earls, the
supervisor and the receiver. The supervisor was probably the senior, and
fulfilled duties which on other estates would be those of the chief
steward. He would be mainly responsible for all legal business, the
conduct of courts, and questions concerning the transfer of land. It will
be noticed in these accounts that all the references to the supervisor
concern his responsibility for land sales and leases. In the 1395 account of

the receiver, Thomas Knyth, reference is made to a payment to John More *supervisor terrarum domini,* a clear indication of the separation of the two offices. Dugdale, however, refers to John Verney, Dean of Lichfield Cathedral (mentioned three times in the accounts), as supervisor and receiver-general, quoting an account now no longer extant.[28] This seems to be an abnormal combination, and Dugdale may not have meant to imply that Verney held the two posts concurrently. The Earl of Warwick's Household Book of 1432 refers to Verney as supervisor only.[29] The duties attached to the two posts were dissimilar, and the financial and legal aspects of estate administration were usually kept separate, as on the Lancastrian estates.[30] It will be noticed that there is no reference in the 1480 accounts to a supervisor or equivalent official of the Neville and Clarence periods, nor to one at the period of the accounts. This does not mean that the office had disappeared, though when the estate was in the hands of the Crown the work of a supervisor may have been done by government officials.[31]

Before the estate came to the Crown the receiver's duty was to receive the cash income from the accounting officials of the different manors of the estate, and to issue money for the various uses of the owner, as well as for the payment of fees, wages, and incidental estate expenses such as were not met locally by reeves and bailiffs. The money was collected at various periods throughout the year, mostly coming in at the fixed terms set for the payment of rent. When the estate came into the hands of the Crown the internal financial administration did not change. The receiver continued to collect the cash revenues through his subordinates. Now he was an official of the Crown, and the money collected went to swell the Crown revenue, not to support a noble household. It seems likely that the receiver in 1480 paid his money into the Receipt of the Exchequer. At any rate the accounts must have been presented in the Upper Exchequer, for we are told that the previous year's accounts of Warwick, Sutton, Erdington, and Brailes had remained in the Exchequer in order that proceedings could be taken against various debtors. For that reason no total of arrears carried forward could be given in the 1480 accounts. It should be noted that one of the auditors of the accounts was the Exchequer auditor John Clerk, a Baron of the Exchequer.[32]

Procedure against debtors through the Exchequer must have been a slow process. For this reason a proposal was made in 1484 for the more expedite collection of Crown revenues, recommending in particular that accountants and other debtors should have no more than four months' respite. More radical was a proposal in the same memorandum that extraordinary revenues from estates once separate from Crown demesne but now in Crown hands should not go through the Exchequer. These estates, known as the King's 'foraign lyvelode', consisted of those of Wales; the Duchies of Cornwall, York, and Norfolk; the Earldoms of Chester, March, Warwick, and Sarum; and all forfeited lands. It was proposed that they should come before 'forayn auditours' rather than before Exchequer auditors, so as to enable the Crown to get the money quicker, and so as to make it possible for the stewards, auditors, and receivers to make annual surveys of the estates. The accounts would eventually be deposited in the Exchequer, but only for record purposes.[33] The diversion of these sources of revenue from the Exchequer was an aspect of the revival of the Chamber as an instrument of royal financial policy, more efficient and expeditious than the Exchequer. Henry VII promoted this policy most vigorously, but (as with other aspects of Tudor policy) it was foreshadowed under the Yorkists. However, the fact that the Warwick accounts of 1480 were still presented to the Exchequer suggests that the memorandum of 1484 was not in all respects, as has been thought, a tightening up of existing practice, but a proposal for innovation.[34]

The principal local officials of the estate were the stewards and the bailiffs. The stewards appear in the accounts only as responsible for presiding over the manorial courts. It is unlikely that there would be a separate steward for each court, and in fact only three are mentioned by name. They are John Barbour, William Berkeley, and John Huggeford, stewards respectively of Lighthorne, Erdington, and Brailes. Like an earlier official, Nicholas Rody, who was steward of both Morton and Lighthorne, they probably had responsibility for other manors than the one from which they derived their title. Stewards were usually drawn from the gentry. Whether they were men with local interests or caught up in government business, the work of steward could only have been a part-time occupation. Bailiffs, on the other hand, as responsible accounting officials, had heavy and continuous responsibilities.[35] Financially they were responsible to the receiver for the payment of monies and to the auditors for the rendering of account. Both receipt and account seem to have taken place at Warwick,[36] though it is possible that money collected by John Heywood, deputy to John Luthington the receiver, was taken from the bailiffs at their manors at times of the year other than Michaelmas. In addition bailiffs would also be subject to the control, as far as general estate management was concerned, of the supervisor. His supervision may well have been partly delegated to the local stewards, since the courts[37] over which they presided dealt not only with internal manorial discipline, but also with transfers of land.

We have said that the estates which fell for one reason or another into the hands of the Crown continued to be administered as units rather than to be absorbed into the general body of Crown lands. Nevertheless there can be no doubt about the completeness of royal control. Experienced Exchequer officials were put in charge of the estates as soon as they came into the hands of the Crown. True, Henry Harper, one of the Duke of Clarence's auditors was confirmed at first in his post by royal letters patent, but he and his fellow John Tooke were quickly superseded by royal officials. Although Harper was granted the post of auditor in 1478, and sat on a commission of inquiry into the Clarence lands in

Herefordshire, John Howyke and Peter Beaupie were appointed auditors of Clarence lands in the same year. Howyke was an experienced man at the job, having held the post of auditor of the lands lately of Henry Percy, Earl of Northumberland as early as 1461, and of the Duke of York in 1471. Beaupie, a clerk of the green cloth (according to the letter patent of 1478), is described in the accounts as a royal commissioner and councillor. He was appointed at various times to responsible posts, including those of J.P. in various West Midland counties, and feodary in Gloucestershire, Warwickshire, and Worcestershire. In 1480 Harper and Tooke were finally superseded as auditors by Howyke and John Clerk, the Baron of the Exchequer already mentioned. These two appear as auditors in the preamble to the accounts and as successors of Harper and Tooke in the list of allowances at the end of the Sutton Coldfield account.[38]

John Luthington, who appears as Receiver in the 1480 accounts was also a royal financial official, with experience going back to 1458 when he was made an auditor of the possessions late of Edmund, Earl of Richmond, and of the temporalities of the Bishopric of Durham. From that date onwards we find him in frequent government employment as auditor, commissioner of inquiry, receiver, and bailiff.[39] References to incidents and other persons in the accounts show the extent to which royal officials and servants took over the Clarence estates. The bailiff of Warwick rode up to London during the course of the year to discuss various matters concerning the lands and tenements in his charge with various royal officials, including Beaupie and William Essex, an Exchequer official of long standing.[40] Central Exchequer control of the estate seems clearly indicated from this reference. But the King also gave positions to others of his supporters who were not so concerned with the financial machinery of the State. William Berkeley, an esquire of the body, who in 1478 was made steward of Erdington, was accustomed to performing similar functions. He was also constable of the King's castles at Winchester and Southampton, steward of Ringwood and Christchurch in Hampshire, and of Solihull, Yardley, and Perry Barr in the Midlands. The demesne farmer and warrener of Brailes, John Hethe, was a yeoman of the King's chamber and also held the office of bailiff of Chadlington Hundred in Oxfordshire. Degory Heynes, the bailiff of Warwick town, is described in a pardon of outlawry to one of his debtors as a goldsmith of Coventry. He was also a yeoman of the Crown. David Madock, bailiff of Yardley and Erdington, is described as yeoman of the Crown; William Selby, janitor of Warwick Castle, as yeoman usher of the household; William Turnour, marshal of Tanworth stud, as king's servant and one of his farriers; Henry Wedehok, warden of the Warwick armoury, as king's servant and keeper of the King's armour in the Tower.[41] These posts were not of course granted solely to ensure royal control of newly acquired estates. They were also rewards. This method of payment was well recognized. Edward IV's own household book, which gives a brief account of the expenses of different ranks of the nobility as well as of the King, speaks of marquesses as follows:

> These Lords rewarde theire knyghts, chapeleyns, esquiers, yomen and other of theyre servauntes after theyre deserts....for the secular men, stewardshippes, receivours, counstables, portershippes, baylywikes, wardenshippes, forresters, raungers, verders, vergers, shreves, eschetours, coronners, custumers, countrollers, serchers, surveyours, beryngs of yeres, gifts, wards, marriages, corrodies, parkers and warreners. And this causeth lordes to rule at neede.'

The King was still to a considerable extent dependent on the same sort of resources as his fellow landowners.

Of course, there were still local men who had been attached to the Warwick estates through many changes of regime. John Huggeford, constable of Warwick Castle and steward of Brailes, was granted those offices by royal letters patent in 1478, but was a member of a family intimately concerned with the Earls of Warwick since the end of the fourteenth century at least. His father before him had been constable of Warwick Castle, receiver-general of the estate, and an executor of the will of Earl Richard.[42] Huggeford seems, however, to have been the only official of importance who had strong links with the past. Some smaller officials still remained, no doubt, who were not simply royal servants. Such, for instance, was John Knight, bailiff of Berwood and custodian of Sutton Chase. In the royal letter patent by which he was granted this office he is described as 'late servant of the Duke of Clarence'.[43] Generally speaking, however, although the old administrative structure was kept, the replacement of personnel and the establishment of central control was complete.

5

The Leger Book of Stoneleigh Abbey

I *The Manuscript*

The Leger Book of Stoneleigh Abbey, sometimes called the Register,[1] is the property of Lord Leigh of Stoneleigh Abbey whose ancestor acquired the site of the dissolved house in 1562, and with it much of the abbey's store of muniments. It is to be presumed that the book was written round about 1392, the date of composition given by the author in his preface.

The book is not a simple cartulary, as will be realized from the author's description of its purpose and from a perusal of its contents. The plan of the work does not appear at first glance, but after some study it is possible to discern that it is composed of three unequal parts. (i) The charters and other evidences arranged chronologically and contained within the framework of a short and inaccurate chronicle of English history; (ii) A summary statement of the court procedure and customs of the manor of Stoneleigh with some illustrations from court cases; (iii) A rental and survey of the lands and tenants of the manor of Stoneleigh at the time of the book's compilation. This begins with a survey of the lands held by the Augustinian Priory of Kenilworth, the appropriator of the parish church, and ends with the perambulation of the bounds of the manor. The whole work is concluded by a short history of the outstanding acts of successive abbots, incomplete for rather curious reasons, as will be seen.

As in the case of most medieval cartularies there are many additions made subsequent to the completion of the main text. Some of these are inserted in the middle of the text where opportunity in the shape of a blank page presented itself. Others are added at the end. Some of the more interesting additions will be discussed below. This description of the manuscript may be concluded with the reminder that this book, being only the first one of four which the author compiled, or intended to compile, deals fully only with part of the abbey's possessions, that is, the nucleus of the estate in the parish of Stoneleigh. Although there are incidental references to parts of the estate elsewhere in Warwickshire, these are not described in detail. A glance at the description of the Stoneleigh Abbey estate in the *Valor Ecclesiasticus* (a version of which was added to this book), shows that although the bulk of the revenue came from the hamlets of Stoneleigh parish, there were other possessions in neighbouring villages (such as Ashow, Hill and Leek Wotton,

Cubbington, Leamington, and Stivichall) and an important exploitation at Radway on Edghill in south Warwickshire. The full evidences and detailed description of these properties were contained in those parts of the author's work which are no longer extant.

II *Stoneleigh Abbey*

The Abbey of Radmore in Cannock Chase, later known as Stoneleigh Abbey, was founded, like many English Cistercian houses, during the unfortunate reign of King Stephen (1135-54). This was the period when the international reputation of the Cistercian order was at its highest, due amongst other things to the great reputation of Bernard, Abbot of Clairvaux (1090-1153), the most famous Cistercian of his day.[2] The endowment of any religious community was thought to bring spiritual rewards to the giver, so that to give to an order outstanding for its asceticism and piety would naturally be an act especially productive of otherworldly returns. An additional advantage was that Cistercian communities expected grants only of uncultivated land, whereas a new Benedictine foundation would require grants of property already worked by tenants. The acquisition of special spiritual honours at a low cost would be a particularly attractive proposition for the brutal and superstitious nobility of the period of the Anarchy.

The normal process by which a Cistercian abbey was founded was for an abbot and twelve monks to be detailed for the purpose from an existing mother house, and to establish the new community on land provided by a benefactor. This was not the way in which Stoneleigh Abbey was founded. The community was originally founded as a settlement of hermits in Cannock Chase, and did not for some years apparently adopt any regular rule of monastic life. Such hermitages were not unusual at this time and it will be noticed that the small estate of the Hospitallers in Fletchamstead, in the soke of Stoneleigh, also began as a hermitage in the reign of Henry I. The peculiar circumstances of the origin of Stoneleigh Abbey, however, have made the exact sequence of events doubtful. Even the medieval tradition recorded by Thomas Pype, the author of the Leger Book, is unclear.

Pype's narrative of the foundation is interwoven with a confused chronicle of national events and is repeated, with curious differences, in the *Acta Abbatum* at the end of the Leger Book. His story is as follows. The Empress Mathilda, daughter of Henry I, gave to the hermits of Radmore the place where they had established their hermitage in Cannock Forest, and some land at 'Melesho'. No date is mentioned, but it is implied that it was earlier than 1140, when the hermitage was converted into a Cistercian abbey. This gift was confirmed by King Stephen, the evidence quoted by Pype being a notification by Roger, Bishop of Chester. In this notification the names of two of the hermits,

Clement and Hervey, are mentioned. Some time after this, William, Prior of Radmore, went with his brethren to the empress and to her son Henry to repeat complaints, first made in 1133, about conditions in the forest.[3] Their complaint was that they were oppressed every week by the comings and goings of the Cannock foresters and they asked for the place of their hermitage to be changed. Mathilda would only agree on condition that they adopted the Cistercian rule, a condition which they accepted. The date of this change is given as 1140. But instead of being moved immediately from Radmore as they had petitioned, they were simply confirmed in their possessions in Cannock Chase and elsewhere. At this point two charters of the future Henry II are quoted which could only have been issued in 1153.[4]

The next stage in Pype's narrative is to describe the actual transfer from Radmore to Stoneleigh. According to him they spent thirteen years being pestered by the foresters; so after Henry's coronation they went to see him and, acting on his mother's advice, he gave them a home in his ancient demesne land at Stoneleigh in exchange for their old home at Radmore. They actually moved, says Pype, on 19 June 1154—an impossible date since Henry was not crowned until 19 December, 1154. The act which they regarded as their foundation charter, confirming both the grant in Stoneleigh, and some other Warwickshire lands that they had acquired when still at Radmore, was issued by the king in 1155.

It has been suggested[5] that the author of the Leger Book confused the date of the adoption of the Cistercian rule with the date of the very first settlement of the hermits. If this were the case, then the hermits first went to Radmore in 1140,[6] suffered from the royal foresters for thirteen years, and adopted the Cistercian habit in 1153. They then reapplied for transfer from Cannock to the newly crowned king and moved in 1155 or 1156. This version of events clears up some obscure points, particularly the oddity of the introduction of Henry's charters of 1153 as if they immediately confirmed an act which is stated to have occurred in 1140.

All elements of doubt are not removed by this suggested reconstruction of the process of foundation. The introduction of the year 1133 in the *Acta Abbatum* may have some basis in fact, so we need not accept as the foundation date of the hermitage Pype's date for the conversion into an abbey. Although he tells us that this was 1140, this part of his narrative comes after his account of the reign of Stephen has ended, when (as mentioned above) he also introduces the charters of Henry Plantagenet of 1153 as the immediate consequence of this bargain with Mathilda. In any case, the year 1140, when Mathilda was keeping to Bristol and Gloucester until the news of Stephen's capture at Lincoln (February 1141), seems an unlikely time for the hermits of Radmore to have approached her. Her charter to Radmore cited earlier on in this account by Pype was certainly later than 1140. It was issued by her as 'Anglorum domina' at Devizes, some time between July 1143 and 1148.[7]

The charter to the hermits of Radmore by Mathilda may have been sought by them for precautionary reasons during this confused period, but the hermitage with its possessions may already have been in existence for some years. Stephen gave the hermits a charter, which was not necessarily a confirmation of Mathilda's grant. It is not cited in the Leger Book. Instead the notification of it to his Staffordshire officials by Roger de Clinton, Bishop of Chester, is quoted. This is difficult to date. But it must have been sent out when the bishop was on good terms with Stephen. He was one of the bishops who went on Stephen's behalf to Rome in 1136, but was with Mathilda by 1141,[8] no doubt following on the attack on Roger of Salisbury in 1139. Sir Frank Stenton refers to him as 'well known supporter of the Empress', although he witnesses a charter of Stephen again, possibly in 1147.[9] It may be, then, that Stephen's grant to Clement, Hervey and the other hermits of their place in Radmore was made before 1139. Bishop Roger also granted two hides in Radway to the 'monks and brothers' of Radmore, not referring to an abbot, and therefore possibly (though not necessarily) before the conversion to the Cistercian rule. This charter is difficult to date except within wide limits. It could not have been earlier than 1135, the date of foundation of Buildwas Abbey, whose abbot was a witness, and it could not have been later than 1147 when the bishop went on the Crusade, never to return. The only other grant to the Radmore community in which an abbot is not mentioned was by Geoffrey de Clinton, the younger. Here again the dating is uncertain, the witnesses being mostly the local Warwickshire personalities who are found witnessing the younger Geoffrey's charters to his father's foundation at Kenilworth, but to whom precise dates cannot be given.[10]

It seems possible, therefore, that the hermits officially acquired their place of retreat in Cannock Chase from King Stephen in the early years of his reign, and that they subsequently obtained confirmation of this possession from the empress. No hint of the community's status as a Cistercian abbey is mentioned in Mathilda's charter of 1143-8, so the date 1140 given in the Leger Book for this event must be wrong. It must, as suggested by the Brookes, have been nearer to 1153. However, the other charters granting land to Radmore as an abbey are unfortunately not more closely datable.[11] The charter evidence of the grant of Stoneleigh is in Henry II's foundation charter of 1155.

The dating given by Pype for the actual move is, as has been seen, very confused. If the land at Stoneleigh were granted after the coronation of 19 December 1154, an anticipatory move on 19 June of the same year is unlikely. Pype gives the correct day of the coronation in the Roman fashion, the fourteenth calends of January, giving the year of grace, 1154. The day given for the subsequent event in the narrative, the move from Radmore, the thirteenth calends of July (19 June) is also put in 1154, although in fact the 19th calends of January (19 December) in this case was towards the end of 1154.[12] Hence the date of the move must be 19 June 1155, and this fits in with the date of issue of Henry II's charter at Bridgnorth in the summer of that year. Pype's confusion continues. He says the monks first settled at Cryfield, but soon moved to Echills Wood, the first stone of the church being laid on the Ides of April (13 April) 1154. This of course could only be 1156.

In view of the hesitations about the exact site, the move may have been prolonged. An occupation in stages is conceivable. According to Eyton,[13] Abbot William was still styled 'of Radmore' in 1156, so he may have been the last to move when advance parties had made full preparations.

At this point a postscript should perhaps be put to this discussion of the foundation of Stoneleigh Abbey. Although the abbey's principal Warwickshire possessions were given to it by King Henry II, it was to John's charters that abbots were obliged to appeal when they were defending their privileges. Henry gave them his 'dominium' in Stoneleigh and defined it in terms of land. But royal officials by the end of the twelfth century still asserted that the king was the lord of the manor, of its court, and of its view of frankpledge. It was to the king's bailiffs not the abbot's that royal writs initiating pleas between tenants were addressed. So Abbot William of Tyso in 1204 bought the whole soke of Stoneleigh. The word soke is not used in John's first charter, but to the recital of the possessions of the house is now added the privilege of quittance from shire and hundred courts and from the usual royal exactions. In the second, shorter, charter issued on the same day the phrase 'totam sokam de Stanleya' is employed and is subsequently used with some frequency.[13] Freedom from royal or official interference was, however, by no means fully won.

The later history of Stoneleigh Abbey is only of interest because of its situation as a small landowner holding former Crown property under special legal conditions. These aspects of its history are discussed further in this introduction. But it was a poor, obscure house and seems to have played no part in English history outside its immediate neighbourhood. Nor was it significant in the annals of the Cistercian Order. It was hardly ever brought to the attention of the Chapter General of the Order,[14] and its dissolution was not attended by any circumstances out of the ordinary.

III *The Author of the Leger Book*

The author of the Leger Book announces himself, in his introductory dedication to the reigning abbot, Thomas of Haltone, as Brother Thomas Pype, adding that he too, though unworthy, had previously held the post of abbot. In the *Acta Abbatum* at the end of the volume, Pype is the last abbot of the list, having succeeded Robert of Atherstone in 1352 as a young man. The reader might assume from this that at a venerable age Pype had retired to make way for the man who, as Pype tells us, instructed him to compile this register of the muniments, charters, and memoranda of the house. Thomas Pype's further mentions of himself in the Leger Book are confined to references to those necessary occasions when, as abbot, he was involved in such transactions as leases, purchases, and sales of abbey property. These references are numerous, in fact Pype mentions himself much more frequently than any other abbot. And although each event which is described is in itself quite colourless, the over-all impression is that here was an abbot who conducted himself with great vigour in defence of the property rights entrusted to him.

However, careful attention to the dates of indentures and charters issued by Pype and other abbots, and recorded in the Leger Book, show that although the last date of such an official act by Pype was in 1381, his tenure of office could not have been unbroken since 1352. An abbot William Aston is referred to as having released a holding in perpetuity to a tenant in Kingshill in 1367-8 which Pype subsequently reacquired. Other references are made in the Leger Book to an abbot John Colshulle or Coleshill, who was issuing deeds in 1383-4, 1384, and 1385. John Coleshill's dates do not of course imply, as do William Aston's, a break in Pype's tenure of office, but it remains odd that he is not mentioned in the list of abbots. How long could the break in the period of Pype's office have been? The last of Pype's acts, before the reference to Aston, is dated 1363-4 and the first reference to his acts, after Aston, is dated 1372. What was happening during this period?

When we look beyond the Leger Book for evidence about Thomas Pype we get a very different impression of him from that which he seems to have wished posterity to deduce from the records he selected for registration. It is not precisely known who were his parents, but it seems likely that he came from a family of local gentry, like so many monks of the later Middle Ages. This family's lands seem to have been in Moreton Morrell, Chesterton, and Erdington, and Thomas, who was perhaps in his twenties when he became abbot in 1352, may have been the son of John de Pype, who was a prominent subsidy payer in these three places in 1332.[15] Whatever his origins, it would appear from reports of his behaviour, which appear in the public records, that he did not take his monastic profession very seriously.

Apart from certain recognizances of debt in the Close Rolls, to which reference will be made shortly, Pype's first appearance in the public records is in 1363, when a commission of oyer and terminer was appointed to inquire into a complaint by the Prior of Kenilworth against Pype and a number of monks, lay brethren, and tenants for assaulting his tenants in Leek Wotton and Stoneleigh. In itself this need not be taken too seriously, since accusations, as in this case, that the tenants were terrorized to such an extent that their lands remained uncultivated, were frequently highly exaggerated. The root of the matter may simply have been an attempt by the abbot to make Kenilworth tenants attend the Stoneleigh view of frankpledge by the process of distraint. However, we must bear this accusation in mind when we read of further accusations against Pype, leading up to his deposition and the taking of the abbey into the king's hands in the autumn of 1364.[16]

The reason given for handing the administration of the abbey estate to two wardens (Richard of Stafford and Richard of Pyryton, Pyryton shortly being replaced by the Duke of Lancaster) was the existence of 'misrule by granting corrodies to improper persons, improvident demises of lands, and the excessive and unfruitful expenses of the presidents' (that is, the abbots). This drastic step (not, however, by any means unheard of)[17] follows closely on a pardon for the unlicensed alienation of Millburn grange and other property, but at about the same time the Crown was also taking the precaution of appointing commissioners to inquire into various alienations of property for which the abbot was said to be responsible.[18] The report of one of these commissions was presented to the justices of King's Bench by the chancellor himself, and gives ample grounds for the resumption of the estate into the hands of the Crown. The facts were given to the royal commissioners (Sir John Pecche and Simon Pakeman)[19] by a jury of local men. The jury was no doubt fairly carefully picked, for none of them seem to have been involved in dealings with the abbey.[20] They may have been retailers of the gossip of the district, but there are no reasons for supposing that they had a special interest in either supporting or denigrating Abbot Pype.

Their answer to the question as to what property given by the king's ancestors to Stoneleigh Abbey had been alienated, to the detriment of the chantries and pious works they should have supported, was quite precise. According to them the principal beneficiary of these illegal alienations was Isabella of Beausale, the abbot's concubine, and John, their eldest son. This grant consisted of a life estate in a messuage, a ploughland (probably to be understood as about a hundred acres), and ten marks rent in Finham, handed over without any payment for the lease and without any rent being due to the abbey. This grant, made out of 'voluptuosa affeccione', led Pype into further difficulties. Fearing deposition as a punishment for his uncanonical behaviour, he alienated Millburn grange, worth £20 a year, to two of his servants, Adam of Stokke, cook, and Roger of Cotes, for their lives, to be held in trust (ad opus et proficium) for Isabella and her offspring.[21] Finally, he alienated a ploughland in Canley and Hurst in fee simple to Richard de la Cloude, who had previously held as a tenant (presumably by the custom of the manor). A rather obscure background to this latter transaction is described. Originally the abbot had brought a suit against Richard and had recovered the holding, apparently on the basis of a document forged by a monk, John of Weston, who later confessed he did so under duress from Pype.[22] Such is the story reported by the king's commissioners. Writing the story up nearly forty years later, Pype gives the affair of Richard de la Cloude an innocent interpretation. Richard was the heir to the lands of the Robert of Canley who had been deprived by royal intervention of a usurped lordship in Canley. Pype's original proceedings against Richard, according to his own account, were based on the illegality of an alienation of the tenement at an earlier date. These proceedings, says Pype, were successful, but he allowed Richard, for a money payment, to hold the tenement, and quotes an indenture to this effect. According to this indenture Richard was to hold this land in Stoneleigh for 5s. 1d. instead of all services except fealty.

Pype's story may not be entirely untrue. But the royal commissioners indicate that the disputed land was in Canley and Hurst, not in Stoneleigh (Pype's story comes in the Canley section of the rental). There is an indenture among the Early Deeds in the Leigh Collection[23] which does deal with Richard de la Cloude's land in Canley and Hurst, and which clearly states that the terms of tenure were to be converted from customary to fee simple, that is, the same money rent will be paid, but fealty only is substituted for suit of court, heriot, and other customs. This confirms exactly one of the accusations against Pype. It is also of some interest that the date of this indenture, and the list of witnesses, are identical with that of the indenture quoted by Pype about land in Stoneleigh where no change of tenure is mentioned. On the most favourable interpretation Pype was suppressing reference to this aspect of the affair. On the worst interpretation he is rewriting the evidence.

The evidence of the jury is supported by entries in the Close Rolls made some time before the inquiries of this commission. These are recognizances or acknowledgements of debt whose recovery would be made easier in view of their official enrolment. It is well known that in many cases these acknowledgements are not of commercial debts, but are a form of sanction to enforce various agreements including title to land. In other words an alienor of land going back on his alienation could be sued by the alienee for the sum named in the recognizance, with the extra right of distraint on the alienor's goods and chattels if the money were not forthcoming. A series of such recognizances by Abbot Pype and the convent in favour of various persons including Adam Stok, Isabel Heynes (of Beausale), and her sons and daughters, suggests that steps were being taken as early as 1360 to make Pype's settlement in favour of his mistress and offspring as watertight as possible. He even caused to be entered on the Close Rolls his alienation of Millburn grange to various feoffees, at a peppercorn rent, dated 7 July 1362.[24] The eight persons named as feoffees in the Close Rolls do not include the two mentioned in the later official inquiry, but the jurors were of course only speaking from hearsay, and the essential point for them was that the persons to whom Millburn grange was alienated were simply Abbot Pype's agents.

The inquiry into the affairs of Abbot Pype was made in January 1364. The king had taken the abbey into his own hands by October of the same year, and as was normally the case, the income from the estate, after provision for the sustenance of the monks and of a moderate number of servants, was to be devoted to the succour of the house, probably paying off debts. Corrodies and such like charges on income (probably to Pype's friends) were to be suspended.[25] Pype and his accomplices meanwhile had left the abbey, but were still in the neighbourhood, for the king had to take the remaining monks under his protection for fear of them. During 1365 the king withdrew his keepers and an abbot, Alexander, was elected. Trouble with Pype and his party was not over. Abbot Alexander denounced Pype as a vagabond in secular habit to the king, who sent out a general order for his arrest. According to another complaint by Abbot Alexander, a group of persons including Isabel Heynes, Adam Stok, and others who were feoffees of Millburn grange, broke into the abbey premises and made off (inter alia) with the abbey seal, deeds, and muniments. In 1368 inquiries were ordered into robbery and destruction of abbey property, and in 1369 six more monks of Stoneleigh were reported as vagabonds in secular habit. William Aston was now abbot, having succeeded Alexander in 1366 or 1367.[26]

For some years after this the affairs of Stoneleigh Abbey were free from the intervention of the royal authority. As we have seen, Pype reappears as abbot in 1372. In 1380 there seems to have been a renewal of previous disputes, for at the same time as the abbot got a royal licence to lease abbey lands for life or term of years the king took the house into his hands again and placed it in the custody of the Duke of Lancaster. The reason given was the suits and controversies between the abbot and his adversaries. Malefactors, presumably belonging to one or other of the factions, seized the abbey seal and used it to lease out manors and grant out pensions. But the abbey must have been restored to Pype for a time because the king confirmed by *inspeximus* a lease granted by him in the spring of 1381 to some Coventry merchants, of lands in Bockyndene grange. By 1382, however, he had retired (voluntarily or otherwise), for in that year the abbot and convent were pardoned for the unlicensed alienation to a group of feoffees, mostly prominent gentry, of Cryfield grange, to the use for life of Sir Thomas Pipe, former Abbot of Stoneleigh.[27]

IV *The Leger Book as Historical Evidence*

The scope of the Leger Book or Register is described by the author in his introductory dedication. It is clear from what is said there, as well as from the contents, that the purpose of the book, as in the case of the many similar registers and cartularies of other monasteries, was the registration of the documentary evidence of the possessions and privileges of the house. Like all medieval landowners, Stoneleigh Abbey was much involved in litigation with neighbours, tenants, and temporal and spiritual overlords. The fourteenth century had been a troubled time and difficulties had arisen not only from these inevitable conflicts but from the dispersal of these documentary evidences. As we have seen when we examined the career of Thomas Pype, the author of this register was himself not blameless, for the conflict between him and his opponents in the abbey in the middle of the century seems to have involved raids on the muniment chest of the house.

Unhappily three out of the four books which Pype claims to have compiled have not been found. The first book is clearly recognizable from the description in Pype's preface as that which we have here. The analysis of the contents of this first book shows that the practical purpose of providing evidence for the defence of the abbey's rights was not lost sight of in spite of the apparently confused and miscellaneous character of the material registered. It is true that the chronicle which acts as a sort of framework to contain the essential materials from the abbey muniments is, strictly speaking, unnecessary. However, for the purposes of subsequent defenders of the abbey, this chronicle framework would no doubt give an historical perspective which would make easier the comprehension of the abbey's standpoint.

No further reference to the use of the Leger Book before the Dissolution has been noticed, though it was no doubt a handy reference book for estate administration. At any rate quite a few extra jottings of charters and other matter seem to have been added in the fifteenth and early sixteenth centuries.[28] But it did not fall into utter disuse after the dissolution of the abbey, for someone practised writing the letters of the alphabet on a fly-leaf at the back, giving the date 13 June 1560. There is also some evidence that it was in demand again when Sir Thomas Leigh finally acquired Stoneleigh.

One of the documents among the Leigh Collection[29] is a list of instructions, probably drawn up by, or for, Sir Thomas himself. These instructions direct some unnamed recipient to inquire what were the legal rights attached to the Stoneleigh property. If the list emanated from Sir Thomas, it probably falls within the period between the purchase of the abbey site (1561) and his death in 1571. Another paper in a different hand seems almost to be the reply, or part of the reply, to the instructions. It records the liberties attached to the former monastic lands. The Leger Book must have been a primary source for this information. We can go farther, however, in proving the interest that was taken in the Leger Book at this period. There is also a complete English translation of the book, in manuscript, beautifully written in a hand which mostly adopts a secretary style, but which occasionally uses the italic.

The date of this translation is not given but it can be guessed at with fair certainty, for there are some other documents in the same hand which are reasonably datable. One of these is a copy of bailiffs' accounts for various of Sir Thomas Leigh's manors collected together in a single book. Some of them are called rentals, but their form suggests that they were in fact based on annual accounts. The whole book was probably drawn up as a rental for the newly acquired property. The accounts used are for years between 1553 and 1570. Then there are some more fragmentary papers, again in the same hand. These are copies of court rolls of two Gloucestershire manors (Bledington and Maugersbury)[30] for 1561 and 1562 to 1571. The copy of the Maugersbury court roll contains an elaborately decorated initial letter which could only have been the work of the scribe of the translated Leger Book.

There is a fair presumption then that these collections of estate evidences were probably written up for Sir Thomas Leigh or his successor in the early seventies. It is not easy to find a certain owner of the hand in which the papers are written. Extant signatures of Sir Thomas Leigh's sons, Rowland and William, are in an italic similar to that used by the scribe we are discussing.[31] There is, however, another signature which is equally possible to identify with the scribe's writing, and its owner is a more conceivable compiler of these various evidences. This signature is on the original perambulation of the parish of Ashow, a parchment pinned to folio 193 of the translated Leger Book.[32] It is in fact the only original signature to the perambulation, the other witnesses having made marks. The signatory is Roger Vicars, parson of Ashow between 1572 and 1575.[33] He also signs a deed of 1569, and may (judging again by the writing) have added the record about Chesford Bridge at the end of the medieval Leger Book (fols. 191 to 193b). Vicars must have been presented to the living by Sir Thomas Leigh's widow shortly after his death. It seems very likely that he was in the family's service before his presentation, an obvious person to be employed in the arrangement of the records of the newly acquired estate.

Whoever it was that translated the Leger Book and copied out the accounts and court records of Sir Thomas Leigh's manors must have had a predominantly practical interest in these documents, though in view of the elaborate care with which the English version of the Leger Book was decorated, an antiquarian turn of mind may be suspected. Sir William Dugdale, however, seems to have been the first person who used it as historical evidence.

Dugdale used this book considerably in the making of his *Antiquities of Warwickshire,* for the most part, of course, in the description of Stoneleigh and its hamlets.[34] He appreciated the importance of the statement of the customs governing the relations between the abbey and its sokemen, and draws attention to the special character of the relationship between the crown and this alienated portion of its demesne. However, the antiquaries of Dugdale's day, with rare exceptions, did not have the same interest in the economic, social, and legal aspects of local history that have occupied later historians. It was not until 1892, when Sir Paul Vinogradoff, still Professor in the University of Moscow, used the Stoneleigh Register in his pioneer work *Villainage in England,* that one of the most important aspects of the document for the general historian was brought to light. Even Vinogradoff, mainly interested in the book for the help it gave him in elucidating the special conditions on the ancient demesne of the Crown, gives only a partial indication of its value. Just as Dugdale's outlook was inevitably restricted by the predominant interest in genealogy of his day, so Vinogradoff was principally interested in the definition of legal status of the different classes of rural society.

Although other aspects of the Leger Book than those which concerned Vinogradoff are of equal importance to historians today, it will, of course, be examined by scholars to see how its evidence, now available in full, supports or refutes the penetrating criticism made recently by Professor R. S. Hoyt[35] of Vinogradoff's theories of the origin of the special conditions on manors of the ancient demesne of the Crown. The evidence of the Stoneleigh Leger Book provided much of the groundwork for Vinogradoff's description of the peculiarities of the ancient demesne.[36] He was particularly interested in the legal protection that was given to the sokeman tenants of Stoneleigh. According to the Stoneleigh customs this rested on two special privileges. First, they had access to a royal writ, the 'Little writ of right close', for the protection or recovery of holdings. Cases initiated by this writ were, however, to be pleaded, not in the public courts, as in the case of common law free tenures, but in the Stoneleigh manor court. Secondly, they could obtain on complaint to the king a writ 'Monstraverunt' which would secure their holdings on the terms by which they were held when the manor was still in the hands of the Crown. Vinogradoff suggested that this special protection, dating back to the Conquest period, had the effect of preserving on the royal demesne alone the peasant conditions of late Anglo-Saxon England. These conditions, presumed by him to be better than those of the majority of peasants at the end of the thirteenth century, were protected from deterioration by the insulation of the royal demesne from the effects of landlord oppression during the late eleventh, twelfth, and thirteenth centuries.

Professor Hoyt, on the other hand, argues that the royal demesne only began to be treated differently from other lands from about the reign of Henry II onwards. He finds that the special category 'ancient demesne of the crown', meaning that which was *Terra Regis* in Domesday Book,[37] only appears towards the middle of the thirteenth century and that appeals to Domesday Book to determine ancient demesne status do not become common until Edward I's reign. Royal justices itinerant at the beginning of the thirteenth century might take an interest in cases of dispute on alienated royal manors, but in their administrative rather than in their judicial capacity. The famous ancient demesne writs had not yet made their appearance. Professor Hoyt's explanation of the appearance of the category of ancient demesne is simple. The Crown was interested primarily in revenue. Although income from the royal demesne was not sufficient for the king 'to live of his own', it could be enough to give him some financial independence of the baronage who claimed the right to give their consent to the extraordinary taxation which was becoming more and more necessary to keep government going. Apart from the

direct profits of demesne lands leased out to farmers the demesne also
yielded revenue when its inhabitants were tallaged. Now the Crown did
not lose interest in demesne that was alienated to other landowners, as
Stoneleigh was to the monks of Radmore. Dugdale, as well as
Vinogradoff, noticed that in spite of John's charter, the king continued to
interfere in Stoneleigh affairs as if the abbey were a farmer rather than a
tenant in frankalmoin.[38] It was clearly in the interests of the Crown, if it
was to continue to exercise rights of tallage on alienated demesnes, to
enlarge as far as possible the category of ancient, that is former, demesne.
It could hardly choose a wider category than the Domesday Book *Terra
Regis*. It was this expedient of the thirteenth century, rather than the
continuous preservation of the demesne in its Conquest period condition,
that Professor Hoyt thinks was the basis of the special conditions in
ancient demesne manors. The peasants of alienated ancient demesne were
protected from the oppression of new landlords, not in honour of any
ancient heritage of freedom, but because they could be more profitably
tallaged by the Crown if their immediate lords were prevented from
over-exploiting them. Vinogradoff's theory about the pre-Conquest
origin of ancient demesne tenure was added on to his description of
ancient demesne conditions in the thirteenth century without being
essential to it. He was well aware that the Crown's interest was largely
fiscal. The Stoneleigh evidence, with its emphasis on the recurrent
attempts by the abbots to stem royal intervention and to keep the profits
of tallage, has nothing in it which contradicts this aspect of Vinogradoff's
views nor the general line of Professor Hoyt. On the other hand, it offers
no support for the theory of pre-Conquest origin. The custumal, after
all, though not dated, is part of a late fourteenth-century compilation.
The compiler states that his sources for knowledge of the customs consist
of old court rolls and information from suitors to the court. The latter
presumably were his contemporaries, and the court cases quoted towards
the end of the custumal are all of the late thirteenth and early fourteenth
centuries. This was the period when the ancient demesne concept had
reached full definition, and had become sufficiently well known to be
frequently cited by peasants all over England who saw in it a method by
which they could delay and prevent rent and service increases.[39] The
earliest document quoted in the Leger Book which uses the term
antiquum dominicum is a royal writ of 1253 allowing the tallage of the men
of Stoneleigh to the abbot when the rest of the demesne was tallaged.
The remaining few documentary references (as distinct from statements
by the Leger Book's author) all fall in the latter part of Henry III's and in
Edward I's reign.

The principal advantage for tenants was protection from arbitrary
exactions by the lord (or by the king's officials where the demesne was
not alienated), and also the security given to tenure through the right to
plead by writ. It is admitted by Vinogradoff that otherwise conditions of
tenure often resembled ordinary unprotected villeinage. Indeed he asserts

that there might be unprotected villeins side by side with privileged villeins on an ancient demesne manor. Even so he stresses the aura of ancient freedom that seemed to cling to the man on ancient demesne, the 'stock of freedom . . . which speaks of Saxon tradition'.

Now, the conditions of the tenants of Stoneleigh seem to support this view. Although some of Pype's disquisitions on the primitive tenurial conditions of the neifs and free tenants in sokemanry and little sokemanry do not inspire much confidence in view of what we suspect about the artificiality of ancient demesne privileges, we have independent testimony in the results of that official inquiry of 1280 called the *Rotuli Hundredorum,* which we shall examine in more detail farther on. At this point we may simply make the point that according to this document only seven out of over two hundred Stoneleigh tenants are called villeins, and that the conditions of these villeins in fact seem indistinguishable from those of the vast numbers of cottars and other smallholders. These hold mostly for life, some at will, but all for money rent and at most a few days' service at the autumn reaping. In other words their tenures were very like free tenures. Then there are thirty or forty privileged free tenants or sokemen, so called by either name. They were also bound to do services at harvest, of a supervisory capacity. Was this, then, a special community of peasants enjoying an archaic freedom, protected by the Crown from the depressing effects of the yoke of Norman landlordism? Of freedom from some of the traditional incidents of villeinage[40] there can be no doubt, but this same inquiry of 1280 shows that this was almost certainly not due to the protection of the Crown.[41] In village after village in east central Warwickshire we find the same predominance of free tenure, irrespective of whether the manors were of ancient demesne or not. It was the consequence, as has been shown elsewhere, of the vigorous extension of the cultivated area in the old woodland of Arden. It occurred during the two centuries between the compilation of Domesday Book and of the royal inquiry of 1280. It was not a matter of Anglo-Saxon freedom preserved, but of new freedom won.[42]

V *Other Stoneleigh Evidence*

The Leger Book is undoubtedly the most interesting of the Stoneleigh Abbey materials which have come down to us, and (as Vinogradoff demonstrated) it is of considerable importance even taken by itself. There is, however, a considerable body of further manuscript evidence for the history of the medieval estate.[43] Although this introduction is not the place for a history of Stoneleigh Abbey based on these materials, it is important that the material should be described and some indication given of its value. The majority of these manuscripts are with the Leger Book itself at Shakespeare's Birthplace, Stratford-upon-Avon. They consist of two collections of original deeds, a fragmentary cartulary, and a number of court rolls. Unfortunately there are no account rolls. At the

Public Record Office there are a few more charters amongst the collection of Ancient Deeds and some late medieval court rolls. At the Public Record Office, too, there is an unpublished manuscript copy of the *Rotuli Hundredorum* of 1280 to which we have just referred. It covers the Hundreds of Stoneleigh (subdivision of Knightlow) and Kineton, and contains a description of all the Warwickshire lands and tenements of the abbey. This document is also referred to as the 'Notyngham Inquest', from the name of the head of the commission of inquiry, Henry of Notyngham.

(a) Stoneleigh Abbey Charters

The Stoneleigh Abbey charters naturally include important grants made by the king and by prominent secular and ecclesiastical persons. Most of these are transcribed in the Leger Book and few originals of them have survived. No further comment about them is necessary here. By far the greatest number of charters and other deeds concern quite small land transactions. It is from these that a detailed picture of the consolidation of the estate, of the nature of the agrarian system, and of the local social structure, could be drawn. Many of them contain quite detailed descriptions of the location in the fields of the land transferred. Rents and services are naturally specified, and in a number of cases the selling price of the land is stated. From the names of grantors, grantees, and witnesses a considerable knowledge can be obtained of the local peasant families. For some villages and hamlets on the estate charters and deeds are abundant, for others relatively scarce. However, the local centre of gravity of evidence is different for each of the three collections of charter material, so if taken in combination a representative selection is available. The charters transcribed in the Gregory Leger Book mostly derive from the south Warwickshire villages of Radway and Ratley. One of the collections of original charters, also from the manuscripts of the Gregory family, has a preponderance of Kingshill (Stoneleigh parish) material. In the other main collection of originals, belonging to Lord Leigh, the hamlet of Canley and the village of Stoneleigh provide many more examples than any other place. But each collection contains deeds concerning other villages than those from which the bulk is derived. The few charters among the Ancient Deeds in the Public Record Office derive from a variety of places. Some of them are in fact originals of those transcribed into the Gregory Leger Book.[44]

i. The Gregory Leger Book

The Stoneleigh material in this book is bound together with a miscellany of other material in a single volume, some of whose contents have been described elsewhere.[45] There seem to be copies of 137 charters in this collection. The reason for doubting the exact number is that after the sixty-ninth charter (p. 224) the inner edges of the pages are badly decayed, the decay being so bad between pages 234 and 241 that it is not easy to be certain how many charters are copied here. There appear to be thirteen. If this is so, only charters 92 to 104 are illegible; charters 70 to 91 vary in the degree of legibility; and charters 105 to 137 are for the most part as completely legible as the first sixty-nine.

Only a dozen of the charters are also to be found (with no, or insignificant, differences) in the Leger Book,[46] and mostly concern major endowments. The others, with a few exceptions, deal with small areas of land alienated by lesser local landowners, alienations which are stated in some cases simply to be purchases by the abbey for cash down, and which in many other cases probably were cash transactions even where this was not stated. Since these charters were regarded as title deeds, those copied also include alienations between previous owners before the final alienation to the abbey.

About fifty of these charters (including confirmations) concern land in south Warwickshire,[47] principally in the villages of Radway and Ratley, on Edgehill. A few others record transactions in the adjacent Oxfordshire village of Hornton. These charters of Radway, Ratley, and Hornton describe endowments or purchases which laid the basis of a working estate in south Warwickshire, consisting, by 1280, of four ploughlands in demesne in Ratley, and two ploughlands in demesne in Radway. There were at that date no tenants of the abbey at Ratley, but sixteen of various grades in Radway. The original endowment in Radway was that of two hides made by Roger de Clinton, Bishop of Chester before the Radmore monks left Cannock Chase. It was when visiting this property from Radmore that they lodged with the Cistercians at Bordesley and became familiar with their rule. The subsequent acquisitions, as recorded in these charters, were from a variety of sources. Local landowners, such as Osbert the Huntsman (Venator) of Radway and his relatives, Ralph Butler of Butlers Marston, and others gave land by charter. One of the charters, by Hamon Lenveyse, granted Stoneleigh Abbey the advowson of Radway church and is to be dated 1220-5.[48] Most of the Radway grants seem to be of the early thirteenth century. The Ratley charters were mostly issued by members of the Arden family, who were lords of the manor. The most important grant was that by Hugh of Arden and his wife of three ploughlands, a grove, and pasture for 300 sheep. Hugh was brother of Henry and Osbert of Arden, perhaps the Osbert who gave the monks some land in Marston before they left Radmore.[49] The Ardens also gave small quantities of land in their manor of Ryton-on-Dunsmore, near Coventry.

Somewhat more than forty deeds (thirteen of the illegible ones are probably to be included) concern property in the villages of the Stoneleigh soke. These are mostly of the late thirteenth century and reflect the buying up by the abbey of lands of its own free or sokeman tenants, presumably in order to add them to the demesne or to re-lease them for terms. One charter shows the abbey pressing this policy rather hard. In it Michael of Hurst quitclaims his right in a third of a two-virgate holding in Cryfield, for which he is pleading by royal writ in the county court at Warwick. For this quit claim—in anticipation of his success—he is given ten shillings, because he is hard up (in urgente necessitate mea), and when he gets the land he is to make it over to the abbey by another charter within eight days. If he is not successful, he pays back the ten shillings. If the writ called 'Pone' has to be bought, the abbot will get it. A Michael of Hurst, living in 1280, is mentioned in the Leger Book. Another Stoneleigh free tenant, John fitz Geoffrey, is the originator of charters for small amounts of land to the abbey.[50] He too was living in 1280, for he is one of the Stoneleigh men referred to as a free tenant in the Hundred Rolls.

The Radway-Ratley and the Stoneleigh groups of charters constitute the main bulk of the contents of the Stoneleigh Abbey material in the Gregory Leger Book. There are other charters, some of which are useful in solving minor problems. For example, there are some difficulties about the land in Marston given by Osbert of Arden to the monks when they were still at Radmore. The grant was confirmed by Ranulf, Earl of Chester (d. 1153), and a grange at Marston is referred to in the foundation charter of Henry II and in King John's charter. There is no further reference to this land in the Leger Book, nor in other extant surveys. Some documents in the Gregory Leger Book throw some light on the question. Hugh, Earl of Chester (d. 1181) confirmed a grant of thirty-four acres in Kingsbury (near Tamworth) made by Robert fitz Walter and his wife Amabilia (granddaughter of the Osbert mentioned), in free alms, to Stoneleigh Abbey. Two other charters, by Robert fitz Walter and his wife, unfortunately somewhat defaced, suggest that they gave this land in place of the land at Marston originally granted by Osbert of Arden, because they (Robert and Amabilia) were unable to warranty it. It seems likely that Marston near Kingsbury, in the parish of Lea Marston, is the place referred to. The land in Kingsbury was occupied by sitting tenants, so no doubt that was the end of direct agricultural exploitation by the monks in North Warwickshire.[51]

The date of compilation of this fragmentary cartulary is not easy to determine precisely. The charters to which certain dates can be given are those issued by prominent persons. The latest of these are earlier than the middle of the thirteenth century.[52] But most of the deeds are issued and witnessed by local men. As students of the Leger Book will notice, there was as great a tendency amongst peasants as amongst barons for the same Christian names to be used generation after generation, and this makes the dating of local charters extremely hazardous. I would, however, suggest that on the basis of the dating of some of the Stoneleigh soke charters quoted above and on palaeographical grounds, the cartulary was made before the end of the thirteenth century.[53] Its evidence was no doubt used (or was intended to be used) by Thomas Pype in the compilation of his second volume.

ii. The Original Deeds

The two collections of original deeds are a good deal more

heterogeneous in character and chronologically more scattered than the fragmentary cartulary just described.[54] There is little reason to consider them apart, for each contains materials from the thirteenth to the sixteenth centuries, of the same type and from the same villages. The only distinguishing feature of the two collections is their separate provenance.

Although the deeds include documents from the late twelfth century to the period of the Dissolution, the greatest concentration of material is between about 1250 and 1350. Many types of deed are represented, including straightforward grants, quitclaims, and agreements and leases by indenture. A large number of documents still retain the original seals, and a study of these would reinforce existing evidence about the wide variety of social types who used seals.[55] The impression, however, is that the majority of transactions of which these deeds were the evidence involved the wealthier peasants of the Stoneleigh parish hamlets, those referred to sometimes as sokemen and sometimes as free tenants. Apart from being the originators of many of the deeds, these men appear time and time again as witnesses to deeds, no doubt in their capacity as the leading men of the court of Stoneleigh. A phrase here and there suggests the court as the place where the final formalities at any rate of some of these transactions took place. In one deed the list of witnesses is completed by the phrase 'et tota curia de Stanleia'; according to another the relatives of the seller of land abjured their rights to it *coram helmot domini regis apud Stanleiam* (a reminder of ancient demesne niceties).[56] But these references to the court are only occasional, and the very existence of these deeds poses a difficult problem.

According to the statement of manorial custom in the Leger Book, the sokemen were not permitted to alienate land by charter. If they wished to alienate, and acquired the lord's permission to do so, the land had to be surrendered 'ad opus ementis' in court, when it would then be reissued, heriots and other obligations having been acquitted by the alienor. The compiler of the custumal is particularly emphatic about the veto on alienation by charter, and mentions this on two occasions other than in his description of the proper method of alienation by surrender. Yet deeds were issued by sokemen on behalf of other sokemen, and on behalf of the abbey itself as if their lands were held in common law free tenure. Nor is it a question of the sokemen alienating freehold land other than their sokeman holdings, for the deeds quite often mention that the land transferred is to be held according to the custom of the manor.[57] In other examples land transferred by deed was clearly not held by normal free tenure in view of the mention in the deed of litigation about it in the abbot's court.[58] The beneficiary of these deeds, as one would expect, is in many cases the abbey itself. The deeds naming the abbey as recipient as well as those describing previous transactions between tenants were, of course, kept among the abbey muniments as necessary evidences of title, a curious practical repudiation of the insistence in theory that this type of land could only legally change hands by surrender in court, with enrolment on the court record rather than charters as the written evidence of tenure. The alienations by charter suggest that the sokemen occupied a more favourable tenurial position than that attributed to them in the custumal. The custumal may, therefore, reflect an attempt by the abbey to prevent sokeman tenure from assuming the alienability of free tenure, by insisting on its customary character. If this is so, the abbey would be just as interested in stressing certain supposed characteristics of ancient demesne as the crown, particularly that all land should be dealt with in the manor court. The other way in which the abbey tackled this problem was to acquire the land of the sokemen so that it could then, if it wished, reissue it for life or for lesser terms. It got royal permission to do this in 1291 and 1380.

An episode recounted in the Leger Book concerning tenants in Canley shows not only what a shadowy division there was between free tenants and sokemen, but how under favourable circumstances a free tenant could make himself into an overlord. As will be seen, the whole story depends on the statements of the accused and of jurors about events at least a century old. But the story has some verisimilitude. It is the story of a wealthy free man, Ketelbern of Canley, who offered to pay his neighbours' rents to the king their lord, and whose successors, going from strength to strength, partly by a successful marriage, arrogated to themselves the lordship of Canley hamlet. The head of the family at the time of the inquiry into the usurpation in 1266, Robert of Canley, had even tried some years previously to bring an action 'de nativitate' against these neighbours. The king's justice decided that there had been a usurpation and ordered the resumption of the abbot's lordship over Canley hamlet. The usurper was stripped of his lands but by favour of the abbot was allowed to resume his own two yardlands, hereditarily, for the old services. The subsequent descent of the holding is traced by the author of the Leger Book. Some surviving original deeds confirm and extend the story. A deed of 1258 is a quitclaim by Robert of Canley, describing himself as lord of Canley, to Alexander son of Guy of Canley, the first of the supposed tenants of Robert mentioned in the 1266 case.[59] In it Robert renounces all claim for services and customs from Alexander beyond a money rent and 'secta curie mee ut alii liberi homines mei de iure facere debent'. This is probably a quitclaim that Robert had to make to all 'his' Canley tenants on the failure of the 'de nativitate' suit, but it will be noticed that he still claims his court. By 1280 the representative of the family was Robert's second son, Master Thomas of Canley, a chaplain holding according to the royal inquiry[60] a messuage and two and threequarters of a yardland. In this document Master Thomas and five other leading Canley tenants (four of whom were once Robert of Canley's supposed tenants) are described as 'sokemen' with the characteristic services of the Stoneleigh sokemen, that is, three-weekly suit of court and supervisory duties at the bederepe. But other deeds preserved by the abbey show as early as 1258 a number of enfeoffments and quitclaims within the Canley family, and in 1270 a lease by Master Thomas to the Abbot of Stoneleigh of most of his Canley property for a ten-year period, in the usual form with rights of distraint in case of rent arrears, and prohibition of waste, sale, or destruction in Master Thomas's wood. Amongst other things the abbot has to maintain the 'domos curie de Caneley', implying that Thomas's house was still a sort of Canley manor house. Another deed shows Master Thomas's property further extended by a grant in heredity, after 1277, by the abbot, of approved waste in Canley. These transactions within the Canley family, between members of the family and other persons, and with the abbey, give the impression of operations analogous to, if not identical with, those undertaken by common law free tenants—in spite of the description of Master Thomas in the 1280 inquest as a sokeman and in spite of the restriction on sokemen's alienations stated in the custumal.[61]

The late thirteenth and early fourteenth-century material in the two collections of original deeds includes evidence about many other aspects of the Stoneleigh Abbey estate history. The considerable collection of Kingshill documents in the Gregory manuscripts, for instance, includes a large number of deeds in which descriptions of the land transferred permit a reconstruction of the hamlet's field system. These will be considered later in the topographical section of this introduction.[62] Another interesting group in the Leigh Collection, Early Deeds, shows the abbey letting off small portions of waste in Westwood to men of the adjacent parish of Berkswell in the early years of the fourteenth century. These were grants in heredity for a moderate money rent, but including a renunciation by the grantees of all common pasture rights in Westwood.[63] But the value of these collections is not confined to this period. Although less in number there are some important deeds of later date. These include leases of demesne lands, mills, and granges. Some of these leases are for very long terms. Half a dozen or so for terms of seventy to a hundred years will be found in the Leger Book. They recur during the fifteenth century,[64] become more frequent in the early sixteenth century, and continue little changed in character when the leasing authority becomes the Augmentations Office. Many of the indentures of demesne leases have no doubt been lost, but there is among the Gregory manuscripts a number of late-fifteenth century rent rolls. These include separate lists of *firme* and *molendina* in addition to the rents from the hamlets and indicate the extent of demesne leasing at the period.[65]

(b) Stoneleigh Abbey Court Rolls

In view of the great interest taken by the author of the Leger Book in legal action to prove rights to land it is unfortunate that only a few manor court rolls earlier than the date of the book's compilation survive. On the other hand we are fortunate that so many cases are in fact recorded in the book. The surviving court rolls are mainly of the fifteenth century and constitute another body of documentary evidence for the medieval history of the Stoneleigh Abbey estate.[66] There are about fifty rolls containing records of sessions of the manor court, views of frankpledge and 'bederepe' courts. In most of them the business is like that of many other manorial courts and views of frankpledge.[67] Of course, from the point of view of economic and social history, the matter of the minor civil pleas, of rural misdemeanours, and of surrenders and reissues of holdings is of considerable interest. Pleas of debt reveal disputes about wages between employers and labourers; a report on the abandoned holdings of servile tenants (in 1481) gives a hint of one aspect of the problem of vagabondage, for these tenants were 'transientes de villa in villa ad manducandum' and died without chattels; a plea of detention of chattels between 1481 and 1491 shows a man from Chipping Warden (Northants.) putting white cloth to be fulled by a Stoneleigh fuller. The 'bederepe' court rolls on the other hand are unusual in form, if not in content. The earliest extant roll records a court of the summer of 1480 and the last a court in the summer of 1493. These courts were held in the fields, usually in August,[68] and consisted of a sort of roll call of those owing bederepe services. Defaulters were presented, hamlet by hamlet, and in fact the defaulters were always in a majority. This must have been expected, so the court was very likely held mainly for the assessment of fines for non-attendance. The distinction, which will be found in the Leger Book, between the sokemen who came to superintend and the lesser tenants whose reaping they superintended[69] is still maintained in these court records. But the whole business must have been little more than an archaic relic by the end of the fifteenth century, if only because of changes in the character of the tenantry. For example, at a court held in June 1487, William Halley, member of an old Fletchamstead family, surrendered the holding in sokemanry which he had in Fletchamstead and paid a licence fee of ten shillings to sell it to John Smith, gentleman, of Coventry, who was to continue to hold the land in sokeman tenure. Smith, however, appears in the rent rolls compiled a few years later as a large-scale lessee, and is mentioned in the records of the depopulation commission of 1517 as having emparked 100 acres in Fletchamstead in 1493. His son Henry converted another 160 acres of arable to pasture in Fletchamstead in 1497, and made even larger enclosures in other Warwickshire villages.[70]

This Henry Smith figures in one of the latest and most interesting of the documents classified with the Stoneleigh Abbey court rolls, although it is not a court record. This is apparently the reply of the inhabitants of Stoneleigh to certain articles. It is undated and not further described. But the nature of the replies suggests that the articles were questions about depopulation and the conversion of arable to pasture, and the names of the persons accused of such acts —post-Dissolution lessees—suggest that the articles were those of the inquiry of 1548. The information to some extent (for instance that concerning Smith) duplicates that already given in 1517. Other information is new. It shows that the active promoters of sheep farming here, as no doubt elsewhere, were not only the immediate lessees of monastic land from the crown but also their sub-lessees whose names are not to be found in the public records.[71]

(c) The Warwickshire Rotuli hundredorum of 1280

No discussion of the various materials for the history of Stoneleigh Abbey and its estate would be complete without some further consideration of one of the most interesting inquiries into local conditions made by the medieval English government. Two references are made in the Leger Book to the inquiry that was held in 1280 in Coventry by Henry of Notyngham and his associates. The twelve jurors used in the inquiry simply stated, according to the author of the Leger Book, the main facts about the principal endowments of the abbey. To these facts they added the names of two servile tenants of the manor and referred to thirty-four other tenants, cottagers holding for life.

In fact the results of the inquiry were much more comprehensive than this. They include not only the names and details about the holdings and rents of these cottagers in Stoneleigh village, but similar details about all landholders and their sub-tenants in the whole of the Stoneleigh soke. The inquiry was, of course, part of that comprehensive government survey whose extant findings are known as the *Rotuli Hundredorum* and which for the most part have been in print for many years.[72] The survey was probably intended to cover the whole country, though only returns from the counties of Cambridge, Huntingdon, Buckingham, Bedford, Oxford, and Warwick have survived. The Warwickshire returns, which were not printed by the Record Commission, do not represent the whole county but only the Hundred of Kineton and the Stoneleigh subdivision of the Hundred of Knightlow.[73] For our purposes, however, they are of great interest, as the returns include all the places in the rental which comprises the second part of the Leger Book.

The main importance of the information collected in the 1280 inquiry is in what we are told about tenants and holdings rather than in that about the demesne possessions of the principal landowners. Information about demesnes is brief and lacking in detail; that about tenants is often as detailed as that to be found in manorial rentals. In fact the 1280 inquiry is superior to the manorial material in that it lists sub-tenants, whereas the manorial rentals almost invariably ignore them, since the lords either did not recognize or were not interested in sub-letting by their own tenants. It need hardly be stressed that the existence of two detailed surveys of rents and tenures, separated by a century which experienced the most serious demographic and economic crises of the Middle Ages, can permit comparisons of considerable interest. It is not our purpose here to make a detailed comparative analysis, which should perhaps wait for an adequate edition of the 1280 survey. But some general conclusions can be suggested from a preliminary comparison of the two texts.

The plagues of 1349-72 took their toll of the Stoneleigh population, as elsewhere. There must have been many families like that of John le Heyr of Stoneleigh, which was wiped out, or like that of John Campioun, sokeman of Fletchamstead, three out of four of whose sons died in the first plague, and one grandson in the second.[73] Since a fall of as much as forty per cent. of the population has been estimated for the period of the plagues,[74] we should expect the number of tenants in the rental of 1392 to be less than the number in 1280, when the medieval English population was supposedly approaching its peak. This is not, however, the case. In 1280 there were about 170 tenants and about 50 sub-tenants in the villages and hamlets of Stoneleigh, Kingshill, Canley, Finham, Fletchamstead, Hurst, Cryfield, Millburn, and Stareton, including a few tenants of the Knights Templar in Fletchamstead. In 1392 there is no information about sub-tenants, but there were about 180 principal tenants in these same villages and hamlets. The similarity of the over-all figures conceals a slight fall by the later date in the number of tenants in Stoneleigh, Canley, and Kingshill, the same number at Stareton and an increase in Fletchamstead, Hurst, and Cryfield.

Even more surprising at first glance are the comparative figures of rent income. During the fourteenth century, and especially after the plagues, landlords' rent incomes generally tended to fall. From the Stoneleigh villages, however, the abbey was drawing in 1392 about four times the amount of money rent that it was drawing in 1280 (roughly £100 to £25). The increase was greater in some of the villages than in others— fortyfold at Milburne, tenfold at Cryfield, eightfold at Fletchamstead, sevenfold at Hurst, fourfold at Stoneleigh and Canley, but only between two and threefold at Stareton and Kingshill.[75]

It is not difficult to explain this apparent population stability and rise in rents. During the twelfth and thirteenth centuries there had been a much more rapid increase of population in the Stoneleigh division of Knightlow Hundred than in the south Warwickshire Hundred of Kineton.[76] There were two reasons for this increase. First, the Stoneleigh area was in the Arden woodland, where there was a rapid extension of the cultivated area during the period. South Warwickshire was settled much earlier than the Arden country, but its agricultural potentialities were inferior and many of its younger sons must have moved north of the Avon where there was good virgin land to be ploughed. Second, in the middle of Arden was the rapidly growing town of Coventry which by the fourteenth century was not merely the biggest industrial centre in the Midlands but the fourth biggest town in the country. Coventry's industrialization was not confined within its walls but spread to the suburbs and the nearby villages. This population growth in the Stoneleigh region probably continued after 1280, reaching a peak perhaps on the very eve of the Black Death. The woodlands belonging to Stoneleigh Abbey certainly continued to be opened up to cultivation during this period, and this explains the increase in the number of tenants in Fletchamstead, Hurst, and Cryfield, forest villages which were at the same time very close to the walls of Coventry.

The increase in rent is to be explained in several ways. First, it follows from what has just been said that there was an increase in the rent-yielding area. Secondly, although there had never been enough labour services to yield much extra revenue when commuted[77] the abbey had leased out much of its demesne property to farmers by 1392. In Stoneleigh village, for instance, nearly half of the total rent was received from the farmers of various demesne mills and fisheries. In Fletchamstead the manorial lands of Whobberley and Horewell were held by farmers, again accounting for about half of the total rent from the hamlet. Morhalle manor in Canley, Bockyndene grange in Hurst,[78] Millburne grange, Helenhill (or Kingshill) grange, and the grange in Stareton were all leased out. The Home grange was still kept in hand, as was Cryfield grange, but at Cryfield the watermill with its pool and meadows was leased out.

Between 1280 and 1392 there was a great reshuffling of holdings, so that it is almost impossible to compare the rents of like with like, though smallholders' rents on the whole seem to have been higher at the earlier date. But if significant comparisons of individual rents at these two widely separated dates can hardly be made, the comparison of sizes of holdings indicates that important changes in economic and social structure had occurred. The most important feature of these changes was an increase in the number of big peasant holdings. The figures calculated are only approximate since in 1392 a number of holdings were described in such a way that their exact size is doubtful. All the same, the trend appears clearly enough in the following table.

Date	Small holdings (under 7 acres) and cottages	Between 8 and 15 acres ($\frac{1}{4}$ to $\frac{1}{2}$ a yardland)	15-30 acres ($\frac{1}{2}$ to 1 yardland)	Between 1 and $1\frac{1}{2}$ yardlands	More than $1\frac{1}{2}$ yardlands
1280	62%	9%	15%	8%	5%
1280†	61%	9%	18%	8%	2%
1392	46%	8%	15%	10%	23%

†—allowing for redistribution among sub-tenants

The reason why the second set of figures for 1280 shows a reduction in the number of larger holdings is because some of those holding fifty or sixty acres in chief from the abbot did not work their whole holding but sub-let to other tenants. Whether the distribution in 1392 would be much altered if we were able to take sub-letting into account is impossible to say. The proportion of smallholders holding directly from the abbey in 1392 is much reduced, but it is, of course, possible that tenants of bigger holdings were themselves sub-letting to cottagers.[79]

It must, of course, be appreciated that the pattern of landholding may have been quite different from that of occupation. One fact pointing to this conclusion is that many abbey tenants in the Leger Book held land in more than one of the villages or hamlets of the soke. Another is that well over half of those living in the hamlets of Millburn, Hurst, Cryfield, Fletchamstead, Canley, Finham, and Kingshill who paid poll tax in 1379 (or their heirs), held no land in these hamlets from the abbey. They must either have been landless or sub-tenants. Conversely, only a quarter of the tenants of land mentioned in the Leger Book in these hamlets are in the tax list. There were in fact half as many tenants again as there were tax-payers. This excess of tenants over tax-paying inhabitants suggests that sub-letting was complex, including leasing by small tenants to the larger as well as the other way round.[80] But even if this were the case, the great increase in the proportion of bigger tenements held directly from the abbey is very striking. The concentration of tenures was even bigger than appears from the table. In 1280 all of the bigger holdings were less than three yardlands (ninety acres) in area, while in 1392 about a third of the holdings in the category 'more than 1½ yardlands (45a.)' were bigger than three yardlands.

The comparisons we have made between the tenants' holdings in 1280 and in 1392 have suggested some general conclusions about population growth and the concentration of holdings during the intervening period. But as we have mentioned above in our brief discussion of the question of ancient demesne, the 1280 returns also give some insight into the legal and social status of different groups in the Stoneleigh population at that time. Since these facts may throw light on the material contained in the Leger Book, a further brief analysis of the description presented to the royal commissioners may be of some use.

The 1280 return is somewhat defective in that it is not made clear throughout which tenants were holding land in which of the various Stoneleigh hamlets. With the help of the Leger Book it is, however, fairly easy to identify the groups of tenants in different places. The distribution of tenants is as follows:

	Tenants	Sub-tenants
Stoneleigh	78	8
Kingshill	17	7
Canley	15	10
Finham	5	5
Hurst	12	4
Cryfield	5	12
Milburn	1	—
Fletchamstead	28	2
Stareton	23	1
Total	184	49

The most interesting feature as regards the status of the tenants is the way in which those tenants who are described in the Leger Book as holding in sokemanry are also distinguished in the 1280 returns. They are usually referred to as free tenants rather than as sokemen, although this last term is applied to a group of six in Canley. But this was entirely a distinction of nomenclature, not of substance. The characteristics of their tenure are the same, whatever name they are given. They owe money rent for their holdings. Some of them pay at a rate of 2s. 6d. a yardland, that is one penny an acre. Others pay more, especially tenants of less than a yardland. When (as some of them do) they hold as sub-tenants, the rents per acre are much more. In addition to money rent these tenants owe suit of court at the abbot's court at Stoneleigh every three weeks. They come mounted for one day with their staves (*virge*) to attend the bederepe at Stoneleigh and to supervise the reapers. On that day they eat twice with the abbot, that is at his expense, as they used to do when the manor was in the king's hands. They have husbote and haybote and are quit of pannage for their pigs in Dalle, Westwood, and Crackley Woods. Finally they are quit of toll.[81] In a reference to the abbot's fishing rights in the Sowe and Avon rivers it is also said that the free tenants too may fish these for themselves but not for sale.

There are thirty-seven of these tenants: two certain, perhaps three, in Stoneleigh, three in Finham, three in Kingshill, six in Canley, eight in Fletchamstead, ten in Hurst, and four in Cryfield. Apart from appearing in the lists of names, they are mentioned again in a sort of summing up at the end of each group of tenants in the various hamlets.[82] Their privileged position is apparent from their supervisory role at the bederepe,[83] their common rights in the three woods, and their comparatively low money rents. But it is worth noting that there are more of them in those woodland hamlets which were probably populated latest, another feature difficult to reconcile with the theory that they were privileged villeins of Anglo-Saxon origin.

The remaining tenants—the vast majority, that is—are described in varying detail. Terms of tenure are given for Stoneleigh tenants, but only rarely in the other hamlets. In Stoneleigh, apart from the two villeins, they were mostly cottagers and smallholders, nine holding at will, four hereditarily, one for twelve years, and the remaining sixtyfive (apart from some half-dozen whose terms are not specified) holding for life. Some of them (about thirty) had to take charge of persons imprisoned at Stoneleigh; almost all of them owed suit of court twice a year, that is to the view of frankpledge, and from one to five days' reaping at harvest time. In the other hamlets, although smallholdings also predominate, sub-tenancies were more common and holdings and rents were more variable. But here again, where specified, biennial suit of court and harvest work was the rule, particularly in the case of sub-tenants of the sokemen-free tenants.[84]

We know from the Leger Book that there was more to be said about conditions of tenure than was written down by the king's clerks in 1280. We have seen that the free tenants of Stoneleigh were not holding by common law free tenure, since they were expected to litigate only in the manor court at Stoneleigh. This was not necessarily an inconvenience. Apart from the ancient demesne writs already mentioned, pleas of dispossession could be dealt with by the assize of fresh force,[85] as it is called in the custumal in the Leger Book, or in 'forma brevis nove disseisionis secundum consuetudinem manerii', as it is put in a court roll of 1373.[86] The abbey court rolls also show that pleas 'in forma brevis convencionis' and final concords were also dealt with in the manor court, presumably at much less expense than in the common law courts. Other tenurial peculiarities are fully dealt with in the Leger Book. But the results of the 1280 inquiry show quite clearly that, for practical purposes, the purposes of a peasant community, the social status of the men of Stoneleigh was much in line with the free status that was generally enjoyed in the Forest of Arden.

VI *A Topographical Survey*

The Leger Book contains a large number of field and other local names. Although, with the help of old maps, some of these can be located, the majority of them may never be more than vaguely placed in the area of the Stoneleigh soke. Yet even without a precise reconstruction of the distribution of fields at the end of the fourteenth century we can get some idea from the Leger Book and other Stoneleigh Abbey sources about the nature of the field system.

A number of factors seem to have determined the character of settlement and of the agrarian system. Although the soil, especially in the north-west of the parish, was good, it was heavily wooded until late in the Middle Ages. In 1086 the woodland was described as adequate for feeding 2,000 swine, being two by four leagues in dimensions.[87] The royal inquest of 1280 refers to 1,000 acres of common wood called Dalle, Westwood, and Crackley (Crattele). This woodland, though no doubt discontinuous, nevertheless must have occupied a considerable proportion of the north-western part of the soke or parish. West of Stoneleigh village and south of the Finham brook, the name of the common field (Wood Field) suggests that this part of the parish too was once well wooded. The loop of the river which contained the abbey and the fields of the Home Grange was originally occupied by Echills Wood. To the south was (and still is, in reduced form) Bericote Wood. East of Stareton was Waverley Wood which at one time also stretched well into Stoneleigh parish at the south-east end.

The woodland in this region was not, of course, neatly contained within parish or manorial boundaries. Hence there were necessarily inter-commoning arrangements between the men of Stoneleigh and those of adjoining manors. These arrangements are described in the Stoneleigh custumal,[87] and one may see from them how near to the streets of Coventry the woodland of Arden must have been in the fourteenth century. Hazlewood, which Stoneleigh tenants pastured in return for rights in the north of Stoneleigh parish enjoyed by Coventry and Stivichale men, bounded the whole south-eastern quarter of the city.[88] Another inter-commoning arrangement with the tenants of Kenilworth gave Stoneleigh tenants access to the Kenilworth woods of Odybarn and Frythe.

Within the soke of Stoneleigh at the time of the abbey's foundation there were probably six nuclei of settlement: Stoneleigh village on the river Sowe; Stareton, a mile to the south-east on the Avon; Finham farther north-east up the Sowe from Stoneleigh; Cryfield, three miles north-west; Canley, a mile north-east of Cryfield; and Fletchamstead two miles north-north-west of Cryfield. By 1305 when a tallage of the tenants was taken, we can be more precise, since the lists of the taxed householders are recorded in the Leger Book. The recognized hamlets of the soke were Stoneleigh (32 taxed persons); Finham, opposite Finbury (which does not appear as a hamlet) on the north side of the river Sowe at the mouth of the Finham (or Millburn) Brook (7 taxed persons); Kingshill, (Hulle or Helenhulle), a mile north-west of Finham (10); Fletchamstead (13); Canley, a mile northeast of Cryfield (16); Millburn (Melburne), two miles west of Finham (11); Cryfield (16); Hurst, a mile west of Cryfield (17); and Stareton (11). The rental in the Leger Book shows that in the late fourteenth century these were still the recognized divisions of the soke. In addition to these settlements of cultivators there were also the granges of the monks: the Home grange, and those of Stoneleigh, Bockyndene, Cryfield, Millburn, Helenhull, Stareton, and Horewelle. Some of these granges, such as Stoneleigh, Stareton, and Cryfield, were probably manors taken over by the monks. Others were granges in the specifically Cistercian sense, new centres of cultivation pioneered by the monks and their servants.

The hamlets and the granges appear in the records at different dates. This is not simply an accident of documentation, for the appearance of a new settlement was of course correlated with the opening up to cultivation of new land. The earliest precise indication as to what areas of the soke were cultivated is in the abbey's foundation charter from Henry II. According to this document the whole of the king's 'dominium' in Stoneleigh was handed over. It consisted of twelve ploughlands. Six of these were in Stoneleigh itself and six were elsewhere in the Stoneleigh soke (two at Dullesworth and four at Cryfield). As we have seen, there was also land at Radway and Marston, which does not concern us here. Stareton, in the middle of the twelfth century, had already been alienated by King Henry II to Simon the Cook (also known as 'of Arden' as were his descendants),[89] and was not to fall into the abbey's hands until the middle of the thirteenth century. Part at any rate of Fletchamstead (one ploughland) had been given by Henry I to a hermit from whom it passed to the Templars as part of their Preceptory of Balsall. Canley, as we know, was a hamlet already containing a group of tenants in the reign of Henry II. Their descendants at the time of the lawsuit of 1266 were cultivating eight virgates and a number of small assarts. But much of the rest of the lands of the soke, included in neither the land granted by the king nor in Stareton, Fletchamstead, or Canley, was probably un-cultivated. The old parish area is given as 10,000 acres. Stareton arable in 1392 was about two ploughlands, so we may give seventeen ploughlands as the maximum cultivated acreage in the twelfth century. At 120 acres of arable to the ploughland, or 2,040 acres in all, nearly 8,000 acres would be left. A good deal of this would consist, of course, of unenclosed pasture necessary for the arable cultivation of the ploughlands mentioned in the foundation charter and of the holdings in Stareton and Fletcham-stead. But there would still be a vast expanse available for assarting.

The author of the Leger Book, basing himself on tradition 'ut audiuimus et didicimus a senioribus predecessoribus nostris',[89] tells us the names of the fields that comprised the twelve ploughlands of the royal 'dominium'. Not all of these fields can be placed, but from those that can we may have a fairly certain notion of the location of the original nucleus of cultivated land in the soke. In Stoneleigh ten fields or furlongs are named. Of these only two can be placed with confidence. They are Washford furlong, which was in what was later called Wood field,[90] on the west bank of the river towards Stoneleigh; and Stockynglond, which was on the west side of the Sowe, north of Stoneleigh. Mulnefeld was probably near the mill on the Sowe, opposite Stoneleigh grange, which was probably the centre of the royal manor before Henry II gave it to the Radmore monks.[90] Stanydelf, which means 'quarry', may have been near the later Quarry meadow just east of Stare Bridge. Culvecroft, which must be the same as the 'Coolvercrofte' of an early sixteenth century deed,[91] was near to the grange, but Le Heyze and Struttespece (alias Cornhill in the deed) cannot yet be identified. Conyngger-furlong, Conynger, and Conyngerpece cannot be placed. They were still part of the arable lands appurtenant to Stoneleigh grange in the early sixteenth century, and ought not to be identified with the 'Conygre' near the abbey site which appears on a late-sixteenth-century map.[92] The arable lands that were cleared near the abbey and provided the agricultural basis for the Home Grange were quite separate from the Stoneleigh grange lands. The remainder of these six ploughlands consisted of two cultures, by the quarry, running from le Cloude, south of Cloude bridge, to Stare Bridge. From this it would seem that the original Stoneleigh village arable lay lengthwise and perhaps discontinuously on the banks of Avon and Sowe, following the river Avon's curves from about a third of a mile southwest of Sowe mouth, round to Cloude Bridge and with a portion (a continuation probably of the line of Washford furlong) following the line of the Sowe up north of Stoneleigh village.

The other six ploughlands of the king's 'dominium' were in Dullesworth and Cryfield. Dullesworth is a name which only occurs in the foundation charters, but the author of the Leger Book explains that the two ploughlands of Dullesworth were attached to Cryfield grange. The name 'Dulsforde' ('Dulisforde', 'Dolisforde') appears as a Canley field name in fifteenth- and fourteenth-century deeds,[93] and this may suggest that the Dullesworth land was on the Canley side of Cryfield. Fields called Dowsford Close and Upper Dowsford, on an eighteenth-century Stoneleigh estate map, lie between Cryfield and Canley.

The fields attached to Cryfield grange (including the Dullesworth property) were, according to the Leger Book, Dallefeld, Hurstfeld, Mulnefeld, Parkfeld, and Cotefurlong. Dallefeld, in one description, is associated with Burystede Wood, and since Burystede was next to Cryfield grange, this field must have been near to the grange. Whether this Dallefeld was included in the Dullesworth land is doubtful. It is true that there was a Dallimoor immediately east of Dowsford in the eighteenth century. But place names containing the element 'Dalle' are also found south of Cryfield grange. Dalle wood must at one time have been of considerable extent. Hurstfeld would probably be to the north-west of Cryfield grange. Parkfeld and Cotefurlong cannot yet be placed, but there seem reasonable grounds for supposing that Cryfield grange lay roughly in the centre of the six carucates attached to it, the two in Dullesworth being to the north.

The foundation charter also states that the king's grant included not only the twelve ploughlands of his 'dominium' but also the 'bruillum' or woodland called Echills (Echels). This wood, whose name is still attached to a small spinney near the abbey, probably filled the whole of the loop of the Avon, and stretched over the Coventry road to the south of Stareton. It may even have been continuous with the southern part of Waverley Wood. The author of the Leger Book gives the names of those fields which were brought into cultivation from Echills wood to form the Home grange lands. Some of the field names in the Leger Book are identifiable in the Avon loop from seventeenth- and eighteenth-century maps—Herdwyc (Great and Little Hardwick), Midulmedewe, and Gatebridge (Garbridge) meadow. 'Blakehulle' and 'Bocheresmedewe', possibly identifiable with the eighteenthcentury field names 'Black Hills' and 'Bocher Hill', are just to the east of the mouth of the Avon loop. 'Holbrokfurlong' and 'Farnhull' were probably farther east towards Waverley Wood, for the description of the bounds of the soke mentions Holbroke pools and Farnhull as landmarks on the southern boundary, near to Waverley Wood. The date at which these fields were won from Echills Wood is not given but no doubt it was a piecemeal process which was still going on at the end of the thirteenth century. Abbot William Heyford (1277-93), we are told, brought the Stoneleigh waste into cultivation against the wishes of almost all the big men of the district.

The next group of fields named in the Leger Book, in connexion with the charters of Henry II and John, are those assarted from Waverley (Wethele) Wood, which, we have suggested, may once have been joined to Echills Wood. Among the arable land taken by the abbots from this wood was a furlong or *cultura* of thirty-six selions (probably about nine acres) called Stywardespece, which was annexed and enclosed by the steward of the adjoining manor of Bubbenhall. The exact location of this field cannot be pinpointed but the general vicinity of this and the other fields is clear, being bounded by the common fields of the surrounding villages of Stareton, Cubbington, and Bubbenhall and the roads known as Leicester way and Coventry way (Cubbington to Coventry). One of them, 'Bradelefeld', an assart, is probably identical with the 'Bradley' of the eighteenth-century estate map.[94] Nor were the monks the only pioneers in bringing Waverley Wood into cultivation. Of the four fields with characteristically 'assart' names ending in breche and broken, Nywebroken survived in the eighteenth century as 'Newbrocken' and the others simply as 'Breach'. All of these were cultivated by the tenants of Stareton and probably assarted by them in the first place.

The author's attempt to describe the original endowment ends with a reference to the assarts of Hurst, first mentioned, like Waverley Wood, as being part of the abbey possessions in John's reign. The names of these assarts are not given but we are told that Bockyndene grange was made from them by the monks.

In the second half of the twelfth century, then, it would appear that the oldest centres of arable farming in the Stoneleigh soke were in the Avon and Sowe valleys, around Cryfield, and perhaps on a smaller scale in Canley and Fletchamstead. More recently, however, assarting by both monks and peasants had added land from Echills and Waverley Woods to the abbey demesne known as Home grange and to the holdings of the men of Stareton. Assarts at Hurst extended the Cryfield nucleus of cultivation westward but the date of the foundation of Bockyndene grange from these assarts is not given. There were still left the considerable woods and wastes of Westwood, Crackley, Dalle, and Armeley,[95] as areas for the further expansion of cultivation. Many of the smaller tenements in the hamlets north of the Finham Brook are described in the Leger Book's rental as assarts from the wastes. The larger scale assarts are to be found in this area as well—fifty acres from Westwood, forty acres from Dalle wood called Kannoc, Dallemoor approved from Dalle waste. Horewelle grange was made from assarts from Westwood and Millburn grange from Dalle wood, just as Bockyndene grange was created from the assarts of Hurst.

Land assarted from the wood and waste was often kept in severalty and even enclosed. Although assarted land could be and often was added to existing open fields, there are reasons for supposing that in the woodland of Arden as in the Worcestershire forest of Feckenham, arable severalties were found in considerable numbers from the twelfth century onwards. But if assarts in severalty were the most characteristic form of clearance in the later Middle Ages, we might nevertheless expect to find some sort of open field agriculture in the immediate vicinity of the settlements of earliest date. An eighteenth-century copy of a late sixteenth-century map of the manor of Feckenham in Worcestershire,[96] in country very like the Arden country of Warwickshire, illustrates this point. Here we find a few common fields with intermixed strips in the immediate vicinity of the village, encircled by a considerable number of small arable fields in severalty, each of only a few acres in area. A phrase in the Leger Book seems to describe, in words, the same situation in the Stoneleigh soke—'Et in quolibet hamletto manerii de Stonle sunt octo virgate terre et non amplius. Et si quod amplius habent hoc utique habent de approwacione et assartacione vastorum.' The word 'virgata' or yardland was in the later Middle Ages, it is true, often used simply as a unit of agricultural land of whatever field layout, but originally had implied a holding composed of scattered ridges in the common fields— to quote another Leger Book phrase 'illa tenementa fuerunt unum mesuagium et due virgate . . . quia distinguitur terra particulariter per seliones et acras'.

Where were the open fields of the Stoneleigh soke and where were the enclosures and severalties? The seventeenth- and eighteenth-century maps which are of some use in tracing field names must be regarded with a critical eye when we seek to reconstruct the field system. Fields that were open and common in the early eighteenth century were probably open and common in the Middle Ages, but enclosures shown on eighteenth-century maps might be medieval or modern. They were being created in the sixteenth and seventeenth centuries on a greater scale than they were in medieval times. We have already seen that the Tudor enclosure commissioners had discovered that this was happening in Stoneleigh and there is no reason to suppose that it stopped after 1548.

Enclosure in the sixteenth and seventeenth centuries diminishes the value of the seventeenth- and eighteenth-century maps as evidence for enclosure in medieval Stoneleigh. The evidence, therefore, on which we must base our estimate of the relative importance of common open field and enclosed cultivation before the sixteenth century must as far as possible be itself medieval. The Leger Book, and in particular the rental, provide a considerable amount of material. It may of course be supplemented from the older field maps as well as from the charters of the thirteenth, fourteenth, and fifteenth centuries in the Stoneleigh archives.

We have already seen from our analysis of the Leger Book's description of the original endowments that in Stoneleigh and Stareton there was a considerable amount of land which was colonized from Echills and Waverley Woods, some to be attached to the Home grange and some to become tenants' holdings in Stareton. The Home grange fields were almost certainly kept as enclosed severalties, as were the additions, from Waverley Wood, to the lands of Stareton. On the other hand the arable land around Stoneleigh village, whether by Avon side or Sowe side, seems to have consisted mostly of intermixed strips composed of arable ridges or 'selions'.[97] The tenants in Stoneleigh of the Prior of Kenilworth as rector of the parish must have been holding some of the oldest tenements of the village, since the church was given to the priory thirty years before the monks of Radmore arrived in the Stoneleigh soke. These holdings are described in the Leger Book. The total amount of land was 257 acres, counted as $8\frac{1}{2}$ virgates plus 2 acres (at 30 acres per virgate). It is described in 10 groups of parcels according to location. The total number of separate parcels (of arable) was 53. The number of ridges (or selions) in each parcel varied considerably but with 603 selions it works out at an average of about 11 or 12 ridges a parcel and rather more than 2 selions an acre. The average of ridges to a parcel is rather meaningless, however, since there was as much variation as from 2 to 44 selions a parcel. The bigger blocks of selions imply a good deal of consolidation. These Kenilworth Priory tenements in Stoneleigh village are clearly part of an open-field system of some sort. The only severalties belonging to them were the curtilages attached to the homestead which could be found in any open-field village. But whether the peasants holding these lands in the Stoneleigh open fields were practising the traditional distribution of their rotation courses in two or three main fields is another question to which we must return.

The lands of Stoneleigh village were not all open and common. A number of small tenants held crofts as well as curtilages in severalty. These tenants were often smallholders with no open-field land. In other cases we find enclosures surrounded by hedges made within the open fields. A big tenant, John Schukeburghe, among his thirtyeight acres, most of which lay open and intermixed, had one acre 'inter sepes' and 'viii seliones cum foreriis pro iiii acris unacum sepibus' lying in between two hedges. Another big tenant, John Bacoun, holding 6 acres and 2 acres of meadow, has 23 selions and 2 headlands in a croft in a furlong called Middle Stockynglond. The croft is 'inter quatuor sepes'. However, in this case the necessary rider is added that the croft 'est commune et seminandum cum Starhulle'. The vicar of Stoneleigh is another tenant with his land enclosed by hedges in Stockynglond. This field may have been one in which well-to-do tenants had consolidated their strips together and then put up hedges without having managed to eliminate other men's common of shack.

The other hamlets whose fields seem to have been predominantly open were Stareton, Finham, and Kingshill. That is to say that the tenants' holdings are described either in terms of yardlands and parts of yardlands, or, when fragmentation seems to have taken place and small pieces of land are described, these are frequently shown to consist of a number of selions. In addition to the evidence of the Leger Book rental, the original deeds confirm this impression, especially for Kingshill. There are over a hundred deeds relating to this hamlet, ranging from the middle of the thirteenth to the end of the fifteenth century, but mostly concentrated in the late thirteenth and early fourteenth centuries. Hardly any of them concern land held in severalty or enclosed. On the contrary, a fairly complete picture of a field system of the open type can be reconstructed, consisting of three main fields (Brookfield, Little Field, and Wood Field) subdivided into furlongs. A typical holding which was the subject of a deed of transfer in the early part of the fourteenth century consisted of twenty-six 'londes', of half an acre each in most cases, each being in a different furlong.[98] The main concentrations of land enclosed or in severalty, apart from the Home Grange severalties, were away from the Avon and Sowe rivers towards Coventry. This was the wooded zone occupied previously by Westwood, Dalle, and Crackley Woods. Here the familiar small enclosed fields of the Arden country, the consequences of assarting, were already in existence in 1392. At Cryfield, a royal manor before the grant to the monks of Radmore, and subsequently an abbey grange, all of the arable attached to the grange consisted of separate enclosures, which, since they were not tithable, must have been of ancient date. The tenants' holdings, as one would expect in so old a settlement, consisted partly of open field land (or at any rate of land described as yardlands or fractions of yardlands). But severalties are prominent as well, though unfortunately the acreage of tofts, crofts, separate fields, and wastes is not given. In the fields of the adjacent hamlet of Hurst, described as 'the assarts of Hurst' in the earliest documents, and from which the sitting tenants had been evicted in the earliest days of the abbey, enclosed severalties were predominant. In the description of Hurst holdings we find the term yardland used, not of open-field land, but of closes: 'unum mesuagium cum curtilagiis et croftis et clausis pro duabus virgatis terre cum pertinentiis', or 'unum mesuagium cum curtilagiis et croftis in quibus continentur dimidia virgata unum quartronum una acra et dimidia terre cum pertinenciis.' Hurst lands, including the abbey grange of Bockyndene, probably consisted entirely of enclosed land by 1392. One lessee, Robert Lytelmon, paying the considerable rent of £4 for an assortment of crofts, fields, assarts, and closes, was in fact obliged by the terms of his lease to keep all the closes properly enclosed.

Some of the fields of Hurst had been taken from the great wood of Westwood. Fletchamstead, the northernmost of the Stoneleigh hamlets, that which contained a Templars' (later Hospitallers') manor was also largely carved in severalties out of Westwood, although there seems to have been a small common field as well. But the few acres in the common field appear insignificant by the side of the wastes and severalties, for many of which in Fletchamstead the acreage is given, ranging from crofts taken from the waste of two acres, to the Earl of Pembroke's sixty-four acres taken from Westwood, held by him of the abbey as lord of the neighbouring village of Allesley. In Fletchamstead again we come across the use of the open-field terminology of yardlands applied to holdings in severalty. A field with a moor appurtenant to it contains sixty-six selions *pro dimidia virgata,* rendering, moreover, an annual rent of fifteen pence 'sicut quelibet virgata terre manerii de antiqua tenura reddit'. The compiler of the rental summarizes the distribution of land in Fletchamstead as follows: 193 acres of waste; 3 ploughlands; and 11 yardlands, of which 3 had been assarted at various times. But the 3 ploughlands composed the demesne of Horewell manor, now leased out, and were in 2 closes 'de approwacione bosci de Westwode'. Even if 8 out of the 11 yardlands consisted of open-field land (which is unlikely), the greater part of the Fletchamstead arable acreage must have been in severalty. For we must not misunderstand the terms 'waste' and 'moor'. When used as descriptions of portions of holdings they mean land taken from the waste and the moor and turned to agricultural use. The rents paid for them by no means permit the idea that they remained in an uncultivated state.

At Canley, much of which was assarted from Dalle Wood—the large enclosed waste called Kannok for instance—there was again a core of open-field land. The description of some of the holdings reveals the names of a number of furlongs divided into arable ridges of mixed ownership. Seventeen such furlong names are found in the description of the holding claimed by William Halley and his mother. But this holding, besides these dozen or so acres in scattered ridges and two half-yardlands that might have consisted of open land, also included seventeen or so tofts, crofts, and wastes in severalty, their acreage unfortunately, for the most part, not being stated. Most of the Canley holdings are composite after this fashion, though Robert Litulmon, whom we have met as a tenant in Hurst, had a 'moor' of thirty acres called Dallemoor, approved from Dalle waste at the end of the thirteenth century by Abbot William of Heyforde as part of Cryfield grange.

The cultivated land in the Stoneleigh soke must, at the end of the fourteenth century, have presented a varied appearance of hedged and ditched enclosures, other severalties which as yet had perhaps not been fully enclosed and ridges of open-field arable in intermixed ownership. In some parts of the soke the open field predominated, in others it was almost entirely enveloped by severalties, hidden no doubt by the innumerable hedges which as yet were only an occasional feature of the English rural scene. But was the open-field agriculture that persisted of the traditional type? Were the ridges of open-field holdings evenly distributed throughout the fields so as to permit a regular cropping system?

No information about the way in which crops were sown and fallowed in the Stoneleigh hamlets survives. The references to common fields, to common pasture rights, and to the sowing of the various commonable crofts at the same time as certain common fields,[99] imply some sort of rotation, no doubt including a fallow. But of course within the broad outlines of such a system, infinite variations might occur.

Sometimes, as H. L. Gray has shown, the rotation pattern can be inferred from the pattern of distribution of the parcels of the holdings. Can his method be applied to the Stoneleigh material?

In the Leger Book seven holdings in Stoneleigh village lands are described, parcel by parcel, and such is our knowledge of the location of the Stoneleigh fields that we can, at any rate roughly, determine the whereabouts of the various portions of the holdings. The first point to make is that although we become aware of 'fields', such as Wood Field, which are subdivided into furlongs, there is no regular division of the whole arable area into two or three or four large fields, with 'furlongs' as subordinate entities. Some pieces of arable which at first glance might be thought to be furlong subdivisions turn out to be clearly of equivalent status to fields. Hence Cloudebridge furlong seems to be treated on a par with the 'Field towards Baginton Mere', just as Lower, Middle, and Upper Stockynglond are equivalent to Wood Field. This contrasts with the deeds concerning transfers of land in Kingshill, where three main fields with their furlong subdivisions clearly comprise all the open land of that hamlet.

The Stoneleigh village holdings show no regular partitioning of the arable land which would indicate a rotational scheme based on the alternation of cropping in two or three big fields. Two yardlands held by John Bacoun contain 70 acres of arable (68 according to the incorrect addition in the Leger Book) and 2 acres of meadow. Twenty acres lay in various fields between Cloude Bridge and that part of the parish boundary running south-east from the Sowe at Finbury to the Avon near Bubbenhall Bridge. Sixteen acres were in Wood Field and Sychenhale (a culture either contained in Wood Field or adjacent to it). Twenty-six acres were in the three Stockynglonds, twelve of which lay together as a croft in Middle Stockynglond. Eight acres were in a croft by Armeley, that is, near the Stockynglonds. The only indication of cropping arrangements—little enough, but more for this holding than for any others—is that the croft in Middle Stockynglond was sown with Starhull and that the parcels in Lower Stockynglond were sown with Stanydelf. Although the exact location of both these places is conjectural, they were probably near Stare Bridge, and possibly on the Stareton side of the bridge—well away from the Stockynglonds. The oddity of these cropping arrangements may be the reason why they were singled out for mention; but the fact that widely separated furlongs were cropped together may also imply that we may not treat as single units the fields in the Baginton Mere-Finbury-Cloud area, the Wodefeld area, and the Stockynglond area. At any rate it seems impossible to apply the two- or three-field scheme to this holding.

When we analyse Thomas Blakenhale's holding it is even clearer that traditional schemes did not apply here. The fifty-two acres of open arable belonging to this holding were, it is true, divided between three fields in the proportion $14 : 14\frac{1}{2} : 23\frac{1}{2}$. The three fields, known collectively as Eyrsfeldes or Heyresfeldes because of their association with Robert of Stoneleigh alias le Eyr[100] at the beginning of the fourteenth century, were in the triangle formed by the Sowe, the Avon, and the road from Stare Bridge to Stoneleigh village. Their individual names were Starbrugge Field (Stare Bridge Field), Grove Field, and Heyresfield. The fourteen acres of common meadow attached to the holding were in Starbrugge medewe. In other words none of the arable of Thomas Blakenhale's holding lay anywhere near that of John Bacoun, in spite of the considerable size of both holdings. On the other hand, a half-yardland of William Staleworth, containing seven acres of arable in the three Eyresfields, and an acre of meadow in Starbruggemedewe, also included land in the same arable fields as John Bacoun's—in the Finbury-Cloud area ($7\frac{1}{2}$ acres) and in Upper Stockynglond (1 acre).

The other Stoneleigh holdings for which details are given in the Leger Book have most of their land distributed over the cultures in the Finbury—Baginton Mere-Cloud area and in the Wood Field area, but in apparently random proportions. Richard Broke's holding was mainly in these two localities in the proportion 12 acres : 6 acres, with 1 acre in Eyresfeld, and another at will (the main holding being a life estate) at Cloudebrugge. The meadow held by this tenant was a separate leasing from demesne. John Werkmon's land was distributed between the Baginton—Cloud area and the Wood Field area in the proportions 6 : 1, and John Smith's 3 : 2. A deed of the late thirteenth century, included in the evidences for the Staleworth holdings, shows the parcels of a small open-field holding distributed over three fields as follows : Wood Field 5 acres 1 rood; 'another' field (probably in the Cloud area) 3 acres; a 'third' field, at Aylewardesclyf (unidentified) 1 acre.

This apparent irregularity in the distribution of parcels makes it, for lack of evidence, almost impossible to guess how the cropping plan was worked in relation to field layout, even if we assume that the almost universal rotation scheme, fallow—winter corn—spring corn, was used. In many cases a man's arrangements would be affected by the fact that some of his land was in severalties not subject to common rights. Richard Broke, for instance, had two crofts, unfortunately of unspecified acreage, in addition to his open-field parcels. Other tenants too, as we have already mentioned, had crofts which presumably were in severalty, since they were not specifically designated as being in common. This irregular distribution of open-field parcels may have been due to more than one cause. Some arable cultures, in individual ownership originally, though subject to common rights, may have been divided up through inheritance and alienation so as to become like any other open fields with intermixed holdings. The Eyresfields may have followed this course of evolution. But we must also remember that by 1392 a considerable amount of buying, selling, and exchanging of land had taken place, alienations partly recorded in the Leger Book and further evidenced by many of the 150 or so surviving charters already mentioned. The tendency of such a market in arable land would be to consolidate parcels, and to judge by the evidence we have just considered, to concentrate holdings in one part of the arable area of the village. This seems to have happened not only in Stoneleigh but in Kingshill, where, as we have seen, surviving deeds seem to show an ordinary type of three-field system. But the parcels of the holdings were not equally distributed over the three fields (Brook Field, Little Field, Wood Field) but in irregular proportions, such as 12:9:6; 3:1:1; 7:3:4; 2:1:1. One could of course imagine a two-field rotation with Little Field and Wood Field considered as one. On the other hand, by 1345, according to a deed of that date, holdings were described according to the furlongs in which the arable lay, without reference to the fields.

6
A Rare Evesham Abbey Estate Document

Those interested in the social history of medieval England frequently sigh with frustration at the uneven survival of evidence from the great lay and ecclesiastical estates. This is usually an accident of post-medieval history, for only rarely were early modern landowners prepared to keep documents whose importance they regarded as relevant only to the year in which they were written. In Worcestershire, it is no doubt our good fortune that much land was held by two almost immortal institutions, the cathedral chapter and the bishop, who preserved the bulk of their records until our own day. We have had no such luck with the records of the great Benedictine abbey of Evesham, though we must, of course, be grateful for the two cartularies of the twelfth and thirteenth centuries, the chronicle of the doings of the abbots (long since in print), and the fifteenth century register of Abbot Bromsgrove. So far, however, and unlike the neighbouring abbey of Pershore, no manorial documents such as account rolls and court rolls have survived, although the earlier Evesham cartulary contains manorial surveys of the late twelfth century.[1]

This is particularly unfortunate because in spite of earlier difficulties, the monks of Evesham seem to have established a grip on the countryside in which their estates lay, unparalleled in the west midlands. As everybody knows, like many other ecclesiastical institutions Evesham abbey suffered from the attentions of land-hungry laymen in the eleventh and twelfth centuries, resulting in considerable alienations of estates which it had acquired in the tenth century and earlier, when it was the monks who were on the offensive as far as the acquisition of estates was concerned. The abbey made a remarkable come-back in the thirteenth century, after the confused situation caused by the disputes during the abbacy of Roger Norreys had settled down. This come-back was described in the jejune entries of the abbey chronicle (so lacking in narrative power compared with Thomas of Marlborough's description of the conflict with Norreys). These entries show that the abbots were not only investing in estate capital, but buying up land, a policy which continued until the end of the fourteenth century. In a number of cases the buying of land consisted in fact of buying back freehold properties on the abbey estate. Consequently, by the end of the middle ages, Evesham Abbey was in pretty well undisputed control of most of the villages on its estate, whereas, by contrast, on the estates of the abbeys of Pershore and Westminster or of the cathedral priory or of the bishop himself, every village was riddled with sub-manors and freehold estates whose very existence, of course, considerably diminished the economic strength of the ecclesiastical overlord.[2]

If we had manorial accounts, we would be able to see how this policy was matched by the economic management of demesnes and peasant tenants. If we had manorial court rolls we would be able to see how the jurisdictional powers of the monks were used to control the tenurial conditions of the peasants and to make monetary profit from the policing of their villages. But unfortunately there is nothing so far discovered to compare with documents of this type which we have even for so relatively unimportant a religious estate owner as Bordesley Abbey. There is, however, one small exception to this general situation of dearth, which is the object of this note.

There is among the manuscripts deposited by Lord Leigh at the Record Office at Shakespeare's Birthplace, Stratford-upon-Avon, a battered, torn and partially illegible document consisting of two membranes of parchment sewn to each other. It contains two (possibly incomplete) lists of leases, heriots and entry fines drawn up when Roger Yatton, later abbot, was cellarer. The first list has a heading from which the date is torn, but a second list, perhaps of the year following, has a heading which shows that the entries were for the normal financial year of the period, in this case Michaelmas 1368 to Michaelmas 1369. The membranes are written on both sides and there are indications that a third missing membrane was sewn on to the end of the second. The headings are short and simply read: 'Fines of lands and tenements and admissions to them from (date) to (date) for one complete year in the time of Brother Roger Yatton, cellarer.' The handwriting could be contemporary, though extracts of items from court rolls such as these were sometimes made for the sake of providing precedents many years afterwards. Since Yatton eventually became abbot, it is possible that (he being simply described as cellarer) the document was drawn up at any rate before his abbacy, which began in 1379.[3]

The individual items are short and (except where torn and faded) the village to which the transaction refers is entered for convenient reference in the margin. The heriot and entry fine, where appropriate, are also repeated in the margin. There are between ninety and a hundred entries, the exact number being difficult to count owing to the illegibility of parts of the manuscript; over twenty of the discernible items are either totally or partially illegible. Eighteen places are mentioned, but they by no means cover the whole of the abbey estate. They are mostly in the Vale of Evesham proper, the ancient core of the property. Such are Evesham, Bengeworth, Wickhamford, Lenchwick, Hampton, North and South Littleton, Offenham, Aldington, Bretforton, Willersey, Honeybourne. Other anciently held properties near Evesham which are mentioned are Abbots Norton and Sambourne. But there is only one reference to the very important Gloucestershire part of the estate, that is to the manor of Bourton (on-the-Water). Saintbury and Talton, in

Tredington, which were acquired at the end of the thirteenth and beginning of the fourteenth century, figure quite prominently. There are two references to Stanley, a manor bought by Abbot Boys (1345-67) and sold by his successor John Ombersley (1367-79), and one to Kingswynford (Staffs.). The explanation for the apparently incomplete cover of the abbey estate is, of course, that these were the manors which were attributed to the cellarer, whose expenses were greater than those of any other obedientiary.[4]

The overwhelming majority of the entries refer to land transactions in the villages, only nine being concerned with non-agricultural tenements in Evesham. For the most part, these transactions concern holdings which came into the lord's hands through the death or flight of the tenant, through the tenant surrendering the holding or through confiscation by the lord. Re-issues of these holdings were either to the customary heirs, or, where these could not be found or were considered undesirable by the lord, to other persons. The type of holding involved is normally described. Most of them (thirty-nine) consisted of a messuage and a yardland, in other words the plot in the inhabited part of the township on which the dwelling house and other buildings would be situated, and the parcels of land distributed in the open fields. The meadow and pasture rights normally attached to a yardland or a fraction of a yardland are not mentioned, almost certainly because they would be understood to be appurtenant. In addition to these yardlands, there were four half-yardland holdings, two quarter-yardlands, one holding of three-quarters of a yardland (though this is a little obscure), one big holding of two yardlands, and two cotlands. In addition there are three holdings which are more vaguely described as the lands appurtenant to a messuage. The acreage of yardland in the Vale of Evesham was possibly twenty-four, judging by a statement in a late twelfth century cartulary, but there may have been variations from village to village.[5]

The principal question that one naturally wishes to ask about the evidence of this document is: what effects does it show of the demographic collapse of the third quarter of the fourteenth century, when the population may have been reduced by between a third and a half? We know that in the long run the bargaining power of tenants and agricultural labourers against landowners and employers was considerably enhanced, so that rents tended to come down and wages to rise. But this long-term trend was not necessarily inconsistent with contradictory short-term movements of rents, wages and prices. There are reasons to suppose that the immediate reaction of lords to the difficulties which they faced was to attempt to get at least as much rent and other payments out of the tenants as before. Certainly the lords in their other capacity as justices of labourers and justices of the peace applied the provisions of the Statutes of Labourers as strictly as possible and may have been able temporarily to hold back wage increases. The outcome of the tensions which were inevitable when natural economic forces were being dammed by judicial and administrative action was the revolt of 1381, an episode normally thought to be mainly confined to the south-east of the country. Discontent, however, was so strong in Worcestershire that the prior of the cathedral monastery had to excuse himself from attendance at the Benedictine General Chapter of 1381.[6]

There are various facts about the land transactions in the document which are of interest. First is the predominance of yardland holdings. It is true that the surveys of the Evesham Abbey manors in the late twelfth century cartulary also suggest that the yardland holding was the basic unit for the assessment of rents and services. Names of tenants of the majority of the customary yardlands are not given and it could be that already these holdings were being divided between two or even more families, largely as a result of population increase. This increase on the Evesham estates was about 70 per cent in the century after the Domesday inquest of 1086 and, judging by the evidence of the Bishop of Worcester's estate documents of 1182 and 1299, the rate of increase was similar during the thirteenth century. The general tendency by the beginning of the fourteenth century was for the typical peasant holding to be the half-yardland rather than the yardland. There is no reason to suppose that the Evesham estate would be exceptional. When, therefore, we discover evidence showing that most transactions at the end of the 1360s were in full yardlands we must assume that it was the surplus of land resulting from the deaths in the various outbreaks of the bubonic plague that made this possible, rather than that the yardland had been the typical peasant holding before 1349.[7]

But if we admit that the average size of holding had probably recently increased, it would seem that the monks were still trying to maintain old conditions of control as far as possible. The great majority of holdings that came into the lord's hands were explicitly stated to be held in bondage, a term which is self-explanatory, or *native*, that is in 'neifty', a term also meaning servile tenure. They were mostly re-issued on the same customary terms, by which the tenant remained *justiciabilis de corpore et catallis*, justiciable by his body and his chattels. This meant that the sanction for the effective exercise of the jurisdiction of the abbot, or his representatives, over his serfs was his power over their bodies and their goods, which he could detain in order to enforce judgment. When holdings were issued in bondage according to custom, this means that the established rents and services were to continue. Unfortunately we do not know what the customary obligations were by this time. There was certainly an element of labour service on demand, but at the end of the twelfth century the option of demanding from the tenants a full range of labour services (five days a week on most manors) or a money rent of 4s. or 5s. a year per yardland, and a reduced scale of services, had already been exercised by the lord. Judging by other estates in the neighbourhood, customary tenure in bondage implied a ratio of money rent and labour dues varying from year to year.

Other forms of tenure are found in the document which represent an apparently unwilling modification of customary tenure. These are mostly leases for life, for which the rent is mainly cash, together with certain labour services at harvest and haymaking, such as four attendances at the lord's boon reap. The life leases are often qualified with the statement that at the end of the tenant's life it must revert to the old customary terms. Thus Henry Philippes of Poden (a now deserted settlement near Honeybourne) took up a yardland in South Littleton for 18s. a year, four autumn boon reaps, mowing services on the meadows, the obligation to provide adequate buildings and reversion of the holding's obligations after his death to the ancient custom of bondage. The money rent for these life leases of yardlands varies from 13s. 4d. to 20s. a year, partly perhaps due to differences in the quality of the holdings, partly due to the bargaining between the tenant and the lord's agent. It is not possible, for lack of comparative evidence, to say whether these rents were high for the time or not. It would be unsafe to suggest that tenants necessarily regarded them with favour, even though the lord stipulated an eventual return to customary tenure, since no entry fines were paid for life leases, though quite heavy fines were paid for customary holdings.

Apart from rents and services, the cash or goods which the lord drew from the tenants on surrender and re-issue was not inconsiderable. Whether the holding came to the lord's hands by death or by surrender, the tenant's best animal was taken as heriot, normally an ox, which was valued. These valuations vary considerably. Most were worth between 10s. and 20s., though oxen were put as high as 40s. and 42s., and as low as 8s. The entry fines paid by incoming tenants also varied. They could be as low, for a yardland, as 5s., for instance when the customary heir was inheriting. But when an unmarried man was acquiring a holding by marrying the sitting female tenant, he might have to pay as much as 20s. A new tenant could find himself with burdens other than those paid to the lord. Such was John Frankes, an outsider who took over a yardland in Saintbury, in customary bondage, for the previous rents and services. He paid an entry fine of 13s. 4d. and agreed to provide a home for the previous tenant, who had surrendered the holding, with provision of three quarters of grain every year. Another Saintbury yardland holding was surrendered the same year by John Bonde for the benefit (*ad opus*) of a relative, Agnes Bonde. A suitor, John Chapellein, paid 20s. for her entry fine, and another 20s. to take her as a wife, and the holding with her. He agreed to let John Bonde have a room over the byre, with free entry and exit, an acre of growing wheat at his choice, and three quarters of grain (two of wheat, one of drage) each year.

The level of rents and entry fines suggests that Evesham Abbey was by no means losing its grip as a landlord. Other indications reinforce this impression. Although the lord emphasised customary obligations, he was prepared to over-ride custom. We find that the right customary heirs came to the cellarer's court to claim succession to the holding. This was sometimes allowed. But the cellarer also sometimes insisted on the heirs surrendering their right into his hands. For example, a tenant of a quarter-yardland at North Littleton surrendered his holding. He named the nearest heir, a smith in Lenchwick, and the second nearest, a ploughman or carter in Hampton. Both of these surrendered their rights, and the cellarer chose the smith who, as we have seen, was in any case the nearest heir. The holding was let to him and his blood, on customary terms, the tenant to be justiciable in body and chattels. What we have here is not so much a breach of custom, as a warning shot by the cellarer that, if it pleased him, he would over-ride custom. Another excellent example of the cellarer's determination to maintain control is his exaction of a fine of 20s. 8d. from a tenant of Talton in Tredington for permission to employ his own brother, an Evesham Abbey serf. This is explained by the labour situation at the time. Parliament, representing the interests of lords of manors, had insisted in the Statute of Labourers that these lords should have first call, as against other employers, on wage labourers who were members of their tenant families.[8]

A form of lease which was to become of increasing importance was that for a term of years. Such leases were, of course, nothing new but, as far as peasants were concerned, they are found in the fourteenth century mainly in inter-tenant transactions. Customary tenure, later to become copyhold, was overwhelmingly predominant on estates such as that of Evesham Abbey. There is, however, one case of a lease for a term of years in the document before us, of interest for various reasons. It is a lease for 20 years to John Prynche, by the cellarer, of the manor house at Bengeworth, the attached garden, the arable demesne (less such parts as had previously been rented out) and the separate and common pastures. This lessee got the Bengeworth demesne as a going concern. He was given the claim on the tenants' ploughing services and other manorial labour services, the grain in the barns and the livestock in the stable, and four draft animals. It may be that the description of livestock is incomplete, for there is a blank space in the manuscript and no details of the farmer's rent are given. However, it is clear that this type of manorial lease does not significantly modify the character of the local agrarian economy. Demesne management of this type, by farmers, occupies the history of the big landlord estates in medieval England for a much longer period of time than the direct management through reeves and bailiffs which occurred in the thirteenth and early fourteenth centuries.

Comment on this interesting document has so far been concerned with the light which it throws on agrarian conditions. The entries concerning Evesham itself are few, and almost entirely of purely topographical interest except that, although surrenders and issues of urban property were made in the overlord's court, the tenants' obligations were primarily to the bailiffs of the town. It would seem that the obedient-iaries who owned house property in Evesham were entitled to their rent, but that the bailiffs, in their dual capacity as agent of the abbey and of their fellow townsmen, had claims over the urban tenants of an administrative and constitutional rather than an economic character.

Reference may finally be made to an interesting entry which illustrates the recruitment of the lay officials of the abbey. It will be remembered that a John Bonde, a serf of Saintbury, surrendered his holding to a female relative whose husband engaged to keep him for life. This appears in the first year's list of leases, of whose date we are uncertain. In the next list (that of 1368-69), a John Bonde of Saintbury appears again. He is granted, in full court, the office of 'Bernward' within the abbey barton, that is the supervisor of the central grain store. He was to have the customary stipend and livery (that is, payments in kind) and cloth from the wardrobe, as for the abbot's officials, for his tunic and hood. It is not impossible that this was the John Bonde who surrendered his service holding in Saintbury the year before, but it does not seem altogether likely that a servile tenant in retirement, who had made humble provision for his keep, should be occupying an important office appropriate for a free man. The co-existence side by side of free and servile families in the same village with the same family name is by no means unknown.

Clearly, sweeping conclusions should not be made on the basis of a single document. There are too few sources for the history of the Evesham Abbey estate of the second half of the fourteenth century. On the other hand, there is no need for complete agnosticism. There is evidence from comparable estates, both lay and ecclesiastical, in Worcestershire and other West Midland counties, not to speak of the evidence from England as a whole. This other evidence entitles us to fit the Evesham Abbey document in the general perspective of historical development between the Black Death and the Peasants' Revolt. It confirms the impression of a conservative institution attempting to preserve customary relations between itself and its tenants when the conditions which had permitted these customary relations to develop no longer held good.

7

A Thirteenth-Century Poem
on Disputed Villein Services

Bodley MS. 57 is a collection of miscellaneous documents, mostly of a theological nature. In this collection (fos. 191d-192) there is a poem of eighty-three lines in a late thirteenth-century hand, telling the following story. The foolish people of Stoughton, tenants of the abbot and convent of Leicester, desire a greater freedom, and complain of a thousand indignities inflicted upon them. A group of tenants decide to go to the king's court to present their case. They return empty-handed. Other malcontents follow them, but are equally unsuccessful. For when they arrive at the king's court an advocate advises them that they stand little chance against their lord, and against the decision of a well-informed jury. One of the more acute of the villagers points out, moreover, that the cost of a pleader would be too great, and would reduce them to beggary, and that their present condition is preferable to that. This argument tells with his companions. They admit defeat, bewail their fate, and curse their ring-leader. One of the canons, who was apparently looking after the interests of the abbey in the case, reprimands them severely, and they follow him home weeping. The poet declares social advancement for villeins impossible, and concludes with a tag in law-French to the effect that custom still forms law in the king's court.

The Bodleian Catalogue suggests that the poem may be the work of a canon of the abbey of Leicester—a likely surmise, considering the point of view expressed. A fairly precise date may be given to its composition from the legal record of the case described. The poem itself gives the impression of having been written very shortly after the conclusion of the incident. It is by nature topical. It is the sort of poem the author might well have read out to amuse his fellow-canons, who, as the lords whose rights had been unsuccessfully challenged, would enjoy a scurrilous attack on their opponents, and particularly one which reflected so accurately their general attitude to the agricultural lower strata.

The case on which the poem is a comment occurs in the Coram Rege Roll for Michaelmas 4-5 Edward I.[1] Although we are not informed of the course of the dispute before it came to the king's court, it seems likely that the tenants had attempted to put their case first in the manor court, and having failed, had had to resort to the royal court. The abbot of Leicester was attatched to answer Philip Attechurch, Robert Makeles, and twenty-eight other tenants of the abbey in Stoughton on a charge of illegal imposition of unjust services. The abbot (William Schepished, 1270-91) replied that he was not bound to answer, but that, to expose their malice he would do so. The plaintiffs, through Philip and Robert,[2] claimed to be free 'sokemanni', owing for each virgate of land 5s. rent, two appearences a year at the abbot's court of the vill, and an appearence every three weeks when no writ or complaint was impleaded. They went on to allege that the late Abbot Paul of Leicester (1186-1205) had made them do villein services, and that the present abbot distrained them to do similar services to their loss of £20 *per annum*. To these charges the abbot replied that 'they were his villeins and ought to perform the same as they had done at the will of his predecessors, before his predecessor Paul was made abbot, and before King John's time.' The plaintiffs denied this. The abbot 'put himself on his country.'

The following January, at Shottesbrook (Berks), before the royal justices, two of the accusers, Hugh of Attewell and Ivo of Friseby, admitted that though they were freemen when they had come to the abbot's land, they held land in villeinage, paying merchet ('redemptio carnis et sanguinis'),[3] and owing other customs according to the will of the abbot. Four others then acknowledged that their ancestors had been villeins, and that they owed villein services not only because they held land in villeinage but because they were of villein blood. Following on these admissions, the jurors swore that William the Carter, Ralph Syre, and others, not only owed the customs which had already been acknowledged by their fellows, but 'other works with forks and flails as villeins do'.[4] The jurors traced the villein condition of these men back beyond the reign of King John to the days before the earl of Leicester, Robert le Bossu, granted the whole village of Stoughton to the Augustinian abbey which he had established in Leicester in place of secular collegiate church of St. Mary in the castle.[5] In those days said the jurors, Stoughton had been a member of the great manor of Groby, and whenever the earl came to Groby it was the duty of Stoughton villeins to thresh corn and oats, and to make malt as often as his bailiff demanded. And so these men were still the abbot's villeins: and though some of their services had been spared this was only at the will of the abbot, and, moreover, they were tallageable, though they had been spared hitherto. Their land could not be freely held, because it was not held by fixed service ('per aliquod certum servicium') At Easter three more of the plaintiffs acknowledged themselves dependant on the will of the abbot; and at Michaelmas, the eleven remaining plaintiffs followed suit.[6]

All the persons named in the case do not appear in the poem, though most of those mentioned in the poem are to be found in the legal record. It would seem that the abbey wit made the most prominent of the villagers concerned in the dispute the special butt of his humour. The Philip Attechurch, who with Robert Makeles (also mentioned), first claimed relaxation of services on behalf of the others at Michaelmas, seems to have been the ring-leader attacked in the poem :

> Sit maledictus Philippus nos quia fallit.

It is interesting to note that Philip appears to have been the village reeve—not only the official link between the tenantry and the lord's officials, but also the leader of revolt against the lord :

> Gessit vexillum : credo quod penitet illum...

It is also natural, in view of the current(and particularly the ecclesiastical) attitude towards women, that two of the women involved, Christiana and Mathilda (Mald or Maud), should also be singled out for special ridicule.[7]

Increased exactions of labour services were a characteristic of the agricultural boom of the thirteenth century. In spite of the fact that villeins were not supposed to sue jointly or through representatives,[8] it is noteworthy that this peasant protest was apparently well organized, and that it was expressed in a legal claim. It was an attempt to take advantage of the supposed tacit encouragement of liberty in the royal courts, and it was an attempt which in practise failed. However, it is significant that it should have been attempted at all, and the poem indicates (for whatever such evidence may be worth) that the villeins had considerable confidence that they would succeed. But equally significant are the words put by the poet into the mouth of the pleader, Allan, who tells the villeins how little chance they stand, because they are villeins :

> Cum domino certare tuo non consilium do
> Rustice, victus eris dominum qui vincere queris.
> Tu debes ferre tibi quod dat regula terre.

The poem affords an interesting sidelight on the social attitude adopted by the canons of Leicester as members of the landowning class. Here is a particular expression of that general hierarchical conception of a society divided into social classes, stratified into a system of castes, admitting of no social mobility :

> Quid faciet servus nisi serviet, et puer eius ?
> Purus servus erit et libertate carebit.
> Iudicium legis probat hoc et curia regis.

And in so far as any change in social status had to be legally sanctified, and sought through legal channels, the high fees charged by the professional pleaders were a considerable obstacle across the path of social advancement, as Robert complains in the poem :

> Pro me vix unus loquitur nisi dem sibi munus.
> Quisquis mercedem petit a me regis ad edem,...

and decides to stay as he is.

There is an interesting background to this case. The people of Stoughton were protesting against a real social degradation. They were only two or three miles away from the free air of the borough of Leicester. Villein tenants elsewhere on the Leicester abbey estates were not so heavily burdened. In fact, the condition of these plaintiffs compared badly with the general level of villein conditions in the whole of the county. Leicestershire was a region where, on the whole, there does not seem to have been a heavy exploitation of demesne arable,[9] and the demand for heavy labour services was correspondingly low, as no other form of cultivation requires so great an application of labour. On twenty-nine lay manors surveyed between 1272 and 1335[10] labour services in no cases included week works. It is definitely stated in eight of the surveys that the villeins owed no works at all. Other works consisted of no more than seasonal boon works, and not many of these were demanded. Similarly, on the largest estate in Leicestershire, that of Leicester abbey, there were no week works demanded from the tenants, and boon works were fairly light, except for one single manor; and that was the manor of Stoughton, in the village of Stoughton, practically all of which was owned by the abbey.[11]

Apart from a number of seasonal boon works such as were demanded from other tenants in other Leicester abbey manors, the virgater at Stoughton was obliged to work twice a week from Michaelmas to the feast of St. Margaret (20 July), and four days a week from the feast of St. Margaret to Michaelmas—in other words, to perform extra work, apart from boons, during haymaking and harvesting seasons. In addition he ploughed a day in spring and winter, and owed mowing and reaping boons as well. He had to carry the hay he had mown and the corn he had reaped to the granges, as well as doing other carting services. These services in terms of toil were unmatched elsewere on the estate, and probably in the county. Merchet and heriot, of course, were common to all villeins. But again it was only the Stoughton villein who had restrictions on his power to sell wood and trees, and male foals.[12] Even the Stoughton services were not, of course, remarkable compared with those demanded from villein tenants on big ecclesiastical estates further south, such as those of Ramsey abbey, or St. Paul's, or any number of others. But in Leicestershire, and on the Leicester abbey estates, they were abnormal, and their imposition was probably of recent date—there is no reason to disbelieve the claim of the tenants that it was Abbot Paul who increased the services—and resistance was natural. The emotional reaction of the lords of these villeins, quite apart from the inevitable legal conflict recorded in the poem, was also typical of the attitude of the feudal landowners who were faced with this type of social conflict, whether expressed in Latin verse, in the vernacular, in the chronicles, or in the pulpit.[13]

MS. BODLEY 57, fos. 191*d*-192

Post incarnatum verbum de virgine natum
Non fuerant gentes fatue nimis[14] insapientes
Ut gens Stoctone caret omnimoda ratione.
Plebs in Stoctona dedit incassum sua dona :
Quando frui more captabant liberiore,
Gens dixit ville 'patimur discrimina mille :
ecce sumus gentes in consilio sapientes,
Omnes prudentes,magnum solamen habentes,
Nulli servire volumus : dum possumus ire,
Ibimus ad regem qui nobis vult dare legem'.
Omnes expresse dicunt 'sic volumus esse'.
Mus furit in messe dum catum sentit abesse.
Human Henricus, Radulphus et eius amicus
Rusticus antiquus Rogerus, et alter iniquus,
Isti dixerunt quod pergere mox voluerunt.
Protinus fuerunt : vacuis manibus redierunt.
'Ad regem vadam' dixit miserabilis Adam;
'Coram rege cadam, causam scriptam sibi tradam'.
Ibant psallentes, magnum risum facientes,
Sed redeunt flentes, fiunt sine fine dolentes.
Ad regem vadunt, quia sperant esse magistri,
Coram rege cadunt, fiunt sine fine ministri.
Providus urbanus dixit narrator Allanus
'Rustice Willelme, causam, tibi supplico, tel me :
Ad quod venisti sensu sine credo fuisti.
Tu male discernis, reus es quia dominum spernis.
Cum domino certare tuo non consilium do,
Rustice : victus eris dominum[15] qui vincere queris.
Tu debes ferre tibi quod dat regula terre.
Bis sex barbati, stantes iurare parati,
Isti iurati, de causa certificati,
Contra te dicent, quod servus eras tibi dicent,
Et labor et lis et dolor et vis, causa pudoris,
Crescit et imminet et male terminet omnibus horis'.
In medio turbe Robertus dixit in urbe,
'Pro me vix unus loquitur nisi dem sibi munus.
Quisquis mercedem petit a me regis ad edem :
Plus prodest caula mihi regis quam facit aula.
Vestes res percudes dispendo meas meliores.
Ecce domi pergo, vos omnes deprecor ergo,
Cras discedamus et ad abbatem redeamus;
Huic servire volo, conventum spernere nolo.
Plus valet ante mori sub fortuna meliori
Quam mendicare vel mendicando rogare,
Si victi simus, omnes sine fine perimus.'
'Verum dixisti', dixerunt protinus isti,

Ivo de Freseby, Willelmus Page, Johannes,
Human Henricus, Astel Rogerus, et Hugo,
Robertus Makeles, Radulphus Syre, Thomasque,
Rogerus montem super, et Rogerus et Honney.
Stat Christiana cum pellicia veterana;
Verba minus vana loquitur quasi turgida rana;
Mald velud insana stetit ut foret una diana,
Hac sibi nec lana valuit piperis modo grana.[16]
O dulcis Christe, dixerunt sepius iste,
Quid faciemus? pane caremus, iam venit estas,
Dampna videmus, farre caremus, crescit egestas.
Sit maledictus ubique Philippus, nos quia fallit:
Exul abibit, raro redibit, et 'heu' modo psallit,
Prepositus ville perversus proditor ille:
Rusticus est hippus victus sine fine Philippus:
Sillaba putressit phi sordida,lippus acressit:
Phi nota fetoris, lippus gravat omnibus horis:
Sit procul hinc lippus, sit phi procul, ergo Philippus
Sit procul a terra: nunquam vixit sine guerra,
Philos fertur amor, equus ippus, et inde Philippus
Sortitur nomen, amisit nominus omen.[17]
Costans Rogerus, est frater in ordine verus,
Defensor bonus est, quicquid loquitur bene prodest;
Tantum defendit, insensatos reprehendit
Donec discedunt: victi plagendo recedunt:
Amodo plectuntur, Rogerum flendo sequuntur:
Quilibet ex illis sibi dicit 'Do that ti will is'.
Ville maiores sunt omnes inferiores,
Divitiis plenus nuper, sit pauper egenus,
Et modo mendicat vix est sibi qui benedicat.
Postquam regnavit Salomen de semine David
Non fuit in villa discordia turpior illa.
Quid faciet servus nisi serviet et puer eius?
Purus servus erit et libertate carebit.
Iudicium legis probat hoc et curia regis.
Uncore a la curt le rey, usum menie la ley.

8

Medieval Peasants: Any Lessons?

A rich complexity of issues arises from the impact of capitalism and imperialism on peasant societies. A student of the medieval peasantry, in face of this evidence, may be forgiven for wondering whether the experience of peasants in feudal Europe can throw any light on modern problems; or conversely, whether the experience of contemporary peasants helps the historian to understand what was happening in the remote and relatively undocumented past. Any serious historian has to classify and generalise social phenomena and is not likely to get very far unless he works from a theory of social development which will provide him with hypotheses. These hypotheses have the function of acting as organising principles for the direction of his research. They will naturally have to be checked against the data and if necessary modified. It is generally assumed by those historians whose work is theoretically oriented, rather than being purely empirical in character, that social formations, like feudalism, and the classes within them, like landowners and peasants, embody certain regularities which justify the comparative method. By this, I mean the illumination of unknown or unverifiable features of one society by the known aspects of another, provided those societies belong to the same social formation, even if separated by time and space.

I believe that this method of work is necessary and justified, but I also think that it can be made ridiculous by being extended too far. The main danger at the moment seems to me to be the result of current over-simplifications of the stages of social history. For example, there is a strong tendency, resulting partly from a reaction against Marxism, to see history as divided simply between 'traditional' and 'modern' or 'post-industrial' societies. This is basically the same theory as that which supposes that 'peasant society' or 'peasant economy' is one complete social formation, provided peasants constitute a majority of the population and irrespective of the characteristics of the other social classes, even the ruling class. It is on the basis of this elimination of the distinctive features of different types of pre-capitalist society that we see the now fashionable habit of explaining say, seventeenth century English marriage customs by reference to the researches of anthropologists into contemporary African or South American habits. This form of comparative study has been acutely and justly criticised by E. P. Thompson.[1]

I am not, of course, suggesting that there are not important continuities of economic organisation and culture between succeeding stages of social evolution. European feudal society had many features which it inherited from the ancient world; European capitalism is likewise riddled with feudal relics. Nevertheless feudalism and capitalism are distinct social formations, based on different modes of production, legitimised by different ideological systems, and dominated by struggles between social classes distinctive of each formation. The medieval peasantry's structure, its class battles and its outlook are to be explained in terms primarily of the overall characteristics of medieval feudalism.

The characteristics of the mid-nineteenth century French peasants, described by Marx in the *18th Brumaire of Louis Bonaparte,* were, as he clearly emphasised, specific to that period. They were not even to be compared with the feudal peasantry of the Ancien Régime, let alone to the feudal peasantry of the medieval period.

To what extent, if at all, can one compare medieval and modern peasantries? This being as much a task for the students of the modern as of the medieval peasants, my contribution had best be confined to a statement of (as I see it) these three main aspects of this class during the medieval period:

- its internal constitution;

- its articulation in the general class structure;

- its struggles with the other classes.

I. *The Internal Constitution of the Medieval Peasantry*

It is obviously difficult to generalise about medieval European peasants in view of the great variation in economic conditions, for instance between the *culture arbustive* of the Mediterranean region and the extensive cereal production of northern Europe (including England); or between old settled areas and areas of new colonisation. All the same, surprising similarities existed even in contrasting areas. Even in periods and places of relatively great urbanisation, the peasant economy was first for the subsistence of its members. The interesting economic variations arose from the different ways in which the surplus over subsistence needs was disposed of; in simplest terms, whether or not it was converted into cash, and if so, by whom? The peasant or the appropriator of the surplus? The next point is that the basic socio-economic unit of all peasantries was the family household. Not enough is known about peasant family structure before the twelfth or thirteenth centuries, but by this period when documentation becomes abundant, each household at the most seems to have contained grandparents, one married pair of the next generation, their children, perhaps an unmarried uncle and/or aunt and sometimes a living-in servant or two depending on the wealth of the group. This would be the composition of the household at the period of its fullest extension. It could be drastically reduced in size by the death of the grandparents and the departure of the unmarried son(s) and daughter(s). The households are only rarely found in isolated dispersion. The hamlet or village was the unit of settlement in which most people lived. The economy, though usually based on the individual family possession of arable land, also had a collective element of varying importance resulting from the need for access to various types of common right in woodlands, marshes, rough grazings, quarries, etc. Much of the formidable cohesion of medieval village communities was based on this. But does this mean that these villages and hamlets were communities of equals? It has been suggested that the main hierarchical division was determined by age and sex.[2] As far as the medieval European peasantry was concerned, this view is not justified by the evidence, although age and sex did have a role in the differentiation of functions. There was clear social stratification by the time we have written records. The reasons for early stratification need investigation, although later stratification (in which the market played a big part) has been more thoroughly researched. The division between rich and middle peasants with land and equipment (especially ploughteams) adequate for subsistence and poor or landless peasants without enough land for subsistence is found very early.

This hierarchy retained its contours for a very long time. The reasons for this stability were rooted in the nature of the landlord-peasant economy. The lord of the village controlled the land market which meant that the accumulation of properties by an alliance of lineages could not take place, except between free families holding in free tenure. The lord prevented such accumulations and was helped in this by the conservative elements in the village community. Through the courts of the manor either the lord or the village notables operated a deliberate policy of breaking up accumulated peasant holdings to prevent too great an enlargement of the property of individual families of the upper stratum.

At the other end of the social scale, another feature helped to maintain the contours of this social hierarchy. Although wage labour was important, certainly from the thirteenth century onwards, it was nevertheless socially diffuse. Firstly, some wage labour came from smallholding families who merged into the middle stratum. Secondly, although there might be a number of people in the village dependent on wages, they tended to be distributed in ones and twos among the richer households. The wage labourer in this type of peasant society was thus a living-in member of a peasant household. A third reason for the dilution of wage labour as a social force was that quite a lot of work in the village which one might expect to have been done by wage labourers was frequently done as contract work between householders. This is seen in litigation about non-performance or nonpayment in manor court records.

The hierarchy of the village was not, of course, entirely static. When population grew faster than productivity in the twelfth and thirteenth centuries, the gulf between the peasant upper stratum and the landless or near landless was deepened. Production for the market further exacerbated these divisions. But conflicts between village rich and poor were never as important as the conflict between the peasants as a whole on the one hand and the landowning class and its institutions on the other.

II. *Articulation of the Medieval Peasantry in the General Class Structure*

If production for the market played an important part in the peasant economy and if the peasantry was by definition an exploited class in the sense that other social groups appropriated the surplus over subsistence, the question of the 'autonomy' of medieval peasant society arises. I doubt whether the concept of autonomy is at all useful in this case. It is often said that the peasant community had a culture which was completely separate from the rest of society. There was no greater separateness of medieval peasant culture from the culture of the ruling class of European society in the Middle Ages than there is a separateness of the culture of the modern working class from that of the middle and upper classes of modern capitalist society. There was, indeed, a cultural separation between rulers and ruled in the Middle Ages, but this was not specific to the separateness of peasant from the rest, but something which was specific to the class divisions within society.

It is true that the peasant household and economy did not in principle need lords, in the same way that the modern industrial proletariat in capitalism needed capitalists: the village economy could carry on without the other social classes. In practice, however, it is not the case that the society of the feudal lords was, to quote Mendras [*1972*]: 'a global society with its own logic independent of the organisation of agricultural production'. In fact, the society of the rulers was in every way dependent upon the organisation of agricultural production and on the way in which peasants reacted to treatment they received from landowners. The nature of the feudal aristocracy was bound up with the way they dealt with peasant society, as can be demonstrated by such things as the development and decline of serfdom and the issue of private jurisdiction, where the feudal lords stood between the developing apparatus of state and the majority of the population. Although the peasantry could be considered in terms of medieval politics as a voiceless mass, in fact the landlords reacted according to shifts in such things as the land-labour ratio and many other factors, which gave peasants greater or lesser grounds for action or pressure against them. In other words the concept of the peasantry as an enclosed community in relation to outside society looks like a euphemism for the relationship between the exploited and the exploiters.

Apart from the fact that it is impossible to think of the peasantry as being autonomous from the rest of society and in particular autonomous from the structure of the feudal rulers, there are other aspects of the relationship between the village, the peasant householders and the world outside the village not directly related to the exploitative relationships with landowners. There were many threads leading outward from the village to the locality, to the region, to the state, not only economic but ideological and cultural as well. The medieval village was contained within an ecclesiastical unit, the parish, which performed an extremely important cultural function. There were certainly many absentee vicars and rectors who drained off the main part of parish revenues. But there were normally two or three resident wage-earning parish priests, not necessarily drawn from the peasantry, but men who were in close contact with them. These priests, in the exercise of their penitential duty, as well as in the exercise of their duty as preachers of the gospel and of the social doctrine of the church, were very important conveyors of the ideology of the rulers of society to the peasants. This was demonstrated very clearly in the limited ideology of the peasantry in times of revolt, when they found it impossible to break away from the traditional tripartite image of society which was promulgated by official ruling society mainly through the church.

The market was a very important meeting place in medieval Europe, not simply for peasant vendors of agricultural produce and the small merchants of the local market, but for men, merchants and others who came from the great cities. The local market acted as a focal point where village and city met.

Another factor which served to convey the ideas and gossip of the ruling class into the village was the peripatetic and open nature of the great households of the feudal nobles and gentry. Great nobles lived a public life surrounded by their entourages of retainers who were usually noble themselves and had their own entourages of lesser retainers. This openness was one way in which the peasantry gained knowledge of political issues, at a national or regional level; and although in times of revolt the political slogans of the peasantry were simple, many in fact hit the nail on the head from the point of view of what were the important issues at the time.

Although there was very often a quite clear relationship of hostility and separation between the peasant and the landowner, certain elements amongst the peasantry did enter into the followings of the local gentry in quite an important way. This is difficult to document, but the criminal records of fourteenth and fifteenth century England which listed the names of members of gangs, very often led by lesser or middle nobility, indicated that there were elements from the peasantry in these gangs who in this way again entered into a much wider sphere than the village itself.

III. *Struggles of the Medieval Peasantry with Other Classes*

In spite of the great changes which took place in the thousand years of the European middle-ages, the great basic fact which determined the most crucial social relationships was the transfer of peasant surplus to the landowning class in the form of rent in money, labour, kind or the profits of jurisdiction. Some modifications to this situation were, however, of considerable historical significance. From the thirteenth century onwards we find the urban communes in north and central Italy usurping the position of feudal landowners as exploiters of the peasants. Peasants were also exploited by usurers through high interest rates and by merchants through unfavourable terms of trade in exchanges between town and country. There were also periods when the squeezing out of peasant surplus was less easy than at others, for example the fifteenth century. As states developed their bureaucratic and military apparatus, taxes were added to the rent burden of peasants. Public authorities might even try to restrain the extraction of rent by landowners so as to preserve the taxable resources of the peasants.

The ideological mystification which justified the transfer of peasant surplus was mainly promulgated by the clergy. This social group occupied an ambivalent position. On the one hand it was presented as an order of society separate from nobles, townsmen and peasants, having the function of securing the salvation of all by its prayers and its administration of the sacraments. On the other hand, it reproduced within its ranks an image of the class structure of secular society. At the top its popes, bishops, abbeys, nunneries and cathedral chapters were wealthy landowners recruited from and enjoying the same sort of landed income as the feudal nobility. At the bottom a large number of parish priests were not even beneficed, but were wage earners. All, however, with a few exceptions, preached, year in, year out, century in, century out, the doctrine that the social order which was divinely ordained, consisted of mutually supporting groups, or estates, each of whose functions was necessary for stability in this world as a springboard for the next. It was difficult, and rare, as was suggested above, for even quite revolutionary figures to get away from this conception. Sometimes, however, the propaganda backfired. The duty of the nobility to protect the rest of society was sometimes not fulfilled, as in France in the fourteenth and fifteenth centuries. This intensified among the peasants a feeling of hostility to the noble class. In this custom-dominated society, rebellious feelings were often generated when custom was broken by the ruling groups.

Social movements which were caused by the conflict between peasants and other classes and which had aims specific to the peasant class assumed very different forms according to changing circumstances. Throughout the medieval periods there were conflicts concerning the level of rent, usually a peasant reaction against attempted increases in the amount or variety of labour services, in the quantity of produce demanded from the holding, or in the cash level of rent where this was in monetary form. This appropriation of the peasants' labour or the product of his labour was so direct and open a form of exploitation that the coercion needed to achieve it had to be legitimised. Disputes about rents therefore merged into disputes about personal status. If a man was a serf, that is, somebody else's property, then the product of his labour must belong not to him but to his owner. Peasants also made claims to free access to what they considered to be unappropriated natural resources, that is, the hunting of game and the fishing of waters. If they were serfs, such claims would be invalid. The issue of freedom and serfdom was therefore a major element in peasant movements from the ninth century until the end of the Middle Ages and beyond.

The power a lord had over a servile peasant was usually expressed in jurisdictional terms. In addition to rents, lords of serfs as well as of free men subordinated to them, exacted a range of payments and obligations which hindered the development of the peasant economy. This was felt particularly sharply as peasants became integrated with the developing market economy, especially in Italy and in France. It is of considerable significance that some of the sharpest clashes and some of the most advanced peasant gains were made in those areas where peasants were producing the most important and marketable cash crop of medieval Europe, wine. These gains were usually expressed in the peasant community's achievement of a fixed monetary obligation to the lord; a commutation of labour services; a relaxation of the more servile aspects of the lord-tenant relationship; sometimes even a modicum of self-government, analogous at a lower level to that of the urban commune. The peasants had to buy these privileges and they mainly benefited the rich peasants who paid for them.

The pressures for lower rent, more freedom and more control over the peasants' own economy (including free access to the market) were characteristic of stable peasant communities confronting seigneurial power. These movements were sometimes violent, sometimes character- ised by non-violent pressure. They were often waged by individual communities, more rarely on a regional or national level. A good example of the latter is the war of the Catalan *remensas*[3] in the 15th century. Other movements were reactions to situations in which peasants were uprooted, disoriented. Such movements were sometimes expressed in forms of thought and action remote from practical issues about rents and conditions of tenure. They also merged with movements of non- peasants. The crusades from the late eleventh century onwards frequently contained a popular chiliastic element directed into orthodox channels. But the movement of the Pastoureaux (herdsmen) in mid-thirteenth century France was similar, though it ended as an attack on the social order. The rising of Fra Dolcino in the first decade of the fourteenth century in Italy was a millenarian movement probably given force by peasants whose communities had been disintegrated by the urban communes. Another form of peasant disorientation resulted from the pillaging of the armies of the nobility during war. This was behind the Jacquerie of 1358 whose only known form of self-expression was a violent hatred of the nobility. The English peasants' rising of 1381 combined many features: a straightforward fight for low rents and freedom; a protest against taxation; but also a vaguely adumbrated utopia with millenarian undertones.

In spite of the millenarian element in peasant movements of the middle ages, whose importance should not be overestimated, the leadership is found most often in the richer elements (including some who had become clerics), those who are mostly closely connected with the market. Their enemies were lords, governments, and church authorities whose modes of exploitation of the peasants were, by the fifteenth and sixteenth centuries, archaic. The peasant rebels, some of them, were going to become part of the class which would supersede the feudal potentates. Medieval peasants lived and struggled in a world composed entirely of family-based agriculture and industry. Merchant capital was confined, mostly, to the international trade in luxuries. However fierce and oppressive were feudal lords and governments, they cannot be compared with the governments of modern imperialism and the international corporations.

9

Peasant Movements in England Before 1381

'Aux yeux de l'historien ... la révolte agraire apparait aussi inséperable du régime seigneurial que, par example, de la grande enterprise capitaliste, la grève.' Marc Bloch, *Caractères Originaux de l'Histoire Rurale Française*, p. 175

I

The dramatic character of the Great Revolt of 1381, the collapse of the government, the concerted action of peasants from parts of the country remote from each other, have made us regard that event as unique in English history. It is certainly true that at no other time was the English peasantry able to make itself felt politically as in May and June of that fateful year. But because of the uniqueness of the movement we are inclined to regard the Revolt as a bolt from the blue. We recognise and analyse the social, economic and political causes of mass discontent, but we mistakenly conceive of them as operating on a hitherto passive population which only shows its exasperation in this one explosive outburst, the first and last of its kind. There are very good reasons for rejecting the idea that the Revolt of 1381 was the last of the great peasant revolts. From the years immediately after the suppression of the Revolt[1] to the Midland Revolt of 1607, agrarian discontent is at the bottom of many movements usually considered to have primarily political or religious causes, and this fact is being more widely recognised by historians.

I am not concerned here to examine the course of peasant discontent after 1381, but to re-examine the period preparatory to the Revolt, a period whose beginnings I see, not at the time of the Black Death but at the begining of the thirteenth century. In order to place this peasant discontent in its proper perspective, before indicating the evidence for it in the period to which I refer, it will be necessary to make some general remarks about the economic and social position of the English peasantry in the Middle Ages. This will seem to many a well-trodden field, and I am conscious of the risks in attempting to reassess the work of such eminent workers as Seebohm and Vinogradoff, or, to come to contemporary scholars, Professors Postan and Homans.

What was it in the agrarian relations of feudal society that made peasant revolts, as Marc Bloch implied in the quotation I have set at the head of this article, inevitable? In order to answer this question, we must simplify the broad outlines of that society by (for the moment) ignoring such important intermediate social strata as the burgesses and certain of the free tenants. Is not feudal society after all fundamentally determined by the relations between a landowning military aristocracy on the one hand, and a vast class of peasant-producers, working individual family holdings but also organised in village or hamlet communities, on the other? I am aware that there have been many important modifications made to this simple picture,[2] but I maintain that the picture remains fundamentally true even for economies of widely differing character, in so far as it describes the basic social relations between the two main classes of feudal Europe. I must, however, further define these social relations as they affected the majority of the peasants and the feudal lords.

The fact that the peasants were organised in an organic community and that they were in effective possession of their own means of subsistence is of the greatest importance. This fact contradicts, as it were, the legal claim of the landowners to the monopoly and free disposal of the arable, the meadow, the pasture, the woods, the rivers and the waste. The landowners were not, however, powerless. They were militarily an extremely powerful class, and whether the state power which they controlled was decentralised into private jurisdictions, or centralised under the direction of the most eminent of the feudal landowners, the king, they had all the means of coercion in society in their own hands. Their sustenance as a non-producing class depended on the transfer to themselves of the surplus produced by the peasant, above what the peasant needed to keep himself and his family alive, and to ensure the reproduction of the agricultural routine year in and year out. There was no economic reason why the members of the peasant communities (many of which existed before feudal lordship developed) should transfer their surplus to their lords. The lord-serf relationship was in fact primarily a political relationship. It may originally have contained within it an element of *quid pro quo* by which the lord protected some of the peasants during the chaos of the ninth and tenth centuries, but that the element of protection was of minor importance by the eleventh and twelfth centuries is shown by the legal status of the majority of the peasants. Their surplus has now to be transferred under coercive sanction, and therefore they are unfree.[3]

The transferred surplus is rent, and the rent can be in many different forms without losing its essential character. In the period of transition from tribal to feudal society, in England in the eighth and ninth centuries for instance, rent as defined above is hardly distinguishable from the food tribute once rendered freely to the king and the warrior leaders of the tribe,[4] and rents in kind remain throughout the Middle Ages as an important component of total rent. Most lords, especially the ecclesiastics, could rely on at least eggs at Easter and hens at Christmas from their tenants as late as the fourteenth and fifteenth centuries. Another form of rent is labour, often regarded as the most typical rent of feudal society. Here the peasant's surplus is transferred to the lord in the form of labour on the lord's own domanial reserve. It should be noted that labour rents do not only involve a transfer simply of labour, but often the application of the peasant's own equipment and seed to the lord's demesne. When the lords are not concerned to cultivate their demesnes directly—and this decision is not, as was once thought, the necessary reaction to the growth of the markets—they might,[5] according to local circumstances, appropriate the peasant surplus either as produce or as money rent. The produce rent of the twelfth and thirteenth centuries must be distinguished from the ancient customary renders of pre-feudal origin. It is sometimes a proportion of the total harvest (the French *champart*), but this is uncommon in England, where more often a fixed amount was demanded. The money rent was regarded for the most part, and should be regarded by us, as a commutation of other forms of peasant surplus. Whilst it is true that by the fourteenth century some demesne and assarted land was being leased at what are sometimes called 'economic' rents, the level of most money rents was determined primarily, as in the case of food and labour rents, by the political relationship of lord and peasant, and not by free bargaining on a land market. Even the level of the 'economic' rent must be assumed to have been considerably affected by this political factor.

Naturally these different forms of rent existed side by side. Examples abound. Let us take the rents paid by the half-yardlanders of Childe-hampton, a manor of the nunnery of Wilton in Wiltshire, in 1315. The money value of labour rent performed during the year was about 6s., the money rent paid was 5s., and customary (probably pre-feudal) produce rents consisted of a cock, three hens, and a grain payment for churchscot.[6] We must also remember that if we regard rent as being the transfer of the peasant's surplus to the landowner, other payments not normally described as rent should be included. Of these payments the most important was probably tithe, which I do not propose to discuss here. Another payment more to the forefront of peasant grievances was tallage, sometimes euphemistically described as aid. This was an annual tax on the unfree peasantry of a manor for the benefit of the manorial lord. It was sometimes a fixed amount, but more often was determined by the will of the lord. In the second half of the thirteenth century the Abbot of Bec was getting from his manors tallage varying between 13s. 4d. and £4 per manor.[7] Individuals paid varying amounts. The unfree tenants of the Master of the Temple on his manor of Cubbington in Warwickshire were stated in 1279 to owe 2s. per head a year, while a serf of the Prior of Kenilworth at Baginton in the same county paid an 'aid' of 5s. 4d. a year.[8] Arbitrary tallage was the most typical, and to be tallaged 'high and low' was considered to be a mark of servitude. It might also be justifiable to include in the total of rent (as defined here) some of the fines in the manor courts. Entry fines should certainly be considered as rent. Fines for permission to do certain acts which might be prevented by the lord by virtue of his political power may well come in this category, although they are principally a by-product of regulations aimed at restricting the movement of peasants and their property.

The main concern of the lord in his relations with the peasants was to get his rent. In view of the ability of the peasant communities to stand on their own economically, it was necessary for the lords to exercise their coercive power in order to guarantee the payment of the rent. A group of regulations operated in the manor courts and ultimately guaranteed by the threat of force was designed to secure the lords' claims. These were restrictions on the movement of the unfree population; restrictions on the movement of their chattels; and restrictions on the transfer of land between unfree peasants. Intended to guarantee the conditions under which the peasant surplus or rent could be transferred, these restrictions came to be the very marks of legal servility; a clear indication of the close relation between the status and the economic obligations of the peasantry.[9]

The restriction on the movement of the medieval serf was not identical with the binding to the soil of the peasant population of the late Empire, in spite of the fact that the author of the *Dialogus de Scaccario* refers to the villein as 'ascriptitius'.[10] The serf, as Marc Bloch has pointed out,[11] was bound, not to the land but to his lord, and it is noteworthy that whilst referring to the unfree peasantry as 'ascriptitii' Richard Fitznigel stresses that they can be moved from place to place, sold and otherwise alienated at the will of the lord. However the fact was that there was such a shortage of labour in the Middle Ages that in practice the effort was always made to fix the peasant to his holding so as to guarantee the payment of rent and the performance of services. Hence the unfree peasant could not quit the manor without permission, and even when given permission had to pay an annual chevage from wherever he might be, to remind him that the lord might recall him at will. The offspring of serfs had to obtain a licence to enter holy orders, or to receive schooling, which amounted to the same thing. The marriage of serfs' daughters, and sometimes of their sons, was additionally controlled, and the obligation to pay *merchet* or, as it was sometimes called, *redemptio sanguinis et carnis,* was regarded as a hall-mark of servility. As a corollary *leyrwite,* the fine for unchastity out of wedlock, was imposed not so much perhaps to compensate for loss of marriage-ability, and therefore of *merchet,* but because bastards were considered to be born to free status.[12] The restrictions on the villein's right freely to dispose of his movable goods was generally covered by the doctrine that such goods were in fact, like the villein himself, the property of the lord. Hence manumissions were always paid for by a third person.[13] More particularly, the villein was forbidden to dispose of beasts without licence, a restriction often linked with the obligation to pay *merchet.* The object of this restriction was probably to maintain the number of plough and draught animals needed to perform services on the demesne. Restrictions on the right to dispose of grain by sale are not found, for the peasant had to sell on the market in order to get the cash with which to pay his money rent. Abnormal sales were, however, prohibited. A villein on the Abbot of Ramsey's manor of Houghton in 1307 sold his movable goods and the crops on half a virgate of land to a merchant from Erith. The abbot's bailiff was instructed to seize all the goods.[14]

Restrictions on the free disposal of produce are capped by restrictions on the free disposal of land. Particularly when labour services were assessed on the yardland or half-yardland tenement it was necessary for the lord to maintain the integrity of the holding. Control of villein land alienations was achieved by making all land transfers illegal except by surrender and release in the manor court under the supervision of the lord's steward, recorded on the court roll. Villeins were strictly forbidden to exercise the right enjoyed by free tenants to transfer land by charter. Land 'in fee' could not be acquired by villeins, for its descent could not be controlled by the lord and it escaped from the rules governing land in villeinage—and the villein might escape with it.

It has often been said, sometimes in an attempt to provide something of a moral basis for the existence of this form of social relationship, that the villein was in practice protected against the extremes of extortion by a tenacious manorial custom which the lord could not override. There is some truth in this statement, but it must be realised also that manorial custom was not fixed. It was in fact a shifting compromise between peasant resistance based on the mutual solidarity produced by common interests and a common routine of agriculture on the one hand, and the lord's claims on the other, more or less urgent as they might be, and backed up by more or less political and military power. But although custom—and in particular the rent demanded—was not fixed, neither did it fluctuate rapidly or arbitrarily. If the rent that was taken had represented the whole of the peasant family's surplus above subsistence needs it would necessarily have varied from year to year, and from holding to holding. This was by no means the case. It was usually constant over a long period of time. And though a fixed level of rent might, and probably did often mean that the poorer peasants in bad years were driven even below subsistence standards, it meant also that the richer and more fortunate could accumulate a surplus of goods, or money, and when the opportunity occurred, could convert that surplus into land and extend their farming operations.

Even when manorial discipline on the English estates was most strict it was not possible for the rigid framework of obligations to suppress this constant movement of differentiation among the basic producers of society participating as they did, like their lords, in production for the market. Because the peasantry was thus separating into elements with differing economic interests, the reactions of different groups to seigneurial exploitation were quite differently motivated. The poor and middling peasants, whose agriculture was only above subsistence level in so far as they had to sell their produce in order to pay their rent, resisted increased demands because they pressed on their already low standard of living. The richer peasants, accumulating both movable and landed property, struck against all aspects of seigneurial control because at every point they found their road to economic expansion blocked by the innumerable devices whose object it was to transfer as much as possible of the surplus from the holding to the lord in the form of rent, by hindering any movement and any progress which might take the peasant or his property out of the ken of the lord. But though the reasons why these groups resisted seigneurial pressure differed, the direction of their resistance was the same, and this accounts for the extraordinary force revealed by a class otherwise so much divided.

II

Peasant resistance to seigneurial pressure seems first to become significant in England in the thirteenth century. This is partly due to the fact that the documents from which we derive our information became very abundant at this time; and partly due to the fact that there was a considerable, and possibly sudden, intensification of the exploitation of peasants by their lords. This intensification was probably much greater than that which is said (on much slenderer authority) to have resulted from the Norman Conquest. It may be remarked that the intensification of exploitation and the increased documentation are not unconnected, for the magnificent series of court rolls, manorial accounts, rentals and surveys, for which this country is the envy of continental medievalists, were a by-product of the administrative activity involved in the organisation of the thirteenth-century baronial estate[15]

Apart from these records of private administration, the official records of the activities of the royal courts and of the chancery become available and abundant from the beginning of the thirteenth century. There are many cases concerning villeinage in the *Curia Regis Rolls,* and in the records of the itinerant justices. Some of these are printed in full, but these are unfortunately only a fraction of the total.[16] The old compilation called the *Placitorum Abbreviatio*[17] contains reports of a number of villeinage cases. The notebook of the great thirteenth-century lawyer Bracton also contains many records of villeinage cases, together with valuable comments by Bracton himself.[18] For the later period, the Year-books and records of the courts of equitable jurisdiction[19] provide some information. The Calendars of Letters Patent and Close are especially valuable because such letters issued from the chancery, ordering sheriffs or other royal officials to take action on behalf of landlords against rebellious serfs, often recite full details of the cases with which sheriffs or commissioners were to deal.

It is now well known that in the thirteenth century most of the great estate-owners, lay and ecclesiastical, expanded their demesne production in order to sell agricultural produce on the market.[20] Prices were rising and for many reasons the landowners were striving to increase their cash revenues, both by increasing their money rents and as stated, by producing for the market. Much of the labour needed for the expanding demesnes had to be provided by peasant cultivators, for although there was a considerable increase in the population which swelled the ranks of the smallholders,[21] wage labour was apparently insufficient to supply the extra needs. So labour services were increased, even doubled. This increase in services appears to have been almost universal (in England), and it was inevitable that there should be resistance by those of whom more was being demanded.

The earliest signs of this resistance are to be seen in the records of the royal courts, a resistance at first put up by individuals rather than by groups, though the individuals who faced their lords in the courts may well have represented test cases for their fellow peasants. In theory villeins had no case against their lords in the royal courts. They held their land at the will of the lord, and so far as the king's justices were concerned (most of whom, like their master, were also serf-owners) disputes about services should be dealt with in the manorial courts, if the tenants were unfree. But although this theory does not appear to have been challenged, the question as to who was and who was not a villein could always be argued about, and the additional complication of free men holding by villein tenure brought another element of doubt into the situation.[22] Consequently the trial of pleas *de villenagio* or *de nativitate* was often in practice the concluding stage of a dispute about increased services. The cases as argued in court are full of interest for those concerned with the definition of legal status, and Miss Cam, Sir Cyril Flower and Mr Lane Poole have recently discussed the evidence at some length.[23] It is with the local struggles revealed by these cases that I am concerned, and I will quote one example typical of many in the records—and no doubt typical of even more that never reached the royal courts.

Bracton tells us[24] that in 1224 a case came up in court at Oxford between the Abbot of Battle and William the son of Andrew, a tenant in the village of Crowmarsh. The abbot claimed that William should do services as of villeinage, while William, though admitting his liability to services, claimed to be a free man, so that his services should be fixed and that the abbot had no right to increase them arbitrarily. The abbot was in fact claiming double services from this tenant, as well as the right to tallage him. The case went against the tenant because the abbot showed that he had a second cousin who was a villein, and because, although William claimed to be free himself, he recognised that all the other tenants (except one) were villeins. He admitted that he did labour services with them, and that he contributed to a tallage levied on them—though he claimed that his contribution was an aid given of his own free will. Once William's villeinage was proved, his case passed beyond the ken of the royal justices. I do not doubt, although no evidence appears, that although William tried to disassociate himself from the villeins of Crowmarsh, the doubling of labour services against which he was protesting had been imposed also on the other tenants.

Individual clashes such as these were but the heralds of the storm. It was collective action which was to be most disturbing to the social order and which was the training ground for revolt on a large scale. Some of the earliest instances of collective action have been recorded as a result of circumstances similar to those which produced the record quoted above. Groups of tenants were only able to find a legal basis for resistance to claims by the lord for increased services by denying that they were of ordinary villein status and so subject to the lord's arbitrary will. So in some cases they claimed to be protected as tenants of the ancient demesne of the Crown, in other cases to be of long-established free condition.

Certain villein tenants on manors that were demesne of the Crown at the time of Edward the Confessor, even though subsequently alienated to other lords, could claim royal protection against an increase in services beyond those rendered before the alienation. The appeal against the increase of services was pleaded before the king's justices by the writ or plaint *monstraverunt* and the decision as to whether a manor was of ancient demesne or not lay in the higher courts. Although not all villeins on ancient demesne were entitled to the writ *monstraverunt,* the distinction between 'pure' villeins and the privileged villein sokemen was often ignored.[25] So the privilege of ancient demesne was often claimed by peasants who saw old fixed services transformed in the interests of manorial profit. This peasant habit of litigation *par colour de certeins exemplificaciouns hors de livre de Domesday* was, as is well known, a matter for complaint in a statute of 1377.[26] It was a habit that was then at least a century old, and a number of cases are known to us from the latter part of the thirteenth century, an example of which I quote from the Patent Rolls. In 1278 the villein tenants of the alien Priory of Harmondsworth impleaded their lord the Prior that he should not demand from them customs and services in excess of those they owed when the manor was in the king's hands. Domesday Book was searched and it was shown that the manor did not count as ancient demesne. The tenants were therefore declared tallageable at the will of the lord and liable to *merchet*. The sheriff of Middlesex was ordered to assist the abbot to distrain and to tallage his rebellious tenants.[27]

Appeals of this sort to a not necessarily mythical or remote past are to be found in other cases in which proof of past conditions was necessary, not involving a plea of ancient demesne. What Vinogradoff calls 'a very definite case of oppression'[28] is summarised in the *Placitorum Abbreviatio,* recording an inquisition at Northampton in 1261. The tenants of Mears Ashby made no claim of ancient demesne, but simply to be free men, to have the right to buy and sell land freely, to be amerced only by the judgement of their peers and to pay a fixed tallage. They complained that though their lord, on first acquiring the manor, had for seven years observed the old customs, he had then reversed these conditions of freedom and tallaged the whole village arbitrarily. They eventually obliged him to restore their rights, by extra-legal pressure it must be assumed, shortly before his death. The inquisition appears to have been taken because his widow once more attempted to impose servility upon them.

I have described elsewhere[29] an attempt by some Leicestershire villeins in 1278 to prove the illegality of a demand by their lord, the Abbot of Leicester, for increased services. In this case too, we find no appeal to Domesday Book, but conscious perhaps of the Danish-influenced social structure of the area in which they lived, they claimed not to be villeins but sokemen. They claimed therefore that their services should not be arbitrarily increased, as had been done, by Paul, one of the abbot's predecessors (1186–1205), but the abbot was able to produce a jury with a legal memory going back to the first half of the twelfth century, and so to defeat them. This jury may very well have been intimidated by the abbot's officials into remembering so much from so remote a period. Local intimidation of this sort must have stifled many a movement of protest. What, for instance, could have been the local circumstances in a Northamptonshire case in 1273, when the men of Weekley got as far as the King's Court to claim the rights of tenants of ancient demesne against an increase in services, but let the case go by default? An examination of Domesday Book was ordered by the court, but the tenants did not come to hear the answer.[30]

A diligent search of the still unprinted records of the royal courts would, I believe, reveal many more cases of such litigation,[31] provoked by increased services, but taking the form of disputes about status. Even all this evidence could not, however, reveal more than a tiny proportion of the existing social discontent. Behind this litigation we become conscious of a continuous day-to-day struggle between lord and villein, almost the only evidence of which is to be found in the records of the manorial courts. Although a number of manorial court rolls have been printed, this is a source of evidence which has not been used as extensively as, for instance, the accounts of manorial bailiffs, and manorial rentals and surveys.[32] Even a cursory examination of some of the best known of the printed rolls, with the problem of peasant revolt in mind, provides some very striking results.

Professor Levett has already drawn attention to the evidence for mass withdrawals of service contained in the Court Books of the Abbey of St Albans. She has shown that these movements were occurring as early as 1245 on the manor of Park.[33] We can see the same forces at work on the manors of the Abbey of Ramsey somewhat later, and can illustrate them with some figures. Between 1279 and 1311 there were twenty-one sessions of courts held in various of the abbey's manors, in which cases concerning manorial labour discipline were dealt with. There resulted one hundred and forty-six separate convictions for the deliberate non-performance of labour services, apart from cases of what may have been equally deliberate cases of bad work.[34] The individual offences are not exceptional, and might occur even where ordinarily the most harmonious relations prevailed between lord and serf. Typical of these offences are refusal to obey a summons to the ploughing service; absence from the autumn boon-work; refusal to thresh the lord's wheat; non-performance of carrying services. It is the number of these offences that makes them significant, and even more so, the clear indication of deliberate, concerted refusal to do the labour services. At the Cranfield view of frankpledge of 1294 twenty-six tenants were amerced for not coming to the lord's ploughing. At the manor court of Houghton in 1307 eighteen tenants, including the reeve, were amerced for not coming to turn the lord's hay when summoned. In the following year, at the same place, fifteen tenants were amerced for going and ploughing their own land after dinner instead of doing a boon-ploughing for the lord.[35]

Such small-scale collective actions are of great importance. The predominance of collective activities in the ordinary routine of the medieval rural communities must have made the organisation of joint action for the representation of grievances to manorial lords[36] or before royal courts easy and natural in the first stages. But without the fighting spirit generated in these obscure local clashes, would the members of an oppressed class, constantly reminded of its inferiority, have been able to force themselves on to the attention of tribunals where they had no legal standing and where the scales of justice were necessarily heavily balanced against them?

The peasant struggle for liberty and for a reduction in rents and services was conducted illegally as well as under the colour of ancient rights. This was necessarily so. Royal courts would protect the rights of men who were uncontrovertibly free, for free men, like knights, were precious assets to the machinery of local government.[37] But it would be foolish to imagine that projects for the general emancipation of the unfree could be entertained by government officials or royal judges, whose social and political outlook was that of their class. So if no general legal redress was possible for the peasants, their action against their lords must either cease, or become violent and illegal. The consequences of the Harmondsworth ancient demesne case mentioned above[38] are an instructive illustration of this point. The Letter Patent which describes this case was in fact a commission of oyer and terminer to certain individuals instructing them to deal with events that happened after the failure of the villeins in their appeal to Domesday Book. Some of them, including one John le Clerk, had then broken into the manor house and carried away charters, other writings and goods, of which they were still in possession at the time of the issue of the commission. In addition they had threatened the prior and his household as to their bodies and the burning of their houses.

It was in this year, too, that a dispute between the Abbot of Halesowen and his tenants, as to whether they were protected from increased services by the privileges of ancient demesne, appears to have culminated in violence. The tenants had failed to prove their case in the King's Court on appeal to Domesday Book. 'Worsted at law', says Mr Homans,[39] 'they resorted to direct action', and were excommunicated for laying violent hands on the abbot and his brethren.

A similar case is recorded in the Patent Rolls of the year 1299.[40] The Prior of St Stephen's, Hempton, had acquired a writ instructing the sheriff of Norfolk to help him to distrain his villeins of Worsted to do their due and accustomed services. The king's common minister for the execution of writs was dispatched to the scene of the disturbance and was manhandled on arrival by no less than sixty-six persons, all of whose names are given in the Letter Patent which, in ordering proceedings against them, tells the story which led up to the assault.

Such violent defiance of both private and public authority continues in the fourteenth century. Miss Morgan has described the development of a revolt over a period of many years, from litigation to open defiance, on manors in England of the Norman Abbey of Bec.[41] The appeal of the Ogbourne tenants to the privileges of ancient demesne was made before 1309, and the movement did not culminate in the wholesale refusal of services until the year of upheavals, 1327. A year after this, we find bitter struggles taking place at Darnhall, a manor of the Cistercian Abbey of Vale Royal in Cheshire, between the abbot and the villein tenants. The villeins appear to have been fighting against a real social degradation following the recent gift of Darnhall to the Cistercians by the king.[42] The tenants' refusal to grind at the lord's mill, their objection to restrictions on the leasing of land, their denial of bondage, in 1328 led to imprisonment, submission and fines. But the movement started again in 1336, and with an incredible persistence the men of Darnhall combined both legal and illegal forms of struggle against their lord. They beset the Justiciar of Cheshire, the king himself, and even Queen Philippa in their search for redress at law, but at the same time some of them went as far afield as Rutlandshire, in arms, to seek out and attack the abbot and his entourage. In spite of some initial encouragement of the peasants by royal and official personages, the abbot was always able to intervene in high places against them with success, and gradually all were brought to submission.

The conspiratorial aspect of peasant revolt which the government and the nobility found so alarming before, during, and after 1381 is stressed in all accounts, official and unofficial, written by those hostile to peasant aspirations. The malicious plotters of Darnhall assembled together *at night* to plan the overthrow of the rights of their lord; in 1336 they *conspired* to obtain their liberty. The tenants of Great and Little Ogbourne not only formed a *conspiracy* in 1327, but supported it by a common purse—as must the Darnhall men, for they would not only have needed money to present their petition at Westminster, but also to pay the 'persons skilled in the law' who represented them at Chester. A commission of inquiry was appointed in 1338[43] to investigate the refusal of the villeins of Hayling to pay to the alien priory of the same place the due ransoms (that is, *merchet*), fines and other services and customs. The outline of the case in the Letter Patent speaks of this refusal as the consequence of a *confederacy* entered into by the villeins. Even the agitator from outside makes his appearance in a case in the year 1352.[44] A commission of oyer and terminer was appointed to deal with three named persons and their supporters, who had not only stolen goods of the Bishop of Worcester and assaulted his servant, but had *conspired* with his bondmen at Hanbury, that they should refuse to do the services owed to him. The conspiracy must, to a point, have been successful, for the bishop had to spend money in order to compel his men to do their services.

Mutual support among the peasantry does not only show itself in conspiracies to acquire benefits for all bondmen in a community. It also prompts action to protect individuals from the consequences of seigneurial justice. In 1338 a bondman of the Prior of Tynemouth's manor of Elstwick was arrested for trespassing with his beasts on the lord's land. He was being taken by the Prior's officer to judgement, when men from Newcastle and elsewhere rescued him. Not content with this, they invaded Elstwick, took possession of the manor, and prevented the Prior's servants from entering to collect rents and levy distraints.[45] In 1349 two bondmen of the Countess of Pembroke were arrested at Foxley (Norfolk) for 'disobedience and rebellion'. On their way to Denny (Cambs), where they were to be 'chastised in the usual manner', they were rescued by their friends who also assaulted the Countess's officials.[46] In the same year, the Prior of Ely complained of the fate of his steward whom he had sent to Melbourn (Cambs) to bring a recalcitrant bondman to judgement. The steward put the bondman in the stocks. Nine named persons with others then lay in wait for the steward, captured him, and forced him to seal a letter ordering the deliverance of the bondman from the stocks.[47] After 1349 such cases multiply, for one of the punishments for breach of the Ordinance and Statute of Labourers was to be put in the stocks.

III

The reasons why peasants, who were living on, or just above the level of subsistence, should resist demands for extra rents and services with bitterness and violence are obvious. The difference between a fixed and an arbitrary tallage taken by the lord at Michaelmas might be as much as the poor peasant's reserve for the winter. The loss of a plough-ox as heriot would tax the dead man's family at the hardest moment of its existence. The lord's demand for extra boon-work at haymaking or harvest might take labour away from the peasant holding at a moment crucial for the crop. But it was not only the poor and middling peasants who took part in movements of revolt. They were joined by the wealthy husbandmen, favoured by fortune and inheritance with more and better land than their fellow villagers. The participation of these men brought a different element, one perhaps of calculation and strategy, an ability to formulate programmes as in 1381.

The growth of a rich upper stratum among the peasants has been well enough documented in recent agrarian studies.[48] Whether we look at peasant life in the south-east, in the Thames Valley, in East Anglia or in the Midlands, we find standing out from the ordinary run of tenants with their fifteen or twenty-acre holdings, a small group of families, sometimes free, more often serf, holding a hundred acres or more. These holdings are composite in character—perhaps a couple of yardlands on customary terms; some land assarted from wood or marsh; portions of the holdings of extinct or bankrupt families; and in the fourteenth century after the final decline of demesne farming has begun, portions of the lord's demesne. But in most cases the economic prosperity of the holders of these extensive farms is in sharp contrast to their legal status. In one of the earliest villeinage cases discussed by Bracton, the villein holding consisted of a hundred acres of arable land and fifty sheep.[49] Among the convictions for the non-performance of labour services on the manors of Ramsey Abbey mentioned above, we find that six men at Houghton in 1294 were amerced for withdrawing *their men* from the autumn boon-work.[50] Now these men must have regarded the restrictions of serfdom in a very different light from the poorer peasants whose legal status they shared. Most irritating to them must have been the hindrances to accumulation, rather than the fear of starvation. Consequently, and especially during the period of seigneurial withdrawal from active participation in productive activity, the issue of the right to buy and sell land freely comes to the fore. For this involved the right to convert surpluses made in buying and selling into landed property, acquired for the purpose of buying and selling on an even larger scale.

It will be remembered that the Northamptonshire case of 1261 quoted above[51] contained a plea by the tenants for the free disposal of land, whether as gift, sale, pledge or exchange. These men who claimed to be free recognised that as villeins they would not have that right—*sicut nec villani possunt*. Ramsey Abbey tenants were frequently being fined for unlicensed leases and exchanges of land among themselves,[52] most frequently of small quantities rarely exceeding an acre, and for short terms, such as for two crops. From 1312 onwards land alienations by charter made by villeins without the abbot's permission on the St Albans manor of Barnet were being attacked by the estate officials, and in 1345 the charters had to be surrendered in court.[53] The 1320 Visitation Articles of the Cathedral Chapter of St Paul, London, order an inquiry to be made as to whether villeins and customary tenants had been leasing, selling or giving customary land, with or without charter to fellow-villeins, without the consent of the farmer of the manor, and not in full court or hallmote.[54] When the tenants of the Canterbury Cathedral manor of Monk's Risborough claimed privileges of ancient demesne in 1336, amongst those mentioned were the right 'to sell their tenements by charter as they wished without the lord's permission'[55]

The lord's action when these transfers took place was to enter on the illegally acquired land.[56] Even if the land was acquired in fee, and could not be claimed by the lord as his villeinage, confiscation was his right. References in the Patent Rolls show this. In 1339 the Priory of Spalding got a licence for acquiring in mortmain a messuage which its bondman had acquired in fee, and which the Priory had consequently appropriated. Similarly, pardon for unlicensed acquisition in mortmain was given in 1366 to the Abbey of Waltham Holy Cross because it had entered into thirty acres of land acquired in fee simple by its bondman 'as was lawful for them to do'. In an exemplification of various suits in 1348, there is mentioned a lay lord's appropriation of sixteen selions of land 'as tenements acquired by his villein'. A manumitted bondman in 1359 had to obtain a royal pardon for the unlicensed acquisition in tail, presumably while he was still unfree, of an estate of some dimensions—two messuages, two cottages, sixty-three acres of arable land, another plot of land and the liberty of a fold[57]

It was clearly, then, deliberate seigneurial policy over a wide area to stamp out illegal land transfers, for this would rob the lord of entry fines, and to confiscate the land so acquired. It cannot be assumed that the desire to thwart the economic expansion of the thriving peasants was a conscious motive of policy of all lords, but it may have been for some. An instruction to the Steward of the St Albans estate lays down that 'several *(plures)* lands are not to be granted to one man, and if one man now holds several lands, they are to be divided up, if it can be conveniently and decently done'.[58] The tenants of St Albans, as Miss Levett has shown, fought this policy during the whole of the period before the Great Revolt. In 1381 when the abbot was obliged to grant charters of liberties to the tenants on his estate, freedom of alienation was one of the clauses. The tenants of Barnet, having reverted to the practice of alienation by charter during the confusion of the Black Death (only four years after their previous surrender), sought to destroy the Court Book which contained the evidence for transfer by surrender in the manorial court.[59]

The Black Death and the labour legislation following intensified the social conflicts described above. The enforcement of labour discipline directly by the organs of the State had the effect of unifying the discontent, because the target of resentment was no longer the individual lord alone but also the local officials of the government. The different peasant groups were affected in different ways by the labour legislation, just as they had been affected in different ways by the increased stringency of manorial exactions. And here again, for different reasons, rich and poor united against the same enemies.

Naturally those without land, and the smallholders who had to work for wages to supplement their income, did not like the restriction on wages and on the mobility of labour. The middling peasant who did not employ labour but whose energies were entirely occupied with his own holding, would probably be affected by the discontent of wage-earning members of his family. His exasperation would be increased if he lived on a manor where the surviving tenants were expected to perform the services owed from abandoned holdings[60] There was another con-temporary phenomenon, not generally noticed, which must have embittered all grades of peasants against the manorial lords. This was the abduction of villeins by one lord from another's manor. It is well known that one of the consequences of the shortage of labour was for some manorial lords or officials to offer wage-rates above the legal maximum. But this must have been an offence to the principles as well as to the purses of many of the nobility and gentry. Brigandage, however, was not. The looting of persons for ransoms during the French wars was more remunerative than the looting of goods, and the habit was not lost in England. It was often the less warlike ecclesiastical lords who suffered, and there are many echoes of their complaints in the Patent Rolls.[61]

An important and, on the surface, paradoxical consequence of the enforcement of the Ordinance and Statute of Labourers, was the hurt done to the interests of the rich peasants, as was pointed out by Professor Levett.[62] The rich peasants were all necessarily employers of labour, for the farming of some of the larger peasant holdings would have been impossible without hired help, and even the richest peasant did not have the villein services of other peasants under his control.[63] Now a large farm is useless without the hands to till it, so the tenant was prepared to pay high prices for the labour he could not get otherwise. In so doing he would also tend to put up the price of labour for the manorial lords. But there was no need for the lords to suffer from the working of economic laws because they had at their disposal the political power which enabled them to circumvent them. They still had reserves of serf labour, and they controlled the distribution of such available wage labour as there was, in their capacity as Justices of Labourers, or of the Peace.

Rich peasants had little or no political influence, and for this reason we find them taking part in the Great Revolt. But there were some persons who were in exactly the same position as the rich peasants as far as the labour problem was concerned, but who did have political influence. Their complaints were made known to the government and are consequently recorded. We can, though with caution, take these grievances as being similar to those which must have been voiced by the peasants—but not heard. The Carthusian Priory of Wytham was a cultivator without any serfs. Its inmates lived in a close in the forest of

Selwood, and (so the licence issued by letter patent tells us) had no lordship within or without the close. They could get no workers to replace those who had died of the plague. So the king gave them permission to attract labour by offering 'reasonable rates', notwithstanding the Ordinance. In addition, they were to recover any fines which might be levied on their servants under the Statute. This meant that they would be reimbursed for any extra expenditure on wages necessary to attract labour. They were also allowed to ignore the price regulations of the Statute when selling their hides in the local markets.[64] The wealthier peasants were obliged to offer high wages, as were these Carthusians, for they, too, were without lordship. But of course they received no licence, and were liable not only to suffer from the monopoly established in the labour market by the gentry in their capacity as Justices, but additionally from the punishments imposed on those who offered illegal rates.

Another religious house had to seek government aid to enable it to solve its labour problems. The Northamptonshire Abbey of Pipewell was suffering from the local monopoly of labour by the gentry, not in Northamptonshire but in East Warwickshire. The abbot complained in 1351 that the Warwickshire justices of Labourers were forcing his tenants in his granges and in the neighbouring villages to work, not for the abbey, but for its competitors, so that the abbey lands were left uncultivated. Since the Ordinance and Statutes reserved to lords the first claim to the wage labour of their tenants, the king supported the Abbot of Pipewell, and instructed the Warwickshire justices to allow him an adequate supply of labour.[65] The abbot was fortunate in being able to enlist royal support in his fight to get enough workers, but we have no knowledge of how the wealthier peasants would fare in a similar situation, other than a suggestion from a well-known story from the chronicles of the Yorkshire Cistercian Abbey of Meaux. This story primarily concerns the attempt by a family of prosperous villeins to prove themselves tenants of the Crown rather than tenants of the abbey. They were not anxious, it would seem, to claim free status, but to exchange for the immediate pressure of the local, undying, corporation, the remoter control of the king and his officers. The attempt was in the end unsuccessful, in spite of the admirable and undaunted persistence of the villeins. What is relevant to the argument here is that one of the early incidents in the case was a complaint by this villein family to the king that the abbot had taken away by force their ploughmen, contrary to the Statute and Ordinance.[66] This complaint was possibly but a minor incident in the battle over the main issue. Nevertheless, it illustrates the difficulties of the villein employer of labour at this period, and shows the incompatibility of his interests with those of the greater feudal landlords, fortunate in their 'lordship'.

Miss Putnam has quoted sources showing that hatred of the Statute of Labourers and of those who enforced its operation led, in the years after its enactment, to organised attacks on the sessions of the Justices of Labourers—in Middlesex in 1351, in Lincolnshire in 1352, in Northamptonshire in 1359[67] What manner of persons these were, who, as at Tottenham for instance, in 1351, released the prisoners and drove the justices from their session, we do not know. They no doubt included agricultural labourers and town artisans. But they might also have included wealthy yeomen. For one of the most striking features of the revolt of 1381 was the unification in it of all the varying discontents of town and country, so that in many cases the leaders of the revolt were not the poor men made desperate by poverty, but prosperous men anxious to expand their thriving farms. Such men are typified by the Suffolk rebel, Thomas Sampson, whose land and chattels were estimated by the king's escheator after the revolt to include 160 acres under crop and nearly 500 head of livestock.[68] Such men were revolting against the restrictions as well as against the oppression of a financially and politically bankrupt ruling class.

Much stress has been laid here on the economic grievances of the peasants, for these were at the root of all others. It must not be forgotten, however, that just as the landowning classes were obliged to serve their economic purposes by contriving a depression of the social and legal status of the peasantry whom they controlled, so the peasants in fighting against economic oppression were also fighting for wider human rights. They strove not merely for a reduction of rent but for human dignity. They fought quite consciously against a system of society which by the thirteenth century had evolved a clear caste interpretation of peasant status, so that blood became the determinant of social and legal rights. What more poignant and bitter comment on this could there be than the action of a Worcestershire tenant of the Earl of Gloucester in 1293? This man was distrained by the earl's bailiffs to receive land to be held in the earl's manor of Hanley Castle in a servile manner. He had often sworn (so a jury said) that rather than take land on servile conditions he would drown or hang himself. And so he did—for to escape this disgrace he drowned himself in the River Severn at Clevelode.[69]

The abolition of bondage and serfdom was the first of the articles of the peasant programme at Mile End, and was repeated at Smithfield. Everything that was written about these peasants was written by their enemies, but the words attributed by Froissart to John Ball were in essence probably authentic: 'For what reason do they hold us in bondage? Are we not all descended from the same parents Adam and Eve? And what can they show or what reason can they give why they should be more masters than ourselves?'[70] These ideas have their history, so that when we read the statement of a Colonel Rainborough in 1647, 'The poorest he that is in England hath a life to live as the greatest he', we know that here is an expression of an English tradition as ancient as the more publicised traditions of reverence for old-established institutions.

10

Reasons for Inequality Among Medieval Peasants

This paper covers nearly a thousand years of history, which, compared with the contemporary epoch, are very scantily documented. It will therefore necessarily be of a different type from the detailed studies of the differentiation within peasant economies hitherto presented to the seminar. In order to make clear the argument, such statistical and other detail as is available is not to any great extent embodied in the text. If it were, this would be a book not a paper. However, references are supplied to some of the works of detail on which the generalisations are based. Although the evidence for the medieval peasant economy is scanty compared with that for modern and contemporary peasantries, that which survives demonstrates that in most European countries, whether in the early post-Roman centuries or at the end of the medieval period as traditionally defined (late fifteenth century) the peasantry was a markedly stratified class. Late medieval stratification has perhaps attracted the most attention because out of the inequalities developing within this single class were seen to emerge agrarian capitalists who played a significant part in laying the basis for the modern capitalist system. The stratification of the late medieval peasantry was largely attributed to its participation in production for the market. Marxists, heavily influenced by V.I. Lenin's *Development of Capitalism in Russia,*[1] were prominent among those who advanced this interpretation. This, however, could hardly account for peasant economies which also showed a considerable level of stratification when similar market conditions did not exist. For example, in spite of attempts to prove the contrary *[Sawyer, 1965],* the economy of eleventh century England was hardly one dominated by commodity production and yet the contours of a peasantry divided between a wealthy minority, a solid middle peasantry and a significant proportion of smallholders can easily be seen in Domesday Book, 1086.[2] The Soviet historian, E.A. Kosminsky, was well aware of the problem: '. . . it would be wrong to attribute all stratification to the development of commodity and money relationships . . . the deep-seated causes of peasant differentiation probably lie as far back as the disintegration of the prefeudal lands into the ownership of single families' *[1956:207].* But his development of this theme was cursory, not unreasonably so, since his main preoccupation was the English peasantry at the end of the thirteenth century.

There were several different factors other than the development of commodity production which played their part with varying force at different times in determining the degree of inequality between peasant cultivators. These include : the abundance or otherwise of cultivable land; the technical level of agricultural production; the rate of population growth or decline; the structure of the family, including the customs of inheritance and endowment; the customs and practices of agrarian communities; the demands made on the peasant economy by non-producers such as lords, priests, craftsmen, merchants, kings and other public authorities. The evaluation of the relative strength of these factors is no easy matter given the scarcity of source material, especially in early times, not to speak of the fact that the sources often contain only indirect answers to the questions we want to put to them. Documents of a survey or census-like character are very rare and lacking in essential detail, so that quantitative analysis cannot often be made. In particular the documents are invariably made for the benefit of those who stand outside the peasant household economy, who are interested in what can be got out of it but not what takes place within it.

A great dividing line of the medieval peasantry was that which separated the free from the unfree. This should be considered first because it was not only a division which came early chronologically but did not always coincide with that between the rich and the poor (which is the usual criterion for stratification), although the *potential* for the accumulation of land and moveable goods was greater among the free than among the unfree. Unfortunately, the line between the free and unfree was ambiguous and, of course, the meaning of the terms neither was, nor is, by any means clear. We can nevertheless start at the beginning by making a fairly confident distinction between chattel slaves and the rest of the rural population, chattel slaves being possessions, like beasts, who could be bought and sold and who had no property. I am aware that in both Roman and barbarian law they had some rights. Nevertheless, their main distinguishing feature was that as a labour force they were completely at the disposal of their owners, whose only obligation was to feed, clothe and shelter them so that they would be fit for work. It is generally thought that they were declining in numbers in the late ancient world but that the warfare after the collapse of the Roman Empire in the west provided a new source of slave manpower [*Verlinden, 1955; Bloch, 1947*]. Such slaves were not, of course, only possessed by their captors; there was a trade in slaves and their ranks were reinforced by debtors and criminals for whom slavery was a punishment. It is impossible to calculate the numbers of slaves during the dark ages. Analysis of law-codes and charters suggests that the institution was dying out in Frankia by the ninth century, although in central Italy they disappeared in the eighth century and in England may still, in 1086 have constituted nine or ten per cent of the recorded population [*Toubert, 1973 :474 ff; Maitland, 1897; Finn, 1963*]. What was happening late in England and earlier elsewhere, and at varying speeds, was a process which had already begun on Roman latifundia, by which slaves were provided with landed holdings from which they gained their own and their families' subsistence. The upheavals of the early middle ages also plunged many free families of cultivators into dependence on powerful warrior and church landowners. As a consequence, former slaves and former free men and women were merged with the *coloni* (juridically free tenants tied to the soil by late Roman legislation) *[Jones, 1958]* into a class of more or less homogeneous legal condition. The forms of dependence on the landowning class by which they were severely restricted as to freedom of movement, freedom of alienation of land and goods, and freedom of access to public jurisdiction, has led historians to regard them as serfs[3] even though some of them still retained elements of juridically free status. This ambiguity can be illustrated by the fact that by the end of the thirteenth century in many French villages, the *vileins,* who were not considered servile, had very similar conditions of tenure and subordination to their lords to the English villeins who were unfree in the eyes of the law. It should also be said that in all European countries east, west, north and south, there were considerable numbers of free tenants who had complete freedom of movement and disposal of moveable goods and a fair degree of freedom of alienation of landed property. Some of these were families with substantial amounts of land, others mere smallholders who had to work for wages on the lords' demesnes or on the holdings of richer peasants. But even though there were rich and poor among free and unfree alike, legal status must not be considered irrelevant even in terms of economic stratification. Whether in the ninth or the thirteenth century the burden of rent in most European countries from which adequate evidence survives was on the whole greater on unfree than on free holdings. This fact, together with the other restrictions mentioned above had obvious consequences for the potential for accumulation as between free and unfree households.

The distinction between the legally free and the servile was becoming faint towards the end of the middle ages, with localised revivals of serfdom at certain times and in certain places (e.g. thirteenth-century England, fifteenth-century Catalonia, and above all fifteenth- and early sixteenth-century Eastern Europe). This distinction was one which was imposed on peasant society from outside by the dominant and law-creating powers. There was a more fundamental form of stratification which was probably generated within peasant society, and stabilised by the demands of domanial agriculture. This was the division between those peasant families which had enough land for their own subsistence, for economic reproduction and for demands from outside for rents, tithes and taxes; and on the other hand those who possessed only a cottage; a garden plot and perhaps a few acres in the fields. The technical equipment matched the landed endowment. The better-off families had a plough and plough-animals, the poor worked with their hand-tools, spade or hoe. It is possible that this is the basic form of stratification inherent in any peasant society in the temperate zone, that is in any agrarian system where the unit of production is small enough to be worked by family labour but where, at certain times of the agricultural year, the addition of temporary labour is required. This extra labour is only needed at peak periods (especially hay-making and cereal harvest) and is paid for by wages in money or kind from the product of the larger holding. At other times of the year the smallholders who provide the extra labour support themselves from their own holdings (too small for year round subsistence) and perhaps from craft-work, gathering and some grazing.

This division of the peasant community was well adapted to the needs of the manorial home farm or demesne. The more substantial peasants brought their own ploughteams to cultivate the demesne arable. The smallholders did other essential work, hedging, ditching, harvest work, spade cultivation in the gardens.[4] Witold Kula has suggested, on the basis of early modern Polish experience, that in this type of domanial system it was the demands of the demesne which were responsible for the division of labour and land distribution. The explanation is doubtful for the medieval period. In the first place the predominance of the domanial system is to some extent a documentary illusion. This system, characterised by the close relationship between demesne cultivation and tenant labour (owed as rent) is certainly well recorded in early medieval Europe. Many estate surveys survive from as early as the ninth century, including those from rich church landowners and from the imperial fisc.[5] But they cover in all only a small fraction of the total area under cultivation. There were many areas where the lords' incomes were mostly from rents in kind or even money, not to mention areas where free allodial property predominated. In the second place, the division between ploughteam-owning peasants and spade or hoe-cultivating smallholders was not simply a feature of settlements which were part of the domanial system. It long survived the disappearance of manorial demesnes; it is to be found in areas where the system had little hold; the conclusion must be that it was a fundamental feature of medieval peasant agriculture, early and late.

The fact that the division within the peasantry to which we have referred suited the needs of the demesne does not mean that it was willed by the estate owners, although they encouraged it, as we shall see. Nor did the better-off peasants will the existence of a useful reservoir of seasonal labour to help on their own holdings. The internal economic divisions in peasant society developed independently of the will of either lords or peasants. It was not, however, an even process. It cannot be too strongly emphasised that at all periods during the middle ages, the bulk of the cultivated area was contained within peasant holdings and that these holdings were managed as family concerns. Even in the ninth century on highly organised demesne-oriented estates like that of the Abbey of St. Germain-des-Prés near Paris, the arable land in the peasant holdings was nearly four times as great as that in the lord's demesnes, and as we have seen such estates were the exception rather than the rule. The average size of the peasant holdings varied from time to time according to variations in the land:labour ratio. When land was abundant the proportion of smallholders fell; when land was scarce (given a stationary technology) it increased. In the early post-Roman period we become aware in the various regions of a basic unit of family property, usually described in Latin documents as the *mansus* (the word itself indicating the family dwelling), but with local variations in nomenclature such as English 'hide', German *Hufe* [*Perrin, 1945; Bloch, 1966; Charles-Edwards, 1972*]. I do not propose to discuss Celtic and Germanic antecedents of these units. However, attempts to suggest that they were mere creations of the domanial needs of the estate owners or the fiscal needs of the state are not, in my view tenable [*Verhulst, 1966*]. They clearly represent the basic peasant family subsistence holding in the period of relative land-abundance of the early middle ages [*Duby, 1973:44-46*] and ranged, according to soils and other local conditions, between 30 and 100 acres in size [*Ganshof, 1949*]. But what was this family? Bloch and others thought it was an 'extended' family [*Bloch, 1966; Perrin, 1940*] consisting of co-residential descendants of at least common grandparents. They also believed that the disintegration of the manse and its replacement by peasant holdings of half or quarter—or even less—of its original size was a function of the replacement of these extended families by nuclear families.

Historical evidence, however, suggests that the nuclear family was the basic component of peasant households both early and late. Co-residence of one nuclear family together with the older generation, the grandparents, was fairly frequent but for short periods of time only, depending for its life-span as a co-residential unit on the life-span of the old people. At certain periods, more than one related nuclear family might occupy a holding (though not necessarily live in the same house). This, however, was not an early stage of an evolutionary process from bigger to smaller family groups but a response to certain social and even political conditions which appeared from time to time.[6]

The average manse (hide or *Hufe*) was, then, much larger in the early middle ages than the average peasant family holdings of the tenth or eleventh century. For example, the sixth-century English hide was probably at least 100 acres; the eleventh-century average holding was a yardland of around 30 acres. This does not mean that in the early centuries there were none of the smallholdings to which reference has been made. Some such holdings were the by-products of seigneurial action, that is the complete or partial emancipation of slaves with landed endowment *(servi casati)*. The holdings could be mere *portiunculae* carved from the demesne whose tenants would still need extra sustenance as a payment from work on the demesne or on the bigger holdings. On the other hand they could be subsistence holdings, but smaller than those possessed by free families [*Charles-Edwards, 1972*]. Family size on these holdings was smaller than on the bigger holdings, a fact noted for the Carolingian period *[Coleman, 1972]* though the correlation between small holdings and small families is found throughout the middle ages. The sons of smallholders delayed or renounced marriage because of inadequate landed endowment; their sisters became servants in lords' or rich peasants' households and their expectation of life was short.

In areas of land abundance in the eighth century (such as Latium in Central Italy), differentiation, other than that resulting from slave emancipation, was slight *[Toubert, 1973]*. Population increase resulted in the creation of new holdings. Existing holdings were not overcrowded. In other areas, for example northern France and the Seine basin, the limits of expansion were being reached. Many manses were occupied by more than one family, at least 40 per cent in the St. Germain-des-Prés villages. The break-up of the old tenemental system was under way. After being occupied by two or three nuclear families, manses were broken up into halves or quarters or less. There were various causes. The end of the old domanial system, dependent on labour services from the holdings, meant that lords cared less about maintaining the integrity of the holding as a labour service rendering unit. Partible inheritance customs obtained freer scope. Technical improvements may have allowed less land to support the same number of consumers. Alternative-ly, if there had been in the earlier period a tendency to under-utilise landed resources, less land might now bear more people because they had to work harder *[Sahlins, 1964: Ch. 2]*. This might result from the increased pressure by the ruling class for more rent and more transfer of income from peasants to lords through the strengthening of the *seigneurie banale.*[7] It has even been suggested that the size of the manse declined because of the emancipation of slaves owned by the free families possessing the manse *[Perrin, 1940]*.

Some historians think that there may have been a temporary halt to population growth in some areas in the eighth and ninth centuries *[e.g. Fossier, 1968: 239]*. But since population growth in periods of little direct evidence is usually measured by indirect indices *[Genicot, 1965]* such as evidence of the creation of new holdings, especially assart land, it is possible that, at first, growth took place un-noticed within the old framework. If landed resources were relatively abundant, the early marriage of offspring would be possible, thus increasing fertility and the older generation, well fed, would live longer. But whatever the exact situation in the eighth and ninth centuries, between the tenth and thirteenth centuries, population growth was reflected in an increased number of peasant holdings. As we have seen, the traditional units fragmented. Apart from smallholders of ancient descent, younger sons of rich and middle peasant families were added to the smallholding group, either by being endowed from land acquired by the family, or by assarting land from wood and waste. The average size of holding diminished, though not always or everywhere at the same rate. The ploughteam-owning peasant subsisted on 15 to 20 acres at the least, but the number of tenants with dwarf holdings increased considerably. The division of the rural population between what the French call the *laboureurs* (ploughmen, tenants of a *ferme à une charrue*) and the *manouvriers* (the smallholders with no ploughteam) already visible in some areas in the tenth century [*Fournier, 1962 : 263-72*] was carried to an extreme degree. In areas of high population density between 40 and 70 per cent of peasant holdings were insufficient for subsistence (that is below about 8 acres),[8] so that the tenants had to rely on wages from the demesne or from rich peasants or from by-occupations.

Now this period was the culminating point of a period of considerable urban development, not merely of giant towns like Paris, Florence, Venice or Genoa with populations around 100,000 or more, or even of substantial places like London, Ghent or Cologne with populations around 50,000, but of a vast network of smaller market and craft centres, many of recent foundation. It might well, therefore, be asked : was there not a considerable market for agricultural products and therefore a market for land ? The existence of large numbers of town dwellers who must have bought their food, as well as country people who did not supply their own subsistence needs, already implies a market in agricultural products. We could in any case conclude this from the high level of money paid over by peasants who would have to sell their surplus to pay rents and taxes. Was there therefore a process of differentiation between the various strata of peasant society attributable rather to market than to demographic and other factors ?

The answer would seem to be that the interplay of the land market with the other factors confirmed and further deepened the existing divisions to which we have referred. The well-established and substantial peasant households maintained and improved their position *vis-à-vis* the smallholders not simply because they were better able to profit from production from the market but for other reasons as well. In the first place, their economy was, even apart from questions of scale, better equipped. They had livestock in addition to plough-animals which provided not only manure but milk, cheese and wool. As village notables they got preferential access to common rights. They were in a position to lend cash and equipment to poorer neighbours. Their labour resources were superior, for the well-to-do family was larger than the poor family. They were therefore able, when opportunity presented itself, to take extra land on lease, such as fragments of demesne or the abandoned land of the unsuccessful.

We must also emphasise that the stratification of the peasantry was also promoted by the outside pressures of the lords and the government tax collectors, partly because their demands fell differentially on rich and poor. It is true that the very poor were exempt from the taxes on moveables, though there are indications that those rich enough to bribe tax collectors got off lightly [*Harvey, 1965 : 105-12*]. More to the point, it has been shown for England, and is probably true elsewhere, that the burden of rent on small holdings (of about 6-8 acres) was nearly twice as much per acre as that on the more substantial holdings of 24 to 30 acres [*Kosminsky, 1956:244*]. Paid labour on the lords' demesnes was a much more important component of the income of smallholding families than for those with adequate holdings, and wages, especially for the unfree, were low at the end of the thirteenth century. The better-endowed peasants, although heavily enough burdened with rents and taxes, ran their family enterprise with little effective seigneurial intervention. More important, in practice the seigneurial administration had to rely on the village notables, that is the well-to-do peasants, for running the collective aspect of peasant affairs. These notables, as has been mentioned, controlled the commons, declared local custom, and maintained order. In the village, as in society at large, jurisdictional and political power was an economic force. The lords' powers might in general be operated against the whole peasantry, but in particular some of those powers were used within the village by the rich against the poor . As we have seen at an earlier period, so long as the lord was interested in the demesne, and perhaps even afterwards, he was interested in maintaining the basic integrity of the various rent- and service-owing tenements, with this additional proviso that it was in no way against the lords' interests that smallholdings should multiply since these provided not only extra rent but cheap demesne labour.

Given all this, it would nevertheless be a mistake to exaggerate the capacity for largescale land accumulation by already well-to-do peasants. Apart from the land market, some customs, such as inheritance by primogeniture, might seem to favour accumulation, as opposed for instance to partible inheritance. However, there seems to have been a strong tendency within peasant society towards the equal treatment of all offspring. It may be that in the sixteenth century, younger sons and daughters were given their shares in cash rather than land, thus encouraging them to settle where cash rather than land was at a premium—in the towns, in commerce or in industry. In the thirteenth and early fourteenth centuries, however, families which had the resources, even where some form of unigeniture was the rule, tended to establish younger sons on, and to dower daughters with, purchased land. It even appears that in nearby villages in Norfolk, which had opposing inheritance customs (primogeniture and partible), much the same sort of division and re-combination of land took place, the land market playing a significant role in the adjustment of property between members of succeeding generations [*Williamson, 1976*].

The records of the English manorial courts, which acted *(inter alia)* as registers of transactions of land held by customary tenure, give a better insight into the peculiar nature of the peasant land-market than can be obtained from documentation in most other European countries. These records give some evidence of land accumulation by leading peasant families but more interesting, perhaps, is the fact that the transactions recorded were normally concerned with very small quantities of land. This active exchange applied to freehold land at the peasant level as well as to customary land *[King, 1976: Chs. 3 and 6]*. But it was a market which acted as an agency for adjusting the relationship between the landed families of the peasant communities according to norms which were also mirrored in inheritance and other customs, namely the maintenance of the traditional property divisions between the peasant strata. It is quite possible that customary prejudices against accumulation, which are certainly found later, were in existence at this period.[9] The production of agricultural commodities for the market, with the object of making a monetary profit, which in turn would be reinvested for expanded reproduction, was not yet a driving force within peasant society. The proliferation of poor smallholders was therefore not so much a consequence of unequal market opportunities (though this did enter into the situation), but was rather the consequence of the long term cyclical movement by which the family labour force tended to increase faster than agricultural productivity. Agricultural productivity was declining because of the falling proportion of pasture to arable and because poor land had already been taken into cultivation. The weight of rent, tithe and tax still further removed the possibility of improved levels of production. Since there was no good land to which the surplus population could escape, since it seems likely that the limit of urban expansion had been reached, the turn of the thirteenth century saw the distortion of the 'natural' stratification of peasant society. It was, therefore, peculiarly vulnerable to the natural and man-made disasters of famine, plague and war, and this applies more especially, of course, to the mass of impoverished smallholders *[Postan and Titow, 1959]*.

The enormous reduction in the size of the European population in the fourteenth century, beginning probably even before the bad famines of 1315-17 and on a catastrophic scale in 1348-9, transformed the land : labour ratio. This had two main consequences for the peasantry. More good land became available and the rent burden on holdings diminished. From Tuscany to England, rent revenue fell in the century after the Black Death at varying rates, from 40 per cent (the Tuscan contado) to 70 per cent (Normandy and parts of Flanders). Rents paid as a share of the crop fell from a half to a seventh or an eighth.[10] At the same time real wages went up. In England they doubled during the same period *[Phelps-Brown and Hopkins, 1956]*, placing a much greater burden on the seigneurial than on the peasant economy, which largely depended on family labour. The fall in rents was partly due to peasant pressure, and partly (especially in war-devastated areas) to the anxiety of landowners to attract tenants to keep land in cultivation. The rising money wages of agricultural workers was no doubt the immediate consequence of their scarcity (though the demand must also have fallen) but could not have been sustained at the high level without a considerable increase in the productivity of labour. This was the consequence of the abandonment of marginal soils, the increased availability of pasture and the increased number of animals.

The consequences of these developments for the internal stratification of the peasantry were as one would expect. The number of smallholders was considerably reduced; the middle stratum was strengthened; the rich peasants also improved their position but not so consistently as did the middle peasants. It is probable that the reduction in the proportion of smallholders was of the greatest significance. This resulted partly from a general increase in holding sizes, consequent on the greater availability of land, partly from a general upwards promotion of all groups. It was also due to factors reducing recruitment to the smallholding stratum. Replacement rates fell overall after the middle of the fourteenth century, an average of 1.4 being one of the best calculations based on English material, as compared with 2.8 in the seventy years before 1350. These rates are consistent with other English calculations for the 1400-50 period [*Razi, 1980; Thrupp, 1975*]. In the area around Lyons, rates fluctuated between 0.6 and 1.9 between 1350 and 1430, and the average between 1330 and 1410 was similar, at 1.39 to the English figures [*Lorcin, 1974: 220-25*].

More significant for our purpose are the differences in family size according to the socio-economic position of the family. The English figures, from a group of family reconstitutions from North Worcestershire, show the following family sizes (offspring over 12): rich 3.0; middle 2.0; poor 1.4. In the fifteenth century Lyonnais, well-to-do families had replacement rates of 3.1, the poor of 1.8. Hence, the families of smallholders were more likely to die out than those of the better-off peasants and what with larger holdings and smaller families the heads of richer households could endow their sons without depressing them into the smallholding class. Some English figures illustrate the decline in the number of smallholders. An extreme case is the peasant population which held the land of the Cistercian Abbey of Stoneleigh in the Forest of Arden, where in 1280, 61 per cent of the tenants held under 8 acres, a proportion reduced to 46 per cent in 1392. More representative are figures from five Midland counties in 1280 where the average proportion of smallholders was 46 per cent. By the late fourteenth and fifteenth centuries the proportion of smallholders in various Midlands manors was down to between 11 per cent and 28 per cent.[11]

Smallholders, as we have seen, constituted a hired labour reserve for the lords demesnes and the rich peasant holdings. Servants and labourers in the period of population decline were not (perhaps never had been) a homogeneous group. There had always been a considerable number of living-in servants, mostly female, in middling and richer peasant households. These were often the younger offspring of other peasant families in the same or adjacent villages, their position being ambiguous, like apprentices or foster-children. They are not to be confused with the smallholding labourers who had their own independent households. This is the group which diminishes proportionately during the century, especially after 1348. These were the people who pushed up wages and were generally regarded as an insolent and demanding group. Because peasant pressure and the lords' convenience over the years had led to the commutation of labour rent, lords had to rely largely on the labour of these independent workers for the cultivation of the demesnes, as had the richer peasants for their holdings. It is likely that the cost of labour was largely responsible for the abandonment of demesne cultivation and it is possible that, at any rate before the latter part of the fifteenth century, high labour costs restricted the expansion of the economy of the large holding, except in those areas of central and southern France where there was a reversion to joint holding by related nuclear families *(communautés taisibles, frerêches) [Le Roy Ladurie, 1966: 163; Boutruche, 1935; Neveux, 1975: 86].*

Hence it is possible that the century after the Black Death was the golden age of the middle rather than of the rich peasantry (the yeomen).

I have tried to show elsewhere how the history of the English peasantry in the century 1350-1450 had rather unusual features *[Hilton, 1975]*. It was not simply that this was a period of relative land abundance. As we have seen, relative land abundance was to be found in the early medieval period, when holdings on the average were large and smallholders only in moderate proportions (as late as the Domesday Book only a third of the recorded peasant families were small-holders). But this earlier period was also one of the strengthening of the power of the landed aristocracy and of considerable pressure for rent, service and jurisdictional profit.[12] Between 1350 and 1450, on the other hand, we find that relative land abundance was combined, for various reasons, with a relaxation of seigneurial domination and a notable lightening of the economic burden on the peasant economy. Peasant society, in spite of still existing within (in broad terms) a feudal framework, developed according to laws of motion internal to itself. The village community was dominated by the richer peasant families, who ran the manorial court in its jurisdictional, punitive and land-registration functions. The limits on rents and services were firmly fixed well below what the lords wanted. There was a certain level of commodity production but a good deal of non-commercial exchange of services between households. Limits were consciously set on the accumulation of property within one family, though it is possible that other factors (such as low replacement rates) limited, as yet, the development of a stratum of agrarian capitalists.[13]

This prosperity of the middle peasants has been noticed by some French historians. They dominated Languedoc during the fifteenth century. It was they who best survived the troubles in Normandy in the middle of the fifteenth century *[Le Roy Ladurie, 1966:151-2; Bois, 1976:150-1]*. But on the whole this 'marking time' phase has not been as much explored by historians as it deserves. On the one hand there has been the natural tendency to focus on the minority of rich peasants, the 'yeomen', because they seemed to be the group which would evolve into the capitalist tenant farmers of the later period. On the other hand there has been the natural pre-occupation of continental, and French historians in particular, to concentrate on the problems of the devastation by war and the subsequent recovery of the economy.

The problem of recovery from war devastation has an additional interest. If a rural society is so devastated that most of the livestock is slaughtered, crops are ruined and whole villages are abandoned, is it not possible that nothing like the old social structure would re-emerge? In the event, it would appear that in France, at the end of the re-construction period, the social and economic structures of both the badly devastated and the less badly affected areas, were, by the end of the fifteenth century, very much of the old type. Seigneurial hierarchies, after having been badly shaken by war, plague and famine, had firmly reestablished themselves. Peasants returned to the villages and started up the traditional round of cultivation. Traditional peasant strata re-appear. The immigrants from as far apart as Brittany and Auvergne take up in the Entre-Deux-Mers region the holdings of the *laboureurs* either as nuclear families or as *communautés taisibles*. In the Rhone valley the land:labour ratio was once again declining, producing an increasing population of smallholders and joint family occupiers. In eastern Normandy by the beginning of the sixteenth century, following an expansion of cultivation in the previous four decades which reached early fourteenth century levels, the smallholders here too begin to multiply again. Fragmentation of holdings was once again the rule in the Paris region. And in southern Germany is an echo of similar themes. In the region of Ravensberg the population was rising and tensions were already displaying themselves between the established peasant households and the increasing number of smallholding labourers—largely recruited from the younger sons of the main families [*Boutruche, 1936; Lorcin, 1974; Bois, 1976; Fourquin, 1964; Sabean, 1971*].

The French historians stress that in spite of the upheavals of the fourteenth and fifteenth centuries, the old social relationships persisted. The *laboureur-manouvrier* dichotomy returned, the *coqs de village* reasserted their local supremacy. Even in regions influenced by big towns urban capital does not seem to have effected economic or social trans-formations. It was certainly invested, but the investors were largely passive. It may be that, since the recovery in France had to be achieved in conditions of military struggle it was inevitable that it should be under the control of the nobility and that this explains its conservative character. At any rate, and in spite of the yeoman-like *laboureurs* in north-east France, there seem to be no clear movements in the direction of agrarian capitalism.

The situation in England at the turn of the fifteenth century is evidently different, if by no means clear. The fact that the country was not devastated by war must, during the long period of the prosperity of the middle peasantry, have made possible accumulations of wealth such as would not have been possible elsewhere. We know, of course, that livestock was among the despoiled resources of the rural economy in war-devasted France, and it is no doubt significant that the grazier appears as one of the quasi-capitalist figures of the late medieval English countryside. There were also rich peasant as well as—perhaps even more than—gentry lessees of the abandoned demesnes of the aristocracy,[14] though whether these in fact laid the basis for the capitalist-tenant farmers of the future is a matter for local investigation. At any rate, in England, as in France, by the sixteenth century the smallholding labourers were once more growing in numbers [*Thirsk, 19: Ch. VII*]. Whether they should be considered a phenomenon repeating the cycle of deprivation of the rural poor within an overcrowded peasant economy or a proto-agricultural proletariat ready to be exploited by a new type of employer is beyond the scope of this paper.

11

Popular Movements in England
at the End of the Fourteenth Century

In this paper I attempt to analyse the popular movements in late fourteenth century England in a specific fashion. Without giving a narrative account of the movements, I attempt to evaluate the threat to the existing social order which was posed, on the one hand by peasant movements, on the other by movements in the towns. It must be understood that I am concerned with the English situation and that although my remarks may have some general relevance I do not assume that my generalisations will necessarily apply to other countries, especially the highly urbanised Mediterranean lands, such as Italy.

I have assumed, perhaps wrongly, that the events of the rising of 1381 in England will be familiar to all.'In view of what is to follow, I should say that although I consider that the peasant element in the rising presented the most serious threat to the feudal monarchy, I would nevertheless wish to stress that the movement involved much wider strata of the population. The rising was sparked off by the Poll Tax of 1380, coming after a sequence of heavy taxes. It affected the whole of East Anglia and the counties around London (especially Kent). These were the areas of the greatest population density and contained new centres of cloth production. It provoked the renewal of dormant class conflicts in many towns and received the support of the London poor. The rebel armies occupied the capital and for a few days in June paralysed the royal government. At the same time other armies were dominating Norfolk and Suffolk. The rising was not simply a lower-class riot, but was (for the epoch) remarkably disciplined. John Ball and other radical clerics had through their preaching disseminated an ideology which was reflected in the demands put forward by the rebel leaders at meetings with the King at Mile End and Smithfield. These demands included the abolition of serfdom and of servile rents and dues. They envisaged the abolition of both secular and ecclesiastical class hierarchy. Although the details reach us only through the medium of hostile chronicles, there is a certain coherence about them which demonstrates how seriously we must take this movement, even if it was defeated militarily in a very short time.

England, like other European countries in the second half of the fourteenth century, was troubled and divided by many political and social conflicts. We must not, however, assume either that such conflicts were peculiar to this half century or that they were uncharacteristic of feudal society. The feudal monarchy and the aristocracy were engaged in warfare, which was part of their natural existence and which they had been waging on and off against the French, the Irish, the Scots and the Welsh, not simply since 1337, but for centuries. Between about 1340 and the 1370s, factional struggle among the nobility was relatively muted in the interests of pillage abroad but was resuming already by 1376 and would reach a climax with the deposition of Richard II in 1399, not unlike the events which had led in 1327 to the deposition of Richard's great-grandfather Edward II. These conflicts were not simply to be explained as a natural consequence of the struggle for landed wealth, power and lucrative marriages, inherent in late medieval 'bastard' feudalism, as in earlier 'tenurial' feudalism.[2]There were aggravating features in the fourteenth century economy and society which may be crudely but justifiably described as a crisis, resulting from falling landed incomes and increasing landowners' expenses, made worse, of course, by the increasing costs of war.[3]

It is important to remember that the 'popular' movements which we are to consider did not erupt in an otherwise tranquil society. The social harmony, which ecclesiastical, political and social theorists constantly idealised in their writings and their sermons, never in fact existed. The fragility of the political system (that is, the political system of the monarchy and the nobility) must be taken into account when we analyse the impact as well as the origins of movements among those outside that system.

When we insist on the long-lasting, even traditional character of social and political divisions within the ruling class, we do not yet touch on the problems which are fundamental to a consideration of the role of 'the people'. Who were 'the people'? To what extent did they constitute an antagonistic class or classes to the ruling gentry and nobility? These are important questions, because currents of discontent, which can be found in any society, do not necessarily constitute a threat to the social order. Such a threat only exists when the discontent is directed against the relations of production which are at the heart of the social order.

The definition of 'the people' and therefore of 'popular movements' is not made easier by the speculations of medieval political theorists and their modern interpreters. Here the *populus* is presented as those over whom sovereignty is exercised by rulers, usually kings, emperors or tyrants. The theorists do not normally go even so far as Marsilius of Padua, for whom 'the people' are the whole body of citizens, defined negatively as everybody other than children, slaves, aliens and women.[4] Medieval social theory, which on the whole remains strangely separate from the more abstract theories of politics was, as is well known, based on the theory of the functionally related and divinely ordained orders. It began, not later than the end of the ninth century (Alfred of Wessex's translation of Boethius), with the concept of the tripartite division of society between the prayers, the fighters and the workers, that is the clergy, the military aristocracy and the peasants. Future comment and satire multiplied the numbers of orders or estates, particularly as a result of the development of towns with their merchants and industrial craftsmen.[5]

In fourteenth century England, estate theory had its peculiar political embodiment in Parliament, from which the clergy as an estate were excluded, although they had their own Convocation, and their leading members (bishops and abbots) sat in Parliament with the secular lords. The assembly of the Commons which was part of Parliament could be, indeed was, presented as if it consisted of the representatives of 'the people'. The term 'Commons' as against 'Lords' is rather ambiguous. The members of the Commons' house were so called because they represented certain communities rather than because they represented 'the common people', as contrasted with the aristocracy.[6]But in any case, the dominant political element in the House of Commons consisted of the knights of the shire, representing in effect the lesser aristocracy of the counties, who in France and elsewhere would be counted among the nobility. The other representatives in the Commons' house were the 'burgesses', representatives of the urban élites. By the and of the fourteenth century these included lawyers and gentry who got themselves chosen as M.P.s for small towns.

From this brief description of the English Commons it may be deduced that neither knights of the shire nor burgesses could be thought of as a 'popular' element in the political system. The attitude of the House of Commons to what we shall recognise as popular movements makes it clear that they considered themselves as part of the ruling, not the ruled, class of fourteenth century society. My emphasis on a certain political dimension whilst considering the definition of 'popular' is of course because what is at issue is not only social discontent but power.

The ruling class consisted of the landed aristocracy (that is the nobility, the gentry and the ecclesiastical landowners) and the merchantile governing oligarchies of the chartered boroughs. The ruled classes consisted of tenants of land, both free and servile, whom we will term 'peasants', and industrial craftsmen, who were mostly, though not exclusively, living in towns. The king in his role as sovereign (rather than as the lord of the Crown estates) ruled through his central and local officials and through the royal law courts. The aristocracy and the gentry ruled their tenants partly through their private (manorial or seigneurial) jurisdictions and partly through their command of the royal network of control at local level. The merchantile oligarchies ruled the craftsmen, apprentices and journeymen through the agency of officials such as Mayors and Aldermen who presided over borough courts.

The income of the ruling class and the state was derived overwhelmingly from rents, dues and taxes paid by peasants. By the late fourteenth century the rent income of the landowners was almost entirely in cash. Comparatively little was in labour or in produce. The same was true of state taxation. Consequently that part of the product of peasant agriculture which was taken in rent and tax had to be marketed first by the peasants. Local markets had of course existed for centuries in order to enable peasants to exchange farm produce for commodities which they could not produce. But local markets were also the urban manifestation of the peasant response to the demand by landowners and the state for cash. At another level, markets which sold luxury goods, arms and other supplies for the aristocracy were the urban manifestation of the expenditure of the cash surplus which had been extracted from the peasantry.

This means that it was the relation between peasant producers on the one hand, the landed aristocracy and the state on the other which was crucial for the social formation of late fourteenth century feudal England. Any hindrance to the flow of rent and tax would not only undermine the position of the monarchy and the nobility, it would also seriously affect the urban sector of society. This emphasis on the primacy of the peasant—landowner relationship in England is of particular importance in a conference which primarily concerns the rebellion of sectors of the urban population of Florence.

It can be argued, that in spite of the early modern absolute monarchies the power structures of European feudal society were not fundamentally transformed until the bourgeois revolutions of the seventeenth century and afterwards.[7]The tendency has been to regard the medieval town as the location of the dynamic element in feudal society, partly by reading back the later bourgeois revolutions and partly by emphasising (perhaps over-emphasising) the anti-feudal character of the urban communal movement of the eleventh and twelfth centuries. I wish to argue that in so far as there was a potentially revolutionary anti-feudal class in medieval society it was the peasantry,—and their friends and relatives, the village craftsmen—*not* the urban craftmasters and *not* the urban wage workers.

I must, however, emphasise the phrase 'in so far as' because the medieval peasantry could not in fact be a generally and successfully revolutionary class (in spite of the history of Switzerland) because it was based on scattered small scale productive enterprise, which would either be static and self subsistent or, if involved significantly in market production, constantly differentiated into antagonistic social strata.

Why cannot we regard the urban classes in the same way as we regard the peasantry, that is as a class capable of seriously undermining the feudal order?

The very rich merchants and bankers who were involved in international trade were mainly providing goods for royal and aristocratic courts. As financiers they were the creditors of royal governments and of aristocratic or ecclesiastical spenders. In other words their economic success depended largely on the success of the landowners and the monarchs in keeping up their income, which was based on the extracted surplus from peasant production. The merchants are typified in England by the aldermanic class of the city of London. They were not, of course, exempt from the risks involved in being identified with particular aristocratic or royalist factions, as the careers of the grocer Nicholas Brembre or his rival John of Northampton clearly show. But they posed no general threat to feudal order.[8]

Lesser merchants of the capital and the merchantile elites of lesser towns had some stake in the royal and aristocratic demand for luxuries. Many of them, especially the provincial drapers, acted as middlemen for cloth exports which were of growing importance after the 1340s. The bulk of the exported cloth was expensive and destined for an upperclass market. They also serviced the general urban demand but given the general dependence of the towns on the health of the seigneurial economy, there was no antagonism between any of the strata among the class of merchants and the landowning ruling class,—accepting again that (as in fifteenth century Norwich) merchants might line up with rival aristocratic factions.[9] It is also remarkable to what extent the urban oligarchs in their daily lives emphasised, with all the elaborate and ecclesiastically legitimated ceremonial that they could afford, the virtues of hierarchical subordination—of course, of their inferiors to them, but also, of themselves to the nobility and gentry.

What however of the subordinated classes in urban society? These were mainly the manufacturing craft masters, the retail traders in foodstuffs, the apprentices, the journeymen or skilled workers, and the unskilled labourers. Their interests were by no means identical. For example the craft masters and the hired workers were interested in low food prices and were consequently in opposition to the providers of fish, bread, ale and other victuals. Skinners and fishmongers in mid-fourteenth century London often fought in the streets. And so complex was the politics of London that the contours of class conflict are often blurred by other antagonisms. However in London as in the provincial towns it seems clear that the organised craft masters were in the nature of things opposed to the ruling oligarchies of merchants. This was fundamentally because of merchantile control of access to raw materials and sale of the finished product, at any rate where the finished product was sold to a wide market to which the craft masters did not have access. But it was also because of the monopoly of political control exercised by the merchants. Manufacturing craft masters at best were allowed representation on advisory councils while the effective government was in the hands of mayors and aldermen (or their equivalents) who were merchants. The gilds of the craftsmen were as much policing organizations supervised by the mayor and his associates from above, as they were organisations representing the craftsmens' interests.[10]

But the craft masters were in a difficult position. They needed the support of the merchantile oligarchs to keep their employees (apprentices and journeymen) in order, especially during our period when the laws concerning wage limitation and the free movement of hired labour (the Statutes of Labourers) were exercised by the urban oligarchs in the role which they were given by the government as Justices of the Peace. Skilled journeymen, especially in towns like London and Coventry, where cloth was manufactured on a large scale, did not hope to acquire their own workshop and tried to form their own organisations. These were always suppressed by the town governments with the support of the craft masters—and of the royal government. The terminology used of these organisations by the authorities includes words like 'rebellions' 'conspiracy' and 'subversion' to such an extent that it might seem that here there was genuinely a threat to the social order. All the more so because below the ranks of the skilled workers was an incalculable mass of unskilled labourers and marginal people of all kinds who were outside the recognised structures of urban society.[11]

It tends to be assumed that urban populations are quicker acting, more conscious of their rights and generally more politically conscious than peasants. This may be a reading back from modern capitalist societies. But even if it were true of the fourteenth century, what objective conditions would political consciousness need to reflect? What was the place of merchants, master craftsmen, skilled and unskilled workers in the relations of production? As we have seen the merchants were largely dependent on the aristocratic market, but was there an analogy between the role of the peasant and the role of the industrial artisans? In some senses, yes. Agricultural production and industrial production were both based on small scale units which reflected the existing levels of technology. The labour force of the peasant holding, as of the master craftsman's workshop, tended to be based on the nuclear family (of four or five people at the most) with a hired labour force seldom exceeding two. No doubt the similarities of small scale production produced similarities of outlook, especially since urban populations were kept up by rural immigration rather than by natural increase.

But the analogy ends at this point. The peasant economy produced the surplus over its subsistence and reproduction needs which went as rent, services and tax to maintain the landed aristocracy and the state. It was a transfer of surplus which was guaranteed not only by jurisdiction but by the institution of serfdom. The income derived from merchant capital was a profit on alienation. Some of it was skimmed off the profits of artisan production, and those profits derived partly from the exploitation of apprentices and journeymen. But that exploitation was not at the heart of the feudal social order. Trouble in the town, at any level hardly affected society's rulers. Trouble in the country affected them immediately, and they knew it.

It follows from our argument so far that some popular movements would be more serious for the ruling class than others, and briefly that peasant movements would be more important than movements of urban artisans or journeymen. Fourteenth century England saw movements of all types, which converged during the summer of rebellion in 1381. Before considering these movements we should briefly examine the conjunction of economic and social trends in the period after the first visitation of the bubonic plague in 1348-1349.

The underlying conjunctural features during this period which might influence the popular movements can be summed up as follows: rents; prices; wages; employment. I will attempt very briefly to summarise the movement of these elements, although one cannot pretend that the available data makes it possible in most cases to give satisfactory statistics. *Rents*: it seems possible that there was an overall fall in rent payments in the *century* after 1349 of between one third and one half. This was due to various causes—a drastically changed land :labour ratio (more land and fewer tenants); tenant resistance; falling agricultural prices. However it seems clear (although not easily quantifiable) that at first lords attempted to use their seigneurial power to maintain rents and services. This policy could not be sustained and before 1400 was being abandoned. *Prices*: agricultural prices were high in the '50s, very high in the '60s, dropping in the '70s, '80s and '90s. Agricultural costs, already outstripping agricultural prices in the '40s continued to rise. The biggest gap between prices and costs was in the '70s and '80s. *Wages*: between the pre-Black Death decade and 1400 real wages of artisans went up 50% and of agricultural labourers possibly more. *Employment*: the rise in real wages (especially in agriculture) probably reflected an increase in productivity, but also in demand. In spite of annual fluctuations, total cloth exports went up consistently until the mid '80s, dropped a little then continued to rise until the middle '90s. This reflected a significant growth in cloth production, in the countryside as well as in the big towns.[12]

It would seem from these figures that popular movements during the late fourteenth century can hardly be explained simply as a response to poverty and deprivation. It is true that, without a repetition of the famine conditions of 1315-1317 there were very high food prices in the '60s, but by the period of rebellion, food prices were down and wages were rising. It is clear that an explanation of the movements has to be made in structural rather than conjunctural terms. The incompatibilities within the social structure came to a head in 1381. Instead of rehearsing the well known events of that year it will be worthwhile to distinguish the different contributory trends during the previous decades. In so doing, I will see to what extent we can evaluate, comparatively, the challenges made to the social order by rural and urban rebels.

As is well known, there is ample evidence in both private and public records for a long continuing conflict between lords of manors and their unfree tenants. This conflict was, before 1381, localised, in the sense that rebellions, protests or law suits were confined to individual manors. Nevertheless, over the years they were widely distributed over the country. Basically the quarrels were about the level of rents and services and freedom of movement. We know about most of them because they gave rise to law suits in the royal courts or to appeals by lords to royal authority for help in their suppression. Since the principal legal guarantee for the high level of rents and services and restrictions on freedom of movement was the fact that the tenants were either claimed as personal serfs or holding in unfree tenure, the disputes were expressed in those terms. To improve one's standard of living or to have greater opportunity to produce for the market, one had to reduce or abolish the incidents of serfdom. An economic issue became one of legal status and, as the demands of the popular preachers and of the rebel leaders in 1381 show, freedom became a central feature of peasant class consciousness.[13]

These village rebellions by no means ceased after the defeat of the rebels in 1381. The defeat was not as crushing as might have been expected because some rebels still held out in the countryside away from London and others were galvanised into consciousness by news of rebellion after it had ended in London. Moreover the government and most of the lords were prudent and prepared to offer pardons to most of those involved. Nevertheless there was inevitably something of a feudal reaction which, in combination with continuing peasant militancy, explains the many local conflicts in the two decades after 1381. By the beginning of the fifteenth century, in fact (and partly as a result of the lords' abandonment of direct management of the demesne), the improvement of peasant conditions was noticeable. Rents continued to fall, perhaps faster than before, and villeinage (serfdom) began to wither away.

There was another component of peasant incomes additional to that which was retained from the product of the holding after the payment of rents, taxes and so on. This consisted of wages. Even after the change in the land: labour ratio in the late fourteenth century, many peasants supplemented the incomes from their holdings by working for wages, either on lords' lands or on the holdings of richer peasants. As has been mentioned, wages increased appreciably from the middle of the century and (according to certain figures from southern England) agricultural real wages increased appreciably higher than those of artisans, especially in the post-rebellion period. But these increases were obtained in spite of serious attempts by the government and the local justices (drawn from the county gentry) to hold them to the pre-plague level. These attempts resulted in frequent punishments and sporadic outbursts of violence. Here was an additional element in the rural class conflict which—in so far as they were not all part of the same class—would bring peasant producers and wage workers together, as was manifest in 1381. There is a clear reference to the labour legislation in the Mile End programme. There was, as one might expect, a post-1381 seigneurial backlash on this issue (the Statute of Cambridge of 1388),[14]but it was ineffective in keeping wages down.

Peasant resistance to seigneurial demands contributed significantly to the difficulties of the landowning aristocracy and the state during this period. The ability of agricultural labourers to keep up their wages, in spite of the labour legislation, forced the majority of landowners to lease out their demesne lands, often to richer members of the village community. The interests of peasants and landowners are revealed as fundamentally antagonistic, an antagonism which was at the root of the 1381 rising.

However, some historians have supposed that this rising was as much urban-artisan as peasant. Can this view be supported?

One can answer, equally justly, in positive and negative senses. The rebel army was admitted into London as a result of the intervention of their supporters in the city (and here I do not mean the supposed 'traitor aldermen').[15] We have lists of names of Londoners to whom the authorities refused the general pardon after the end of the rebellion. Furthermore there were social and political conflicts in a number of provincial towns which, if not part of the rebellion, were at any rate able to take advantage of the disarray of the central government. On the other hand, it could be argued that the urban contribution to the rebellion was opportunist, limited and did not present any serious threat to the feudal order. These problems need more attention if we are to indicate our suggested resolution.

At this point, something should be said in general about English medieval urbanisation, for it could perhaps be argued that it was so under-developed that those who suggest that there was no intrinsic challenge to the feudal order from the English towns are simply emphasising the backwardness of English urban life as compared with that of continental Europe, especially Italy. And in truth, English towns were rather small. London, however (which we will consider separately), was comparable in size and function to some of the bigger continental towns. Its population at the time of the rebellion was at least 35,000 (cf. Florence, possibly 50,000 on the road to recovery after 1348). And that figure should be increased considerably to take into account Southwark and Westminster which were part of the metropolitan complex. It was a political and ecclesiastical centre as well as being a focus of international trade and of industrial production. The next biggest town was York, about 11,000 inhabitants, followed by a number of provincial 'capitals' and county towns between 2,000 and 10,000 inhabitants. The biggest of these were Bristol, Coventry and Norwich.[16] But one of the features of English urbanisation which should also be emphasised was that throughout the country there were very many small market towns, many with less than 1,000 inhabitants, which nevertheless were commercial and industrial, not agricultural communities. Perhaps half of the country's urban population was contained in these places. England therefore was, in a *sense,* under-urbanised, but partly because of the dispersal of marketing rather than because of the backwardness of market production.

There were sharp social conflicts in a number of towns at the time of
the 1381 rebellion which throw some light on the nature of urban class
antagonism in the fourteenth century. The pattern varied from town to
town. We will consider them primarily so as to evaluate the relative
threat which they posed to the social order. First, we should mention
those urban rebellions which seemed to be part of that general assault on
the authority of the landowning nobility and the state which has so far
seemed to us to have been mainly of peasant origin. These came from the
borough communities of Bury St. Edmunds and St. Albans. Bury St.
Edmunds was a developing cloth manufacturing centre of some 3,500-
4,000 inhabitants; St. Albans, whose size is not known, was certainly a
growing market town, probably the biggest in its county (Hertfordshire).[17] Both these towns were ruled directly by the rich Benedictine
Abbeys of the same name and had never acquired the chartered
privileges which other towns of similar size had enjoyed for two
centuries. They had been at loggerheads with their lords for many years
and naturally took advantage of the rural revolt to attempt to achieve
elementary urban rights. Even though the government took a severe
view of their action (especially that of Bury) they were not seeking to
overthrow the feudal order, but simply to take the place within it that
most of their co-burgesses in other towns had occupied for many years.

Certain other urban disturbance were aspects of the class antagonisms
inherent in medieval urban society, which may schematically be described as the conflict between merchant capital and small scale craft industry.
In York, the governmental functions were concentrated in the hands of a
narrow mercantile oligarchy while even quite rich craft masters,
organised into strong and self conscious fraternities, had only an advisory
role in the constitutional structure. As often happens, the manifestation
of craft masters' demands came about through their support of a mayoral
candidate of mercantile origin, though as often in these cases, it is not
certain who was manipulating whom. The struggle began before the
general rebellion and continued after it, resulting in a fine being imposed
on the whole city (as in the case of Bury) by the Crown. The
government, of course, was always sensitive to any disturbance to the
hierarchical order whether in town or country. The harshness of its fines
on delinquent urban communities reflect, however, its greed for money,
as much as any particular fear of urban as against rural discontent. This
was again illustrated at Beverley, a Yorkshire cloth manufacturing town
of some 4,000 inhabitants. In 1381, the craft masters attempted to take
over the leading offices of the town from the mercantile families who
normally monopolised them. The merchants eventually regained
control, but the Crown exacted an even heavier fine than that paid by
York.[18]

It has been suggested by Bronislaw Geremek à propos Paris, that in
medieval towns the dangerous classes were not those who were part of
the regular institutional structures (—and this of course would include

the craft masters in their gilds as well as their apprentices and regularly employed journeymen—) but the 'marginal' element, mostly immigrants from the countryside.[19]These would be employed sporadically as unskilled workers, would often be unemployed and be involved in crime of various sorts. In periods of high mortality, many country people did move into town so that we may find a deceptively successful maintenance of urban population levels. London's pre-Black Death population is estimated at about 40,000.[20]The 1377 population was about 35,000, suggesting a population decline of about 10%—a good deal less than the minimum 40% overall which is now suggested as the bubonic plague mortality in the second half of the fourteenth century. It implies considerable immigration, and this may have happened in other towns as well. It has, in fact, been suggested that in Canterbury at the time of the 1381 rising the rebels and their supporters were *intrantes,* that is immigrant traders and craftsmen who had been coming in great numbers since 1350 and who were discontented because not able to acquire the privilege of freemen of the city.[21]

The question of the relative importance of rural and urban social movements for English society as a whole during the late fourteenth century cannot be solved without consideration of England's largest town, London. Historians have, quite correctly, regarded as a very important task to define the social content of the fierce political struggles during this period. They have analyzed the divisions within the ruling elite, broadly (though inadequately) definable as between the victualling and the manufacturing interests. In fact, of course, oligarchs of both parties were involved in international trade in commodities (like wool) which had nothing to do with their supposed occupations; were involved in government finance; and were considerable owners of urban and rural real property.[22]The manufacturing interest led by John of Northampton, a draper, managed to harness the resentments of the craft masters, perhaps in their joint interests in keeping down food prices (and therefore wages). But in spite of the bitterness of the factional struggle and its involvement in the conflict between the Crown and the noble opposition, it cannot be regarded as in any way subversive of the feudal order. The craft interest did not manifest itself with any political force beyond agitating (with only temporary success) for a Common Council (in any case with no power) elected on a craft rather than on a territorial basis.

Perhaps one reason for the timidity of the craft masters was that they had their own problems with their apprentices and journeymen and needed the oligarchic city government to keep them in order. The craft masters, represented in the Common Council, tried to get the Mayor and Aldermen to keep up the price to be paid by journeymen in order to be admitted to the franchise of the city and thus to set up as masters.[23] And in fact it has been calculated that only a quarter of the city's inhabitants were enfranchised citizens, that is with the right to trade retail and the other political rights of citizenship.[24]The masters also relied on the city government and its courts to prevent the journeyman from organising, mainly to keep up wages. There are, especially after 1349, many cases of prosecution under the Statute of Labourers. Action by journeymen themselves ranged from short term organisation to the attempt to set up religious fraternities. A spurriers' fraternity, dissolved early in 1381, was said to have lasted for nine years. It aimed to control piece-work rates, to keep outside workers from employment and to control its members by regular meetings and oaths to obey the fraternity's ordinances. A fraternity of journeymen saddlers, organised according to their masters *under the false colour of sanctity* was said by the masters to be thirteen years old, but by the journeymen to be much older. Its object was to raise and to maintain wage rates. The Mayor and Aldermen ordered its dissolution.[25]

Journeymen in London (and elsewhere, for example Coventry) were imitating the organisational forms of the master craftsmen. It could well be argued that in spite of the basic nature of the confrontation between those who paid and those who received wages, the small scale nature of craft enterprise and the aspirations of the journeymen towards master's status inevitably meant that they were not even a revolutionary element within the urban economy, let alone with regard to the wider society. But was there in London a significant number of unskilled and marginal elements who could have produced a seditious, if not a revolutionary ferment? The records of the London courts which operated peace-keeping jurisdiction give some insight into this problem. It should be said that in spite of the troubles arising from the factional struggles of the '80s (between the supporters of Brembre and those of Northampton), it is in the three or four decades *before* the rising that there is evidence of generally disturbed conditions. But what this means is that the city authorities were paying particular attention to criminal elements, 'night-walkers', 'travelling men' and their inevitable companions in the stews (brothels) of Southwark. One cannot say, however, that they seem to have presented a serious problem of law and order. More violence seems to have arisen from internecine strife between recognised gilds (saddlers versus woodworkers [fusters] ; skinners versus fishmongers; fishmongers versus goldsmiths).[26]

Nevertheless, it may well have been men and women on the edge of recognised commercial and craft society who identified with the rural rebels in 1381. There is a list in the records of Parliament of Londoners who were exempted from the royal pardon to rebels after the defeat of the rising. With some caution, we may assume that these would, if anything, be well known and therefore active ringleaders. Out of 148 named persons, 33 have no given occupation at all. The highest number in this list (and in a contemporary list in the city plea rolls) are described as servants. A small majority (about 60%) are in occupations outside the 111 recognised (in 1422) by the Brewers Company as respectable.[27]

There is a wide scatter over some 50 separate occupations, but with a significant concentration in textiles, especially weavers. This may have been a result of the attacks that had been made on Flemish weavers, though it might also reflect the fact that textile workers were particularly at the mercy of merchants as middlemen, and were in fact obliged to sell their product to drapers rather than direct to the ultimate consumer. But we must echo the general conclusion reached many years ago by Ruth Bird, that there was no strong party of support in London for Wat Tyler and his followers, however much sympathy (such as would ensure the rebels' entry) there might have been.

In this paper, I have concentrated on a particular though fundamental problem, namely the relative threat to the social order by peasants on the one hand and the lower strata in the towns on the other. I have tried to show that because of their position in feudal society as the payers of the 'feudal rent' which constituted the bulk of landowners' income, the peasants posed a much greater threat than did the townsmen. To pose a threat is not, however, to make a revolution. I do not think it will be dangerously teleological to suggest that peasants could not at this stage have provided an alternative ruling class to that of the feudal monarchy and its aristocracy. It is obvious, in the first place, that a scattered class of small producers dependent on a seasonally varying way of life would have great difficulty in permanent political mobilisation at a national level. Furthermore, a class of small producers would, as production for the market developed, more or less rapidly differentiate and lose its temporary solidarity. It is also important that the political vision of the rebels' leaders had not developed into a clear picture of an alternative social order. It is true that they had clearly thrown overboard the doctrine of the hierarchy of social orders. They wished to abolish the landed aristocracy, to disendow the Church and to destroy the ecclesiastical hierarchy. But they had not apparently envisaged any role for the towns and could not think of a political regime other than vague schemes for a popular monarchy.

The ideology of the rebels was under the influence of such preachers as John Ball, already similar to that of the later Lollards. Although the Lollards were usually quietist rather than politically militant, the ruling class, as been well shown by Margaret Aston, identified Lollardy with sedition because of their memories of 1381.[28] So Lollardy itself, though mainly developing in the fifteenth century, should also be thought of as a popular movement, with more connection with the 1381 rising than is usually thought. In so far as one can identify its social base, however, it seems to have been urban and artisan rather than peasant. And whatever the future association between Puritanism and revolution in England, the Lollards did not present a serious challenge to the social order as (for instance) did the Hussites in Bohemia.

12

Some Problems of Urban Real Property
in the Middle Ages

There has been, over many years, a good deal of discussion among economic historians about the part played by the ownership of real property as the source of the initial capital for the development of trade. W. Sombart, misled, according to his critics, by the study of the backward towns of medieval Germany, thought that the foundation of the fortunes of the urban patriciates was the income received from ground rents. Pirenne's persuasive writings substituted a theory of early urban growth which attributed merchant fortunes to the exploitation of long-distance trade. Sapori and others follow Pirenne, and minimize the real property contribution to early merchant and urban fortunes.[1]

But there has also been a swing away from Pirenne, without, necessarily a return to Sombart. Contemporary historians are not inclined to underestimate the great development of international commerce in the twelfth and thirteenth centuries. However, they tend to see some continuity between the developed patriciate of the period of efflorescence and the petty nobles, feudal officers and other small urban landowners of the tenth and eleventh centuries. Even if the urban oligarchs of the era of the so-called 'commercial revolution' were primarily bankers and merchants, there may have been, at an earlier date, an important element of real property in their family fortunes. Furthermore, as Pirenne and others have emphasized, merchant fortunes, whatever their origin, were frequently invested in land.[2]

Although there has been among historians a general interest in the problem of the part played by landed property in laying the basis of early mercantile wealth, there has been less interest in the distribution of urban landed property in the central and late middle ages, as though this were no longer of practical or theoretical interest. In view of other well-documented features of the social, economic and political life of towns from the thirteenth century onwards, this is perhaps natural. It would, however, be of some interest to establish whether or not rent from urban real property continued to form an important part of the incomes of the mercantile and industrial upper classes; whether or not there was any tendency for the concentration of ownership of urban real property; and if so, whether this concentration was in the hands of a recognizable and distinct social group.

An enquiry on these lines is rather different from those which, by examining the histories of individual merchants, show how successful families often acquired properties and even merged into the landowning aristocracy. It would start from the standpoint, not of the individual, but of the total available amount of real property in the town—or as near to the total as documentation will allow. It would not concern itself with the investment of merchant capital in agricultural land. To make significant generalizations, we ought, of course, to draw on evidence from a wide range of towns. In medieval Europe there was enormous variety, ranging from big centres of industry, banking and trade to minor market centres. One should not expect similar answers about real property holdings from them. This essay will be confined to a few towns of the English midlands for which there is some useful evidence of the type required. One of them, Coventry, was, from the thirteenth century, a prominent cloth manufacturing centre, perhaps by the second half of the fourteenth century the fourth largest town in England, after London. Even so, it was, by (say) Italian standards, small. The others, Gloucester, Worcester and Warwick were administrative centres and regional market towns with a certain manufacturing element. Though smaller than Coventry, they were fairly representative of the middle rank of medieval English towns. Between the eleventh and the thirteenth centuries, there was evidently a considerable expansion of the urban occupied area. Not only did the built-up area spread laterally and spill beyond the town walls into the suburbs, but unoccupied land within the walls was also used for building. Perhaps the latter provided the more significant multiplication of living space. How far can we measure this? It is easier to guess what was happening than to give exact figures.

The earliest units of urban land of which we have medieval records sometimes give the spatial dimensions of the plot without indicating what, if anything, was built on it. An example is the *haga* or haw, or enclosed plot along the north wall of Worcester granted by the Bishop of Worcester in 904 to the alderman of Mercia and his wife Aethelflaed, daughter of Alfred of Wessex.[3] It measured twenty-eight by twenty-nine by nineteen rods. If we take the risk of assuming that these rods contained five and a half yards, the haw was between three and four acres in area. But this example comes from a period which many historians would regard as pre-urban. Most regard the eleventh century, at the earliest the tenth (in Italy for example), as the initial phase of the great period of urban growth. In England it may (hesitantly) be measured in Domesday Book (1086), the most comprehensive and reliable piece of quantitative evidence from any European country at that date. In this record, many different terms are used for the basic units of tenure in the towns-messuages, houses (*mansiones*), tenements, burgages among others—but in all cases it is almost certain that the term referred to an area of land rather than to the buildings (if any) on it. The term 'burgage', indicating a tenure which gave rights as well as implying obligations, became generalized in succeeding years, but continued to imply an area of land rather than the dwelling or other building. The area varied from place to place. In Lincoln, at the time of Domesday Book, it seems that there were six or seven burgages to the acre.[4] The burgages of those towns, many newly founded, of the twelfth and thirteenth centuries, which were given the laws of the Norman town of Breteuil, usually contained more than half an acre, in one case six acres.[5] When the Bishop of Worcester founded Stratford-on-Avon, round about 1196-8, he divided the borough area into burgage plots of three and a half by twelve perches, just over a quarter of an acre.[6] At Worcester, according to some deeds of transfer, some urban tenements were of considerable size. In 1250 a draper sold to a cleric his capital messuage of nearly four acres. In 1307 a house and a three-acre garden were sold. Both of these sites were within the town wall.[7]

Whatever the variations in the surface areas of these early haws, messuages or burgages, it is obvious that they were usually much more extensive than the ground-plan of the average medieval two- or three-bay house.[8] By the end of the thirteenth century, at the peak of a period of urban as well as rural population expansion some plots may not have been built on, may even have been cultivated. Most, however, had been split up, sub-let and built over by houses, cottages, shops, inns, workshops and stables of varying size and rental value. Topographical research, based on deeds and rentals, can illuminate this process by which the intra-mural area of our medieval towns were built up.

But other problems arise as well, of economic and social rather than of topographical history. Some of the midland urban rentals may in part solve some of these problems, while posing others.

In the early Norman period, in the midland towns as elsewhere, the principal ground landlords were the king and the ecclesiastical and secular nobility. In Worcester, the bishop had ninety 'houses' *(mansiones)* half of which were sub-let to Norman nobles, the most important being the sheriff, Urse of Abitot. The Abbot of Evesham had twenty eight messuages and the king and five nobles had fifteen between them. In Warwick, the king had 113 'houses', his barons (of whom the most important was the Benedictine Abbot of Coventry) had 112, and nineteen burgesses owned their own messuages. At Gloucester, 542 'houses' were distributed between the royal demesne (300), the archbishop of York (60), St Peter's Abbey (52) and some twenty other lords.[9] Stratford-on-Avon, of course, had one principal ground landlord, the Bishop of Worcester. Coventry was divided from the twelfth century between the Benedictine Abbey (which became the cathedral priory) and the Earl of Chester.[10]

These principal landlords drew varying rents from burgages (or whatever else the unit of tenure might be termed). Some were only a few pence, as in the case of the Gloucester 'landgable' payments.[11] A higher rent was not uncommon. In newly-founded towns, and elsewhere, 12d a burgage was not uncommon. This was the burgage rent at

Stratford-on-Avon. By comparison with the rent from arable land this was considerable.[12] But, of course, it gave burgess privileges and was in lieu of all services. The fact that landlords were able to attract settlers with these relatively high rents illustrates the twelfth century urban boom. But with the considerable rise in prices which continues to the end of the thirteenth century, these burgage rents became much less valuable to the principal landlords. It was the burgage tenants who sub-let who were in the best position to profit from the rising demand for town property, as we can show by a comparison of burgage chief rents with the rents of sub-let properties.

An official survey of 1280 of Coventry[13] gives a number of examples of the subdivision and sub-letting of burgage tenements. Master Richard Burton and his wife Petronilla had a holding consisting of nine burgages, many of them subdivided; three watermills; half a dozen cottages; a couple of crofts; and a complex tenement held by a sub-tenant. For these holdings they were both paying rent to the overlord, and receiving rent from sub-tenants. The complications can be simply illustrated from one group of holdings for which they paid 34s. 6d. to the Prior of Coventry, overlord of his own half and lessee at that date of the half of the borough which had once belonged to the Earl of Chester. This payment was for four burgages and a watermill. Unfortunately the rent of the watermill cannot be separated from that of the four burgages, but burgage chief rents were seldom more than 2s.[14] We may safely assume that the four burgages were responsible for not more than 10s. of the combined rent paid to the Prior. But these four burgages were sub-let, one complete for 5s., one with two cottages for 9s., the rest being sub-divided into thirty cottages and thirteen curtilages or garden plots. The total rent from the sub-letting came to nearly £5. Another example is from the property holdings of Peter Baroun who had seventeen and one third of a burgage and two cottages for which he paid to the principal ground landlords 14s. 1d. These were not sub-divided to the same extent as the Burton property; twelve burgages were sublet complete, fourteen cottages being carved out of the rest. Even so the total rent from the sub-letting was 39s. 2d. If we knew about the sub-sub-letting which undoubtedly happened, but which is not recorded, the total profits from the property would be seen to be even greater.

Similar profits accruing to intermediate tenants can be observed at the same date in Warwick. As one would expect in this smaller and less wealthy town, the recorded subdivision of burgages was much less developed.[15] Thomas Payn, a Warwick burgess who bore the ephemeral title of 'mayor', held a dozen burgages for low rents from the Earl of Warwick and from a number of ecclesiastical landlords, as well as three of which he was principal landlord. His rent income from his sub-lettings was nearly four times as great as the rent he had to pay out. The average burgage rent that Payn paid to the Earl of Warwick and to St Mary's Collegiate Church averaged just over 8d. though he had to pay between

1s. and 4s. to his monastic landlords. He was, however, sub-letting some of his burgages for 8s. to 10s., although some other rents for sub-let burgages were kept at a traditionally low level. In these two surveys of 1280 we see considerable remnants of the burgage system of the earlier period. In Warwick, in fact, the whole tenanted area, apart from eighteen tofts and four cottages, were reckoned in whole or fractional burgages, possibly occupying much the same surface area as at the time of the Domesday survey. At Coventry, while there were many tenements, messuages and cottages which may or may not have originated in whatever original area it was that was divided into burgages, the burgage system was still prominent. At Stratford in 1252, as one might expect from the date and circumstances of its original foundation the burgage tenements were still the only ones that counted, apart from a few stalls and shops. But this information is in the bishop's rental, and he would not necessarily be interested in sub-letting.

By the fourteenth century the 'burgage' is less prominent. If the towns were filling up with buildings, especially buildings of a more permanent character than those of the twelfth century, it would follow that, in the later rentals and deeds of transfer, houses and shops rather than burgages should feature largely, although often enough the house and the land are described together. In Stratford there are no more rentals for the whole town after that drawn up for the episcopal overlord in 1252. But in the fourteenth century begins a series of rentals of the Holy Cross Gild and the other gilds which were soon to be amalgamated with it, probably the most important property owners in the town. The earliest of these is dated about 1328, and they continue until the sixteenth century. In the middle of the fourteenth century, the Holy Cross Gild was still sub-letting burgages, half burgages and tenements as well as buildings, but as time goes on, the buildings rather than the house sites predominate. The contemporary gild accounts, mainly occupied with building and house repair costs, show clearly that the gild recognized the importance of house rents. From about £6 in 1355 the gild income from its urban property rose to nearly £50 by the end of the fifteenth century. To begin with, an element in this increase resulted from the amalgamation of the gilds, but it was mainly due to the buying up of property, the improvement of existing property and to the erection and letting of new buildings. Rents varied a great deal according to factors which cannot be calculated, but the impression is that they were, in general, going up in the fifteenth century. The contrast between the old, low, burgage rent and that paid for new houses still occasionally appears. In a rental of 1446, for instance, the gild lets out two burgages, one in Evesham Lane for 8d. and one in Rother Street for 1s. 8d. But a new tenement in the corner of High Street, sub-let to a tailor and a shoemaker, and which certainly occupied less space than a burgage, was bringing in 36s. 8d.[16]

Two Warwick rentals of the fifteenth century, drawn up for the principal ground landlords, St Mary's Collegiate Church and the Earl of

Warwick, present interesting contrasts to the 1280 survey which we discussed above. In 1424 the College was receiving rent from some eighty or ninety tenements, cottages, crofts and gardens in the urban area.[17] Rents varied greatly. In the absence of details about the rented property there must be some doubts as to the reasons for these variations. It is probable, however, that the frequent rents for 1s. or less are old burgage rents of the type we have been discussing, and in a rental of this type there are naturally no indications of rents taken from sub-tenants. There are, however, some recent economic rents which were paid to this chief lord, such as 18s. paid from a newly built tenement in the Horsecheaping, leased for a term to the tenant. In the Earl of Warwick's rental of 1482[18] much of the archaic burgage framework was artificially· preserved. This is partly because this is a rental of an ancient principal ground landlord still drawing income from burgages which had undoubtedly been long since sub-let by the tenants. Partly, too, the relative economic stagnation of Warwick in the fifteenth century must have slowed down the break-up of the old tenurial system. The burgages were only paying small sums, normally less than 1s. However, the earl's rent income from some hundred and sixty or seventy tenants included a number of improved, or economic, rents, called farms, not, of course, from archaic burgage tenements but from buildings. Since these were economic rents, signs of very recent change show them moving in a downward direction. Even so, cottages were let at 4s. or 5s., messuages for sums varying between 8s. in Castle Street and 26s. 8d. in High Street.

Moving to the more active economic milieu of Coventry, we find these tendencies further advanced. Already by the middle of the fourteenth century, the deeds which bear witness to land transactions indicate an abandonment of the 'burgage' terminology still used in 1280. Apart from the original and copied deeds, the main sources are early fifteenth century rentals of the urban properties of the Coventry Cathedral Priory cellarer and pittancer,[19] and a late fifteenth-century rental of the property of the powerful Holy Trinity Gild.[20] In 1411, about a quarter (thirty-six) of the properties held from the priory's pittancer were held 'in fee'. Many of these, as well as tenures in fee held from the cellarer, paid 1s., others less. These may be relics of burgage tenure. Sub-tenancies are occasionally mentioned but there is no information about the rents paid by the sub-tenants to the priory tenants, so there is no knowing exactly what was the increase in rental value implied in the difference between the rent in fee and the rent paid by the sub-tenant. However, two-thirds of the pittancer's tenants were in fact holding for life or lives or at will, and these of course would tend to be the same sort of economic rents as sub-tenants of tenants in fee would be paying.[21] Peter de la Mare held in Gosford Street by indenture for life a big tenement with a tavern built in stone, called the New Inn, paying 20 mks (£13. 6s. 8d.), and three other tenants each held for life, a shop, hall and chamber above (*super*) the said tavern for 33s. 4d. a year each.

Margaret Halle held a tenement for life, with a tavern, for £4. She sub-let to Adam Swelte, a cardmaker, but for what rent is not stated. A Chandler, James Fynche, paid £4 a year for a tenement in Smithford Street which he held by indenture for life. John Barrow paid £3 for a big tenement and two cottages with a garden where there had once been six cottages. He had a sub-tenant, William Stille, but this sub-tenant's rent is not given. These are among the highest rents for which there is evidence, and the rental of the Holy Trinity Gild for 1486 suggests a similar level. In this rental, as in those of the priory, precision is impossible because the size and nature of the property is not given in sufficient detail. However, cottages fetched between 4s. and 12s. and some of the wealthier tenants, great merchants with familiar names, were paying over £4 for their tenements.

There is a Gloucester town rental of 1455 which was principally compiled to record the old, low, landgable rents payable by the principal tenants to the town authorities from the original building sites. The real rents actually paid by sub-tenants for houses, shops, stables and the like are only recorded for Southgate Street and the Mercery, and only incompletely for these. The landgable payments vary a great deal since the original burgages had become much sub-divided. Even so, they contrast strongly with the current house rents. For example, the Priory of St. Bartholomew paid the town authorities a landgable of 1s. 2d. for a certain tenement with a bakery in Southgate Street. The Priory of Lanthony rented it from St Bartholomew's for 18s. and sub-let it to a baker who occupied it for 40s. William Butter paid 7¾d. landgable for two tenements in the Mercery and was able to get 12s. from a sub-tenant for one of them. Although some houses were let for only a few shillings, clearly many houses in the middle of the town were let for £1 and over.

These examples of rents in the later middle ages have been quoted in order to show the contrast between the original ground rents and the rents which were paid for buildings in these sites. They show the possibilities of profit in site development, of which, as we have seen, the Stratford-on-Avon Holy Cross Gild took advantage. Such figures could be multiplied, not so much from rentals, which have their limitations and which are rather infrequent, but from charters and other deeds such as are to be found at Worcester Cathedral, in the Coventry or the Stratford municipal archives. The point, however, is rather a simple one, and leads to the more interesting problem of the importance of income from real property in medieval merchant fortunes. This is a problem that has already been posed by Professor W. G. Hoskins.[22] He quite rightly warns us against assuming that big real property accumulations were permanent, or even typical of the medieval merchant class. This caution seems justified by the evidence of some of these midland towns.

With this problem in view, let us return to the Coventry survey of 1280, drawn up at a period of rapid economic and population expansion. The sub-letting of properties within the original burgage tenements, to which we have drawn attention, points to the existence of a market in house property. It would be important if we could discover if this market in real property led to its concentration in few hands, to such an extent, for example, that income from real property could sustain, wholly or substantially, an important social group. The survey presents some technical difficulties, preventing us from being sure of an accurate count of all persons and all properties. For one thing, since the statute *Quia emptores terrarum* was not yet passed, a real sub-tenant cannot always be distinguished from a purchaser paying a quit rent. However, one must risk mistakes. It would seem that about five hundred persons or institutions occupied or had rights in real property in the town. There seem also to have been about seven hundred separate occupiable premises. The record, as we have seen, is unusual in that it records many sub-tenants, but the disparity between the number of tenants and the number of properties suggests that many other sub-tenants (or sub-sub-tenants) are unrecorded. Out of some two hundred and sixty or seventy burgages, one hundred and eighty are described as if undivided, an unlikely state of affairs. However this may be, the evidence suggests strongly that (below the chief lord, the Prior) there was very little concentration of properties in few hands. Only sixteen persons held more than the equivalent of five burgages. No religious house or other institution held as much as that.[23] Most significant, those people with the biggest real property holdings seem to have derived rather small net incomes from them. Master Richard Burton and his wife got 56s. 8d., Peter Baroun 39s. 2d., and others whom it would be tedious to enumerate even less. In nearby Warwick, a much smaller town of course, the principal accumulators of real property were the Earl of Warwick with the equivalent of about twenty-seven burgages, and the Collegiate Church of St Mary with some seventeen burgages. By far the biggest individual owner among the burgesses was the Thomas Payn whom we have already mentioned. He had a net revenue from his holdings of only 14s. Thirteenth-century evidence from Stratford, Worcester and Gloucester, mostly charters and deeds, gives no indication there of big accumulations of real property.

This thirteenth-century evidence is too scanty to be conclusive, but what there is leads in the same direction. The more abundant fourteenth and fifteenth-century evidence suggests something of a trend towards a greater concentration of real property holdings, but mostly in the hands of institutions.

The mid-fifteenth-century rental of Gloucester enumerates some five hundred and eighty properties of different types. Of these, monasteries had about two hundred and seventy, town churches, chantries and religious gilds about a hundred, and the borough's stewards twenty-five or thirty. Individuals were much less endowed. Only ten had more than five tenements, the most important being Thomas Deerhurst with eighteen tenements and nine cottages. In Warwick by the fifteenth century the Collegiate Church of St Mary had probably increased its property holdings a good deal since 1280. At the earlier date, as we have seen it had about sixteen burgages; by 1424 its tenants held some sixty-five tenements, various cottages, crofts, gardens and the like. In 1482 the Earl (more like an institution than an urban personality) had more than a hundred and sixty tenants compared with his two dozen in 1280. Some of the Earl's tenants were themselves accumulators of property, holding from him and then (presumably) sub-letting. Such were John Huggeford, esquire, with ten burgages, eight messuages, three cottages, two barns, two gardens and half-a-dozen unoccupied sites. He was probably a tenant of St Mary's as well: his grandfather before him had held three tenements in 1424 from that institution. Another lesser tenant holding from the earl was the Warwick Gild which had two burgages, seven messuages, seven cottages and a croft. This gild probably played a part analogous to that of the Stratford Holy Cross Gild. But the Holy Cross Gild, as we have suggested, emerged by the end of the fifteenth century as a considerable institutional property holder, with more than ninety tenements, cottages, shops and barns in the town.

At the end of the fifteenth century (1486), the Gild of the Holy Trinity in Coventry, by this time the most powerful institution in the town, was receiving rents from nearly four hundred tenants, many of whom, as we have mentioned, were leading merchants. This very sharply contrasts with the apparently wide distribution of real property in 1280. The early fifteenth-century priory rentals show that there were at this date some interesting individual accumulations. The biggest of these was in the hands of a draper, John Preston, who had five tenements in Gosford Street, two in Little Park Street, one each in Smithford Street, Great Park Street, and Westorchard, and some ridges, presumably of arable, in an enclosed croft at the bottom of a garden in St Nicholas Street. Unfortunately, we cannot tell what was the annual rental value to Preston. One of the tenements in Cosford Street which had been divided into four cottages was worth 40s., but there is inadequate data to enable the net income to be calculated. Another merchant, Robert Shipley, had holdings of similar extent, seven tenements and six cottages. William Lusterley, fishmonger, had four tenements and four cottages. John Lyrpole, butcher, had five tenements. Other individual holdings were smaller. Now these priory rentals are not necessarily comprehensive as was the 1280 survey, but they do in fact cover a good deal of ground. It cannot be said that individual property holdings show much advance, as far as concentration is concerned, compared with 1280. It would not seem that the net incomes from property would be very important to the individuals concerned.

Although the biggest individual property accumulators in early fifteenth-century Coventry were merchants, it is worth noting that non-mercantile types are also well represented. We know little about the mercantile community of thirteenth-century Coventry, but Mr Richard

Burton as his title shows, probably was not part of it. He does not even appear as a witness in the borough court as does his contemporary and fellow accumulator, Peter Baroun. John Huggeford of Warwick was a member of a family whose principal function was to serve as officials to the Earls of Warwick.[24] Thomas Deerhurst of Gloucester was a lawyer. Whoever they were, one gets little evidence that any of them could have relied on their urban property holdings to give them an adequate income. Presumably mercantile and industrial profits were such as to attract the bulk of urban capital. Some capital may have been invested in rent charges, though on nothing like the scale found in continental towns. The main trend after the building expansion of the thirteenth century seems to have been towards institutional ownership of the bigger blocks of urban real property, safe investments, the income from which served the social purposes of these institutions. These purposes, of course, included the ritual functions of chantries and religious gilds, not to speak of monasteries; but the gilds also acted as credit institutions, burial clubs political and social organizations. By no means enough is known about what they did with their incomes because few of them left accounts; and most of them, of course, were soon to be expropriated.

13
Towns in English Feudal Society

I shall begin by making some general remarks about the small town as a neglected feature of the medieval urban scene. Since these small towns were, for the most part, component parts of large feudal estates, I shall take the opportunity to move to a further stage of generalization about the role of towns in feudal society as a whole.

There is a tradition in the historiography of the medieval town in England which concentrates on the royal boroughs—mainly the county towns—and, of course, on the city of London. In spite of the fact that there is good documentary evidence for many smaller towns, especially those ruled by feudal landowners, this material has not been fully exploited by professional historians.[1] Given the close connection between small market towns and the rural hinterland it would appear that one useful task that historians concerned with the problems of the medieval peasantry could accomplish would be the analysis of these small urban centers.

As I have suggested elsewhere (1975, ch. V), we may recognize two distinguishable patterns of small town development. In the first, we observe towns—at any rate by the later thirteenth / early fourteenth centuries—which seem to be functionally sharply differentiated from the coutryside. These are towns with perhaps a population of 500 to 1000. The functional specialization is indicated by the fact that there was a range of twenty to thirty non-agricultural occupations which were regarded as the primary occupations of the individuals concerned. Such craftsmen and traders might certainly have been tenants of small quantities of arable and pasture land, of gardens and crofts. But the non-agricultural occupation would have been the principal source of their disposable income. In such a town there might well have been one or two peasant farmers, but they would have been a very small minority. Finally, although these small town populations were functionally dif- ferentiated from their rural hinterlands, there was little specialization within the range of non-agricultural occupations.

Toward the end of the Middle Ages, another type of small town made its appearance. These towns began as industrializing villages from primarily agrarian settlements. For various reasons (which have not been sufficiently investigated), market opportunities, the development of rural crafts, the immigration to the villages of urban craftsmen during a period of urban economic contraction—one finds such places developing in East Anglia, the Midlands, and elsewhere. The industry which stimulated such development was usually woollen textiles, although the metal industry, especially the cutlery trades, also figured in a minority of cases. Naturally, the existence of significant concentrations of specialized producers attracted a range of service occupations, especially in food processing and clothing. In towns of this type one still finds a significant minority of peasants, the survivors of the older economy. These places, of course, were the foci of some of the new industrial developments, away from the regulated urban centers, and represented the 'manufacturing' transition to the industrial capitalism of the factories.

The first type of small town, that which at first glance seems most sharply distinguishable from the agricultural hinterland, evidently developed earlier than the second. It was much more widely established than was once supposed—at any rate before the work of M. W. Beresford and H. P. R. Finberg familiarized us with it (Beresford, 1967; Beresford and Finberg, 1973). Furthermore, since most of these towns were parts of great feudal lordships, a considerable (though by no means complete) documentation survives. This provides an opportunity for the English urban historian which is not exactly matched in countries such as Italy, France, and Germany, where, in other respects, there is a stronger tradition of urban history. The small English seigniorial boroughs, in fact, shared some of the well-known advantages of documentation which have made possible some of the considerable advances in English agrarian history. For although seigniorial boroughs have not left annual accounts analogous with those of the medieval manor, there are not a few rentals and surveys. And, above all, by analogy with the record of the manor court, there are records of their urban equivalents, the portmoot or borough court.

In some cases these court records were better kept, and more continuous over long periods, than comparable records of county boroughs, cathedral towns, and great ports. It is true that, primarily owing to the fact that land held in boroughs, unlike manorial customary land, was alienable without license, there is little evidence for an urban land market. Demographic data are also more difficult to compile, since land in burgage tenure did not lapse into the hands of the lord at the death of the tenant. Nevertheless, small borough courts normally recorded the acquisition of burgage tenures by outsiders, and the purchase from lords of permission to trade. They passed by-laws, provided a forum for litigants in pleas of debt, trespass, detention of chattels, and breach of contract, and through the exercise of leet jurisdiction dealt with petty crime and breaches of the assizes of bread, ale, meat, and fish.

I would like to give a brief example of the possibilities of this type of documentation, the more significant perhaps because of the insignificance of the town concerned. The small town is Thornbury, about ten miles north of Bristol.[2] An agricultural settlement, the original Thornbury, was part of the estate, first of the Earls of Gloucester and, from the early fourteenth century, of the Earls of Stafford, later Dukes of Buckingham. It had a market already in 1086 but was in no way urban in character. At an unknown date in the second half of the thirteenth century (probably between 1243 and 1262), Richard of Clare, Earl of Gloucester, made a general appeal to persons who would be prepared to come to Thornbury, to take up burgage tenements and to enjoy the existing privileges of Tewkesbury, another private borough on the same estate.

Given the rural surroundings of the Severn estuary and the dominating position of the great port and manufacturing centre of Bristol, one would not have been surprised if this attempt had simply resulted, at best, in an enlargement of the existing rural settlement. However, the early sixteenth-century antiquary John Leland remarked: 'There is a market kepte weekly in the toune. And there is a mayre and privileges.... [T]here hathe been good clothyng in Thornbury, but now idelness muche reynithe there' (1964, pt. X, 99). This suggests that there had been more to it, and this is confirmed by the records of the borough court (surviving from 1324) and of a number of surveys by officials of the crown.

These records make clear that this was a town conforming to the first type which I have defined. It was functionally separate from the countryside, its inhabitants sharing between twenty and thirty non-agricultural occupations. This included a small textile industry, which may have been dependent on that of Bristol. Some of the burgesses held some agricultural land although there was very little overlap between the burgesses and the tenants in the nearby manor of the same name—even though some shared family names indicate the manor as one source of recruitment to the borough. This agricultural land must probably have been to a large extent associated with the activities of a group of butchers and graziers who constituted a leading element in the population. Otherwise, the elite who made up the jurors and officials of the court were mainly dealers in grain and malt with a certain interest in inn-keeping and in selling victuals retail. It is of some interest that this elite had virtually no connection with what small industrial element existed there. It conducted its affairs through the borough court, which, though presided over by the lord's steward, was concerned much more with the business of the burgesses than with those of the lord, except when certain of the lord's rights—especially concerning market tolls—were involved.

A declaration of intent to consider towns, great and small, in the context of feudal society implies some form of conceptualization and, inevitably, some consideration of the extent to which conceptualization has found a place in English urban history. This is an appropriate moment to raise this question since urban history is a booming field of study in England. Much of the innovative work in this field is on the modern period (the sixteenth century onwards), but there has been enough writing in the medieval field to encourage the publication in the last five years of two general surveys of the medieval English town. I do not propose to consider these works in detail, but simply to comment on their general approach.

The English Medieval Town by Colin Platt (1976) is written by a historian with archaeological experience. *An Introduction to the Study of Medieval English Towns* by Susan Reynolds (1977) is written by a historian working in the Oxford tradition of political and constitutional history. Both works continue the descriptive, non-theoretical tradition of medieval urban history in England. This tradition has undoubtedly its great names, such that of James Tait, whose authoritative *The Medieval English Borough* (1936) seems to have constituted one of those almost impassable mountain ranges or scholarship on whose slopes lesser historians are likely to die for lack of oxygen. The historians I mention continue this tradition, of which the outstanding feature is not simply the absence of any theoretical framework, but even a reluctance to use any but the most elementary type of generalization as an aid to historical understanding.

It is, of course, possible that medieval English urban historians have been somewhat frightened by the urban sociology of the last forty years, a fear which I must confess is understandable and to some extent justified. It is well analyzed by Philip Abrams, a contemporary sociologist, in a critical article in the recently published *Towns in Societies* (1978). Nevertheless, it is surprising to find that even the well-known sociologically oriented survey of urban history—a work after all with many insights—Lewis Mumford's *City in History* (1961), finds no place in the bibliographies of the two books mentioned. Perhaps even more surprising is the omission of Max Weber's *The City* (1958), a work which, however much it may have been misunderstood, must nevertheless be seen as a *locus classicus* for the identification of some of the specific features of the medieval city.

Even if one were to reject the higher-level theory of professional urban sociologists, there are other types of theory at a lower level which could help to orient the historian of the towns of feudal society. F. W. Maitland was a generalizer of genius, which better accounts for his influence than the 'factual' content of his work. He produced more than one theory about the medieval English town, but a central preoccupation was the understanding of the relationship between town and country. One aspect of this was his 'garrison' theory in which he emphasized the role of warrior representatives of landowning aristocrats in urban communities, where the military role, if it did not entirely account for the mechanisms of control of urban life, was nonetheless important in determining the town's topography (the protective walls) and its population structure (the garrison). He also examined the role of the pre-urban envelope of open-fields which relatively big towns retained, with burgess pasture rights over them, until late in the Middle Ages (Maitland, 1897). Although not a necessary consequence of Maitland's work, this led to assumptions of a theoretical cast by which some urban historians tended to regard the town as essentially an extension of the countryside. Even so good an urban historian as Mary Dormer Harris, editor of the *Coventry Leet Book* and author of a pioneering work on that city's medieval history, was curiously dominated by this theory. 'The townsman,' she wrote, 'was a 'rustic', as Professor Maitland has it, who held some ploughlands in the green fields which engirt the town and together with his fellow burgesses claimed grazing rights over stubble and fallow, meadow, and common pastures' (1908, 144). Dr. Platt retains elements of this theory: 'It was not just that the English town was small; frequently it also retained many rural characteristics that blurred its distinction from the countryside' (1976, 15).

The town-country continuum is, in my view, a non-starter as a model of medieval urbanization, and the writer whom I have quoted does not, in fact, develop this theory—or any other. There is, however, a well-known body of theory which both economic and political historians have employed over many years. This is the theory of the town as essentially antagonistic to the feudal agrarian social order within which, like a pearl in an oyster, it grows. For some, such as Henri Pirenne and his followers, it was so antagonistic to the principles of agrarian feudalism that it had to be brought from outside, by the déclassé merchants who introduced silks, spices, and the desire for monetary profit to the static economy of the feudal West (see Pirenne, 1925; Sweezy, 1976). A not totally dissimilar perception of the medieval city is found in the writings of some French historians who were more concerned with political and institutional than with economic history (see Luchaire, 1911; Petit-Dutaillis, 1947). For them the consequence of developing bourgeois self-consciousness was the urban communal movement of the twelfth century and the location of *seigneuries collectives*, that is, discrete political entities within the feudal world, separate from that world, but possessed of 'parcellized sovereignty' comparable to that of the fief holders. It is no doubt by combining the general outlook on the economic role of the town held by the Pirenne school with that of the political historians of the commune that led Professor M. M. Postan in his *Medieval Economy and Society* to refer to towns as 'non-feudal islands in the feudal seas' (1972, 212).

But could it have been possible for so important an entity as a town to embody economic social and political principles not merely other than, but antagonistic to, the social formation of which it is part? I would like to suggest that one can locate the town closely within the structures of feudal agrarian society, (that is peasant household; village community; lordship, or fief) (see Hilton, 1978); and in so doing see to what extent towns are both part of the feudal social formation and involved in its contradictions—without being *the* principle of contradiction. This will involve analyzing the structures of medieval urban society in a manner analogous to that which I have done for agrarian society.

First, however, I would like to suggest a broad categorization of the medieval town. By this I do not mean that familiar classification into country markets, regional markets, specialist industrial towns, towns dependent on long-distance trade, political centers, ecclesiastical centers, etc. These distinctions, however useful, do not relate the towns closely enough to the essential features of the feudal economy.

I define the first category of towns as being those places which arose from the operation of the simple commodity production of the peasants' economy. These were towns where the surplus from peasant family household production was converted into cash. This was partly, of course, so that peasants could buy salt and manufactured goods which could not be obtained in the village, but mainly so that they could obtain cash for the payment of rent, jurisdictional fines, and tax. Such towns therefore were dominated by the produce market, and by a fairly narrow range of manufacturing crafts in wood, leather, iron, and woollen textiles. The agricultural producers of the hinterland constituted part of the market for these craftsmen, but the latter also serviced those whose interests were in the produce market, namely the small town elite. For, as one would expect in an economy where bulk commodities could not be carried long distance, there were many small places of sale rather than a few large ones.

The quantitative significance of these small market centers is not to be underestimated. At least two-thirds, possibly three-quarters of medieval English towns, by the end of the thirteenth century, were of this type and contained over half of the total urban population. Nor was this peculiar to England. N.J.G. Pounds has shown that in northern Europe at the same period, towns with estimated populations less than 2000 constituted 90% of the total number of towns and at least one-half of the total urban population (1973, 358).

The second category of towns comprises the larger urban centers, though in this classification I am not defining them by size. These towns arose from the combined operations of the feudal ruling class, the state (or statelike formations), and merchant capital. They were the urban by-products, not of the conversion of peasant surplus into the cash which became the income of landowners and the state, but of the expenditure of this surplus after its preliminary realization as cash on the small town market. These urban categories are, of course, to a certain extent analytic. In practice, peasant markets were also contained within the big towns of the second category, although not much landowner or merchant capitalist income was spent in the small town markets.

Let us now consider the internal structure of the towns. The urban economy, like the rural economy, was universally based on the family unit of production and distribution, that is, the artisan workshop or small retail shop (or a combination of both). As in the peasant family economy, there were, in addition to blood relatives, one or two servants, apprentices, and journeymen. In the bigger towns, the craft organizations, fraternities, and guilds acted as mediating structures between the artisans and small traders on the one hand and the urban government on the other. In this they resembled the village communities which acted as mediators between the lords and the peasants. Both the craft fraternities and the village communities were dominated by the richer craftsmen and peasants.

If we are to continue this analogy between rural and urban rural structures, we might ask to what extent we can equate the urban elite with the lords of estates and the rest of the ruling class in feudal society. Of what did these urban elites consist? Clearly they were the great, middling, and small merchant capitalists, people who accumulated money capital as a profit derived from alienation rather than from production—crudely put, from buying cheap and selling dear in the local, regional, and international markets. Naturally, they varied considerably, ranging from the great merchant bankers of places like Florence or Bruges, through those in the middling-sized towns who sold manufactured commodities to a market too wide for the craftsmen to have access, to the small town manipulator of the local produce market.

There were certain resemblances between the merchant capitalists and the feudal lords. First of all, there was the distance from the productive process, which was as characteristic of the merchant capitalist as of the feudal landowner, in spite of the former's role in town government in the legitimation of craft regulations concerning quality, labor input, and raw materials. Secondly, neither feudal landowners nor merchant capitalists showed any propensity to invest. This was as much because of the impenetrability of the family unit of production by outside forces as of the subjective attitudes of lords and merchants—not, of course, that these two factors were unconnected.

The differences, however, were considerable. The income of the merchant capitalists did not directly depend, as in the case of the feudal landowner, on the appropriation of surplus labor or the fruits thereof. It depended on the fulfillment of a middle-man function. This function was exercised in the middle- or long-distance sales of such products of artisan industry as could command a wide market, and in the provision of a wide variety of commodities for the population in general at various marketing levels. The big money was, however, primarily in the provision of luxuries for royal and aristocratic courts. Secondarily, it was made in making loans to the aristocracies and the state, partly to tide them over the time gap between the flow of income from rent and tax and expenditure on largesse and the like, but above all to finance military activity, easily the most costly of all state, if not of private aristocratic, expenditure.

Given that much of the merchant capitalists' profit was made from the provision of aristocratic households, it could be said that they were living indirectly off peasant surplus, and would naturally be affected by changes in the balance of power between lords and peasants and consequently in the disposable real income of the landowners. The nature and destination of profit from artisan industry is not so clear, but given the fact that the merchants did not normally invest capital in the craftsman's workshop, we must regard merchant's profit as a middleman's appropriation of part of the gains of the family enterprise. This family enterprise did, however, contain within it certain other forms of exploitation, not simply of the journeyman as a properly paid wage-labourer, but of the apprentice as a labourer who was paid no wages, or very low wages, during the period between the end of his training in the craft and the formal end of the apprenticeship.

A final distinguishing feature between merchant capitalists and feudal lords is somewhat problematic. Did merchant capitalists exercise political domination? This, of course, brings us to the essence of the problem of the role of the town in feudal society. At first glance, it would seem that the feudal powers recognized that their form of political domination was inappropriate in the bigger towns which had acquired various levels of self-government. On the other hand, it could be argued that the merchant capitalists were so dependent on the landed aristocracy and the feudal monarchy as their principal market that they must always have been politically subordinate. But was there, in fact, a political division of labour? What was the direct role of the feudal ruling class in the towns?

A primary role was evidently in the small market towns, to which reference has already been made. The great majority of these towns were 'seigniorial boroughs,' and to them should be added some larger towns which, in spite of economic development, had not obtained the relative autonomy of the royal boroughs. Well-known examples include Bury St. Edmunds of Suffolk and St. Albans (Herts.), which remained subject to the abbots of the Benedictine monasteries of those places, and even Coventry until its mid-fourteenth century incorporation. Whatever the discontents, however, of these bigger seigniorial towns, they did have some considerable measure of self-rule and cannot be taken as typical of seigniorial boroughs as a whole (see Lobel, 1935; Lobel, 1969; Coss, 1974).

What did seigniorial control mean in the case of the smaller towns? Rent income paid to the lord for houses and stalls may not have been of great significance, nor did the conditions of burgage tenure yield any significant profits on alienation or inheritance. However, if a burgage lapsed into the lord's hands for lack of heirs, an incoming tenant might have to pay an entry fine. He, and any persons wanting the trading privileges of burgesses, would also have to pay to the lord a fee to enjoy the 'liberty of the borough.' Such admissions to the liberty also imply an element of seigniorial control on entrants to the borough community. Perhaps the most important financial return was from tolls paid on market transaction by non-burgesses. A money income also came from the exercise of jurisdiction. The borough court was presided over by the lord's steward who supervised the levying of amercements and fines, and maintained the lord's rights. All these were tangible benefits, to which should be added the intangible, probably hardly realized, importance of the market as the place where rural tenants would acquire cash from sales in order to pay rent.

The lord's officials in the borough court were at as much of a distance from the producing and trading population as they were from the peasant family holding. As in the case of the village community, the local officials and the juries of presentment and inquisition who were chosen from the members of the small town community, acted as mediators between the lords and the burgesses. As one reads the records of the three-weekly borough courts and of the biennial courts leet, one perceives the element of control, even under the eye of the lord's steward, which these men must have had as they presented offenders, passed by-laws, and regulated the flow of immigrants. Normally, the lord and burgesses would adjust their interests to each other through the maintenance of the burgesses' monopoly of the market and of the lord's right to toll revenue, although frictions could occur.

If the feudal presence was dominant in most of the small market towns, to what extent was it excluded from the chartered boroughs? Was the 'parcellized sovereignty' which they have been said to enjoy sufficiently complete to separate the burgesses as a political entity from the feudal order? Could the burgesses within this protected shell develop forces, means, and relations of production which would contradict and eventually destroy feudalism?

To answer the question, we should first consider the role of the feudal monarchy. We should not, however, concern ourselves with the crown as the embodiment of public as against private authority. We are concerned with the socio-economic character of the state, not with its administrative or political competence. Therefore we must treat the crown as a particular manifestation of the feudal order. In medieval England the corporate liberties of most of the bigger towns were granted by royal charter in return not only for a heavy lump sum down but for the payment of an annual farm or rent (*firma burgi*). This farm was a composition for the various sums which the officials of the crown as lords of the town had previously collected, consisting of house and stall rents, profits of the market, profits of the courts, and so on. It was paid over to the Exchequer by the elected town bailiffs (whom the crown regarded as its own officials) and constituted a sufficient levy on the town's resources for constant pleas to be made for reduction, especially after the mid-fourteenth-century demographic crisis. At various periods, the hand of the feudal monarchy on the chartered towns was more or less heavy, but this feature of the feudal presence must not be neglected when we consider the place of the town in the feudal social order.

The feudal monarchy tolerated a system of borough courts which was as separate from the crown's jurisdictional system as was the private jurisdiction of territorial landowners, with the usual reservations to the royal courts of pleas of the crown. In fact, borough custom tended as much to preserve archaic elements in law as to innovate. It can hardly be regarded as an anti-feudal force. But in any case, the monarchy used the borough courts in their political and administrative aspects as well as in their judicial function. Out of earlier undifferentiated borough courts there developed not only specialized tribunals, but governing councils. Both were used by the crown as organs of social control. It protected the oligarchic privileges of the ruling merchant capitalist elites against the political discontents of the middling and lower ranks of the craft producers, retailers, and wage-workers. In the early 1390s, when such a conflict broke out in Lincoln, the king appointed a commission of Lincolnshire landowners to settle the matter—in the interests of the 'high and mighty persons' of the oligarchy (see Hill, 1948). This typified royal attitudes to social conflict in the towns. The urban oligarchies were further strengthened when many of them, following Bristol in 1373, were made into counties and the mayor and his close associates given the powers of Justices of the Peace.

In most large chartered boroughs there was also a feudal presence of the older type. The overlords of burgage tenements, who were such a marked feature of the Domesday borough, may have faded somewhat into the background in later centuries, but the aristocratic territorial interest was never eliminated, and in some respects was strengthened. It was, however, of a special character. The principal owners of urban property and jurisdictional enclaves who belonged to the feudal landed ruling class were ecclesiastical persons and corporations. This resulted from a considerable transfer of property from the lay feudality in the form of pious donations as well as from grants of privileges of one sort and another. It is true that some important lay magnates kept property and jurisdictions, such as the Berkeley fee in the industrial suburb of Redcliffe, south of the Avon in Bristol, or the property and jurisdictions exercised in Warwick by the Beauchamp earls (see Seyer, 1823).[3] But for the most part, the most tenacious and independent representatives of feudal landed society were bishops, cathedral monasteries or colleges of canons, and monastic houses.

The most striking jurisdictional and tenurial enclaves in the large towns were those of the bishops and cathedrals, whose tenants had dual loyalties to their overlords and to the borough community. There was hardly a cathedral town where problems did not arise from this ecclesiastical presence. At Norwich and at Coventry, for example, conflict between the townspeople and the cathedral, not over religion but over jurisdiction, lasted throughout the Middle Ages. These two towns were not exceptional. It is also worth noting that the crown normally supported the ecclesiastical side in the quarrels. In cathedral towns and in others, there were also property interests of monastic landowners. St. Mary's Abbey in York, St. Augustine's in Canterbury, Hyde Abbey and two nunneries in Winchester are to be added to the already powerful interests of bishop and cathedral monks or canons. St. Peter's Abbey in Gloucester, St. Mary des Prés in Leicester, St. Werburgh's in Chester are good examples of the social and economic power, as well as the physical presence, of ecclesiastical (that is, in terms of the social formation, feudal) landowners within the larger towns. Most other county towns or towns of comparable size had similar, if smaller, communities of monastic land-owners within their walls or in their suburbs. (See Hudson and Tingey, 1906-10; Harris, 1898; Urry, 1967; Biddle, 1976; Fulbrook-Legatt, 1952; Bateson, 1899; Lobel, 1969, 1975).

There was also what may justly be described as a feudal encroachment on the market in many towns, another aspect of the transfer of resources by pious donation from the lay powers to the church. A well-known example of this is the September fair of St. Giles in Winchester, which monopolized, to the profit of the bishop, all trade in the city and in a seven-league radius for nearly two weeks (see Biddle, 1976). Fairs and markets on a more modest scale, whose profits were appropriated by religious institutions were found in many other towns, such as St. James Priory's fair in Bristol, or the three Norwich fairs controlled respectively by the cathedral priory, the abbess of Carrow, and the Magdalen Hospital or at Northampton the abbot of St. James's fair and the possession of the tithe of the All Saints fair by the priory of St. Andrew (see Bickley, 1900; Hudson and Tingey, 1906-10; Cam, 1930).

The ecclesiastical enclaves were probably the most important aspects of the feudal presence within the chartered towns. We should not, however, forget the town castles, many of which had their origin at the time of the Norman Conquest, when entire quarters of burgess tenements were destroyed to make way for them. The castle area was usually jurisdictionally separate from the area governed by the borough courts. In many towns, it is true, these castles represented royal power rather than that of the feudal magnates. They were often the head-quarters of the country sheriffs. But sheriffs were not impersonal public servants. Recruited from the lesser aristocracy, they were sometimes the direct nominees of feudal potentates (as at Worcester) rather than of the crown. Sometimes the potentates excluded them from the castle in the county town. The sheriff of the jointly administered counties of Warwick and Leicester had his headquarters in Kenilworth Castle. The castles at Warwick and Leicester were occupied respectively (from the late thirteenth century) by the earls of Warwick and earls (later dukes) of Lancaster. There was no sheriff at Bristol before it became a county of a town, but the castle and the royal constable constituted an unmistakable —and interfering—feudal presence in the town. The citizens of Lincoln attempted, for good reasons, to break down the separate jurisdiction of the duke of Lancaster's castle constable in the bail, but they were entirely unsuccessful.

If we consider English medieval towns as a whole, including the market towns as well as the larger centers, it is clear that we cannot think of them as nonfeudal islands within a feudal sea. Nor can we envisage the social and economic interests of the medieval burgesses as being in fundamental and developing antagonism to the interests of the feudal state and its land-owning ruling class. Town elites were, of course, frequently quarreling with feudal lords as well as with royal castellans. But quarrels between holders of rival jurisdictions were a medieval commonplace. We should regard the urban economy as an integral part of the feudal-seigniorial economy as a whole. As we have seen, the various levels of operation of the feudal seigniorial economy produced a variety or urban types. Urbanization at the level of the small market town was the necessary consequence of peasant simple commodity production within the framework of, and subject to, the demands of feudal lordship. At the level of the county and cathedral towns, of the provincial and national capitals, and even of the more specialized industrial towns, urbanization was the consequence of the disbursement of agrarian surplus by crown and aristocracy, and of the profits from the middleman function of large, middling, and small merchant capitalists.

The dynamic, therefore, of feudal society is not to be found in some town-country or burgess-feudal lord antagonism; it is to be found first in the antagonism between lords and peasants in the act of the appropriation of the unretained portion or surplus of peasant production. It is to be found, secondly, in the distance between family-based peasant and artisan production and the feudal and merchant capitalist appropriators, a distance which constituted an inescapable weakness for the appropriators. It was because of this weakness, which the armed power of the rulers tends to conceal, that in the complex conjuncture of social, demographic, and political difficulties of the late Middle Ages, petty commodity production in agriculture and industry was able to thrive, to generate social differentiation, and to lay the basis for transformation of a capitalist character.

14

The Small Town and Urbanisation—
Evesham in the Middle Ages

Evesham in Worcestershire, famed for its abbey, and in modern times as the centre of a market gardening region, does not naturally spring to mind as an example of a certain level of medieval urbanisation. This however is an important aspect of its medieval history as was the case too of its better known neighbour, Stratford-on-Avon. It was part of the estate of the ancient and prestigious Benedictine Abbey of Evesham, and this, like the other Avon valley towns of Warwick, Stratford, Pershore and Tewkesbury was a seigneurial borough, integrated into the system of feudal land ownership (using the term 'feudal' in its wider meaning).

By the end of the peak period of medieval urbanisation in the late 13th century, some two-thirds of the English boroughs were 'seigneurial', mostly small market towns under the rule of a lay or ecclesiastical lord.[1] Probably a half of the urban population of the country lived in these small towns, which, as I have argued elsewhere, were, in spite of their small size, genuinely urban in character.[2]

In the three west midland counties of Worcester, Gloucester and Warwick nearly 90 per cent of the boroughs were seigneurial and most of them were small market towns. Given the poor quality of the evidence for demographic calculation it is very risky to make estimates of population, but it would seem likely that in the later middle ages most of them would have had less than 1000 inhabitants. As we shall see, Evesham was probably one of the more populous. Whatever its specific features as an abbey town and a river-port it can be taken as characteristic of the small centres which were so important in the urbanisation of medieval England.

Let us return to consider those characteristics which made Evesham, quite early on, a borough with a commercial and industrial rather than purely agricultural function.

Evesham had already been granted by the King the privileges of a market and the designation of *port* (market town) in 1055—at any rate according to the writer of the Chronicle of Evesham Abbey.[3] It was not however described as a borough in Domesday Book (1086), nor were its inhabitants referred to as 'burgesses' as they were in Pershore; but as has recently been pointed out, urban recording in Domesday Book is very patchy.[4] Nevertheless, near contemporary evidence suggests that Evesham might, by the end of the 11th century, contain property held by burgess tenure. In one of the Evesham Abbey cartularies a reference is made to illegal grants of *mansure* (house sites) in the borough *(de burgo)* by abbots Robert (1086-1096) and Maurice (1096-1122).[5] It is not impossible that these *mansure* of the turn of the 11th / 12th centuries were those which later became designated as *burgagia* in the 13th century documents in one of the cartularies of the Abbey.[6] But the fact that the term 'burgage' is not used in the earlier (late 12th century)[7] cartulary— where the phrase *'mansuras de burgo'* is continued—does not exclude the probability that borough tenants enjoyed elements of standard burgage tenurial privileges. This means, of course, that they would have freedom of legal status, freedom of alienation and, in general exemption from irksome conditions of tenure characteristic of either military or custom- ary peasant holdings.

As important, in indicating urban status, as these forms of tenure, are the occupations of the inhabitants. In 1086 there was still an agricultural element, as one would expect near a abbey of ancient foundation in a previously entirely rural area. There were plough-teams working the abbey home farm and some of the tenants had plough-teams. These were not, however, the normal type of agricultural tenant—*villani*. Instead the tenant population consisted of small holders *(bordarii)* who were described as abbey servants *(servientes curie)* and 'men' who payed the abbey a fixed money rent. Some of the bordars would, of course, be responsible for agricultural work on the home farm, but much of this population must have constituted a service element brought into existence by the needs of the monastic community.

A century later the rental of the town suggests a considerable occupational heterogeneity which was unlikely to have developed suddenly. There were at least twenty occupational designations of a non-agricultural character attributed to the tenants of properties. These include artisans such as weavers, fullers, carpenters, smiths and a parchment maker, as well as persons in the victualling trades, such as bakers, cooks, fishmongers, vintners and millers. There were two 12th-century mills leased by the millers from the abbey, one at Evesham Bridge and one at Hampton Bridge.[8] These are not, of course, necessary signs of urbanisation but they suggest a concentration of economic activity at the town.

Finally, as a further indication of Evesham's urban status, we may mention that the town sent burgess representatives to the Parliaments of 1295 and 1337.[9] The town was, however, too small to have burgesses in normal medieval parliamentary assemblies, but this representation on two crucial occasions indicates a recognition of the town's burghal character. It might also be mentioned that Evesham also presented offenders before the royal justices of assize as a separate borough within the county.[10]

Evesham grew steadily. Valuation in 1086 was £5 10s.0d, an increase on that of £3 0s.0d in 1066. The valuation of £26 for Pershore in 1086, with its 28 burgesses, cannot be reliably compared with that of Evesham because it is clear that in the Pershore valuation there was a bigger agricultural element than at Evesham.[11]

During the 12th century it would seem that growth had continued. The late 12th century rental already mentioned shows that north of the river there were 234 tenants distributed in the different centres of settlement. These were in 'Evesham', probably the urbanised area around Bridge Street where there were 98 tenants; 'Barton', the area immediately dependent on the abbey, around Merstow Green, with 91 tenants; the 'New Borough', probably west of High Street, 15 tenants; and 'Rynehill', probably north of 'Evesham' on the east side of High Street. There were also 65 abbey servants, some of whom may have been included in the Barton section of the rental. The description of Bengeworth, south of the river, with its sixteen and a half yardlands burdened with labour services, at first sight hardly suggests an urbanised suburb[12] —and yet there were also 27 *bordarii* most of whom were paying the urban-type money rent of 12d. a year. For the most part only fore-names are given, but two of them are described as smiths.

It is interesting to note too that the tenants of the New Borough and Rynehill were paying 12d. money rents, or multiples or fractions thereof. As is well known,[13] the 12d. urban money rent was a common feature of burgage tenure in the 12th century. The appearance of this standard rent suggests that New Borough and Rynehill, perhaps even the lower end of Bengeworth, were planned extensions to the old borough.

The 1206 rentals printed in the Abbey Chronicle[14] give a further flavour of urban life around this time. These show what properties yielded income to the monastic obedientiaries. One of the most interesting of these is the kitchener's expectation of 5s. 3d. every Saturday from the Evesham market—a proportion, no doubt, of income from tolls and stall rents. Not that stalls were only to be found in the market. The sacrist and the almoner each had rents from stalls before the cemetery gate, and the almoner had two ovens in which tenants of the borough were obliged to bake their bread.

By about 1200, then, there would have been in Evesham some 250 to 300 tenants. If these were heads of households with wives, children and servants the population would have been more rather than less than 1000—above average for the normal run of small market towns. This growth almost certainly continued throughout the 13th century, principally by rural immigration. We cannot calculate the population from the tax returns of 1275, but about a quarter of the taxpayers' surnames indicate a rural origin. By the tax of 1332 this proportion was nearer a half.[15]

The lack of reliable population figures does not mean that we are at a loss to estimate growth—not absolute growth but at any rate comparative growth. We can in fact compare Evesham's wealth with that of other Avon valley towns by looking at their relative taxable capacity.

According to the tax of 1275, for which only the Worcestershire returns survive, Evesham had three times the taxable capacity of Pershore and 91 taxpayers as against Pershore's 74. The following figures from the returns of 1334 and 1523-4 give a useful indication of the relative progress of Evesham and other small towns of the region, besides Pershore, such as Winchcombe and Warwick. In particular, Evesham compares well with two Warwickshire towns, known for their dynamic growth during this period, Birmingham and Stratford.

Town	Amount of Tax † in 1334	Amount of Tax ‡ in 1523-4	Persons Taxed in 1523-4
Evesham	£8 5s. 6d.	£25 7s. 0d.	121
Pershore	£4 4s. 0d.	£10 9s. 2d.	78
Stratford	£8 14s. 0d.	£29 8s. 10d.	91
Warwick	£13 3s. 0d.	£14 17s. 11d.	c.130
Winchcombe	£7 2s. 0d.	£8 10s. 4d.	130
Birmingham	£9 8s. 0d.	£23 9s. 6d.	153

†—Stratford, Warwick and Winchcombe were taxed in 1334 at 1/10th of the value of moveable goods. The other places were taxed at 1/15th. The figures have all been adjusted to 1/15th.
‡—The amount of money paid by Warwick in 1523-4 is taken from another list than that giving the number of persons, though purporting to be of the same date.

What lay behind Evesham's growth? The initial impulse and continuing expansion probably owed much to the demand by the abbey for goods and services. At the end of the 12th century, in addition to the 65 servants already mentioned, the monastery contained 55 monks, 5 nuns and 3 clerks. Some of the servants were, of course, producers as well as consumers, such as bakers, brewers, gardeners, tailors, shoemakers and fishermen. Others, such as the porters and the domestic staff, would contribute to the consumer demand. The numbers of monks in the old-established Benedictine houses fell considerably in the later middle ages. Evesham's monastic population, however, stood up well. At the election of Abbot Richard Bromsgrove in 1418, there were still 32 monks, though these included two scholars at Oxford, the Prior of Penwortham and a colleague from Lancashire.[16] Abbey demand like that of any set of consumers of their social class, included imported luxuries. In the 15th century for example, the abbots were bringing wine direct from London. That does not mean that there were no local vintners. Several of them were presented in 1275 probably for serving short measure to local customers.[17] But most important was the abbey's role, direct and indirect in stimulating local production (including cloth), not to speak of food processing.

The abbey's indirect influence as a great local landowner on the Evesham market was probably very considerable. It owned most of the land in the villages of the Vale of Evesham to the east of the town, as well as having important properties in the Cotswolds. The tenants on these estates owed money rent for their holdings as well as paying other dues and jurisdictional fines in cash. Already at the end of the 12th century, the rentals show considerable cash obligations from tenants, as well as labour services. The latter could be, and probably often were, commuted for money. By the 14th century, such information as we have—a collection of leases over the estate as a whole, probably dated 1369[18] and a record of some properties of the chamberlain in the Cotswolds in 1373[19] show the total victory of money rent. The implication of this is, of course, that tenants had to find cash by selling their produce (surplus to subsistence and reproduction) on local markets, either directly or through cornmongers, woolmongers and cattle dealers. Evesham market, as well as such other markets as Stow-on-the-Wold would be stimulated on the supply side. The grain market would naturally flourish, with interesting side-lights. In 1275 we find a local grain dealer prosecuted as a usurer.[20] The offence is not clearly described but it looks as though he was making a loan of grain and charging above the market price in order to conceal the interest on the loan.

One would expect Evesham, situated in a rich agricultural area, to be a market for foodstuffs. What is also interesting is evidence that it was a cloth manufacturing centre. Cloth making was of course ubiquitous. Most towns, even small ones, had some textile craftsmen producing for a local market. The two Evesham Abbey cartularies already cited indicate the presence of textile craftsmen in the 12th century and in the proceedings before the royal justices in 1275 there are references to a dyer and to eight men selling cloth 'against the assize' (possibly short measure again). But some later evidence implies quite a strong textile development suggesting the service of a regional rather than a purely local market.

This evidence is from the accounts in 1400 of the royal ulnager who collected tax on clothes offered for sale.[21] The reliability of these accounts has often been criticized and ulnagers, clearly, were as corrupt as most officials of the medieval state. Nevertheless their returns were more likely to underestimate (in their own interests) than overestimate their receipts. Here there are the numbers of sellers of cloth in various Worcestershire towns:

Worcester	— 46 sellers of cloth
Evesham	— 36
Pershore	— 8
Droitwich	— 7
Tenbury	— 7
Kidderminster	— 3

Ulnagers' returns fluctuate from year to year so that these figures cannot be taken as a permanent record of Evesham's importance, but they nevertheless indicate its prominence as a maufacturing centre.

How was the borough of Evesham governed? The evidence is scanty, so the subject is obscure. From scattered indications it would appear that its government was similar to that of most seigneurial boroughs. A steward appointed by the abbot presided over the borough court, known as the portmoot. If it was similar to other borough courts, it would meet about twelve or thirteen times a year with one or two special sessions of the court leet, or view of frankpledge.[22] The townsmen chose two bailiffs who would be responsible for day-to-day administration. We do not know whether the two parishes (St. Laurence and All Saints) were treated as two wards for administrative purposes, but this is possible. In 1523 they were the topographical units for the collection of the royal subsidy[23]

In some seigneurial boroughs, a gild or fraternity became the focus of the burgess élite, a sort of shadow government additional to the official borough court. Such was the case with the Holy Cross Gild at Stratford-on-Avon.[24] There are some 16th century references to the lands of a Holy Trinity Gild at Evesham. It is not to be found in the gild returns of 1389, nor among the gild and chantry certificates of 1549. But what then was the origin of the Gild Hall said to be located at the south-west corner of the Bridge?[25]

Without the records of the portmoot, it is difficult to say to what extent the abbot maintained firm control of the town, for the power of landowners could be less real than apparent—in a quiet way urban (even village) élites could get their own way. However, there are indications that in Evesham, feudalism was alive and well in the late middle ages. The abbot and convent seem to have maintained their control of the borough land market as well as that of the villages of the rural estate. Such seems to be the conclusion one would draw from the list of leases, already referred to, made in 1369 when Roger Yatton was cellarer (later he became abbot, 1379-1418). But abbots also looked to their seigneurial rights. In 1362, a townsman named William of Tetbury tried to set up his own baking oven. This would have competed with the monopoly enjoyed by the almoner, who (as we have seen) had two ovens in the town to which all inhabitants had to bring their bread to be baked. Abbot William Boys (1345-67) had Tetbury's oven destroyed. In 1389, Abbot Roger Yatton confiscated the querns which various townsmen had acquired to grind their own malt. About the same time he rebuilt the Evesham malt mill[26]

Evesham, like Stratford-on-Avon, was a town subjected to the overlordship of a feudal landowner. Nevertheless, both towns seemed to prosper during the later middle ages. This prosperity can, of course, only be judged in comparison with other similar towns of the neighbourhood, all of which were subject to the same sort of seigneurial constraints. Yet the advance of Evesham and Stratford contrasts sharply with the apparent stagnation of Warwick ad Winchcombe—judging at any rate by the uneven development of taxable capacity between 1334 and 1524. Factors other than seigneurial control must therefore be taken into account, and these could be multiple—ease of communications, prosperity of the immediate region, local competition (Coventry, for example, with Warwick). The prospects for further investigation are considerable.

15

Lords, Burgesses and Hucksters

William Langland's poem, *Piers Plowman,* is famous for being vivid and concrete in its depiction of a range of social types. Whether we should be suspicious of this 'concreteness' is still a matter for discussion. We may be certain that Langland was not interested in presenting a work of social realism. The concern of the poem is mankind's search for salvation. This involves him deeply with the problem of sin. But as any student of the penitential system of the medieval church or of the abundant 'estate' literature well knows, sin for medieval Christians was firmly placed in the context of social obligations. The treatment of sin in Christian poetry hovers ambiguously between symbolism and realism. The sharper the depiction of the social context of the sin and the sinner, the more likely it was to strike home. No symbol would be meaningful if it did not connect with life's experience. The symbols and images of Langland are still powerful because they related to his life and, we must suppose, the life of the people in his audience.[1]

However much Langland, like other medieval poets, may have continued earlier images, we cannot but suppose that his perception of his folk was rooted in his own experience of life, of which we know nothing, outside of what is said in the poem itself. It is of particular interest, given the location of some of the source material for this article, that he seems to have had some connection with the area of the Malvern Hills on the boundary between Worcestershire and Herefordshire. More important it seems likely that he spent time as a minor cleric in London, one of Europe's major cities with 45,000 to 50,000 inhabitants—a capital, an industrial centre, a port. As such his social milieu would have been at the bottom of the social scale, perhaps, not unlike that of François Villon in Paris—though the effect on the work and thought of the two poets differed profoundly.[2]

Like other critical writers of his time, Langland was much concerned with self-interest, corruption, the lust for money. The affairs of Lady Mede are powerfully presented. But these unpleasant vices are not so much represented in his verse by the really big monied people of late fourteenth-century England—rich landowners, merchant patricians, wealthy knights—as by petty traders, those who fill the Fair Field Full of Folk, whom we discover in the symbolic depiction of the seven deadly sins, who are symbolized later in the poem by Haukyn the active man, a baker, representing 'sinful and repentant humanity'.[3] Upper-class types do appear, of course, especially the ecclesiastics, but it is petty rather than large-scale corruption which the author seems to feel most vividly.

This could, of course, be explained in terms of the experience of a poor cleric in a big city. It would be the cheating of the petty trader which would be felt rather than the more remote exploitation by the landowners and the patrician élite, such as those who were indicted in the Good Parliament of 1376 and of whom Langland was obviously aware. But could there be more to it than that? Were petty traders at the forefront of Langland's imagination, not simply because they were inclined to cheat but because they constituted a more important element in the economy and society than historians have supposed? When we think of medieval town life we tend to have in our minds the merchants, craftsmen and journeymen, the producers and the more important traders. We think, too, of bakers and brewers, because the urban authorities, being so anxious to keep down the price of food and the cost of labour, regulated these trades perhaps more than any others. They appear before us, because like the merchants, craftsmen and journeymen, they figure prominently in the documents. But it is in prosecutions against them for cheating that we find them, so that our perception of them is distorted. Does this explain why a translator of Langland converts 'Rose the regrator' (that is, retail trader), wife of Covetyse, into 'Rose the racketeer'.[4]

If Langland knew the Malvern Hills as well as London, his experience of English urban and commercial, not to speak of rural, life must have embraced much more than the streets of the capital. We must therefore consider these other English towns and markets, and thus ask 'How urbanized was England outside London?'.

If we concentrated our attention on the leading boroughs, the places assumed to differ from the countryside by the character of their corporate life,[5] we should perhaps assume a rather low level of urbanization—in the late 1370 only four towns with 8,000 to 15,000 inhabitants, only eight between 5,000 and 8,000, only twenty-seven between 2,000 and 5,000. But then there were some five hundred small boroughs with populations between, say, 500 and 2,000, and probably more market towns without any burghal status.[6] In addition there were many village markets held weekly in settlements where arable cultivation and stock raising predominated, but which by their existence indicated a significant degree of commercialization of the economy. It is best to demonstrate this on a regional scale, partly because the information for all England has not been fully collected, partly because of regional variation and partly because the implications of this commercialization are best appreciated at this limited level. The three west midland counties of Gloucestershire, Warwickshire and Worcestershire, with a geographical, cultural and historical unity which has already been sketched, had 47 towns, or to use the contemporary legal terminology, 'boroughs'. These had occupational structures which clearly distinguished them from the agricultural hinterland. But in that agricultural hinterland there were

112 village markets. We cannot know anything about the volume of transactions going through these markets but at any rate we know of their existence because the lords of these villages had thought it worth while to buy charters which enabled them to profit from them.[7]

Most of these west midland boroughs and markets were—as in other regions—closely associated with the seigneurial economy. There is hardly need now to insist that an incompatibility between a dynamic and market-oriented urban sector, and feudal landed society, is an outdated concept. Nonetheless the general conclusion is worth illustrating at this local and regional level. The west midland example demonstrates well how lords of estates seized opportunities given to them by the increasing market orientation of the economy. To summarize the causes briefly: there were important surpluses produced by the predominantly peasant economy over its subsistence needs; there was a growing number of people ranging from poor wage-earners to well-to-do ecclesiastics who did not produce their own subsistence; the ruling class had an ever-expanding need for cash to spend on military equipment and the luxuries provided by international trade; and (coming round in full circle) there was an ever-increasing need by peasants for cash in order to pay money rent, jurisdictional fines and state taxes. A boom in marketing was inevitable, which, by the turn of the thirteenth century, was reflected in an immense increase in the volume of small change (such as farthings) produced by the mints, as well as being reflected, archaeologically, by increased amounts of small coins found on a whole range of excavated sites.[8]

It has been suggested in other regional studies that the pattern of markets to some extent reflects the pattern of landed estates.[9] Perhaps it reflects even more the nature of seigneurial domination. This certainly seems to be the case if one analyses the social character of the founders of markets and boroughs in the west midlands. These are given as percentages of foundations.

	Markets	*Boroughs*
Bishops	5	4
Monastic lords	23	32
Barons	47	51
Local lords	25	13

Apart from the financial resources available, it might be thought that baronial foundations were to some extent motivated by considerations of status.[10] This would be particularly important in borough foundation. In the case of monastic lords, the permanence of their presence as well as their devotion to estate building would no doubt be a more important factor than status.

It should be emphasized, of course, that the conditions and the reasons for the foundation of village markets on the one hand, and boroughs on the other, were by no means identical. In many cases the chartered market in the village would be the institutionalization of an existing informal market, probably held on Sundays, in spite of frequent official prohibitions.''There would be good reasons for this formalization, certainly the collection of tolls, perhaps a realization that a convenient market would help the flow of money rent by easing sales of agricultural surplus. However, weekly village markets (and the annual fairs with which they were often associated in foundation charters) were occasional events. The borough was intended to be something more. Often preceded by a market grant, it represented an initiative, presumably by the lord or his advisers, aimed at encouraging not only a market but the growth of a stable and permanent body of resident craftsmen, food processors and providers of various services. This was done by offering burgess status, with all its supposed advantages, to the new inhabitants and (this was much cherished) by giving them the monopoly of the market.

Lords, in creating boroughs, also provided the conditions for the operation of petty traders—hucksters—who were the inevitable intermediaries between peasant producers and consumers of various social origins (including peasants). Hucksters aspired, inevitably, to burgess status and not infrequently acquired it. What can we say about them?

Hucksters were largely, though not exclusively, concerned with the provision of food, drink and, to a lesser extent, clothing. These were the items which constituted the major expenditure for those who did not produce, and had to buy, their means of subsistence. These hucksters were particularly prominent in the small and middling-sized market towns, in relation to the rest of the population, *seeming* to be less prominent in the bigger towns. The surviving documentation of the larger towns very much concerns such matters as the control (through craft organizations) of industry and trade in more expensive commodities than those dealt with by hucksters, not to speak of matters of public order, taxation and litigation about debt and contract. Nevertheless there was a preoccupation with the regulation of victuals, that is, of the primary commodities of retail trade.

The mayor of Bristol had a life in which administration and ceremony were much intertwined, described with loving care by Robert Ricart. According to Ricart, once the mayor received his charge at Bristol Castle from the Constable and had processed around the city sustained by cakes and wine, he spent two days hearing the oaths of the leading officials; he then received the oaths of chantry priests and of the newly elected Masters of the crafts. The first, and the only named, crafts were the bakers, brewers and butchers. Then came all other crafts, unnamed. According to another record, one of the mayor's first duties after Michaelmas was to discuss the price of malt with all Bristol brewers and to set a lower price if prices were high due to shortage. Subsequently he was to visit, on the mornings of shifting days of the week, in company with the official ale-conners, all those serving ale. The traditional oath of the mayor of Coventry emphasizes just as clearly the prominence of victualling in official concern. He was to keep the peace, maintain the franchise, regulate the assize of bread, ale, wine and all victuals and do equal right to rich and poor. His only precise commitment, in fact, was victual regulation[12]

One of the unfortunate deficiencies of much urban documentation is the disappearance of those records of the courts leet which state the ordinary presentments by juries of petty offences, especially concerning the sale of victuals and other items in the budgets of the poor. Where they do survive, the prominence of the retail trader once again stands out. The leet jurisdiction of Norwich provides useful figures. The spread of commodities sold retail is well illustrated. There are corn dealers, sellers of dairy products, fishmongers, poulterers, chandlers, cooks, brewers, butchers, bakers and second-hand clothes dealers. The numbers involved are striking—290 brewers fined from six leet areas and 84 fishmongers from one leet in 1288-9, 250 brewers in 1312-13. The brewers, as is well known, were a special case since, more than with other victualling trades, ale was sold from the surplus of production of households which were not full-time brewers but engaged also in other activities. Comparative figures are made more difficult because sometimes all traders are reported as fined—all second-hand clothes dealers, for instance, in Conesford ward in 1312-13. But figures are given for one ward ('Over the water') in the same year—11 grain dealers, 13 dealers in cheese, butter and eggs, 11 second-hand clothes dealers, 7 poulterers, 10 chandlers, 14 butchers, 19 cooks—as compared with 52 brewers from the same ward. Their delinquency varied in character. The victuallers were mainly fined for forestalling the market, the butchers for not using official measures, the chandlers for deficient products, the cooks for warming up food cooked two or three days back, the clothes dealers for dubbing old cloth with fullers' blocks, and the brewers for selling against the assize and by illegal measures.[13]

The burgess élites were, then, well aware of the importance of the food component in lower-class budgets, and in no doubt of the troubles that would arise from shortages, not to speak of the likely effect on wage rates. Hence their strong commitment to the suppression of profiteering in the victualling trade. Is it possible that the anti-huckster ethos, reflected in Langland, was particularly a large-town attitude? In now considering the evidence from two small market towns we may have an answer to this, as well as to other questions.

If, as seems likely, half of the urban population was in small market towns, they should not be ignored by the urban, or any other sort of historian. One of the difficulties about these places is not only that they tend to fall between the two stools of urban and rural history, but that in most cases their documentation is scanty. Even some relatively well-documented small boroughs have little evidence about everyday existence. In the west midlands Stratford-upon-Avon has its Holy Cross Gild records, which are of particular interest for the history of building. Droitwich's records tell us about salt production. We can know something about Cirencester and Evesham from monastic cartularies, reinforced by other useful but discontinuous sources. Pershore, likewise, has cartulary evidence and, more interesting, some borough court rolls, but scanty and with many gaps.[14]

It is, however, the records of the small town courts which, where they exist in continuous form, can tell us more than most other types of record. Seigneurial boroughs, whose lords carefully preserved the court records of their rural manors, in some cases have records which give us an even better insight into urban communities than is available for much bigger towns. We are now aware of what important reconstructions of the evolution of peasantries can be derived from their court records, when relatively unbroken series are available.[15] Similar series—though very few—survive from the west midlands boroughs. Evidence from Halesowen (Worcestershire) and Thornbury (Gloucestershire) will be used to illustrate our theme. And this evidence is by no means negligible in bulk. As in the case of manorial courts, the borough courts met twelve or more times each year. In the boroughs, meetings of the portmoot were most frequent—every three or four weeks. The court leet, embodying the view of frankpledge, met once or twice a year. In the portmoot there was litigation between parties about land, debt, trespass and contracts. By-laws were passed. Inquiries about rights were made. Brewers, bakers, butchers, fishmongers and other victuallers were presented for breaches of the assize. The leet dealt primarily with petty police cases —assault, bloodshed, housebreaking; though, as is well known, the boundaries between the two branches of jurisdiction, from court to court, was by no means clear. The volume of business transacted was enormous and the number of named persons entering the records considerable.

The first of these places to be considered is Halesowen, one of fifteen monastic boroughs in the west midlands.[16] The lord was the Premonstratensian abbot of Halesowen, who created the borough around 1270 and granted it the customs of the city of Hereford. This was not a 'planted' borough but the promotion to burghal status of an existing settlement within a rural manor composed of about a dozen hamlets. The borough court records run parallel to those of the manor, beginning in 1272 and going fairly continuously (except for one serious gap, 1283-93) until the end of the fifteenth century. Some four hundred individuals occur in the record in the first ten years, though these are not all residents of the borough.

What is interesting about this borough is that, as a market centre to a rural area, it was anything but extraordinary. Its ordinariness, its typicality, is an advantage, given this accident of abundant documentation. Another advantage is that the records begin only two years or so after its promotion to borough status and so reveal the nature of the recruitment to a community no longer of agriculturalists but more and more of trades and craftsmen. For the most part, recruitment was from a five-mile radius of the town, mainly that is from the settlements within the manor. There were some settlers from farther afield—Birmingham for instance—but these were a small minority. As far as the majority was concerned, one of the interesting features is that, to begin with at any rate, they retained some interest in their native villages, partly in landholding and also in rights of common. Even apart from those specific interests, the townspeople, long after the establishment of the borough, continued to encroach on the resources of the manor, stealing grain, pasturing their beasts, stealing fences for firewood, fishing on the lord's estates. It hardly need be stressed that this sort of activity did not make (or remake) peasants of them, even though one might sometimes feel 'scratch a burgess and find a peasant'. However, given the medieval towns' dependence for demographic survival on rural recruitment, the same might be true of bigger places than Halesowen.

Apart from the radius of recruitment one or two other aspects may be mentioned. First, a high proportion of those coming into town were women, perhaps three-quarters of the total between 1272 and 1350. Secondly, the flood of recruits resulted in a considerable amount of turbulence, and some violence. One gets the impression that the lord (or his steward) who presided over the portmoot (or 'Hundred' as it was normally named in Halesowen) may have been somewhat overwhelmed by the response to the creation of the borough. At any rate the steward and the jurors, who were drawn from the leading burgesses, were quick to expel newcomers. Not that they were all that successful—those expelled kept on reappearing, would then be told to find pledges for good conduct and might even thrive to stall-holder, then burgess status. The third aspect of the influx was that a very large number of existing householders seem in effect to have turned their homes into lodging-houses and consequently to find themselves named as the good-conduct pledges for their lodgers. This was particularly the case with the large number of female hucksters who entered the borough. By the beginning of the fourteenth century a recognizable shape to the borough can be discerned. All entrants either strived for (or were obliged to acquire) the privileges of the liberty of the borough. This was defined (to quote a somewhat verbose statement from the court record) as follows: 'to have all liberties and free customs, in trading with all merchandise, buying and selling all manner of goods *(mercimonia)* of whatever sort and using all other commodities, as the rest of the burgesses'. The liberty could be obtained by the acquisition of a tenement held by burgage tenure; by hiring a stall; or by temporary purchase of the liberty which could be from one year to life. And what this meant, of course, was access to the market without the payment of toll.

There are no rentals or surveys of the borough, but the continuous nature of the court roll series gives one a fairly precise idea of the occupational structure. There were about thirty-five separate (non-agricultural) occupations, about half being food processing and dealing, and half manufacturing. There seems to have been some specialization in linen weaving. But although these various activities were seemingly separate, there was also a noticeable overlap in that many householders were involved in more than one activity. Many households brewed for ale. Many households whose principle occupation was not linen weaving nevertheless grew and processed flax. In 1300, for instance, the wives of a smith, a tanner, a baker and a butcher, together with a (male) baker and a (male) butcher, were amerced for soaking flax in the lord's vivary. Many of the women who can be defined as hucksters, resident or otherwise, were dealing in foodstuffs, but not all. In 1290 Isabel of Bracton, a dealer in clothes, enters the record, moving from lodging to lodging (including a night in a stable with John of Honeford, one of her hosts). She had quite a range of commodities—hoods, gowns, tapestry and linen sheets. But unlike some of the hucksters who settled in the town, she then disappears, at any rate under the name first given to her.

As has been hinted, the lord abbot may have been somewhat overwhelmed by the eager response to his borough foundation. He seems to have been neither benevolent nor negligent as a lord, which his already bad relations with some of his rural tenants might lead one to expect.[17] Some consequences of the urban development could be expected, even by him. Servants of the abbey, for example, took advantage of the town market and, using burgesses as intermediaries, sold off goods (especially victuals) from the abbey. But one aspect of the relationship between lord and town is particularly significant. Although the abbot must have been aware of the implications for personal status of burgess rights it would seem that he was reluctant to accept the transformation of his unfree peasants into free burgesses.

One of his bad habits was already present in the 1270s—the use of labour service to be performed in the manor as a punishment imposed in the borough court. In 1282 a certain Margery Hall (*de Aula*), who claimed and was not denied the liberty of the borough, was even amerced a day's work in the autumn for the rest of her life. These impositions multiplied in later years, especially in the second decade of the fourteenth century. Another habit was to impose marriage fines, and in 1301 he even extracted a 12d. amercement from a certain Juliana of Illey, who three years previously had acquired the liberty, for having been deflowered. A carpenter, John Gachard, who appears as a juror in 1297, who held a tenement, and was married, with a family, was accused in 1307 of being the lord's serf. He claimed burgage tenure and was amerced because he carried on with his work in his house when it had been declared confiscated (*in manus domini*) —this in the same year when, once again, he was a juror of the borough. Ten years later, in 1317, he has to do work as a carpenter, to the value of 12d., in recognition of his servile blood. A dyer, Thomas Garding, also married and a householder, was instructed in 1308 that he must pay the lord two capons every Christmas in recognition of his servile status.

These pressures clearly led to bad relationships between the abbot and the canons, and the borough community. No doubt the willingness to help abbey servants to bring abbey bread and ale into town was one symptom. More evident are the frequent presentments against towns-people for cursing and defaming the abbot and canons. Accusations for defamation are already beginning in 1274. In 1279 a shoemaker's wife is accused of making hostile remarks about the abbot and canons in relation to women. In 1316 a man hanged a dog on the abbot's pillory. But the bad relations between the abbey and the borough, of which these are simply examples, do not continue. By the middle of the century the court records, which were earlier full of evidence of friction, have very little in them about lord, abbey officials or canons. A distance seems to have been established between lord and borough.

However, it is not to be assumed that the same pattern was universal, as we can illustrate from another small seigneurial borough in the west midlands. This was Thornbury, some ten miles north of Bristol. This borough had a powerful lay lord, prominent in national politics and rarely resident near the borough. It was founded before 1262 by Richard of Clare, earl of Gloucester, and given the privileges of another borough of the earldom, Tewkesbury. Eventually the Clare inheritance was divided between co-heiresses, and Thornbury came into the hands of the earls of Stafford. The evidence is more diversified than that of Halesowen, but the series of court records is much more broken. They do not begin until 1324 and have many gaps, especially before 1360. Nevertheless those which survive are full and detailed and permit useful comparisons with Halesowen.[18]The occupational structure and the marketing and manufacturing functions of Thornbury were quite similar to those of Halesowen, as was the size of the borough—not many more than five hundred inhabitants in the pre-Black Death period. There were about thirty to thirty-five separate occupations with perhaps a slightly higher proportion of craftsmen than at Halesowen. There was a noticeable textile element, though here it was (as one might expect near to Bristol) woollen cloth. The main activity of the leading burgesses, however, was in the grain and malt market, which seems to have been much more prominent here than in Halesowen. Hardly any were involved in manufacture.

Here, too, immigration as late as the 1340s seems to have caused problems. For the most part the main range of recruitment was within a radius of only five or six miles. As one would expect, so long after the creation of the borough (and of the market) this type of recruitment was not the source of turbulence. It was rather the influx of immigrants from further afield, especially the Welsh. It is difficult to quantify this type of entrant, but one suspects that they were people seeking work for wages rather than potential settlers. They appear principally in presentments made against innkeepers, or possibly employers, for receiving them into the borough. Significantly these presentments cease entirely after the Black Death, when (as later also becomes clear) it was labour shortage rather than the flood of immigrants which was the problem.

There are hardly any indications in the Thornbury records of the pre-Black Death period of the hostility to the lord which has been noticed at Halesowen. In contrast it was in the post-Black Death period that trouble began and eventually became focused on that particular type of huckster, the ale-wife. To begin with perhaps, the frictions reflected the slightly more industrialized character of Thornbury, part of Bristol's hinterland. From 1351 onwards we notice other aspects of labour shortage, in addition to the cessation of presentments against lodging-house keepers for receiving outsiders. Now we have cases of the enticement of servants and apprentices. We have a series of orders by the lord (through his steward) forbidding townsmen from leaving the lordship in autumn to find work elsewhere. Those involved were members—younger members no doubt—of well-established borough families, and were presumably attempting to make money from harvest work.

At the same time, other entries in the court records suggest a growing hostility to authority. Suitors of the court refuse to attend in order to elect officials; they refuse to discuss matters with the bailiffs or to obey him. Jurors refuse to make presentments, and even erase the record of presentments from the court roll. The jurors themselves are insulted by the suitors. The lord is insulted by a townsman who calls him 'a skate'. All this evidence of generalized discontent coincides with a curious series of events involving brewers, tapsters and drinkers.

As has been indicated, in towns (and villages) many households brewed more ale than they consumed and offered the surplus for sale. Some households began to specialize. In Thornbury in the 1360s there were about twenty regular brewers and six to ten tapsters (retailers). The way in which the distribution of this vital commodity was controlled dates back, as is well known, to at least the early thirteenth century, the so-called Assize of Ale. What was supposed to happen was as follows. Ale could only be sold after a sign (an 'ale-stake') was put up outside the house of the brewer or brewstress. The ale-tasters, who were manorial or municipal officials, then came to taste the ale to guarantee its quality before being sold. It then had to be sold *outside* the house, on a level step, from sealed and licensed measures of one gallon or half a gallon. All who asked were to be served until the supply was exhausted.

But things were changing in Thornbury—and no doubt elsewhere. In 1369 the court record runs as follows:

> It is given to the lord to understand that all the brewers of Thornbury, each time they brew, and before the tasters arrive, put aside the third best part of the brew and store it in a lower room. It is sold to no one outside the house but only by the mug to

those frequenting the house as a tavern, the price being at least 1d. per
quarter-gallon. The rest is sold outside the house at 2½d. or 3d. a gallon, to the
grave damage of the whole neighbourhood of the town. The lord also understands
that all the ale tapsters are selling at excessive prices, by the mug, at 1d. per fifth or
sixth of a gallon.

There seems to be a link between the more general discontent and the
behaviour of brewers and tapsters. It also seems that the drinkers hardly
appear to be falling at the lord's feet in gratitude for his attempt to keep
down the price of ale. In 1370 we read some revealing items in the court
rolls. Two taverners are forbidden to use their houses or hostelries so that
danger and disturbance of the peace may be avoided. One Juliana Fox,
tapster, (in trouble before) is accused of running a hostelry, of receiving
priests, clergy and laity at unsuitable times, that is, at night. She is, in
fact, accused not merely of organizing a brothel but also of receiving
thieves. The court orders her expulsion from the borough. But, of
course, she soon returned, illustrating not merely that she was not
rejected by the community, but that seigneurial jurisdiction, faced with
rural and urban communities, had a limited effectiveness.

One is reminded of Langland's Rose the regrator:

> I bought her barley, she brewed it to sell—penny ale and pudding ale she poured
> together—for labourers and for low folk, kept separate—And the best ale lay in my
> bower and in my bedroom—whoever tasted it then bought it—at 4d. a gallon but
> not by big measure—but by the cupfull—her real name was Rose the regrator
> —she had been a huckster for eleven years. [19]

—with the exception that Juliana Fox was apparently accepted, perhaps
even supported, by the local drinkers, including Langland's fellow
clerics. However great the concentration of wealth in landed property
and mercantile profits at the top, the late medieval world was dominated
by petty production—peasants and artisans. The small scale of production was reflected in the sphere of circulation by the petty retail trader, as
often as not—or perhaps even more often than not—a woman.
Langland's world was not a world of low life, but of normality.

16

Women Traders in Medieval England

To all appearances medieval feudal society was outstandingly male dominated. Its ruling class of warrior landowners used women as a mode of acquisition and transmission of property; in some more sophisticated circles treated them as cult objects in elaborate games of courtly love; or, insofar as they could fulfill neither of these functions, consigned them to a life of celibacy, out of the world, in nunneries. The ideological legitimation of this social order was provided by a hierarchy of celibate (male) priests, who because of their control of the sacraments, were the sole intermediaries between mankind and God. For them, women, daughters of Eve, were tempters leading men into sin, unless they imitated the virgin mother of Christ and, at the best became nuns or at least became faithful wives producing heirs to prolong the family dynasty.[1]

This bleak picture of woman's lot in the middle ages has, quite rightly, been modified by historians who have looked at medieval society from below, rather than from the aristocratic heights. One should name, in particular, Eileen Power and Marion K. Dale. They, and some others, have drawn attention to the active role of working women in town and country.[2]

It would be wrong to exaggerate the relatively more equal position of these working women as compared with those of the aristocracy. Peasant women, though not rightless (especially if they were widows with property) were still socially and politically subordinated. The husband was automatically assumed to be the answerable head of the household, in control of the holding and of the movable property. In the manorial courts, the legal and administrative focus of rural affairs, single women tenants could be suitors and litigants, but jurors, pledges (sureties) and manorial officials were nearly always men.[3] One result of this is that they are under-represented in the court records, a grave matter for the historian since these are our principal source for rural social life. For example, even in perhaps the fullest documented manorial court of medieval England, that of Halesowen, Worcestershire, women's appearances in the court record between 1271 and 1395 was only 26% of the total, whereas they were probably more than 50% of the population.[4]

In the boroughs, too, women's legal position was similarly disadvantaged. They do not become jurors, councillors, alderwomen or mayors. It is true that some married women could be treated in law as *femmes soles* if they were carrying on a different trade from their husbands, but their socio-legal position in general was no better than that of their sisters in the villages.

What grounds, then, are there for concluding that in their social context working women were better off than upper class women? A main constituent of the answer is to be found in the spheres of production and distribution.

The basic unit of production in the medieval economy was the household, where the labour force was based on the family. The family itself could fluctuate in size and composition over time, ranging from the single couple at the time of marriage, through the familiar two generation family of parents and children, to the three generation family with co-habiting grandparents, children and grandchildren.[5] Additional labour in the wealthier households was rarely in more than twos or threes. Servants in husbandry, apprentices and journeymen were not only in many cases resident in the household but assimilated to the family. Living out servants, though not unknown, were not a major element in the labour force and, especially in the towns, would tend to be marginalised. It would appear that, at this stage, a sexual division of labour within the family labour force was by no means fully developed. If peasant women were regarded as particularly responsible for the poultry yard, they were often found working in supposedly 'male' occupations such as ploughing and reaping. All members of the family labour force, of both sexes, had to work on the holding, otherwise it would not be viable. And in times of labour shortage, women, like men, went off the holding to hire themselves out to richer peasants or to local gentry. This becomes clear if one studies the records of the sessions of the Justices of the Peace in the later fourteenth century when they were enforcing the Statute of Labourers.[6]

A similar situation is found with the urban crafts, where the identity of home and work-place is even more marked than in the countryside. Apart from the famous case of the London silk weavers, a craft dominated by women, it is quite clear that women participated in the same craft processes as men. It is true that the craft organisations were male dominated. This one would expect of recognised institutions that were as much policing organisations as spontaneous gatherings of craft workers. It is also true that in times of economic contraction, especially in the fifteenth century, the craft organisations sought to exclude women and aliens from the labour force, as in the case of the Bristol weavers - though in passing ordinances for this purpose they show that women were in fact part of the labour force.[7] Apart from such regulations one finds sufficient references to women as well as to men in the requirements for recognised levels of skill, to indicate that wives and daughters as well as husbands, male apprentices and journeymen were engaged in the main jobs in the trade. Let us take an easily accessible source from late medieval York, the Memorandum Book. Here we find, in various craft ordinances, that women could be capmakers, glovers, parchmentmakers, dyers, barber-surgeons, bow-stringers or tanners.[8] Their access to the trade was most often through birth or marriage rather than through apprenticeship. Nevertheless, they were participant workers in the household unit of production.

This emphasis on the productive base, as explanatory for a relative freedom from subordination of females to males among the working population of medieval society, does not, however, take us far enough in understanding the female role at the social level. We cannot understand the medieval economy without appreciating the predominance of the household unit of production, but this appreciation is not sufficient in itself. Partly due to the nature of our documentation, we tend to focus on the supply side of the economy. Manorial records tell us about demesne production and tenants' holdings. Urban records tell us about the manufacturing crafts, but as far as the demand side of the urban economy is concerned our attention is mainly focussed on greater merchants, participants in the export trade or in the provision of luxury goods for the feudal aristocracy and predominant in urban politics. Futhermore, most of the towns which have been studied have exaggerated that bias because they are the large towns with organised, supervised and therefore well-documented industrial activities. These are the documents which are preserved. Records of petty trade, especially in the court leet proceedings, have survived very unevenly. This, of course, limits our investigation of women's role in the market economy.[9]

It is clear that from the eleventh century onwards, at the latest, all conditions tended to the monetisation of this small producer economy. The lay and ecclesiastical aristocracy was increasing in size. Its demands for expensive imported luxuries and involvement in expensive wars were increasing even more rapidly. Its cash needs grew correspondingly and were met by increasing money rents, taxes and other monetary exactions. These cash needs were met primarily by peasants producing even greater surpluses beyond their subsistance and reproduction needs. The urbanisation which characterised the period was not only stimulated by upper class demand but by a developing division of labour between town and country. Peasant surpluses were brought to urban markets; urban markets demanded a range of services not only for the markets and their participants but for country buyers of urban craft products. By 1300 there may have been in England 1500 markets; most of these were chartered village markets but many were town markets, both in old established boroughs and in newly found market towns.[10]

Admittedly, many of these new markets, especially in the villages were the reflection of seigneurial illusions about the possibility of toll revenues and collapse in the period of demographic crises between the fourteenth and the sixteenth centuries. Only about half were still active by mid-sixteenth century. The three West Midland counties of Gloucestershire, Warwickshire and Worcestershire had 127 markets at the peak, but only 63 were active in mid-sixteenth century. The county of Lincoln fared worse, the corresponding figures being 97 and 37. Nevertheless, the growth of markets is a phenomenon to be considered seriously as a corrective to an economic history which emphasises the supply side, that is demesne, peasant and artisan production.[11]

When we look more closely at marketing—not simply at the markets themselves but at people who frequented them—we are bound to bear in mind the predominance noted above of small scale units of product-ion. What we find, in effect, is a reflection of these small scale enterprises in the scale of the commercial intermediaries between the suppliers and the consumers. Too long have we been bemused by the merchant princes of London, York, Bristol, Newcastle-on-Tyne and elsewhere. We now need to look at the swarm of retail traders - and this is where women reappear on the scene in some numbers. This is not surprising. If the male members of peasant and artisan families were more likely than the women to be tied to the holding or to the workshop by the exigencies of agricultural or craft occupations, a trading role would fall naturally to the women, though here again we must not assume too advanced a sexual division of labour.

First, something about retail traders. Their position was somewhat ambiguous. The right to retail trade in all commodities without paying toll was regarded as the primary privilege of those who became burgesses or freemen of chartered boroughs, great or small.[12] But the merchantile elites of the big towns, from London downwards, were always uneasy about retail trade. As far as the more expensive items of urban craft industry were concerned, especially textiles which had a wide market, they did not like producers retailing their own goods. They thought they should be put on the market only through the intermediary of the merchants. Thus, here, the 'one man, one trade' ethos [13] implied a separation of marketing from manufacturing as two separate and incompatible occupations. Then again, the urban elites, backed by the royal government, were deeply suspicious of all retailers of victuals. This was no small matter, because for most people who were not agricul-turalists producing their own subsistence, food and drink were probably the biggest item on the expenses side of their budget. High prices of foodstuffs would push up the cost of labour, quite apart from generating discontent.

Hence, although the right to trade retail was the essence of urban freedom, those who so traded were regarded with suspicion, and closely controlled—fortunately for us, because control generates document-ation. A term which authorities often used for these unpopular small retail traders was one with pejorative overtones—'huckster'. According to the Oxford English dictionary, using historical evidence, a huckster was (i) 'a retailer of small goods, ... a pedlar, hawker' and the ending of the word in -ster implied a female; (ii) 'a term of reproach (... regrator, engrosser of corn, broker, middleman)'; (iii) ' a person ready to make his profit in a mean and petty way' ... 'Rose the regrator, wife of Covetise in

William Langland's *Piers Plowman* aptly reflects this predudice. She had spent eleven years as a huckster, she cheated spinsters to whom she put out wool for spinning and she cheated ale drinkers by keeping the best of the ale which she brewed to sell at high prices to her favourite customers in the parlour, while the poor had to be satisfied with small ale sold outside the house.[14]

When we look at the various types of court record—the main source for retail trade—it is clear that it was not easy, then as now, to distinguish the different types of trader. In so far as we can make a distinction, it is mainly between producers selling their own products retail and retailers selling other peoples' products. The latter are the true hucksters.

Craftsmen outside the victualling and textile trades seem on the whole to have successfully ignored the merchantile hostility to their retailing their own goods. For the most part, therefore, they are free from prosecutions by the urban authorities or Justices of the Peace, except for a few cases of blatant profiteering, like the Lincolnshire shoemakers presented for selling at 8d to 11d a pair when the expected price was 5d.[15] In her study of the London grocers, Sylvia Thrupp commented that in that city, retail trading was practically unstoppable, except for the weavers, fullers and dyers who were controlled by the drapers.[16] Alan Dyer, writing about sixteen-century Worcester, noted that the city's economy was dominated by artisan retailers —except in the case of the textile industry.[17] This limitation to the textile workers of restrictions on craftsmen retailing their own goods is illustrated again by the 'poor burgesses' of Newcastle-on-Tyne, who complained in 1355 that the 'rich burgesses' of the Gild Merchant were preventing them from selling their cloth retail.[18]

However, there was another important group of manufacturers who sold their own products retail and received much attention from the authorities, for reasons already mentioned. These were the ale-brewers, a by no means negligeable element in the trading population. Their prominence to us is, of course, to some extent a by-product of the documentation arising from control. Nevertheless, they were numerous as the following figures derived from presentments under the assize of ale will indicate: Norwich (early 14th C) 250-300; York (mid 15th C) 221; Bridgewater (1380) 157; Leicester (1329) 128; Nottingham (1327) 107; Winchester (late 14th C) 50-66. In small market towns obviously there would be fewer—Halesowen, Worcs. (early 14th C) ca. 20; Thornbury, Glos. (throughout 14th C) 15-20.[19] One precautionary note, however, should be made about the high figures for some of the bigger towns. Some of these figures could include offenders against the assize (or licensees, if amercements were in practice, licence fees), who were tapsters or tiplers, that is, retailers of ale brewed by others. The numbers of tapsters as against brewers is rarely given. However, quite unusually the distinction is made in the Oxford presentments, where we find that retailers in 1311 were 45% of all presented for offences against the assize, a proportion which increased during the next forty years (59% in 1348 and 66% in 1350).[20]

The tapsters come into the category of true hucksters, that is persons selling retail other peoples' products. These people acquired their commodities either at the market or by forestalling. Forestalling implied going outside the area of market jurisdiction to meet dealers coming in, who would be willing to sell in order to avoid market restrictions, tolls and other urban inconveniences. The retailers would then sell on the street or in their own houses or shops. Most of the forestalling which is recorded in the prosecutions was of grain, fish and wool, that is to say, raw materials rather than finished or processed goods. It would often have been the case that those from whom the forestallers bought were themselves intermediaries rather than agricultural producers— cornmongers, woolmongers, fishmongers, who went to the source of supply in the villages and on the ships. Some peasants, no doubt, came to the town market with their products, but we must not assume that they were the main direct suppliers. There was a certain amount of retail trade in goods other than victuals, though the under-representation of non-victuallers in the documents may somewhat under-estimate their importance. In the fourteenth century court leet and peace sessions they amount to about 10% of the presentments and a much smaller proportion—perhaps 1% or 2% of persons. The main commodities included tanned leather, whose dealers are found especially in the Norwich and Linolnshire records. In the Linolnshire sheep country, tar and bitumen were commodities whose dealers were frequently presented for high prices or illegal measures. Second-hand clothes dealers are found in the bigger towns —the main fault of the Norwich dealers being the freshening up (presumably to disguise the age of the clothes) by using fullers' blocks. In Coventry, retailers of charcoal were prosecuted, mainly for attempts to establish monopolies.

It is impossible to say whether the predominance in the record of presentments of retailers of victuals reflects more the eagerness of the authorities to control the price of foodstuffs than the actual volume of trade in victuals. There is undoubtedly an element of exaggeration, but given the importance of food and drink in lower class budgets we must not dismiss our impressions as merely a documentary illusion. The obvious preoccupation of urban authorities to ensure prior supplies on the food markets for householders, by excluding retailers and others buying up goods before nine or ten or later in the morning, is a sure indication of the importance of the victualling trade.[21] Who were the traders and what did they sell?

Before coming to the shopkeeper, stall holder or street retailer, attention should be drawn to two special types of providers of food, essentially by retail sales, the cooks and keepers of hostelries. Cooks were not restaurateurs, but probably functioned as managers of 'take-away shops': Some idea of numbers may be given from the Oxford Poll Tax return of 1380.[22] Out of the total of 125 heads of households who were in the victualling trades (themselves about 27% of all named occupations), there were thirteen cooks in the town and its suburbs. Although this figure excludes the cooks of the students halls and religious institutions, the figure may still reflect the special conditions of a university town. In any case, cooks are found more in the big towns than in the market towns.[23] In Norwich, for instance, they were frequently presented for selling re-heated meat and pies and even encroaching on the butchers trade by fattening up pigs, lambs and calves of their own.

Generally speaking, hostelers seem to have been more numerous than cooks and are found in market towns as well as in the bigger centres. Two official counts may be quoted. There were 45 in early fourteenth century York and 197 in late fourteenth-century London.[24] Official figures or even occupational designations indicating professional status *(ostilarius)* do not, however, tell the whole story. It is clear that in towns large and small, householders were receiving lodgers to such an extent that one wonders whether any houses did not from time to time have (probably short term) lodgers. The bigger, more permanent and professional hostelries enter into our survey of the victualling trade, for their owners are frequently presented for brewing against the assize, for selling oats at exessive prices and for encroaching on the bakers' trade by selling their own horsebread, or even sometimes ordinary wheaten bread.

Most of the retailers appear as individuals or as married couples, selling ale (as tapsters), fish, poultry, vegetables, meat, eggs, milk, cheese, butter and (less frequently) grain. Ale sellers are prominent and insofar as brewers did not provide the service, were setting up ale-houses where customers could come in and buy by the mug, instead of having to send out from home to buy by the gallon or half-gallon. Fishmongers are also prominent and are frequently presented for forestalling fresh fish from the ships (especially in coastal areas of the North Sea) as well as salt fish. Poultry and vegetable sellers were common. Terms such as *vegetarius, holcroppatrix* or *garlekmonger* suggest some separation of vegetable sellers from the general run of poultry dealers or sellers of dairy produce. Sellers of meat were usually butchers and, at any rate in the bigger towns, tended to be richer than most victuallers since they had to invest money not only in buying the animals, but in renting grazing grounds in easy reach of the shambles for fattening them.

Reference has been made to the probability that, in certain respects, our sources, being jurisdictional and legislative, consisting of court presentments and ordinances, will overestimate the *numerical* importance of the retail traders. There are grounds however, for suspecting that in some respects the sources may underestimate the *volume* of retail trade. The reason for this is that, contrary to what the king's and urban governments—and indeed social theorists—envisaged, there was considerable fluidity between occupations. The right of burgesses and other persons enjoying the liberty of the borough to trade retail, in itself implies that whatever a person's main occupation might be, retail trading could be another. And we may be sure that the same multiplicity of occupation would apply to retailers of the marginal type who had not yet obtained the liberty of the borough.

As we have seen, hostelers were involved in the sale of victuals as well as being innkeepers. But we may note that in Coventry in 1378, of the 14 hostelers presented before the JPs, one was also described as a 'paltok' (doublet) maker, one as a wright and one as a smith. Coventry brewers included a mason, a woman tailor and a cook. Brewers, far from being one-occupation professionals, were in many cases simply selling the surplus beyond the household's needs, probably quite modest amounts of ale. So, in Kings Lynn in the late fourteenth century, we find a shearman, a mariner and a dyer among the brewers. One brewstress was also a stable keeper and sold wine, oats and horsebread. The Lynn tapsters included a tailor, a weaver a baker and several cooks.[25] In York, a barber kept a 36 bed hostelry, brewed, baked bread and dealt in grain. Nottingham's brewers included a corviser, a cook, a cooper, a tailor, a smith and a clerk. In the small borough of Thornbury, a chaplain, a baker, a butcher a chaloner, a dyer, a smith, a cobbler, a tanner and a weaver were all brewing for sale. At Newcastle-on-Tyne, the 'poor burgesses' whose complaint that they were not allowed to sell cloth retail has been mentioned, also complained that the burgesses of the Gild Merchant stopped them from selling herrings, wine, groceries and wool retail.

Judicial presentments give the impression that a considerable number of retailers were married couples. Since men were legally answerable in many cases for their wives' activities, the men presented alone may in fact have been acting alongside their wives, so that the numbers of couples presented may underestimate the number of jointly active husbands and wives. In addition a significant of single women appear as retail traders. The fortunate survival of court records from the early days of the new borough of Halesowen (1272 onwards) gives us an unusual insight into the migrants from the surrounding villages and hamlets. In the early decades it seems that something like three-quarters of the immigrants were single women. A combination of causes may explain this—population pressure on scarce landed resources, combined with primogeniture and an imbalance of the sex-ratio.[26] These immigrants enter the court record very frequently because accused of 'bad conduct' which is seldom defined, but appears to be unconnected with either rowdiness or breach of sexual mores. It seems, from the sequence of events, and some explicit remarks, that their bad conduct was normally illegal retail trading. The sequence of events referred to begins with this illegal activity; they are then obliged to find pledges for good conduct, usually the tenant of the house where they are lodging The next stage is when they apply to become stall-holders and to enjoy the liberty of the borough, that is to trade retail. Most of them were involved in selling victuals but there is at least one case of a woman who was an itinerant dealer in clothes and other textile products (tapestry,linen sheets).[27] These women traders constituted more than half of the licensed—or un-licensed—traders in the borough.

The importance of women in the retail trade in market towns such as Halesowen is likely to be found elsewhere. These market towns were not, for the most part, industrialized—we are not here concerned with industrializing villages, which were growing into urbanism, in the areas of cloth manufacture.[28] Places like Halesowen and Thornbury did have linen and woolen cloth weavers, as they had tanners and shoemakers, but as a service element in the borough and its hinterland rather than as specialists for a wider market area. The smaller retailer therefore can also be expected to be an important servicer of the market. What, then, of the bigger towns? The craft, mercantile, administrative, professional and ecclesiastical members of the population must have constituted a substantial market for food and drink. In so far as evidence for this survives, it should tell us a lot about women retailers. Unfortunately, the leet records for Norwich, so revealing in many respects, are inadequate for statistical purposes. Presentments of named individuals do, of course appear, but frequent statements by the jurors that, for example, 'all poulterers' have broken the assize, ruin hopes for quantification. It is interesting, of course, that when similar blanket presentments are made against those breaking the assize of ale, we are told that 'all brewstresses' are at fault. The assumption that all brewsters are women is found elsewhere, including some extant versions of the national assize of ale regulations which refer exclusively to *bratriatrices*.[29]

The Coventry presentments of regrators and forestallers for the years 1377-80, on the contrary, name all individuals, so that a sex-ratio is calculable. I exclude figures of hostelers, because as people holding real property there will be a built-in male bias. This done we find that 63 women are presented out of a total of 139, that is 45%. The commodities dealt with are fish, poultry, ale, butter, charcoal, eggs cheese and fruit. At this date, Coventry was third in population ranking order among English provincial towns (after York and Bristol). It was, like Norwich, which was next in ranking order, a textile town, and the pattern of retail trade was no doubt typical of this type of town. It is of some interest, therefore, that the Lincolnshire Peace Rolls of a similar date (1381-96) show a different pattern, with a much smaller proportion of women involved. The area covered is more rural than urban. The people involved in the presentments of victuallers were mainly accused of forestalling fish on a large scale—sometimes buying by the shipload—at the coastal quays. Otherwise, the retailers presented were mainly tanners, ironmongers selling tar and cobblers. There are hardly any presentments of victuallers selling in the local markets. This, of course, represents the preoccupations of jurors of presentment in the countryside as against the towns. But it must also reflect a real difference in the social and sexual composition of retailers.

Reference has been made above to women brewers and retailers of ale and to the assumption, current now as in the Middle Ages, that the very important brewing industry was dominated by 'ale-wives'. The issue is by no means clear. It may be that the pre-occupation with ale wives has had the effect of drawing attention away from the considerable participation of women in retail trade in general. The evidence for a female quasi-monopoly in brewing is, somewhat uncertain. The principal source for quantitative estimates is the presentments by ale-tasters or ale-conners who were appointed by local authorities to supervise the assize of ale. Their duty was to ensure that brewers put up a sign when brewing so that the tasters could come to test the quality of the brew. They also checked on measures and prices. In most towns and villages, the court records name all offenders, the Norwich blanket formula being rather rare. Therefore we often know the proportion of the sexes who were presented. I have already noted that at the village level there was by no means always a female majority among brewers[30] This was also the case in the towns. At Nottingham in 1371, out of 107 brewers offending against the assize, only 21 were women. At Kings Lynn at about the same time, 38 persons were presented for breach of the assize. Eleven were brewers, of whom two were women. The rest were retailers. At Bridgwater (Somerset) in the late fourteenth century, about 10% of those presented were women. In Halesowen borough, in the half-century after 1272, about 30% were women. In early fourteenth century York, about 28% were women. At Oxford, the proportion of women presented (brewers and retailers) was steady at about 22%. This, however, conceals the fact that between 1311 and 1350 women brewers presented dropped from 20% to 15%, while women retailers rose from 24% to 27%.[31]

In view of the frequent assumption by the promulgators of ordinances that it would be brewstresses who would be mainly responsible for ale brewing, it may be that the apparently uncontrovertible ale-tasters presentments conceal the truth. The obvious point to make could be that in many, if not in most cases, husbands were answering for deficiences in the manufacture and sale of ale brewed by their wives. This does not mean that prosecuted brewstresses were all single women. Many were demonstrably not. But the implication that husbands in many cases were answering for their wives should not surprise us. Given the occupational fluidity already noticed and given the fact that in a household-based economy both male and female members were part of the labour force, this element of sex-differentiation may have developed early but unevenly.

It may be worth speculating that women may have played a role beyond the purely economic in the development of the ale-house whether as brewstresses or as as tapsters. Such places were common in early fourteenth century London and by the end of the fourteenth century were to be found in other towns, large and small. Ale-houses were places for drinkers, but they were also places for sociability, for talk, perhaps subversive talk. If we knew more about these places we might discover that the presiding genius was 'mine hostess' rather than 'mine host'. The medieval ale-house, in the particular setting of the household economy, where women in the workshop, women stall-holders, women selling in the street were not as separated from the male worker as in modern times, might well have been a place where women had influence, quite different from the predominantly male working class pub of modern times. Who kept the ale-house where Glutton was tempted to stay on his way to church in Langland's *Piers Plowman?* It was Betty the brew-wife. Who was sitting there? Watt the warrener and his wife; Tim the tinker and his two lads; Hick the hackneyman; Hewe the medler; Claryce of Cockes Lane; the church clerk; Peres the priest with a woman, Purnele of Flanders; Rose the dishmaker; all sitting with craftsmen, retailers (including a garlick-monger) and various rogues.[32]

Perhaps the information in this preliminary sketch about women in retail trade—part of the larger problem concerning working women in medieval society—will seem familiar enough. What I have attempted to do is to give some impression of the scale, both of retail trading and of the female role within it. It is the size and importance of this sector of the economy which needs emphasis, as well, perhaps, as some indication of the wide range of commodities available in the medieval markets.[33]

17

Social Concepts in the English Rising of 1381

The rising in the south-eastern counties of England and in the capital did not begin until the end of May 1381 and, apart from sporadic disturbances in outlying areas, was put down by the King and the landowning class before the end of June. The outbreak was sudden and the organisation seems to have been spontaneous and unplanned. Nevertheless, compared with other rebellious movements of medieval Europe the leadership, if not the mass of the followers, gives the impression of having a rational and coherent even if unrealisable programme. In fact, although there were expressions of elemental class hatred (leading one historian to characterise the rising in Norfolk as 'a vast pillage'),[1] the actions of many of the rebel bands often seemed, in their carefully directed violence, to correspond to the aims expressed by their leaders in their meetings in London with the King and his advisers.

The rising is often referred to as a 'peasants' revolt'[2] but it should be emphasised that it was a plebeian rather than exclusively a peasant uprising, or, as it was put at the time, a rising of the 'commons'. Naturally, in a country the majority of whose inhabitants were engaged in agriculture, the peasants constituted the most important element in the rebel armies and their aims were clearly reflected in the demands put forward in London at the Mile End and Smithfield meetings between the rebels and the King. But it must be remembered that the populations of the counties mainly affected, that is Middlesex, Kent, Essex, Surrey, Hertfordshire, Suffolk, Norfolk and Cambridgeshire, had a special social character. It should firstly be emphasised that these areas were strongly influenced by London, whose population was recruited to a considerable extent from East Anglia. London was an important market for the agricultural products and the manufactured goods of the surrounding counties. Together with Westminster, which was just outside London's western wall, it was the dwelling place not only of persons dependent on commerce and industry—the merchants, petty traders, craftsmen and unskilled workers—but also of the royal court, the bureaucracy, the lawyers in attendance on the central law courts and from time to time of the sprawling households of the politically active members of the nobility. The court and the nobility moved out of London from time to time to their country manors in the vicinity of the capital. And although countrymen fled from manor to city, there were also those who came from London to take up land in the villages.[3]

In addition to London's influence, there were other aspects of the social structure of the areas from which the rebels came which help to explain the breadth of social conceptions to be found in this uprising. The affected counties were much industrialised and urbanised as compared with all but a few other regions of fourteenth-century England, even though many of the settlements did not have the legal status of towns. The chief reason for the industrialisation was that the late fourteenth century was a new period of growth of the wool textile industry. Although a considerable volume of production was centred in the towns, there was now a spread of the industry to the villages. Here the textile craftsman received raw materials from clothiers who marketed the finished product. Although the figures of cloth offered for sale provided by officials called aulnagers[4] have been severely criticised, they nevertheless suggest a significant development of the East Anglian industry. The growth of the industry at the end of the fourteenth century is proved by the considerable rise in the export figures (which are considered reliable).[5] Furthermore, the returns of the collectors of the third poll tax of 1380-1 (the tax which precipitated the revolt) have survived in significant quantity. These returns are unique in that for the most part they give the occupations of the taxpayers. A high proportion of taxpayers evaded the tax collection, but these seem to have been mainly servants and labourers. The returns show that in many villages in Essex, Suffolk and Norfolk there were, in addition to old established peasant households, groups of textile craftsmen. Furthermore, the textile craftsmen (and craftswomen) seem to have called into existence a further group of workers in service occupations (processing of food and clothing, building).[6] These constituted a further non-agricultural element in the countryside, though it must always be borne in mind that persons giving the designation of their principal occupation (e.g. weaver, shoemaker, baker, labourer) could also be in possession of a small quantity of land. There was no gulf between them and the peasantry and many of these artisans from industrialised villages played a part in the rising.

Some townsmen, in addition to the Londoners, also played an important role in the rebellion. Like the London poor, the middle and lower strata of the smaller towns seem to have sympathised naturally with the rebels. Their aims as journeymen and apprentices were expressed in the rebel programme. But in addition, elements from the mercantile bourgeoisie are found temporarily in the rebel camp. It is now considered unlikely that any members of the London patriciate were in league with the rebels[7] but the ruling circles of some smaller towns tried to use the rebels for their own ends. The well known instances are St. Albans and Bury St. Edmunds. Each of these towns was ruled by an old established ecclesiastical overlordship. Another example was Cambridge where the bourgeoisie tried to use the peasants to throw off the jurisdiction and influence of a different type of ecclesiastical institution, the University. With the possible exception of William

Grindcobbe, the leader of the St. Albans revolt, the townsmen shared few of the wider social aims of the rebel movement but were concerned with the establishment of corporate urban privileges.[8]

It is evident from the listings of the confiscated goods and other property of the rebels after the defeat of the rising that there was a significant element of rich peasants, including freeholders, who not only supported the rising but were in leading positions. These persons represent an old established and easily recognisable upper stratum of village society. Their holdings were four or five times the size of those of the middle stratum of peasants who were producing mainly for subsistence and only marginally in order to obtain cash for rent, tax and essential manufactured commodities. The rich peasants, on the other hand, were producing for the market on a scale which indicated the operation of the profit motive. They dealt not only in grain and ale, but in livestock, such as sheep for the sake of the wool and cattle for the urban meat market. The rich peasant's position of leadership in agrarian rebellions was by no means new in 1381 : it is found in England as well as in other countries from at least the twelfth century onwards.[9] However divided the peasant community may have been, those divisions were not as fundamental as that which separated the whole peasantry from the landowning, ruling class. Nevertheless, in 1381 in England as in other mass peasant risings of the later middle ages, we find occasional members of the lesser nobility, that is, of the knightly class or gentry who identified themselves with the peasant cause, even assuming positions of leadership. In England, as elsewhere, the reasons seem to have been personal, rather than social.[10] The gentry as a whole remained faithful to the interests of the Crown and the higher nobility.

Although there is no evidence that the 1381 rising was planned in advance, the English peasants and other plebeians were by no means unprepared for joint action in support of their economic and social aims. As early as 1163 we have evidence of a violent conflict between an ecclesiastical landowner and 'villein' tenants, apparently concerning the performance of ploughing services.[11] During the late twelfth, thirteenth and fourteenth centuries, instances of conflict between lords and peasants became more and more frequent.[12] Sometimes they were confined to litigation in the royal law courts, sometimes they involved violence by the peasants, but in all cases the evidence shows that peasants were acting collectively. This is not surprising, for village or hamlet communities had to act collectively in other matters besides conflict with their lord—in the assessment and collection of taxes; in the management of common rights, such as pasture; in the direction of the rotation, sowing and harvesting of crops; in the presentment of offenders to the royal and manorial courts; in the performance of services on the lord's demesne; in attendance at the royal court of the hundred; in the unwilling and selective performance of military service in the King's army.

The tension between lords and peasants which intensified during the thirteenth and early fourteenth centuries was increased after the Black Death (1349) for two reasons. First, there was a shortage of tenants in relation to the land available. Deaths from the plague resulted in the extinction of peasant families. Lords had on their hands not only the vacant holdings of these extinct families, but parts or the whole of their demesnes which, owing to rising costs, they wished to lease out. The relative surplus of land meant that there was a natural downward trend in rents. In order to counteract this threat to their income, lords used compulsory methods to obtain tenants and to enforce services. They also increased, whenever the opportunity presented itself, the financial exactions to which they were entitled from unfree tenants.[13] These measures exacerbated the natural tensions between landowners and tenants. Second, there was a shortage of labour. This was the consequence of the widespread mortality from bubonic plague. Wage labour became scarce not only because of the deaths among the labouring population but because there was more land available to provide for the subsistence of those who had previously needed to work for wages in order to live. There was increased competition between lords and rich peasants for scarce labour supplies, and the lords found it difficult, it not impossible, to control the movement of those elements among the manorial population who wanted to leave the manor in search of well paid employment. The answer which was found was for Parliament (representing the landowning interests) to pass a Statute of Labourers which laid down maximum wage rates and controlled the movement of labour. It was also laid down that any villager possessing less than an oxgang of land (that is seven or eight acres) and not engaged in an industrial craft should be obliged to work for wages. The Statute was at first enforced by special Justices of Labourers chosen from the landowning class and later by Justices of the Peace also drawn from the same class.[14] The application of the Statute after 1350 further increased the hostility of the peasantry and the craftsmen to the ruling class, for many members of peasant and artisan families worked for wages.

The most important demand of the rebels in 1381 was the abolition of serfdom.[15] It was this demand which struck the hostile chroniclers (mostly monastic) most forcibly. After all, their economic and social interests as landowners were directly affected by this demand. There is no doubt that the peasant desire for freedom was important not only in 1381 but in previous centuries, in other European countries as well as England. Why should this be so? It was supposed by clerical theorists in the middle ages as well as by historians in modern times that the peasant obtained security and protection in exchange for liberty. The statement is justificatory rather than descriptive. Peasants were deprived of their freedom so that they could be exploited, but naturally, to some extent, their 'own' exploiters protected them against the depredations of others. Even this was not always the case. In fourteenth-century England, the organised gangs who broke the law and spread terror in the countryside were those same members of the military aristocracy whose social role was supposed to be that of protection.[16]

The ethos of freedom developed among the English peasants in various ways. The teachings of radical preachers, such as John Ball, were obviously important. Legal concepts learned from common lawyers must also have been contributory. Perhaps most important were the lessons learned in practical struggle.

Conflicts at village level between lords and peasants from the twelfth century onwards have been referred to. These conflicts, as the peasants preceived them, developed because the lords attempted to alter customary practice in order to increase their rent income and the service obligations of the peasants on the lords' demesnes. There seems to be little doubt that increasing aristocratic expenses on war and conspicuous consumption, together with a very sharp rise in prices after about 1180, were responsible for this pressure on the peasants.[17] How did peasants attempt to combat increases in rents and services? They did so either by arguing that they were free or that they had once been tenants of the Crown. The services of free tenants could not be arbitrarily increased by the landowner; former tenants of Crown lands were privileged to retain their old conditions of service even though the King had given or sold the property to another landowner.[18] There were considerable ambiguities about the meaning of free tenure and free status. Those peasants who in the eleventh century were described as villeins (*villani* in Domesday Book, 1086)—about 38% of the population—were still considered to be of free status at the beginning of the twelfth century, even though their tenure was customary. Nevertheless they were not free-holders (*liberi tenentes*) and did not enjoy the protection which royal justice developed for free tenants in the second half of the twelfth century. Another 32% of the population in 1086, described as cottagers or bordars, that is small holders, were of more dubious status, but were still distinguished from the *servi* (about 9%). Social and legal pressures seemed to be leading to the creation of a homogeneously servile peasantry more or less uniformly described in legal and central government records as 'villeins'. By the thirteenth century, villeinage was considered to be a form of unfree tenure, normally associated with the unfree status of the tenant.[19]

The peasantry was not in fact pressed into a homogeneous social mould. At the end of the thirteenth century unfree villeins constituted the majority over all of the peasant population. Within the unfree population distinctions were still made between 'neifs' (*nativi*), probably descendants of the eleventh-century slaves (*servi*), and the customary tenants. More important, there was in some areas a high proportion of free tenants. In some east Midland and East Anglian villages, free tenants could account for a half to three quarters of the peasant population.[20] The process of rural industrialisation in the fourteenth century, which included the immigration of outsiders, increased the free element in the population. Under such conditions, the attempts of villeins to block increases in rents and services by claiming to be free would be further stimulated by observing the relatively favourable economic, as well as legal and social, conditions of neighbouring free tenants: that is, low fixed money rents; freedom of movement; freedom to buy and sell livestock; freedom to buy and sell land; freedom from arbitrary exactions such as tallage, marriage fines, death duties and entry fines.

Freedom therefore was a concept which when embodied in practical conditions of tenure and status was economically and socially advantageous, especially for peasants who wished to produce for the market. It is probable that the concept of the free man became independent of its purely tenurial connotation, but not only because of the Christian concept formulated by John Ball, as reported by Froissart: 'Why do they hold us in bondage? If we all spring from a single father and mother, Adam and Eve, how can they claim or prove that they are lords more than us?' When peasants were involved in litigation about their status, they were obliged to contest their claim for freedom in the King's courts, and consequently to hire a lawyer to argue their case. They collected money for a common purse and dispatched a delegation to Westminster. Although not pleading in person, there can be no good reason for supposing that the peasants were unaware of the case that was being put on their behalf by their lawyer, even though the pleading was made (or at any rate reported) in lawyers' French.

Some of these pleadings have survived and demonstrate how the lawyer temporarily identified himself with his clients' case, expressing their desires in a manner which was as generalised as the formulations of the preachers, but of a different character, striking equally strong roots perhaps in the minds of peasants who were themselves well accustomed to the processes of customary law in the manor court. Such a formulation is found in a record of pleading of 1310. 'In the beginning every man in the world was free and the law is so favourable to liberty that he who is once found free and of free estate in a court that bears record shall be held free for ever.'[21] The second part of this declaration could be of little comfort to a man proved to be a villein, but the first phrase would strongly reinforce the doctrines of the radical Christian tradition. There is no reason to suppose that this was the only occasion on which peasant litigants would hear such lawyers' arguments, and peasants, like others, could select the views which suited their needs.

The common lawyers were not, of course, in any way radical in their social or political concepts, nor did they need to be in order to plead in protection of existing free tenures. Nevertheless the social outlook of the rebel leadership clearly was very radical. We have to piece together the evidence of the remarks of hostile chroniclers about the actions and demands of the rebels in order to obtain some idea of the general conceptions which either originally motivated them or were developed during the course of the rising. There was far more to their programme than simply the demand for freedom of status. The further demands included the end of all homage and service to lords; the distribution of all lordship (except the King's lordship) amongst all—in effect the abolition of lordship; the establishment of popular policing (the law of Winchester);[22] the end of the control of labour; the division of church property amongst the commons; the clergy to have no property but only their subsistence. These items appear in the demands reported by the author of the so-called *Anonimalle Chronicle*[23] the most sober and reliable of contemporary writers, who was probably an official of the central government. Other plausible elements in the peasant programme from this and other sources include such details as the abolition of the whole church hierarchy except for one bishop; the payment of tithes by parishioners to the priest only if he were poorer and more worthy than them; the replacement of existing law by a new law. The extreme hostility to the existing law was shown by the attacks on lawyers and justices, and the determination to end the manorial system was widely demonstrated by the burning of the records of the manorial courts.

The rebel demands run entirely counter to the prevailing theory of society which pervaded the sermons of the clergy from bishops to parish clergy; which lay behind much of the penitential system of the church; which was expressed by the lay nobility in Parliamentary petitions and statutes; and which was found in both courtly poetry and that reaching a wider audience (e.g. William Langland's *Piers Plowman*). The essence of contemporary social theory was that the various orders of society, based on the original tripartite division between those who fight (the nobles), those who pray (the clergy) and those who work (the peasants), were of divine origin and not, therefore, to be changed by the actions of men. Every man and woman must remain in his or her own calling and perform the appropriate duties. The theory was ancient and consequently deeply rooted. It has even been suggested that it was of Indo-European origin, a theory which seems plausible if one looks at some of the early Sanskrit scriptures.[24] It was supported by the most prestigious authorities of the church and few dared to challenge it.

The chronicler of St. Albans Abbey, Thomas Walsingham, suggested that the spread of the doctrines of John Wycliffe was partly responsible for the rising.[25] It is now thought that the spread of his views beyond the narrow confines of the academic world in Oxford would have been too late to have been of any influence in 1381. It is even doubted whether he was much of an innovator as a thinker, even though in the fifteenth century the Lollard heresy was thought to be of purely Wycliffite inspiration and to be subversive not only of the ecclesiastical but of the social order.[26] In any case, Wycliffe was essentially conservative in social theory. His tract, *Of Servants and Lords* repeats the same message which orthodox contemporaries were preaching, a message that each order in society should fulfil its allotted role : 'Lords should live in their estate ... and destroy wrong and maintain poor men in their right to live in rest, peace and charity and suffer no man ... to do extortions, beat men and hold poor men out of right by strength of lordships.' But even though Wycliffe believed that tithes should be held from ill living priests, he said that it was 'a feigned word of Antichrist's clerks that servants and tenants may withdraw their service and rents from their lords ... lords have power of men's bodies and chattels in reasonable manner and temporal sword and wordly power by God's law to compel men to do their service and pay rents'[27]

Wycliffe, then, was not only too late but too traditional in his social teaching to have inspired the rebels of 1381. If the bringing of theory to the movement can be attributed to any one man, that man must be John Ball, though even he may have been one of a number of pre-Wycliffe poor preachers. Ball is variously referred to in the chronicles as a priest and a chaplain. His attacks on the ecclesiastical and social hierarchies are well known, though only the inventive Froissart attributed to him the view that all goods should be held in common (an unlikely peasant aspiration). References to his activities in earlier years occur in royal and episcopal records, indicating that his main spheres of activity were the dioceses of Canterbury and London, though not necessarily in the city.[28] He had been excommunicated by the Archbishop of Canterbury before 1366, but made no attempt to get absolution. Instead he went on a tour of illegal preaching in cemeteries, churches, and market places attacking the Pope, the Archbishops and the Bishop. In the late 1360s and 1370s we find him in Essex, denounced by the church and under threat of arrest by the secular power. As late as April 1381 the Archbishop was still fulminating against him as a 'pseudo-prophet'. The indications are that he was mainly active in the rural areas and it is worth noting that most of the other priests who were involved in the movement were from rural rather than from urban parishes.

We have the names of at least twenty rebellious clerks, mostly in East Anglia, Essex and Kent, and there is a reference after the defeat of the rising which suggests a large-scale participation in the revolt by chaplains and clerks in the archdeaconry of Essex. These clerics may have been influenced over the previous fifteen or twenty years by Ball and could have been a significant element in the transmission to the country people of social radicalism, though not necessarily of doctrinal heresy.

In view of the probability that Ball's ideas, consistently, though in each case only partially, reported by the main chroniclers (Walsingham, Anonimalle, Froissart),[29] were widely disseminated in the rebellious areas, it is not surprising that the Mile End and Smithfield programmes should, in effect, demand the dismantling of the organic society of hierarchically arranged orders.

The question arises, would all the different social strata among the rebels of 1381 be likely to support the different elements of the radical programme of their leaders? If one takes the various individual items presented to the King and his councillors at Smithfield, one might conclude that even the richest peasants would welcome the abolition of lordship, the reduction of rents, the freeing of wage labour, and the abolition of serfdom. Whether peasants would be behind the programme of church disendowment is another question. It is not that such a programme was inconceivable at this period, since some of the gentry in Parliament in both 1404 and 1410 were prepared to advocate far-reaching church disendowment schemes. However, disendowment as a policy tended to be supported (i) by academic clergy, such as Wycliffe, thinking in the Marsilian tradition of lay supremacy, (ii) parish clergy with moral or professional reasons for hostility to the endowment of the regular clergy, (iii) landowners who wanted a better use of landed endowments than the maintenance of the monastic clergy, such as support for military leaders or an increase in the Crown lands, so that the King could live without taxing his subjects.

The attitude of the peasants to the church and to the religious orders requires careful consideration. The policy of disendowment was associated with Wycliffite Lollardy during the fifteenth century and in so far as this was a popular policy among plebeians, it seems to have been confined to artisans and to the middling and lower urban strata. If one is to judge by the popularity of the mendicant orders in the towns —for they were from the beginning primarily an urban phenomenon[30] —the acceptance of Lollardy by urban populations is understandable. Although Wycliffites and friars were enemies, they were both hostile to the monastic possessioners. The propaganda of the friars may have paved the way for the acceptance by the urban plebeians of Lollard views about church property, especially the property of the monks. But popular religion in the villages was different from popular religion in the towns where Lollard evangelical doctrines of a Waldensian type struck roots. In the villages, popular religion tended to be a religion of local cults and rituals which contained many pre- or non-Christian practices.[31] Most of these cults and practices had been comfortably accommodated within orthodox religion. The village priests presided over such fertility rites as the beating of the bounds on Rogation Days. If peasants were to reach the same conclusions about the disendowment of the monasteries and the dismantling of the church hierarchy as the Lollards in the towns, it would be by a different route.

Whatever that route might be, we do have some contemporary evidence about rural attitudes to the monastic possessioners. According to the B text of William Langland's *Piers Plowman* (composed about 1377), the allegorical figure of the sin of Sloth, represented as a parish priest, was ignorant of his clerical duties, but knew well the rimes of Robin Hood.[32] This shows that the Robin Hood ballads were popular at the time of the rising. Their setting is rural—indeed there is a strong element of town-country antagonism in them. The free life of the outlaws described in them is an obvious fantasy for a discontented rural population. The social character of the ballads is indicated in the earliest version, *The Geste of Robyn Hode*, by Robin Hood's listing of the outlaws' friends (husbandmen, yeomen, some, but not all, knights or squires) and enemies (bishops, archbishops, sheriffs, earls, barons, abbots). The focus is narrowed in the ballad story. The evil exploiter is the rich abbot of the Benedictine house of St. Mary's, York[33] and the traitors who betray Robin Hood are successively a monk, whom Little John kills in revenge and a nun who bleeds Robin Hood to death. Now, a great deal of satirical verse of the fourteenth century has as its chief target the rich and luxury loving monks,[34] but these verses were mainly of clerical origin. Obscure though the literary origins of the Robin Hood ballads may be, there is little room for doubt that the sentiments are as near as we shall get, in imaginative literature, to those favoured by the peasantry at the time of the rising. They suggest very strongly that the rural population would have accepted the expropriation of the wealthy possessioners with as much satisfaction as would the urban Lollards of the fifteenth century. At the same time, the Robin Hood ballads express an orthodox piety far removed from other aspects of Lollardy. Indeed, despite the proposals for the elimination of the church hierarchy above the parish level, there is no evidence that any of the rebel priests, including Ball, were heretical in theological doctrine, as was Wycliffe.

If the English peasants and their plebeian allies in 1381 were prepared to dispense with the whole of the clerical order above the level of the parish priests, it need cause no surprise that they also considered that the nobility and gentry did not constitute a necessary order in society. Their programme demanded the end of lordship, their principal theoretician had preached to them about the equality of all descendants of Adam and Eve, and their actions in burning the records of the manor courts showed more clearly their determination to end the system of lordship than any acts of violence against individual lords would have done. This combination of thought and action, implying the rejection of the concept of a society composed of a balance of hierarchically arranged estates is not easy to explain. Peasants and other commons could, and did, rebel because they thought that the other orders of society were not fulfilling their divinely allotted role. Thus it is possible to envisage an English rising which would not go beyond a protest against increased pressure on peasants by manorial lords, judicial harassment of wage workers and excessive taxation. The fact is, however, that it did go further not only as regards the programme of the leaders but, as I have pointed out above, in the actions of the local bands of rebels. I have tried to stress the role of ideas in the history of this rebellion because this remarkable breakaway from traditional thought is one of the most interesting aspects of the rising. It has frequently been emphasised that between the middle of the twelfth century and the growth of Wycliffite Lollardy there were no mass heretical movements in England such as were common on the Continent. But the ideas and programmes enunciated by John Ball and Wat Tyler did not spring unprepared from their heads. Their existence and their acceptance by the rebel following suggests a previous period of unrecorded preaching and agitation of which John Ball's activity is just one example.

18

Feudalism or *Féodalité* and *Seigneurie* in France and England

Féodalité et Seigneurie, the feudal and the manorial systems—the two terms are more frequently used in a linked phrase by French than by British historians, but the conventional wisdom on both sides of the channel is that the institutions which the two terms indicate, though co-existent, must not be regarded as necessarily interdependent. This insistence is an aspect of a modern sensitivity to the broad use of the term 'feudalism', which once embraced both the fief and the manor, *féodalité* and *seigneurie.* This eighteenth-century usage has been prolonged in our era as a result of its employment by Marx who, engaged in his task of penetrating to the essence of the capitalist mode of production, necessarily had to distinguish that mode from others and, in particular, that from which it grew. Since, for him, the essence of a mode of production was the way in which labour was exploited, it came about that some of those who subsequently applied his method to the last of the European pre-capitalist modes of production tended to equate 'feudalism' with 'serfdom', that being the term, socio-economic rather than juridical, which was used to describe the form of labour which produced the surpluses on the basis of which medieval societies were elaborated.

It is not my intention to engage in scholastic dispute. To reduce feudalism to serfdom is as bad as to insist that without the fief there is no feudalism. The social and economic order of medieval Europe is sufficiently distinct and recognisable, with its own laws of motion, to require some term by which it can be distinguished from preceding and following social formations. If we do not use the word 'feudalism' we would have to invent one, and it would have to encompass within its definition both *féodalité* and *seigneurie.*

The feudal organisation which is implied by the word *féodalité* had emerged by the eleventh century in France and England in different ways but with similar contours. Its coherence must not be exaggerated. Even in England, where the feudal institutions of the new aristocracy were formed quickly as a result of the conquest of 1066, and much less in France, there was no perfect, completed hierarchy of mutual obligation between barons and fief-holding vassals owing military service and expecting protection. One should imagine, especially in France, a series of untidy regional groupings dominated by one or two great land-owning families who derived most of their income from the rents and services of peasants. They also held jurisdictional power, not only over their peasants but over their free vassals—landowners, some of noble pretensions, whose male members were either warriors or destined for office in the Church. By this time personal relationships between the great lords and their vassals were assuming tenurial form, the rendering of homage and fealty and the promise of military service, financial aid and counsel in return for fiefs in land.

In fact the mobilisation of military service on this basis, once presented as the essence of feudalism, was in practice by no means general. By the twelfth century, if not earlier, all the best wars were fought for pay in cash and the hope of booty. The persisting strength of 'feudalism' in the narrower sense of relations within the landowning class, was as much ideological as it was tenurial or jurisdictional. The ideology had deep roots in earlier societies before feudal bonds were formalised, arising particularly from the relationship between the leader of the war-band and his following. It was strongest after about 1050 and persisted throughout the whole medieval period, and beyond. Its main tenets were hierarchy, deference, fidelity, military prowess and largesse. It was an extraordinarily strong and pervasive form of class consciousness, given the regional character of the economy, the verticle structures of social relationships, the difficulties of communication and the dispersed location of those centres in which feudal aristocrats could meet. It was also of extraordinary depth, given the great differences in wealth between dukes, counts and barons on the one hand, and petty knights of villages on the other, all of whom shared this ideology.

It is sometimes assumed that the mutual ties of personal dependence and support between lord and vassal, which knit together the regional aristocracies, continued downwards to embrace also the peasantry. There could be no greater error. The dependent peasant was not a small scale vassal holding land for services which happened to be agricultural rather than military. Petty though the village knight might be, he not only shared the ethos of the baron, he also stood with the baron on one side of the great divide in medieval society: both lived from the fruits of the surplus labour of the peasants. The peasants themselves by no means constituted a homogeneous class. Already by the eleventh century there were, on the one hand, families in possession of lands adequate to maintain them as well as to provide rent and service for the lord; on the other hand there were already families of small holders who had to eke out their living by labouring on the lord's demesne or on the holdings of richer peasants, or by doing craftwork, or by gathering or poaching. None of these peasants, rich or poor, lived according to the aristocratic ethos, though it was precisely at this time that the old Indo-Germanic theme of the divinely ordained division of society between those who prayed (the clergy), those who fought (the nobles) and those who worked (the peasant) was being revived in learned theory. This was part of ruling class ideology which peasants *were* expected to embrace and which was preached from a thousand pulpits.

It is in accepting the divide between lord and peasant that we can perceive the distinction between *féodalité* and *seigneurie,* two inseparable facets of the same social order. Without the lordly control over the peasants the feudatories could not exist either as warriors or as holders of power. They could not even exist as an interdependent group, for what was largesse, one of the most imperative of the noble virtues, but the downward redistribution of high aristocratic incomes, extracted from the peasants, to the military retainers and into the ever-open satchels of the clergy?

This feudal social order was once regarded, especially in comparison with capitalism, early and late, as static, only able to change as the result of external stimuli such as long-distance trade. In fact, although the growth of production and population (perhaps 1% population growth per annum at the best of times) was slow compared with the modern era, there was an internal dynamic to the society, a motor of social change which can be well illustrated from the histories of French and English feudalism. But in order to understand the dynamic of the feudal order we should say a little about its structure.

If we look at this predominantly agrarian society over the five centuries which concern us we can discern, in spite of great changes which took place, a number of basic forms of social organisation whose essential characteristics persisted during the period, so giving it its unity as a social formation. The fundamental unit was the holding of the peasant family, combining in its economy varying proportions of arable and pastoral production. The family holdings were surrounded by a periphery (greater or smaller from time to time) of small holders— agricultural labourers, craftsmen, herdsmen, gatherers ... The peasant holdings probably contained within them the overwhelming bulk of the productive forces of medieval England and France, so that whatever happened to them would be reflected in their capacity to pay rents and taxes. This would have reverberations at the summit of the feudal order. For the amount of peasant surplus that was transferred to individual lords and to the state depended not only on impersonal economic factors but on peasant resistance to demands made upon them. It was by no means an easily exploited class. But peasant resistance, insofar as it was successful, was collective, through the mechanism of the village or hamlet community. This fact must make us doubt whether the peasant holding was the key unit of the medieval social structure.

The village community was more than a collective of individual producers. The peasant family holding was an incomplete economy— and not simply because it needed to look outside itself for such products as salt and manufactured goods. It was incomplete because many of its important resources, such as pasture, meadow land, timber for fuel and construction, stone from quarries and fisheries, were controlled as common rights by the village community. Peasant self-consciousness developed to a considerable extent during our period, not only because of the joint use of these resources but because of collective resistance to the claims of the lords. As part of their attempts to strengthen their position as the dominant class in rural society, the lords asserted their ownership of these common resources, not so much in order to transfer them from the communal to the private sphere, but in order to establish that rights of usage were privileges which would have to be paid for.

In some parts of France, particularly near Paris and further east, some rural communes emerged as social and political entities with limited autonomy. In spite of the successes of the village communities, however, we must not see them any more than we see the peasant holding as the essential, distinctive units of feudal society. Any gains made by the rural communes were partial and not widespread. It is rather to the *seigneurie,* lordship or manor that we should look. It was in this institution that the two great classes met face to face —the landowners great and small and the peasants rich and poor, the first to receive, the second to give their labour or the fruits of their labour, in cash or in kind. It was the principal theatre of that act of coercion, sanctified by custom, legitimated juridically in the various forms of dependence, ranging from serfdom to villeinage, by which the infinitely scattered surpluses of the peasant economy were concentrated into the hands of the politically and socially dominant class.

The fief and the lordship evidently overlapped. The fief was a piece of income yielding property held of a superior lord by a vassal who swore fealty, promised military service on horseback, financial aid and advice. It could be very small: some English military tenants in the twelfth century had fiefs in land which were mere fractions of villages. Others contained one or more manors and a manor could encompass more than one village or hamlet community. The concept of the fief as part of a fund of landed property handed down through the feudal hierarchy in order to reward and retain the loyalty of warriors would seem to be well supported by English evidence. But this is only one way of looking at the disposal of the estates of the conquered English. In France, however, many fiefs were family allodial property, the terms of whose tenure was feudally redefined without the family losing its original endowment. The family's grip on its land was hardly weakened—the heredity of fiefs, even in England, though briefly challenged, was never really in doubt. But as property was bought and sold, subdivided and regrouped, the fief as a means of mobilising military service became of little significance, even if the ethos of vassalage and chivalry which was briefly associated with it, became the dominant outlook of all ranks of the feudal hierarchy.

The *seigneurie* or manor, on the other hand, in varying forms persisted, it embodied the organising principle of the whole of feudal society. This principle was that by which the social product coming from the peasant economy was realised, first as landowner income and then, through the mechanism of the market, as the source of demand for craft products and the commodities of regional and international exchange—a demand to which, of course, the peasants themselves also contributed directly. In addition, the *seigneurie*, precisely because of its varied demands on the peasant household, stimulated production and was thus, at any rate in the early stages of feudal society one of the prime movers of economic development.

It is not only a difficult, but perhaps a mistaken task to compare the feudal societies of medieval 'France' and medieval 'England'. Within the modern boundaries of these two countries there were, in the middle ages, such striking regional diversities that in each kingdom there were greater contrasts than between some of the provinces of each. England, south of the Thames, was more like Normandy than it was like the Marches of Wales. The Ile de France was as much like the valley of the lower Thames as it was like Languedoc. But if there were great regional diversities within each country, perhaps, insofar as we can arrive at an overall, generalising view of English and French society the similarities, will emerge the more forcefully in that we recognise these internal divergencies.

To English historians the differences at first seem considerable. The most obvious, partly in our minds as a result of the preoccupation of nineteenth- and early twentieth-century historians with the emergence of the centralised state in the form of the feudal monarchies, is that the English aristocracy never managed to complement their undoubted powers as landowners and lords of tenants with a corresponding jurisdictional and political power. The lesson that we have learned about France is that following the disintegration of the ramshackle and, relatively short-lived power of the Carolingian emperors, the great provincial landowners, the *potentes*, openly appropriated the public jurisdiction they had held as dukes and counts by imperial nomination. The aristocratic families of the regions, tied by vassalage and increasingly by tenure (as their allods were turned into fiefs) to the dukes and counts, themselves underwent an important evolution. Family allegiances with widespread lateral links between agnatic and cognatic connections consolidated themselves into lineages more concerned with direct ancestry and descendants than with collaterals, and focussed more on the male than on the female line of descent. These contracted and consolidated lineages established firm bases of local power, usually focussed on castles. They too appropriated public jurisdictions, whose boundaries, narrower than the county, were defined by the area of domination of the castle. Finally, their vassals, the knights of the villages, consolidated their local power as landowners with varying levels of public jurisdiction, and they too turned their tenants into subjects as they themselves climbed into the ranks of the nobility.

This appropriation of public jurisdiction never went so far in England. Although the ecclesiastical immunity was developed in Anglo-Saxon England, as it was in Carolingian Gaul, and the landed magnates effectively controlled the shire courts, sheriffs and ealdormen were still officials of the Crown. The Norman invaders, though destroying the old English aristocracy, took over the institutions of the English monarchy and from this firm base, in the next two centuries, successfully excluded individual magnates, (except for the lords of the Western and Northern Marches) from developing a baronial jurisdiction, founded on alienated public powers, comparable with that of their opposite numbers in France. 'Haute Justice' in England by the end of the 13th century was dealt out by royal justices of assize, as were most disputes concerned with land held in freehold (including military)tenure. The old franchises, whereby jurisdiction at the level of the hundred court was in private hands, were seemingly denatured in that instead of this being an appropriation of public power by the private lord, the private lord had been appropriated as an agent by the public power

There are good reasons for not carrying this contrast to extremes. First there is the question of scale. England at the end of the 13th century was a feudal kingdom of about four million people in a comparatively small area of land—mostly concentrated south east of the line from Exeter (170 miles from London) to York (200 miles from London). France was a country of 15 million people, evidently distributed with variable densities but with the extreme south by no means lagging behind the Paris region. From the Norman coast to the Mediterranean is about 600 miles, and from Bordeaux to Lyons, 350 miles. Secondly, there is the question of the distribution of aristocratic landed property. In England, in contrast to France, the greater magnates tended to have property scattered rather than concentrated in one region. The Clare Earls of Gloucester, for instance, had their most important concentrations of property in East Anglia, the West Midlands and South Wales. In post-Carolingian Gaul, the collapse of the authority of the state simply revealed that real power was and could only be exerted over an area which was not too big for a duke or a count to rule with the aid of his following. In contrast, in spite of the difficulties of travel, lowland England, where the population was concentrated, was small enough to to be handled by a royal administration, eventually settled in Westminster. Furthermore, the dispersal of property and, consequently, of followings and allegiences, meant that except for the Welsh and Scottish marches, it was more realistic for the higher nobility to exercise power through influence at the King's court than to rely on their regional strength. Their local followings were important power bases, but for the sake of leverage at the centre.

These however, are considerations of most importance for feudal politics and the development of the state, which is not our concern. Our concern is with the downward thrust of feudal power, the thrust which guaranteed the incomes and therefore the existence of the feudal aristocracy. How different was the internal organisation of the feudal lordships in France and England? Here again we must critically examine received knowledge.

Many years ago C.E. Perrin and other French historians showed how in northern France, in the 9th century, the estates of the ecclesiastical aristocracy and the monarchy (the only ones for which surveys survive) were on the edge of disintegration precisely when their traditional form was revealed in *polyptyques* and *censiers*. The principal characteristics from the standpoint of the relations of lords and peasants was that the peasant holdings provided rent consisting of the unpaid and enforced labour services for the cultivation of the demesne, and for the manufacture of craft products needed in the estate. The rent, mostly labour services, but also to some extent in kind, was a payment to the lord in his capacity as landowner and was notionally related to the size of the holding. From the tenth century, or even the late ninth century, as population grew (and coincidentally, of course, with socio-political decentralisation to which we have already referred), peasant family holdings disintegrated and were re-formed, demesne cultivation dwindled, and labour rent was largely replaced by money rent which tended to become fixed by custom— and devalued. But since this was precisely the time when lords, high and low, were appropriating public jurisdiction, including the power of command—that is the *ban* —over all persons within their jurisdictional area, the opportunity arose to organise the transfer of peasant surplus in the form of varied jurisdictional profits—court fines, payments for the use of the lords' mills, ovens and wine presses, *corvées* unrelated to tenure but consequent on the general power of command. In a word, by the 11th century, *seigneurie domaniale* was succeeded by *seigneurie banale*. Counts, castellans and knights were not merely land-owners with tenants but sovereigns with subjects. The whole movement was inseparable from the growth of urban markets great and small, and the conversion of ancient serfdom into *vileinage* (which some might consider to be a change of terminology rather than of substance). As Georges Duby has recently suggested, the *seigneurie banale* became one of the motors of development.

England, as described in Domesday Book (1086) was still a land of *seigneurie domaniale*. Though seldom reaching the high proportions of demesne to tenures found for example on the estates of St. Germain-des-Prés or of S.Bertin in the Carolingian period, the organising principle of aristocratic landed property, at the time of Domesday Book, and in the twelfth century surveys was the cultivation of the demesne by labour services owed from dependent tenures, usually realised economically in the payment of a fixed annual farm in money or kind. After a marginal contraction of demesne in the 12th century, the whole system which had remained virtually intact, not merely since 1086 but since, at the latest, the 10th century, was rejuvenated and expanded under the inflationary conditions of the 13th century. Demesne management was made accountable, managers replaced farmers, labour services were increased and rents were raised. Dependent villeinage, which had not been regarded as servile, was declared unfree in the public courts. Manorial profits rose and the proportion of income from the sale of demesne produce sometimes exceeded the income from rent. The domanial system did not collapse in England until the second half of the fourteenth century. It was almost as if England was three centuries behind France in feudal development, conserving large scale demesne estate management and a mainly landowner : tenant relationship within a polity where the monarchy was strong and the private jurisdiction in the hands of the landowners being little more than a regulatory, customary law of the landed estate. In fact the contrast is misleading. We will leave aside the question of the relative strength of the Capetian and Plantagenet monarchies, and deal only with manor, estate and lordship. Here the similarities are considerable, though our perception of these similarities does not come easily because of differences in nomenclature and historical traditions which have emphasized contrasts. But once the effort of comparison is made, aspects of one country's history are thrown into relief by examining those of the other.

We must for example draw attention to the role of private jurisdiction in England. In some ways jurisdiction can be regarded as the most important open expression of the power of the aristocratic class. As we have seen, for special reasons the English aristocracy, to a greater extent than the French, exercised this power through their influence in central institutions, including the central law courts, whose justices were often their retainers. But they also had an important degree of local private jurisdiction which was directly and indirectly very profitable. It is true that baronial and honorial courts, by the end of the 12th century, were not dealing effectively with either crime or disputes about land held in free tenure, but the courts through which the lords controlled the dependent peasantry were very powerful —and, after all, dealt with most of the issues which affected most of the population most of the time. Enforcement of the terms by which villein tenants held land, performed services and rendered dues naturally flowed from the landowner-tenant relationship. But with the application to once-free villeins of such obligations, well known in France, as merchet (*formariage*), heriot (*mainmorte*), tallage or aid (*taille*), personal as well as domanial dependence was emphasised. The most important landowners acquired hundredal jurisdiction for their manorial courts which gave them policing rights over petty crime involving bloodshed short of felonious murder or assault and over the sale of essential commodoties such as bread and ale. Many of them, in spite of the considerable extension of royal jurisdiction, had gallows on which they were entitled to hang thieves caught red-handed within their jurisdiction. They built mills and ovens and obliged the inhabitants of their lordship to grind corn and bake bread only at those places. The English manorial courts were, as in France, not only important centres of social control, but also institutions yielding monetary profit.

Although we have emphasised the rural base of the feudal order we must also not omit to emphasise another important element of seigneurial power in England of which a study of *villes-neuves* and *bastides* in France reminds us. The larger English boroughs, like the French communes, had a special relationship with the monarchy or other state-like authorities. but there were also hundreds of small towns in England which were focal points of seigneurial, not royal or public power. Some of these were 'organic', some were 'planted', but, whatever their origin, their borough court was analogous to that of the manor, presided over by the lord's steward who concluded affairs as far as possible in the lord's interests, with regard especially to income from tolls and rents from houses, shops and stalls. These seigneurial boroughs were individually small but it is probable that their total population well exceeded that of all of the bigger and more prestigious royal boroughs. More, from the point of view of status, to be lord of a borough was analogous to having a castle (the two were often connected) or being a patron of a monastery. No estimate of the private power of the feudal nobility should ignore their effective control of the centres where the bulk of market transactions affecting the rent-paying rural population took place.

The greater landowning aristocrats of medieval England, lay and ecclesiastical, are remarkably well-documented, not so much in their relationships with their free vassals but as regards the internal structure of their estates and the manors, lordships and jurisdictions which composed them. This is because of the survival of detailed surveys, of annual accounts and, above all, of manorial court records. The lower ranks of the aristocracy—the knights—are less well known in spite of the detailed, painstaking and rather boring compilations of local genealogists. This again is partly due to the fact that the records of their small estates have not survived—if they ever existed—with the same abundance as those of the greater families. In different ways and, in part under the influence of the work of French historians, their social characteristics are becoming better known to us.

A striking time-lag between England and France has been revealed in the development of the knightly class, though this may have been not so much due to the lack of precocity in England as to the political, social and cultural break in 1066. For the pre-Conquest English thegns, who are analogous to the continental *chevaliers*, were already regarded as nobles in the 10th and 11th centuries, whereas many of the post-Conquest Anglo-Norman *milites*, as we have seen, by no means conformed to the traditional picture of local aristocrats endowed with the *feodum militis*. A large number were at best substantial free tenants, probably not ploughing their own lands, but nevertheless in possession of landed property only twice or three times the extent of that of a well-to-do peasant. The class became polarised and an element did prosper, economically and socially. But, whereas the eleventh century was the period in France when the knights, the *chevaliers*, began to be considered as noble and to acquire over the peasants the power of the *ban*, it was not until the late 12th or early 13th century, that this seems to have happened in England. This is the period when they began to be used in administration and judicial process by the kings, when they began to be distinguished as *domini* in charter witness lists from other free men and when—especially by the time of the Montfort rebellion—they were able to exercise collective political weight in national affairs. And no doubt in imitation of their French couterparts they were taken to typify, at tournaments and in the royal and aristocratic courts, those virtues of the chivalric ethos to which we have already referred.

There are other interesting analogies with the French knights. The French knightly class, normally speaking, not only had rather small estates but they were of heterogeneous composition—a castle or manor house, some meadows or vineyards in demesne, groups of tenants not necessarily in the same village, perhaps a mill with suit of mill from the persons under this lord's jurisdiction, and other jurisdictional rights. Similarly in England. E.A.Kosminsky's analysis of the *Rotuli Hundredorum* of 1279-80 revealed a type of small-landowner property, different in structure from the classical manor of the estates of the higher nobility. In particular there was generally little association of tenantry and demesne. The knight's income could consist almost entirely of rents from groups of tenants in various places, or he could on the contrary be an entrepreneur deriving much of his income from a demesne worked by wage labour. And we know from other sources that he could have the advowson of a parish church, patronage over a local monastery, a certain amount of urban property, and exclusive hunting rights in his locality (hare and rabbits of course, not the royal deer).

These lesser English aristocratic landowners, the forerunners of those who will later be called the 'gentry', were becoming less inclined to assume the burdens and the expense of knighthood by the end of the 13th century. They were not a homogeneous group, of course, and it was the poorer, with fewer direct connections, especially military, with the households of the greater nobles, who withdrew from chivalric status. There may have been a revival of knighthood and chivalry during the Hundred Years War, but even then, many minor landowners, if they took part at all, enlisted as men-at-arms rather than as knights. The trend continued, as can be seen from lists of county notables drawn up in 1434 where the knights form only a small proportion of the total. But this was by no means a peculiarly English phenomenon. The petty lords of France, even some of middle status, in peace time as in war time were disinclined to undertake the expense of being *chevaliers*. Nor is this surprising, when one considers the incomes of the minor lords of, say, the Bourbonnais, where a miniature collection of seigneurial rights and property in Livry—a house with a meadow and a warren attached, 4 vines, another meadow, a piece of arable and a dependent holding, part of a tithe, a portion of judicial rights—brought in a mere 50 s.t.a year.

That important subject, the rise and fall of chivalry as a way of life and a symbol of aristocratic prestige, should not deflect our attention from the most important and interesting phenomenon which affected *féodalité* and *seigneurie* in the later middle ages—the economic and social crisis of the late 14th and early 15th centuries. One can discuss 'bastard feudalism'— the replacement of tenurial by cash links between lord and vassal; one can discuss whether in France nobility hardened into a caste or, on the contrary, as in England, remained a class relatively open to upwardly mobile elements from the rich freeholders or the bourgoisie. But the most portentous phenomenon in these crisis years was the changed relationship between lords and peasants, the relationship which we have presented as the essence of medieval feudal society.

The importance of the demographic collapse of the middle of the 14th century and the consequent sharp rise in the land : labour ratio cannot be underestimated. This happened when in both countries the peasantry had already been tested in conflicts with the lords, had achieved remarkable modifications to their dependent condition and even acquired communal rights in some regions in France. No rural commune can be found in England, but the lords' and lawyers' pressure to declare villeinage servile had been fiercely resisted by the peasants though not, in the end, successfully. Nevertheless, in the course of the struggle, village customs had been defined, arbitrary exactions replaced by fixed obligations and self-conciousness of the village communities strengthened.

After the famines and the plagues it might seem that English and French feudalism would then follow rather different paths, given that France was subjected to the devastation of the English armies and the pillaging of the *routiers*, leading to the literal destruction of village communities. Following the English peasants revolt of 1381, English peasant communities continued successfully to exercise pressure on their lords for a diminution of rents and a relaxation of dues and services for 70 years. Did the Jacqueries of northern France, the Massif Central and elsewhere have the same effects. Or was it simply that French lords had to make concessions in order to restore the spoiled land ? In any event, from the Bordelais to the Lyonnais money rents declined, as did the proportion of crops demanded for rent in kind.The peasants in both England and France found more of the fruits of their surplus labour in their own hands; the productivity of labour (reflected also in rising wages) was enhanced and the foundations were laid for an economic revival.

Did the end of the fifteenth century see the parting of the ways between English and French feudalism ? In Normandy, the Paris basin, the Lyonnais and elsewhere in France the seigneurial structures were restored with remarkably little change in their essential character. What happened to the English manor? It, too, had a long history yet to come. After all, copyhold tenures were not abolished until 1922. But there were distinctive features of English development which relate to the peculiar character of the English landed aristocracy. During the course of the 15th century the English manor court was drained of much of its jurisdictional power over persons. This does not mean that the power of the local aristocrats was diminished. In fact their jurisdictional power over local communities was increased, particularly with reference to the control of labour, by the power given by the goverment to the élite of the county gentry who were appointed to royal courts as Justices of the Peace. An important element developing out of the richer peasantry, the yeomanry, some of whom were graziers, others arable farmers, also represented an indirect weakening of the manor. Although some of their land was held by the no longer servile version of villein tenure, copyhold, they mostly held by freehold and in particular leasehold. Their relationship with the landowner began to look more like that of the capitalist farmer of the future rather than simply a well-to-do manorial tenant. What was needed to make them into true agrarian capitalists was a wage labour force and that was yet to come.

In spite of real, and important differences, it would be unwise to ignore the common features of the development of feudal society in medieval France and England. The evolution of the economy, society and institutional forms was often out of phase, France often seeming to be more precocious in development than England. Backwardness, however, could turn into its opposite and not merely because the English devastated France and preserved their own towns and village intact. In the end it may be that the relative weakness of the English manor, as compared with the French seigneurie, gave scope for that spurt in development which enabled the English to anticipate by nearly a century and a half the destruction of feudalism—not to speak of 'feudalism', that is, not only of *féodalisme* but also of *féodalité*.

19

Was There a General Crisis of Feudalism?

Contemporary historians are showing considerable interest in the end of feudal society and in the economic, social and political factors which brought the modern world into existence.[1] There is nothing surprising in their efforts to understand why and how established social orders go through periods of crisis and in the end collapse. Even medievalists cannot expect to be sheltered from the world in which they live. It is quite natural, therefore, to ask oneself whether the feudal order was subject to accidental disintegration, to be gradually replaced by another social, economic and political order—capitalism; or whether its disintegration was speeded up by several unrelated crises, which operated in different aspects of feudal society; or whether there was, in fact, a general crisis of this society because of its inherent weaknesses—a general crisis of which the separate crises which historians examine were simply particular expressions.

E. Perroy, in his recent article in *Annales* on the crises of the 14th century, writes about some of the catastrophes which shook the social order of western Europe; he characterises this society by the end of the century as afflicted by 'mediocrity in stagnation', rather as M. M. Postan, in an article on the 15th century, characterises the subsequent period. And it is, in fact, one of the surprising features to us of the decay of medieval society that it should have lasted so long, accustomed as we are to much quicker cycles of growth and depression. From the 14th century onwards, this civilization was undermined by intellectual doubts, its political foundations were sapped and it seemed to have become socially and morally decrepit. The general picture can be perceived, even though many details are obscure and although the sequence of cause and effect is by no means disentangled, especially as far as demography is concerned.

The European population, no doubt, increased considerably during the 12th and 13th centuries, but in the 14th century, before the Black Death, it was beginning to diminish. At the same time, that is before the Black Death, indications of crisis and decline appear in the most important sector of the economy, agriculture. Land went out of cultivation and that which was still tilled yielded less. There could be no more revealing indications of the crisis of a social order than the inability of its ruling class, demonstrated over a long period of time, to profit in a situation over which they seemed to have complete control. And yet, both the accounts of the great estates in England and the terms of contracts of tenure in France reveal, in the first half of the 14th century, the beginnings of a contraction of seigneurial revenues which lasted for at least a century.

Consequently, the principal market for imported goods in Europe, as well as for many of the continent's industrial products, also contracted. It is no surprise therefore that industry and commerce were affected by the crisis. Thus, underlying the violent but short term oscillations of the textile industry (attributable to political causes) a general tendency to contraction is to be seen. Commercial and financial companies scaled down their activities. Urban populations diminished. There appeared to be no recovery until the end of the 15th century.

One may wonder, however, whether the phrase of E. Perroy, quoted above, 'mediocrity in stagnation', is altogether adequate to characterise western European society towards the end of the 14th and the beginning of the 15th centuries. The phrase certainly cannot be applied without risk of error to the whole of the 14th century, that epoch when society was rent, not only by warfare between states but by social conflicts on a scale hardly paralleled since the age of the Bagaudae. The revolts of maritime Flanders, of the Jacques in France, of the English peasants in 1381 and of the lower and middling strata in numerous Italian, French, Flemish and English towns, are dramatic events which have to be situated in a climate of discontent which historians are only just beginning to study. The most interesting aspect of the major rebellions of the later middle ages is that they no longer simply expressed grievances against local oppression, they were becoming the expression of a revolt against the way society was organised. Whatever might be the differences between the risings of the French Jacques and the English peasants, they had this in common: a manifest hatred of the officials of the State, rather than of those of the manor or seigneurie who had been the traditional objects of peasant discontent. And, of course, even if lords became less involved in manorial production, they still had to cope with the problem of falling revenues. War and pillage were still among the measures used in their attempt to solve the problem but it was the State which organised war and raised the money needed to pay for it. State taxation was added therefore to the burden of rent owed by the peasant and urban taxes bore down on the petty artisans and wage workers of the towns.

To sum up, the profile of the late medieval crisis as it emerges from recent research is of a contraction of the rural and industrial economies operating over a long period and accompanied by a fall in the population. This contraction was probably felt in the first place by the ruling class, given the fact that even in periods of economic expansion the lower classes lived not far from famine conditions. Seigneurial revenues and industrial and commercial profits began to fall. Consequently wars which in the past had tended to stop soon after they began, were prolonged because their protagonists saw in them the chance to compensate by pillage and ransom for the fall in their rent. But the prolongation of these wars made the mobilisation of armies more difficult, complicated and costly, especially since military expeditions had to be paid for in cash rather than raised on the basis of military service. It was not only the burden of tax but the disorganization of the economy in the war zones which had to be borne by the poor, thus provoked to rebellion. Revolt in the towns disorganised industrial production and revolt in the countryside strengthened peasant resistance to the payment of rent. Rent and profits thus dropped even further—a vicious circle.

One has to ask however, how this process began ? Was there a series of unconnected crises which shook the social order to the point at which, however basically sound, it was incapable of recovery ? Or, on the contrary, were there deeper causes at the root of these economic, social and political crises ? This latter explanation seems to us the better. But let us put away one specious hypothesis : that there was some sort of slump in agriculture, industry and finance, similar to those which our own experience of capitalist society suggests should be expected after a period of prosperity.

For here we do not have to deal with a capitalist society. The necessary conditions for such a society did not exist in 14th century Europe. By far the greatest proportion of the products of agriculture and even of industry were always intended for the consumption of the producer or at the most for the local market. Even where production was aimed at a wider market, there was no clear distinction between the capitalist owner of the means of production and the wage earner who had nothing to sell but his labour power. It is true that there were enormous accumulations of merchant capital, made in the course of the circulation of commodities—especially those goods of high price and small bulk of Eastern origin. Together with this accumulation of merchant capital, we must also mention the precocious development of the commercial techniques required in the regular functioning of international trade. The devices of the merchant bankers of the 14th century were developed with subtlety ; the means by which credits were extended and transferred without transfers of specie became very effective ; business men and even some landowners showed considerable initiative in the pursuit of profit. However, their activities were marginal to the mode of production and social organisation and did not alter its traditional character. Hence, theories of economic development which are based on the study of fluctuations in currencies and transfers of precious metals can only, at best, explain a very small sector of the medieval economy. Only in this small sector could we imagine anything resembling the classic succession of periods of expansion and crisis. But a crisis of over-production affecting a whole society, as in modern times, was impossible in the middle ages.

It seems more likely that the prolonged crisis of feudal society in the 14th and 15th centuries more resembles—in spite of important differences—the crisis of ancient society in the last centuries of the Roman Empire than the crises of the 19th and 20th centuries. During the last days of the Empire, as in the late middle ages, society was paralysed by the increasing costs of the social and political superstructure—costs which were not paid for by any increase in society's productive resources. The basis problem is, therefore, to explain this failure of a significant increase in the productivity of agriculture and industry during this period. How can we explain the long hiatus in technological progress between the end of the growth period of the medieval productive forces and the beginnings of the technical progress which laid the foundations for modern capitalism?

Although the word 'boom' is hardly a useful term to describe the expansion before the collapse, there was nevertheless real progress. The researches of Lefebvre de Noëttes and Marc Bloch have shown the development of techniques during and after the 10th century, especially in the use of animal traction and water power. The considerable expansion of the cultivated area of Europe was of great economic importance. It was one of the principal successes of feudal society, as well as being the necessary condition for the development of international trade and of European culture during these two centuries.

We must, of course, consider the negative as well as the positive aspects of the extension of the cultivated area. It was accomplished at the expense of woodland and natural pasture. Even though we cannot produce statistical proof, it is by no means impossible that this lateral spread may have intensified one of the basic contradictions of medieval agriculture. Agricultural productivity was limited by the shortage of manure and the raising of stock was hindered by the lack of winter fodder—a problem not fully resolved until the 18th century. It is possible that by the end of the 13th century, the precarious balance between stock-raising and agriculture was broken by the extension of arable at the expense of pasture.

Admittedly, this is conjectural, for it is generally supposed that the productivity as well as the total yield of agriculture had increased during the 13th century, especially in England. M. Perroy writes of the 'continuous creation of new capital' during this period, so that we might assume that the increase of production followed the reinvestment of profits.[2] In England, when the price of cereals and livestock increased in the 12th and 13th centuries, the demesne economy remained intact, by contrast with France and western Germany. These circumstances made possible agricultural production on a large scale for the market under the direct control of the big landlords. Some of these landlords, in order to expand the area of cultivation, spent money on the draining of marshes and the clearing of forests. Not that they were the only elements in the rural population to do this. Others, such as the lesser nobility and the richer peasants also expanded their cultivated area under the stimulus of increasing prices. However, even though the total production of grain must have increased during this period, there is no indication of a general and permanent increase in yields. What seems to have been a surprising overall increase in the yields of grain on the estates of the wealthy bishops of Winchester in southern England, could in fact be largely attributed to an increase in the amount of seed sown per acre. Figures from other estates in different regions give the impression that there was no increase in agricultural productivity before the 17th century.

The general conclusion must be that there was no sufficient re-investment of agricultural profits which would have *significantly* improved productivity. This was as true when very large profits were being made as when they were not. If the quantity of goods put on the market in the 13th century was greater than in preceding periods, production for the market still did not predominate sufficiently so as to develop competition, leading to a reduction in the costs of production as a result of technical improvements—as in the capitalist process in the 19th century. The greater landowners, because of the very nature of their social existence, were neither inclined to save nor to re-invest their profits. The principal expenses of the nobility, lay and ecclesiastical, were on war, luxury and display for the lords themselves and for their numerous retainers. These expenses reached such prodigious levels that even at the height of their prosperity as landowners, lords were living all the time on the edge of financial failure. In so far as they received credit, it was for consumption, not for productive investment.

But in any case, the great landowners, even in England, and less so in continental Europe, were not the main producers. Most of the cultivated land was in the hands of the peasants. However, in spite of genuine progress made by them, to which we will return, these small producers were the last to be able to increase productivity by investment. First, the lords always strove to appropriate, in rent, the greater part of the surplus product of the peasant. Next, the burden of tax, in the last resort, always fell on them, which still further reduced their share of the surplus product. And finally, as in all primitive agricultural societies, peasants tended to be exploited by usurers.

Similar arguments apply to industry. In spite of the high level of organisation in certain centres of the textile industry, cloth production was always based on the small unit of production. Espinas, for the Flemish industry and Doren for the Florentine, both show that between the 14th and 18th centuries there was no change in the equipment used for the principal processes. S. Lilley, the English historian of science, showed that the rate of technical innovation fell sharply after about 1300.[3] The sectors of industry which produced for local markets also did not evolve technically. Investment was as impossible for the small household enterprise in craft industry as it was in peasant agriculture, and for similar reasons. The restrictive policies of the craft organisation constituted a further hindrance to technical progress. In Flanders, in north and central Italy, and elsewhere, everywhere where merchant-bankers became involved in the industrial sector, the interests of merchant capital would discourage the investment of capital for technical improvement. The merchants were just as inclined to put their money into a cargo of spices, into loans to a ruler or into mortgages on real property as into the textile industry. The only way in which the total product could be increased was by the multiplication of small workshops, but, as Mme. Doehaerd has indicated concerning the Belgian textile industry in the 14th century, 'demographic growth failing... the productive capacity of industry, based on the old techniques, was bound to become stationary with the numbers of the labour force'.[4]

To sum up: the stagnation of productivity during the last centuries of the middle ages, its inability to support the increasing cost of the non-productive expenditure of the ruling classes, were the fundamental reasons for the crisis of feudal society. This stagnation was the consequence of the inability of the feudal economy to generate investment for technical improvement. In the first place, production for the market and the stimulus of competition only affected a very narrow sector of the economy. Secondly, agricultural and industrial production were based on the household unit and the profits of small peasant and small artisan enterprise were taken by landowners and usurers. Thirdly, the social structure and the habits of the landed nobility did not permit accumulation for investment for the extension of production.

This technical stagnation made impossible the demographic growth which had occurred in the 12th and 13th centuries. But this halt in growth cannot solely be attributed to the fact that agricultural production was insufficient to support an increasing population, for the population was not stabilised at the high 13th century level. It declined considerably. The succession of famines and plagues in Europe from the beginning of the 14th century gives one the impression that poverty—resulting from increased exploitation as well as from the fact that medieval agriculture seemed to be incapable of improvement—brought about an enfeeblement of the population's resistance to disease. Thus, the fall in the European population in the 14th and 15th centuries in relation to economic collapse is both cause and effect, since the problems of the agrarian and industrial economies were intensified by the shortage of labour in town and country.

Evidently, this sketch of a theory of the crisis of feudal society is incomplete. We have to deepen our knowledge of new elements in the situation which appeared at the depths of the crisis and which were necessary for the later development of a capitalist economy. Even in the 14th century new elements are making their appearance. The upper stratum of the peasantry, benefiting from the crisis of the seigneurial economy was to become an important factor in the constitution of the class of capitalist farmers in the 16th and 17th centuries, a social group of the greatest importance, especially in England. In England, as elsewhere in Europe, the parallel and partly related development of the textile industry outside the big towns was already well advanced in the second half of the 14th century. One finds an industrial organisation, which certainly began at a lower level than what had been achieved in big centres like Douai and Florence. Nevertheless, it was this rural textile industry, in a sense born out of the crisis, which was to be the direct ancestor of later developing capitalism.

These aspects of the period of crisis are significant: they show that when old societies seem to promise no hopes for change, new forms appear, ensuring future progress.

20

Ideology and Social Order in Late Medieval England

The heavens themselves, the planets, and this centre,
Observe degree, priority, and place,
Insisture, course, proportion, season, form,
Office and custom, in all line of order...
   (W. Shakespeare, *Troilus and Cressida,* Act I, Scene 3.)

The history of European society in the late middle ages, but especially after the middle of the 14th century, continues to excite considerable discussion. The main debate is about the problems of the economy, broadly between Marxists and neo-Ricardians[1] These writers have, on the whole avoided questions of the history of ideology which has been left to the historians of religion. In so far as there is any convergence between them, it has concerned the social interpretation of heresy.

The question as to whether heresy should be seen as a form of social protest or purely as a dispute concerning Christian belief does not concern me here. However, as will appear below, the problem cannot be avoided entirely, given that any form of social philosophy in the middle ages would be expressed within the broad framework of Christian doctrine. Within that framework, however, there were many changing forms of expression about the nature of the social order and the relations between classes which deserve specific examination.

An interesting recent work has proposed an interpretation of class in 15th century England in terms of certain propositions about the nature of social evolution and contemporary social attitudes.[2] One of the merits of the work is that it advances our understanding of an old problem in English social history—the identification of the 'gentry'. I am not concerned here with this class, but with those lower down the social scale who have been somewhat neglected in this book. Nevertheless it is necessary to refer briefly to the reason why the gentry are at the centre of the discussion. It is suggested that the 15th century was above all a period of upward social mobility. The chief manifestation of this mobility was that the old landed aristocracy—those of 'gentle' birth—was being penetrated from below by merchants and other rich commoners. This was why it was necessary to sharpen the definition of social boundaries as was done in sumptuary legislation as well as in legal and other writings. An era of individualism comparable to that of Victorian England was, it would seem, paradoxically reflected in expressions of increased social exclusiveness.

These stricter definitions of social space were not, according to this interpretation, further generalised in social theory, rather the reverse. The indisputable argument having been put forward that western Europe had never known a caste system, as in India, the author suggests that this was 'despite the classic but literary and soon decayed division between those who fight, those who pray and those who labour.' This is an unfortunate formulation. The essence of the social theory which was supposedly decayed was not so much in the tripartite division between warriors, priests and peasants but in the *functional* concept of the social order. In other words, in the 11th century as later, society was conceived as an integrated hierarchy of divine origin, in which each class kept to its own functions without encroaching on those of others.

Naturally, when the social division of labour became more advanced, additional status groups had to be included in the model. Even so, the tripartite image remained powerful. We may see this in Geoffrey Chaucer's General Prologue to the *Canterbury Tales*, where the knight, the parson and the ploughman stand out as ideal types, not subjected to satirical comments as were the other pilgrims. One could also add that that very conscious social analyst, the poet John Gower, prefaced his social satire (*Vox Clamantis*) which was directed against a wide range of social types in the 1380s, with the simple statement 'Novimus esse status tres sub quibus omnis in orbe more suo vivit...'[3] The continuing power of the image was, of course, also due to the fact that those who laboured, mostly the peasants, still saw the fruits of their labour transferred, in the main, to the landed aristocracy, (still identifiable to the villager as armed men on horseback) and to the priests in the form of tithes and other ecclesiastical dues.

I propose, in this paper, very briefly to present some evidence that, although contemporaries may have felt it necessary to define social boundaries, the problem was not one of insecurity caused by increased social mobility. The problem, especially between about 1380 and 1450, was seen by these contemporaries as a general upward move of the whole of the lower class, as much as social climbing by individual parvenus. But before looking at expressions of social attitudes, I must briefly state some contrary views about social mobility as an economic and social phenomenon at this time.

It is difficult to admit that there was any serious threat to the ruling families either of the nation or of the shires which came from immediately below. The problem was demographic. Low family replacement rates, which also affected the supposedly upwardly mobile bourgeoisie, were chiefly responsible for the extinction in the male line of noble and gentry families. This was not even a new problem. Baronial families between 1086 and about 1330 had an average existence in the male line of about three generations, and this was when replacement rates were higher. Nor was the investment of mercantile wealth in rural lordships a new phenomenon, as Henri Pirenne suggested many years ago.[4] Furthermore, any significant move by merchants and others into the ranks of gentility could only be the consequence of a general rise in the incomes of capitalists in London and the major provincial towns. But this was not happening in the 15th century. There were, as always, some very rich London merchants. But if anything there was an absolute decay in urban wealth, especially towards the end of the century. The new wealth that was being created was at levels where no threat was as yet being made against the nobility and gentry at any rate in terms of ambitious families aspiring to gentle status. If there was a threat, it came not from individuals but from a whole class or classes. It may have been a sensitivity to this threat which seemed to harden and to make even more articulate the old and deeply rooted consciousness of status.

There is no space here to elaborate the nature of this threat. It is enough to refer to the combined effect on the late medieval aristocracy, especially between 1380 and 1450, of open peasant rebellion and constant peasant pressure for reduced rents and services. All this is well documented and was observably successful. To it should be added the equally successful upward pressure on wages by labourers. And although the influence of the Lollard heresy on peasants, artisans and labourers may have been restricted to a small minority it was feared by the authorities as a serious subversive threat, not only to religion but to property. It is also worth mentioning that to these fears was linked an apprehension of a subversion which could be seen as equally dangerous—the usurpation of the rights of men by women.

Social attitudes reach us through the written word. But who were the writers? The mass of the people was illiterate. Those who wrote at this time must mostly have been clerics. Some of the clergy had taken part in the 1381 rising. Many may have been sympathetic to peasants and artisans and could have expressed their feelings. But the clergy were also the principal transmitters, through the pulpit and the confessional, of established social theory. It may not, however, be important for our purposes to identify the social origin or sympathies of sermons, poems or other written evidence of social attitudes. What is important is the evidence of social preoccupation. It must also be admitted that seemingly direct references to social types, in particular to 'ploughmen', can be interpreted symbolically, usually with a religious connotation. Nevertheless, symbols are chosen because of their contemporary resonance. It is no accident that the ploughman appears so powerfully, whether as himself or as a symbol in the last century and a half of the middle ages.[5] He had become a *disturbing* figure, and not simply because he rather than the knight now appears as mankind's guide to salvation.

The rebellion of 1381 plays its part in the unease about ploughmen, shepherds, artisans and other plebeians. John Gower, in his dream about the rising sees them as oxen who refuse to be yoked to the plough. Even when they are put once more under the yoke after their defeat, they lie in wait in the hopes of once again bringing the nobility (*genus ingenuum*) to truction. A poet writing in the 1390s compared the rising to two natural catastrophes, pestilence and earthquake:

Theose three thinges, I vnderstonde
Beo-tokenes the grete vengaunce & wrake
That schulde falle for synnes sake...

The refrain of each of the eleven stanzas of the poem is a variation on the theme:

This was a warnyng to be ware:[7]

Stiff-necked peasants, even after the defeat of the insurrection, still refused to pay certain rents and services, especially those with servile implications, even to the most powerful of lords.[8] And although the risings of 1450-2 were not simply peasant and artisan rebellions as in 1381, the fear of peasant upheaval, directed against all lords, was revived. In 1452 a number of Kentish husbandmen, yeomen and artisans were accused, not simply of being supporters of Jack Cade (reputed to be still alive) but of plotting to destroy the king, the lords of his council and the bishops. These sons of the devil and Lollards (as the indictment calls them) further proposed to hold all things in common.[9] The atmosphere which caused the elaboration of such unlikely accusations is evoked in a story by Thomas Gascoigne, once chancellor of Oxford University, writing in the 1450s, in his *Loci e libro veritatum*. Illustrating the decay of *justicia primitiva* he tells us that a thousand tenants of an earl rebelled because of the beating of one peasant. Instead of attacking the responsible individual, they killed several other people, destroyed manor houses, barns full of grain and the buildings owned by a cathedral whose bishop had excommunicated them.[10]

The ploughman who was found to be so disturbing cannot be clearly separated from the ploughman who was exalted as the embodiment of social and even theological virtue. In the poem *Pierce the Plowman's Crede* (mid 1390s) the poet finds that it is the ploughman who will teach the creed better than any of the orders of friars or monks.[11] In this, the poem, with new Lollard overtones, continues the idealisation of the ploughman in William Langland's *Piers Plowman* . 'Ploughing, it is wisdom's way' writes Iolo Goch, a Welsh contemporary of Langland in his poem *The Ploughman*.[12] An anonymous song, probably of the 15th century, with the refrain 'God spede the plowe al day', has as its opening lines:

The merthe of alle this londe
maketh the gode husbonde,
With erynge of his plowe.[13]

But ploughmen are also represented, not only as supporting the world with their labour, but questioning how the fruits of their labour are distributed. Some writings of this type, are, like *Pierce the Plowman's Crede* mainly anti-clerical or Lollard propaganda. In the prologue to *The Plowman's Tale* (circa 1400), the ploughman refers to his supposed duty to sustain the clergy. They, however, provide nothing in return:

> They have the corn and we the dust...[14]

This pious tract is almost echoed by the Satanic Cain in the Wakefield play (before 1450), who refuses to pay tithe on his grain:

> Or it was shorne and brought in stak
> had I many a wery bak
> Therefor ask me no mor of this
> For I have giffen that my will is...[15]

The husbandmen of another poem with the title *Gode Spede the Plow* (15th century) claim that they 'mayntayne this worlde' and then go on to say how the world divides their product: tithes for the clergy; produce taken without payment by the king's purveyors; a fifteenth of the value of moveable possessions in tax; rent for the lord; alms for the mendicants; bribes for the summoner; and so on.[16]

The contrast in many of these poems is between the ploughman at work and the idle clergy, especially the friars. The issue for the poet may be primarily doctrinal. The point for us is that it is the looming figure of the ploughman through whom he makes his argument. The anti-clerical point is emphasised more than once by the ploughman's castigation of monks, priests and bishops as social upstarts, sons of labourers and beggars. But this, of course, further links the symbolic ploughman with contemporary reality, the ploughman, that is, who has to pay high wages to his labourers.

In this period, then, there were more serious threats to the stability of the social order than from a few aspirants to gentility. Those threatened naturally reacted. Margaret Aston has shown how the Lollard heresy was equated with social and political sedition.[17] An important move therefore would be to stop people from discussing unsuitable topics. This theme appears frequently in orthodox writings contemporary with those from which we have drawn illustrations of the ploughman theme. Thomas Hoccleve, in his *Regement of Princes* (early 15th century) might write:

> peples vois is goddes voys, men seyn

but he also advised:

> ..of our faithe noon argumentes meeve

since nowadays:

> a baillif or reeve or man of craft wole in it
> dote or rave...

Even worse:

> Some women eke thogh her wit be thynne,
> wole argumentes make in holy writ...
> (Hoccleve, *Minor Poems*)[18]

A sermon writer of the period preached as follows:

> It is enough to thee to believe as Holy Church teacheth thee,
> and let the clerks alone with the argument.[19]

In an anti-Lollard poem of the early 15th century (*Jak Upland and the reply of Friar Daw Topius*), the friar complained that the Lollards

> with wrenchis and wiles
> wynnen mens wyves
> and maken hem scolers
> of the newe scole...

He warns that:

> ...carpenters ne sowters
> cardmakers ne powchers
> drapers ne cutellers
> girdelers, coferers ne corvysers,
> ne no manere of artificers.
> this sacrament (the Eucharist) mowe treten...[20]

Little wonder that the vociferous if orthodox Margery Kempe was suspected of Lollardy.[21]

The exclusion of the laity and especially of women and plebeians, from discussions about doctrine, was no new thing in Europe, though perhaps unusual—because not previously necessary—in hitherto orthodox England. The same is not quite the case with another remedy for social instability, that is the writing and preaching of the social doctrine of the harmony of the estates. This was commonplace in England well before the end of the 14th century; nor by then was it in any way decayed. So strong, in fact, had the satirical element in estate literature and preaching become that some suspected it of too dangerously pointing out the sins of the rich to the poor. After the late 14th century rebellions the emphasis was laid rather on the preaching of social harmony.

In another sermon, the preacher whom we have already quoted refers to the duties of the three estates: the 'knights and other gentles' to govern in time of peace and look to 'points of arms' in time of war; the priests to learn and preach the law of God; lower men to content themselves with the questions of their own labour. The preacher goes on to say:

> ... if every part of Christ's church would hold them content
> with their own occupations ... then the grace of almighty God
> should flourish ...

The anonymous author of *Mum and the Sothsegger* tells us:

> Ther gomes and the goodman
> beth all eliche grete
> Woll wo beth the wones and all that woneth ther-in[22]

Only slightly later Hoccleve says peace is at risk :

> when the grettir obeith to the lesse

and there is trouble in the land when :

> no wight halt hym content of his estate[23]

The emphasis on hierarchy and on the disasters which follow the overthrow of hierarchy is not new, but it is newly stressed. Hoccleve and the author of *Mum and the Sothsegger* were preoccupied with disturbances at all levels of the social hierarchy. An anonymous poem of the same period makes the point again with familiar but significant banality :

> Eche kyng is sworn to governaunce
> to govern goddis puple in right
> Eche kyng bereth sword of goddis vengeaunce
> To felle goddis foon in fight
> And so doth everons honest knight
> That bereth the order as it wes;
> The plough, the chirche, to maynteyne right
> Are goddis champyons to kepe the pes.[24]

For a lower social level the pompous friar, Daw Topias rebukes his Lollard opponent, Jak Upland :

> For right as in thi bodi, Jake,
> ben ordeyned thin hondis
> for thin head and for thi feet
> and for thin eyen to wirken
> right so the comoun peple
> God hath disposid
> to laboren for holi chirche
> and lordshipis also
> . . . .
> The sonne is holy chirche
> and lordship the moone
> the sterres ben the comuns...[25]

The theme continues, in sermon, prose and verse through the 15th century and beyond. It is not a social theory which would go unchallenged in periods of rapid social mobility and opportunities for individual advancement, but the 15th century was not such a period. However, particularly up to the middle of the century, there was evidently a sharp perception by the writers and by their patrons that peasants and artisans were making significant advances in the social and economic sphere and might well be mobilised politically. To answer this it was important to justify the existing order in term of celestially sanctioned harmony.

21

Some Social and Economic Evidence in Late Medieval English Tax Returns

Historians of the English economy in the thirteenth and fourteenth centuries are fortunate in the abundant survival of manorial and estate records of all sorts. This material has its deficiencies, of course, but so long as the landowners continued their close interest in the internal workings of the manor, the annual accounts of their reeves and bailiffs, the rentals and custumals which were used to check these accounts and the records of the manor courts, give an unparalleled insight into the agrarian economy. Urban records, in comparison, are very disappointing for individual commercial or industrial enterprises rarely left financial accounts; the survival of official municipal records is uneven; and the type of information found in the notaries' registers of Southern France and Italy is almost entirely absent. From the last quarter of the fourteenth century, even the manorial material becomes scanty and less informative as a result of the widespread leasing policy of the landowners, by which demesnes were henceforth cultivated by farmers who either kept no accounts, or if they did, have not left them behind for posterity.

The diminution in the quantity and scope of the manorial material, and the lack of any compensating increase in the evidence for the urban and industrial sectors of the economy presents the historian of late medieval England with considerable problems. For this reason, other types of evidence require a closer analysis; and the taxation records are of the first importance. Even those tax returns (such as the second and third poll tax returns of 1379 and 1381) whose deficiencies have been most ruthlessly exposed can be used, provided their limitations are recognised. A good deal of important work has been done in recent years on this type of evidence. One may refer to Professor M. W. Beresford's use of tax returns to demonstrate the scale of the desertion of village and hamlet settlements in late medieval and early modern times. Of comparable interest is a recent essay by Dr. R. S. Schofield in which he measures the geographical re-distribution of the country's wealth (measured in its taxable capacity) primarily between the fourteenth and fifteenth centuries. And in more detail, with a narrower focus, Professor W. G. Hoskins has shown how tax returns can illuminate the economic development of certain late medieval towns.[1]

In the following study, I investigate the possibility of using tax returns to show population movements and changes in social structure over a relatively small area of the country between 1380 and 1524. I am not concerned with changes in the taxable capacity of individuals as calculated by the local assessors but rather with the number of individual taxpayers, and (insofar as this is discoverable) with their role in the social economy. The area with which I am concerned here is the Cotswold region of Gloucestershire,[2] famous both as a wool producing and a cloth manufacturing area. It may be thought that a type of evidence which some historians think should only be used on a wide scale and in order to arrive at very broad conclusions ought not to be employed so narrowly. However, fairly complete material from the poll tax returns of 1381 and the subsidy returns of 1524 have survived, so perhaps the risk is worthwhile.

As Oman and others have rightly insisted, the Poll Tax returns of 1379 and 1381 show a considerable degree of evasion compared with that of 1377. However, for the area that I have chosen to investigate there are no detailed returns from the earliest Poll Tax. Furthermore, although the last Poll Tax is defective in that many of those who ought to have been assessed escaped, it does at any rate give occupational descriptions of all those taxed. The 1524 subsidy is less detailed but probably more reliable and comprehensive. It also designates those tax payers who were assessed on their wages rather than on moveable goods and land.[3] There is therefore a basis for comparison as regards wage workers the two returns.

Additionally, although total figures of the tax-paying population are unreliable in both cases and not comparable as between the two dates, the distribution of the tax-paying population within the same area at the two dates may be compared. This however, is a comparison fraught with more risks than a comparison of the wage earners at the two dates. It will be noticed from the tables which follow later in this paper that the numbers of tax-payers in the 1524 returns are much lower than the numbers of tax-payers in 1381. This is to be expected, of course. There are naturally more people paying a poll-tax than a tax mainly assessed on property, even when certain wages were also assessed. The tax-payers to the 1327 subsidy were also fewer in number than the poll-tax payers of 1381, in spite of the plagues which reduced the population in the intervening period. All the same, it has to be admitted that even when one is only comparing proportions (in this case of town dwellers and country dwellers), the fact that the total numbers in the later return are less than half the numbers in the earlier must make one cautious about one's conclusions.

Another difficulty may be that different classes of people would be exempt from or would evade assessment to the two different taxes. It has been suggested, for instance, that in 1524 urban evasion was much greater than it was in the villages. This is almost impossible to prove, but even if it were true (and it is not, in the nature of things, unlikely), it was probably equally true in 1381. Then there is the possibility of different types of people being exempt or evading taxation because of the different modes of assessment. Poll tax evaders in 1381, as is well known, were primarily unmarried females in parental households, as well, no doubt as some males without households of their own who could easily be concealed, or move away. Evaders in 1524 could be persons in similar positions but the legally exempt would also include very poor house-holders possessing under the lower limit of 20s of moveable goods. Unfortunately, we have no means of calculating the proportion of those who did not pay the tax in either case. If we had enough information to do so, we would not need to depend so much on the evidence of the tax returns themselves.[4]

I first propose to show how a comparison of the two tax returns yields suggestive evidence about some population movements during the period. It would be possible to go into considerable detail and to compare the relative population strength of every village at the two dates. The returns could be used to illustrate for the Cotswolds what Professor Beresford has done for other parts of the country, the actual disappearance of village communities.[5] They would also show the relative growth of some other rural communities such as those of Lower Swell, Upper Slaughter and Great Rissington. But such fluctuations are best examined in the light of detailed local study based on all forms of archaeological and documentary evidence. More striking, and easily related to existing knowledge, is an examination of the population fluctuations of the urban centres and the centres of rural industry. There are different ways of bringing out these changes, and the employment of calculations on more than one basis acts as a check on conclusions.

We may in the first place take the better known towns of the region, those, that is, for which there is evidence in both sets of returns. These include all of the important Cotswold markets, except unfortunately for Northleach. This little town and manor was owned by St. Peter's Abbey, Gloucester, and its position as a collecting centre for wool is well known. In 1524 its taxed population was about the same as that of Lechlade and Stow-on-the-Wold but unfortunately the taxed population in 1381 cannot be calculated owing to defects in the manuscript. However we have information for both dates about Cirencester, Lechlade, Fairford, Tetbury and Painswick in the South Cotswolds, and about Stow, Chipping Campden and Winchcombe in the north-east. If we estimate the relative strengths of these urban centres at the two dates, we find that the most striking feature is the decline of Cirencester. In 1381 its taxed population was one third of the total taxed population of these eight towns. In 1525 it was only a little more than one-fifth. Campden, Lechlade and Fairford maintained their position. Stow, Painswick and Tetbury declined slightly, but Winchcombe expanded. Its taxpaying population was only two-fifths the size of Cirencester's in 1381. By 1524 it was nearly a tenth bigger.

These are shifts in the relative strengths of the urban population

considered without relation to their rural setting. This, however, is
unsatisfactory, especially since it is said that in the fifteenth and early
sixteenth centuries there was a general tendency for industry to leave the
towns and to be re-located in the countryside. The best known example
of this, of course, in the Midlands, is the textile town of Coventry, whose
population may have been something like 5000 in 1280, 9-10,000 before
the Black Death, 10,000 in 1379 and 6600 in 1521.[6] Stratford-
upon-Avon's fourteenth century cloth industry, small in scale but
responsible for a street of fullers and a Drapery Hall, dwindled
considerably in the fifteenth century, if it did not disappear.[7] The
Worcestershire towns actually got an act passed in 1534 to protect them
against the rural industry, and it is generally assumed that the Cotswold
textile industry was rural rather than urban.

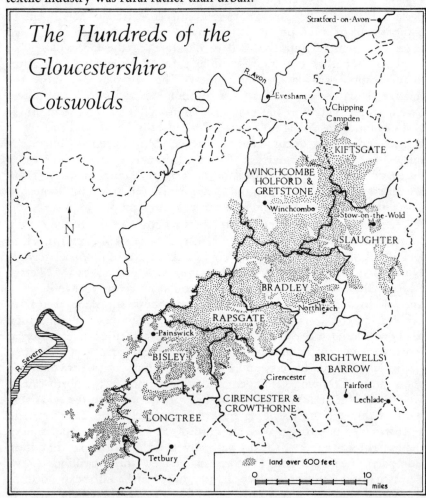

The Hundreds of the
Gloucestershire
Cotswolds

Was there, then, a de-urbanisation process in the Cotswolds in the fifteenth and early sixteenth centuries? To confirm this we must attempt to compare the town populations with the populations of the rural areas at the two different dates for which we have the tax-return evidence. To do this it is necessary of course, to eliminate from the calculations all villages as well as towns for which there are not figures at both dates. This narrows the statistical basis while making it more secure. Fortunately, the returns are least defective and the coincidence of data the greatest for the south-eastern hundreds where there was the main industrial concentration. These are the hundreds of Bisley, Cirencester,[8] Crowthorn, Brightwells Barrow and Longtree. The most defective evidence is for the Hundreds of Bradley and Rapsgate in the central Cotswolds where the only centre which could be thought of as urbanised was Northleach. The figures for the northern hundreds of Holford, Gretstone, Kiftsgate and Slaughter (or Salmondsbury) are more complete, though not as complete as for the south-eastern hundreds. These last cover a continuous stretch of territory from the Stroud Valley to the Thames and the Oxfordshire boundary.

The physical characteristics of these areas which are relevant to economic activity are as follows. The south-eastern group of hundreds (Bisley, Cirencester, Crowthorne, Brightwells Barrow and Longtree), reading from West to East includes 1) The steep valleys of the Stroud area where there is very little room for arable farming owing to the steep sides and very heavy clays in the valley bottoms; 2) the arable land of the main Cotswold plateau, where sheep were as essential an element as an adjunct to arable farming as in producing an income from wool; and 3) the upper Thames valley alluvial meadows where the main dangers were floods and liver fluke. The central Hundreds of Bradley and Rapsgate were mostly typical Cotswolds plateau country but with better land in the Coln and Windrush valleys. Apart from those parts of Holford, Gretstone, Kiftsgate and Slaughter which were also on the oolitic plateau the most important variations were north of the scarp in the Avon valley, and on the East in the vales of Moreton and Bourton where the soils were heavy, lias clays varied with lighter boulder clay and glacial deposits.

The following table summarises the distribution of the taxpaying population in the southern group of hundreds:

	1381	%	1565	%
Total taxed population counted	3152	100	1265	100
Urban population	1159	37	326	26
Cirencester	574	18	119	9
The remaining towns	585	19	207	17

From this it would appear that the proportion of the urban taxed population to the total taxed population fell considerably, and that the greatest decline was at Cirencester, the ancient capital of the Cotswolds, the centre of its communication system and the seat of one of the wealthiest religious houses in the West Midlands. Of course, quite apart from the general reservations already expressed, the figures are not conclusive in view of the omissions that have to be made to keep the data from the two sets of returns as far as possible comparable, and in view of the different character of the assessments.[9] It may be added that Painswick as well as Cirencester seems to have lost severely. This comes out best by relating this town's population to its immediate, rather than the wider, rural hinterland. In 1381 its taxed population comprised one third of the total taxed population of the Hundred of Bisley, whereas it was only seventh in 1526.

The Stroud Valley is in the Hundred of Bisley. The name of Stroud does not appear in either tax return, for those industrialised hamlets which formed the Stroud cloth-making area were all included in the 1524 return under Bisley parish. Some of them are, however, separately named in the 1381 return, which was made on a settlement not a parish basis.[10] When identity of areas is established, we find that the taxed population of Bisley parish, which was about 40% of the taxed population of the Hundred of Bisley in 1381, had risen to about 66% in 1524. It is probably not jumping to extravagant conclusions to associate this population concentration with industrialisation.[11] Already in 1381 there were fullers in some of the Bisley parish hamlets (in Upper and Lower Lypiatt they were the highest assessed taxpayers); and in nearby villages in Longtree Hundred there were other textile workers -a weaver in Avening and fullers and weavers in Woodchester. In Horsley there were cardmakers, craftsmen linking the textile with the metal industry. Horsley had about 8% of the taxpaying inhabitants of Longtree Hundred in 1381, a proportion which had doubled by 1524. Rodborough, another village of the industrial area, also increased proportionally, though not as much as Horsley. Minchinhampton's population probably experienced a slight proportional increase as well.

In the north Cotswolds there is no reason to suppose the growth of an industrial area as concentrated as that of the Stroud valley. Then, as now, the area was probably closely linked economically and socially with the Avon Valley. The northern Hundreds, in fact, took in quite a lot of the southern part of the vale between Evesham and Stratford-upon-Avon. The area was primarily pastoral and agricultural and there does not seem to have been industrial development comparable to that of the Stroud valley. Unfortunately there is less information about occupations in the Poll Tax returns for this area than for the hundreds further south. But one feature stands out as a contrast with those hundreds. There seems to have been no move from the towns to the villages, a fact which may be explained by the failure of the villages of the northern edge of the

Cotswolds to follow the same evolution as those of the west. The table illustrates this point, and emphasises a considerable relative increase in the population of Winchcombe[12]

	1381	%	1524	%
Total taxed population counted	3398	100	974	100
Urban population	679	20	246	25
Of which: Winchcombe		7		13
Campden		9		8
Stowe		4		4

Winchcombe, like many small towns, already had a textile industry at the beginning of the thirteenth century, but there is no indication in the 1381 Poll Tax return of any particular specialisation in cloth manufacture, although fulling was done in the adjacent hamlet of Cotes from the late thirteenth or early fourteenth century until the sixteenth century.[13] It seems probable that the relative population increase was due to the town's increasing success as a market centre at the junction of vale and wold. It has not the repute of Chipping Campden and Northleach as a wool mart, but it is possible that this was one of the commodities sold there. If there are reasons to suppose that in the middle of the fifteenth century the abbey of Winchcombe's wool mostly went to Northleach for sale,[14] it is also worth remembering that some villages near to Winchcombe were by 1524 being depopulated for pasture. These include the abbey manors of Frampton and Naunton on one side of Dumbleton Hill and Didcot on the other side. These are about five miles to the north of the town.

These conclusions drawn from a geographically restricted region and from records which are by no means clear in their meaning must necessarily be very tentative. As there are no Poll Tax returns for the Hundreds of the Severn Vale it is impossible to extend our examination of population movements in an obvious direction—obvious in that the Stroud industrial area may just as well have derived its relative population increase at the expense of the villages of the vale or of other parts of the western Cotswold edge for which there are not extant tax returns at two dates, as from the main Cotswold plateau.

Another possibility to be borne in mind is that there may have been a longer term population movement affecting the general population ratio between vale and wold. To show this it would be useful to have complete tax returns which would enable us to compare population ratios in 1380 and 1524 with those of Domesday Book and of the pre-Black Death period. This comparison unfortunately can only be made for a small area. The lack of Poll Tax material makes it impossible to make the comparison between the wolds and the Severn valley, and the defective returns for 1524 for Kiftsgate Hundred deprive us of the chance of assessing north Cotswold and Avon valley populations at the beginning of the sixteenth century. We can however compare the Domesday figures with those of 1327 and from the north Gloucestershire Hundreds of Holford and Gretstone and Kiftsgate.

The importance of being able to do this is that, as I have mentioned, these hundreds straddle vale and wold. The villages in these hundreds should perhaps be triply classified into those of the wold, those of the vale and those at the scarp edge whose territory embraced the valley from the late thirteenth or early fourteenth century until the sixteenth century. I have excluded the two towns of Winchcombe and Chipping Campden from these calculations partly because there are no actual Domesday population figures for Winchcombe and partly because there is some doubt about the Domesday existence of some of their hamlets. Otherwise there seems to be fairly strict comparability between the areas covered at the two dates. About 18 villages were in the Avon valley, 10 on the Edge, and about 21 on the Wold. I use the word 'about' because in fact in some cases two or even more places were included under one designation. The ratios of recorded population at the two dates are as follows:

Year	Vale	Edge	Wold
1086	34%	25%	41%
1327	45%	26%	29%
1381	47%	29%	24%

From these figures it will be seen that the villages of the Avon valley increased in population considerably in relation to those of the wold during these three centuries, and that the mid-fourteenth century plagues did not alter the general trend. There is unfortunately no means of knowing whether the vale population was recruited from the wolds or from further parts of the vale, or in what direction villagers of the wolds may have gone, or whether the phenomenon is to be explained mainly in terms of different birth rates and death rates.

It would also be most unwise to assume that there was a similar change in population ratios between the wold and the vale of Severn. and that therefore the increased population of the Stroud valley was as much the result of a general trek from the high ground as to industrialisation. Neither the steep sided Stroud valley nor the Vales of Berkeley and Gloucester are anything like so favourable to agricultural settlement as the Vale of Evesham, parts of which constitute such an important element of the north Gloucestershire hundreds. Soil and climatic conditions were almost certainly more attractive in the vale of Evesham than on the plateau, but it may be doubted whether Cotswold farmers would have been equally attracted by the waterlogged clays of the Severn valley.

The second topic that I propose to illustrate by a comparison of the two tax returns is that of hired labour. This is a difficult and controversial subject, but one which can hardly be avoided by anyone attempting to get some conception of the social structure of late medieval England. It is of no less significance for economic history, since the distribution of labour must have been a factor of prime concern in the development of industry in a comparatively unmechanised age.

In view of the different interpretations which can be made of evidence about hired labour during this period, every doubt about quantitative estimates must be fully admitted. Just as manorial surveys can conceal reality so can taxation records, as we have already indicated. Firstly, the lists of taxed persons are incomplete since many persons in the taxed community were either exempt or managed to evade assessment. Although evasion of assessment for the third Poll Tax was probably by members of families of both rich and poor, those escaping assessment would tend to be actual or potential wage workers rather than established householders with land or workshops. The exempt beggars are difficult to define, but one should perhaps think of some of them as potential labourers. Exemption in 1524 was clearly on an income basis, and the high proportion of exempt suggested (in urban communities at any rate) by Dr. Hoskins should for the most part be added to the propertyless, potential wage worker element of the population. In other words, the effect of exemptions and evasions will rather be to minimise the wage earning, property-less element in the population than otherwise.

The second difficulty about the taxation returns is the element of formalism in their compilation. When the Poll Tax assessors described a man's occupation or status, they might to some extent be classifying persons of different standing under a designation which may well have been suggested to them as much by the instructions from London as by local nomenclature. Two general terms seem to be used in the Gloucestershire returns for wage labourers. These are *laboratores* and *servientes*. The position of names in the lists, and the indications as to whether they were married or not suggest that the word *laborator* was most often used for a married man not living in an employer's establishment but in his own cottage. The *servientes* were frequently female and often grouped with their employers as if living in. There is a class, however, of *servientes per dietam* who seem to live out, and perhaps did not work for one single employer. In some cases a man's son or daughter is described as his servant.

The possibility of an element of formalism must also be borne in mind when considering the 1524 returns. The taxpayers are classified according to their income from land, according to the sum of their movable goods or according to their wages, and taxed accordingly. In the Cotswold returns those classified according to their income from land are negligible. There are considerable variations in every village amongst those classified according to the amount of movables, ranging from 40/- to £100 or more. Persons fall into various taxation categories —so many at 40/-, at £3, at £5, at £7 and so on. The round figures look conventional, but this may be because they were assessed to the nearest pound. Whether there was a conventional element in valuations of such movables as cattle or grain, as in earlier subsidies,[15] cannot be said. Of course, the possibility that the amount at which individuals were assessed was conventional, does not mean that the relative scale of wealth in movables was not reasonably accurate. It is equally obvious that the assessment on wages was also conventional. Except for a few men in towns, probably employees of wealthy merchants, the vast majority of those assessed on wages were assessed on 20/-. The lack of variation emphasises its conventionality, this element of formality probably being due to the drafting of the Act. It could not be a real annual income in wages when the normal craftsmen's wage was about 6d. a day. However, what is significant is that there were substantial numbers of taxpayers in town and country who were assessed on wages rather than in the traditional way on movables or land.

There are forty villages in the Hundreds of Kiftsgate, Bradley, Rapsgate, Crowthorn, Cirencester, Bisley, Brightwoldsbarrow and Longtree which have sufficiently perfect returns in the 1381 Poll Tax lists to make possible an assessment of the strength of the wage earning element (*servientes* and *laboratores*). In making this count I have omitted wives and children except when the children (in rare cases) are described additionally as servants or labourers. In other words, the persons counted are either heads of households or independent single persons gainfully occupied. The total number is 1016, and of these 414 are described as servants or labourers. This is a proportion of about 40%.

This percentage is worth noting when one is considering general questions such as the government's wages policy. In view of the considerations mentioned about those exempt from or evading the tax, I cannot regard this as a maximum figure. But even if one were to argue that it should be so regarded, it still emphasises how serious must have been the intentions of those who pressed for the frequent renewals of the Statute of Labourers in the second half of the fourteenth century and in the fifteenth century. But beyond using the figure to emphasise the importance of wages in the late medieval economy, I do not think it merits elaborate discussion, because it is too general. This percentage conceals such great extremes of social structure from village to village that it could be quite misleading. The best way to show this is to quote examples.

In some villages no servants or labourers appear in the tax lists. Bagendon, four miles north of Cirencester, was a hamlet containing four peasant families only. Stonebridge, a hamlet of Bisley, had ten husbandmen (*cultores*) and a shepherd. Elmstree near Tetbury simply had five peasant families. In contrast, we may note the village of Coates near Cirencester, where, to eighteen husbandmen and a shepherd, there were sixteen servants (five *per dietam*) and five labourers. Another contrast is Quenington, near Fairford, where the proportion of wage workers was even greater. There were fifteen husbandmen, two brewsters, a baker, fourteen labourers and sixteen servants.

These wage workers were often fairly evenly distributed among the wealthier cultivators. Where this was the case, the essential character of the peasant household as a family concern was little altered. At Lower Turkdean to the north of Northleach there were three peasant families, two labouring families, and a shepherd with his son who served him in his work. The peasant households had two servants, one servant and one labourer respectively. At Stowell, two miles on the Cirencester side of Northleach, there were five husbandmen, one of whom had two servants, another, one. In addition there were four labourers not attached to any individual household. At Withington on the river Coln, between Northleach and Cheltenham, there was a similarly even distribution of hired servants. Three out of ten peasant households had three, two and two servants respectively, two clerics had a servant each, one out of three tailors had a servant. A carpenter had none.

In other cases, gentry or rich peasant households employed a disproportionate amount of the available wage labour. The manor of Berkeley at Coberley, four miles south of Cheltenham, had five out of the eleven servants in the village, a peasant household had two and the other four were *per dietam*, not attached to a specific household. At North Cerney near Cirencester there were seven peasant households and eight servants, five of whom were employed by one of the cultivators. In the village of Coates already mentioned, the wealthiest peasant household employed seven of the sixteen servants. This uneven distribution of the village labourers is, of course, no surprise. Noble or knightly establishments, as we know from manorial documents, usually employed several fulltime ploughmen, carters and herdsmen. The manorial documents have also made us familiar with the wealthy peasant leaseholders who were now becoming more important than the landowners as the direct exploiters of the larger agricultural units. These to some degree succeeded the manorial lords as employers of labour. All the same, the majority of the servants and labourers were probably distributed in ones and twos among the middling sized households, while most peasant holdings would be cultivated by the labour of the family, with perhaps occasional hired help from outside.

In the 1524 subsidy returns those paying their tax on their wages are usually, though not always, grouped together. It is impossible to analyse the distribution of the hired labour within the village as can be done from the 1381 evidence. All that can be usefully done is to give proportions of those assessed on wages compared with the rest. Out of a hundred[16] parishes in the Cotswold hundreds, 577 out of 1812 taxpayers, about 32%, were assessed on wages. Since it is very probable that those assessed on 40/- in movable goods (the lowest assessed category) constituted in whole or in part a reserve of employable labour, I have counted these as well. There were 349 of these. Added to those assessed on wages, we have then a proportion of 59% of the taxpaying rural population of the Cotswolds who may fairly safely be assumed to be closely affected by ups and downs in wage payments.[17] Any further assumptions about the extent to which this proportion of possible wage labourers indicates a change in the economic pattern depend on closer investigation of the distribution of hired labour between farms. As has been mentioned, this cannot be done from the 1524 returns. However, some additional nuances may be derived from these figures by calculating the proportions of taxpaying hired labourers to the total taxpaying population parish by parish. In forty-seven, nearly a half of the parishes counted, one third or more of those taxed were assessed on wages. In sixteen parishes the wage earners were more than half of the total taxed.

Hundred	Assessed on wages and at 40/-	Assessed on wages only	Total taxed	Comment
Slaughter	198	117	369	Less Fairford
Brightwells Barrow	81	58	179	and Lechlade
Crowthorne and Minty	104	59	274	
Rapsgate	76	44	160	
Longtree	131	56	292	Less Tetbury
Bisley	198	136	318	Less Painswick
Total	926	577	1812	

If we add to the wage earners those taxed on the lowest amount of movables, that is on 40/-, we find that in eighty-three parishes one third or more of the taxed population were in these categories. In fifty parishes they constituted more than a half of the taxpaying population. It will be seen from the accompanying table that some hundreds had a higher proportion of this element than others.

Although the information is incomplete for 1381, it is worth while trying to estimate the proportions of hired hands to the total taxpaying population in some of the towns.[18] Using the same method of calculation as for the country districts, that is elimination of wives and children, the following approximate results are obtained. In Chipping Campden the servant population was slightly under one half of the total taxed. In Stow it was little more than one third, in Fairford an incomplete, because partly damaged, return shows that they were at least one third. In Lechlade, on the other hand, they were only one seventh. Better figures are available in the 1524 returns and are best set out in tabular form.

The low proportion of wage workers in Cirencester, Tetbury and Painswick in 1524 is worth noting since these were towns which, as we have said, seemed to have been declining relatively in numbers during the fifteenth century, possibly because of the proximity of the expanding industrial area of the Stroud valley. Apart from these towns, the general population of wage workers in the Cotswold towns would seem to have been at the beginning of the sixteenth century some ten per cent higher than in the countryside at the same date. But as we have emphasised when discussing the figures for the rural areas, a satisfactory estimate as to the role of hired labour depends on a more accurate knowledge of its distribution among employers. This information cannot be extracted from the 1524 returns, though there are some details in the 1381 lists.

	Assessed on wages and at 40/- %	Assessed on wages only %
Fairford	58	50
Lechlade	54	36
Northleach	50	27
Tetbury	52	20
Cirencester	48	17
Painswick	33	6
Campden	75	66
Stow	50	40
Winchcombe	70	37

The best return for 1381 is that of Chipping Campden. Out of 122 households, 70 were servantless. Of the remaining 52 only 14 had more than one servant. Most of these had two or three. The only big employers were Robert Mors, a smith, with 6; William Grevel, the famous wool merchant, with 6; and Walter Ebyrton, an innkeeper, with 5. Even this degree of concentration is unusual. In the other towns whose entries are legible few householders have more than one servant. A smith in Fairford had two employees, but only four others in the town had more than one, and this is the case in Lechlade and Tetbury (in the latter case again, as far as legible). Even in the newly industrialised areas there is not much sign of a concentration of labourers in the employment of individual masters. The Bisley parish textile workers must have been, for the most part, working in family workshops. The only sign of the employment of wage labour is that two fullers in Lower Lypiatt—the highest assessed taxpayers in the village—have a servant each. In Minchinhampton the employees of the nuns of Caen, the dominant landowners there, are not distinguished, and a merchant is the only sizeable employer, with four servants.

Two poll tax fragments from two larger Midland towns providea comparison and a contrast. A torn part of the return for Worcester city shows that 1432 persons in all were counted but details of only 400 have survived.[19] All the same, they constitute a fair cross-section of the city population, which was almost certainly less industrially specialised[20] than Coventry, Bristol or even Gloucester. A difficulty, however, is that the assessment itself seems to vary in character, probably from ward to ward. The first 99 names of craftsmen and wives are listed with no reference to servants. The next membrane lists 75 craftsmens' households of whom 28 shared 45 servants between them, who seem to have been living in. At the end of this list are 11 servants, unattached to specific households. Most of the 28 households which contained servants had only one servant, a few had two. The only big employers were a fuller and a butcher, each with four servants. Whatever interpretation is given to the servantless 99 households in a block at the beginning of the list, it seems that in Worcester there was hardly a greater concentration of labour employing enterprises than in the Cotswold towns.

A Coventry fragment,[21] as one might expect, shows a rather more advanced concentration of the labour force. This is all the more significant in that the fragment does not cover that part of the city where the textile industry was concentrated. It does, however, include many of Coventry's iron workers, so important as ancillary craftsmen to the cloth industry, as the Coventry Leet Book makes clear. In this fragment are 741 names (excluding wives), and of these 310 are servants. As many as 87 persons employed more than one servant. Of these, 39 employed 2 and 20 employed 3 servants. The greatest concentrations are as follows:

Richard Taylor, tailor	7 servants
Richard Bykenhalle souter	6
Thomas atte Welle, mercer	6
Richard Duddeleys, merchant?	5
John Ardele, merchant?	5
Henry Dylcott, passenger	5
John Shyrleye, wiredrawer	5
John Bunde, ironmonger	5
Richard Marschall, smith	5
Adam of Keresleye, grazier	5

Another fragment of a tax return, almost certainly from Coventry,[22] and probably recording the assessment of 1379, gives the same impression. Although there are no occupational descriptions of the principal taxpayers, the number of servants in each household is given (e.g. X *cum tribus servientibus*). Most of the entries are those of husband and wife, a few are of single male or female taxpayers. No children are mentioned, so the number of servants may include some children of tax-paying age. There are in all 127 entries. Twenty households had no servants, 26 had one each, 41 had two each, 22 had three each. A minority of households employed a more significant concentration of servants: seven with four each, seven with five each, two with six each, one with nine and one with ten.

It is most regrettable that this sort of information, however dubious and incomplete, is only available in the Poll Tax returns. For we know from other evidence that Coventry was a decaying town by 1524, while on the other hand John Leland was to say that Worcester had become the most important textile town in England (evidently an exaggeration, but not to be ignored).[23] All in all, the urban evidence emphasises, as for the countryside, the importance of the class of wage workers as a social group. But at the same time, the fact that they were so little concentrated in individual enterprises must make us appreciate that as yet their presence did not alter the traditional, family scale of the unit of production.

Postscript

As in the case of other articles re-printed in this volume, I have avoided the temptation to update by using subsequently discovered evidence. I must, however, draw attention to a 1380-1 poll tax return for Gloucestershire which was compiled after the main listing. It is clearly an attempt to catch out evaders—almost all servants and labourers. It shows that their numbers were seriously underestimated. See my *English Peasantry in the Later Middle Ages* (Oxford 1975), p.32, citing P.R.O., E 179/113/31A.

22

Capitalism—What's in a Name?

The history of capitalism was once studied by its supporters and its critics on the basis of reasonably common agreement as to what both meant by the term.

The subject of capitalism'[1] wrote Professor M.M.Postan; 'owes its present place in political and scientific discussion to the work of Marx and the Marxians.' Many historians substantially follow him. Mr. E. Lipson in his *Economic History of England*[2] on the whole adopts Marx's definition of Capitalism. He agrees that its essential feature is the division of classes between propertyless wage-earners and entrepreneurs who own capital, in contrast to the characteristic medieval organisation of industry and agriculture on the basis of the small producer who owned his own means of production.

Definitions, both implicit and explicit, which are much less precise have become fashionable in recent years. A characteristic definition is given by Professor Pirenne describing 'the tendency to the steady accumulation of wealth which we call capitalism.'[3] Two leading French historians refer to capitalists and capitalism when writing of large scale landed property in the Carolingian era.[4] And it is surely a looser definition than that of Marx which leads Professor Armando Sapori, the historian of Italian industry and commerce in the middle ages, to write of a 'capitalist revolution' in the time of Thomas Aquinas.[5]

Pirenne's definition referred to the activities of European merchants in the 12th and 13th centuries. Such definitions face the history teacher and student with the puzzling phenomenon of 'the rise of the middle classes' (associated of course with the growth of trade), which seems to start so early, to go on for so long, and to be the explanation of so many different historical movements and events. For although the urban middle class of medieval Europe is said to have begun its notorious career as early as the 10th century,[6] the teacher is faced with the problem of explaining why it was not until the 17th and 18th centuries that this class became the dominant force in society. Why did it take more than 700 years to reach this position if during the whole period it was 'rising'?

Not all historians equate the expansion of a class based on trade in a predominantly agricultural society with the expansion of capitalism. Nevertheless the assumption that the two movements were identical is generally made. It is made with care and reservations by the specialists, but usually more unreservedly by those who feel it necessary to simplify for general teaching purposes. The latter do in fact get plenty of justification from some of the eminent specialists writing on medieval trade. For example, Professor de Roover, an outstanding contributor to our knowledge of medieval banking, speaks of the 'commercial revolution at the end of the 13th century' which paved the way for 'mercantile capitalism, which in most European countries was not replaced by industrial capitalism before the middle of the 19th century.'[7] And most of the contemporary contributions by historians of medieval industry and commerce rest on the (usually implicit) assumption that what is being discussed is 'capitalism.'

Recent researches have shown that an older generation of economic historians who regarded the middle ages as a period of 'natural economy' were mistaken. These historians minimised the extent to which commodities were produced for the market. They also under-estimated the volume of international trade and the repercussions which it had on economic activity. Pirenne, both in his studies of the growth of medieval towns and in his more general works[8] has had a considerable influence on the teaching and study of medieval economic history. He emphasised that the growth of international trade played a key role in the transformation of feudal society. Many current assumptions about medieval capitalism are derived from his work, and his conclusions have been supported by a number of subsequent studies. Only a few need be mentioned here. The most important have been those which have explored the development of trade and industry in the most advanced economic regions of medieval Europe—Flanders and Italy. The researches of Espinas have shown how great was the industrial activity of the Flemish cloth manufacturing centres, adding detailed material to illustrate the more general remarks of Pirenne. Doren, Davidsohn, Sapori and others have shown how the industrial and commercial activity of the Tuscan towns was even further advanced than that of Flanders.[9] These centres were producing cloth for an international market. They bought their raw material far from the place of manufacture. Wool was imported from England, Spain and elsewhere. Dyestuffs were brought from as far afield as the Black Sea. Naturally this shipment of raw materials and the export of finished goods brought into being an elaborate trading mechanism. Up to the end of the 13th century, the great fairs of Champagne formed the greatest among a number of international emporia where buyers from the south met sellers from the north. In the 14th century merchant importers (Italians especially) established permanent agencies in the manufacturing and trading centres. To avoid the transport of bullion and to overcome the difficulties of currency exchange in coin, letters of exchange were elaborated. This permitted the development of credit not to speak of facilitating large and small scale usury and international public finance.[10]

Investigations which revealed the importance of international trade have been accompanied by studies of agrarian life which again have corrected the older impression of a world composed of closed 'natural' economies. The disintegration, from the 11th century onwards of the big estates of the Carolingian era, the sub-division of manorial demesnes, the reduction in the numbers of completely servile peasants and the growth of rent paid in money, rather than in labour or in kind, have been described in works written half a century and more ago.[11] Since then economic historians have tended to link up these features more definitely with the contemporary commercial expansion. Yet less detailed study has been made of the market aspects of agriculture than of industry or trade. One reason for this is that evidence for production for the market in agriculture is comparatively scanty, except for England. The break-up of the big landlord estates was delayed longer in England than France and Western Germany; and so they were the main participants in market production when the demand came, above all in the 13th century. Consequently records of this production for the market have survived in England, as they have not on the continent. Annual manorial and central estate accounts dating from about the middle of the 13th century exist in abundance. But although many valuable monographs concerning individual estates have been written, ccmparatively little systematic investigation of the exact scope of production for the market has been undertaken.[12] Even so, one modern historian at least has concluded that the 13th century English estates were examples of agricultural capitalism.[13]

There is clearly no little confusion in the study of early forms of capitalism. It is therefore well to look back to what Marx understood by the word. He used it to denote what he described as a 'mode of production' of the material wealth of society. He believed that social and political institutions, the ideas and achievements of any society ultimately derive from its 'mode of production.' He therefore saw the heart of the change from feudal to capitalist society in the change from a primarily agrarian society of petty producers, whose most important social classes were the landlords and their unfree tenants, to a society producing commodities for exchange on the market, whose principal classes were capital-owning entrepreneurs and propertyless wage-earners.

Marx' general views are well enough known, and his chapters on the 'primitive accumulation of capital' in Vol. I of 'Capital' (Part VIII) are familiar to most economic historians. But of more special interest to the medievalist are three chapters of Vol. III,[14] which summarise his less well-known views on the genesis of capitalism.

His main argument is that commerce, in money or goods however widespread, and however productive of accumulations of money capital, does not *by itself* transform feudal society. The speed and forms of the disintegration of feudal society, on the contrary, 'depend(ed) on its solidity and internal articulation' as a 'mode of production.' It was rather the inherent contradictions within the society than the impact upon it (as from without) of commerce which were the prime causes of its downfall.

In his view, the only form of capital in the ancient and medieval world was the money capital accumulated by merchants and usurers. The typical medieval capitalist was the merchant who drew his profit from the monopoly of the carrying trade between economically backward and geographically remote areas. This profit might be derived from the import of articles of small bulk and high prices (such as spices) from the east ; or from the exploitation of the different prices of commodities of everyday consumption as between one local market area and another. The usurer's profit also depended on the backward, rather than on the advanced features of the economy. It was drawn from the extravagance of the landowning classes, and from the perpetual bankruptcy of the peasant and the small artisan. It is only when capital 'takes hold of production' that merchant's and usurer's capital becomes subordinate to industrial capital, and only then that it becomes possible to speak of a capitalist 'mode of production.'

This attitude to medieval money capital led Marx to view with scepticism the claim that the growth of money rent in itself had any direct connection with the decay of feudal relationships. He distinguished 'feudal rent' from capitalist ground rent with the same care that he distinguished merchant from industrial capital. The 'feudal rent', paid by the peasant to the landowner, whether in labour, kind or money, is analogous to the 'surplus-value' which the capitalist derives from the wage earner. Ground rent under capitalism is not the main source of the income of the ruling class. It is merely a 'super-profit,' derived by the landlord from the capitalist farmer by virtue of his monopoly of a force of nature, the land.

Marx emphasised the corrosive effect of money on the economy of feudal society, whilst he also pointed to some of the retrograde effects of the action of merchants' and usurers' capital. In the cloth industry, the domination of merchants' capital simply deteriorated the conditions of the artisans, so that in some respects they were worse off than the wage earners. Usury, especially in the countryside, caused a depression without altering the character of existing society. 'The indebted feudal lord becomes even more oppressive, because he is himself more oppressed.' But Marx regarded the growth of merchants' capital as one of the preconditions of the capitalist mode of production.

The most important of these pre-conditions, especially for the development of capitalist industry, was the concentration of moneyed wealth. In agriculture, the development of money rent assisted the stratification of the rural population, and the growth of capitalist farming. When money rent replaced labour rent, the peasants were able to devote all their time to their own holdings, and the richer among them were able to accumulate surpluses. The poorer peasants, on the other hand, were ruined by the effect of continuous demand for money rent, and by usury. When the rent from land was expressed in money, it became possible to put a money price to the land. This promoted the buying and selling of land; and, as more land came on to the market, the resulting disintegration of traditional holdings further assisted the social differentiation of the peasantry.

The test of any such analysis is not whether or not it sounds convincing, but whether it helps to interpret the facts and solve some of the problems which confront the historian of the middle ages. One of the foremost among such problems is how far older forms of economic structure and social organisation persisted, and how far they remained dominant.

The main new developments in the agrarian life of the later middle ages in Western Europe are well enough known. The legal claims of the lords over the persons of their tenants were reduced; a majority of tenants were freed from the obligation to labour on their lord's demesne; money rent predominated; and the total amount of rent paid over to the landlords decreased. In short, the landlords' control over their peasantry was weakened. Ignoring for the moment the exact relationship between these new developments and increased market production, let us briefly consider how far they involved a fundamental change in the character of society. The big demesnes tended to disappear or to shrink, but they had never constituted more than a fraction of the land under cultivation nor did the techniques used on them differ significantly from those which the peasants used on their own plots. Small scale peasant production continued as before. It is true that, from the 14th century onward, a number of richer peasants, and, a little higher in the social hierarchy, many of the lesser nobility, were beginning to farm on a larger scale. Both needed a certain amount of wage labour. But the amount was not yet enough to change the old system. Furthermore, although a landlord-tenant relationship based on the payment of money rent can be seen in the light of later events to have been an important transitional stage in the decline of medieval agriculture, the main features of feudalism persisted. The landlords continued to take rent from peasants by non-economic compulsion.[15] The peasants handed over to their lords a portion of their surplus under the same sort of legal and military sanctions as before (though the growth of the state machine made them much more efficient). The fact that the surplus had to be converted by the peasant into money instead of being rendered directly in labour or in kind did not *yet* alter the class relations.

Small scale production operated also in industry. It was a great change when to the activities of the scattered artisans in the villages was added the productive effort of large numbers of workshops concentrated in towns and organised in gilds. This was part of the general economic expansion of the 12th and 13th centuries. In certain centres producing for export, primarily cloth, groups of wealthy merchants seized hold of both ends of the process of production, the provision of raw material, and the marketing of the finished product. In so doing they destroyed the independence of the artisan. But the big merchants of Douai, Ghent or

Florence did not revolutionise production. Although some centralisation of the preparation and finishing processes was achieved, the greater part of the work of manufacture was done in the family workshops of the master craftsmen. Furthermore although a proletarian labour force of some dimensions existed in both the Flemish and Italian cloth centres, they were normally concentrated in groups of no more than four or five apiece in the central warehouses of the merchants. For the most part they were employed in the artisan workshops by the master craftsmen, by whose side they worked.[16] In some respects the big merchants actually retarded the development of production. They were afraid of production for the market by the artisans themselves. Consequently they forbade any collusion between artisans at different stages of the production process. If weavers passed their product straight on to the fullers and dyers, there was risk to the merchant that an element among the craftsmen might control the process of production from within. This almost happened in Flanders in the 14th century. When the political power of the old merchant-draper patrician caste was broken, the weavers of towns such as Ghent threw up an entrepreneur element which would have taken over the organisation of the industry, had not political factors, the rise of the country industry and the decay of the Flemish cloth industry prevented them.[17] It was to avoid this that in Northern Europe and in Italy, the merchants supplying the raw materials insisted that after the completion of each stage of the production process, the product should be brought back to the central warehouse for re-issue to the next craftsman in the chain. Whilst the artisan remained subordinated to the merchant in this fashion, no change in the traditional small scale methods of production was possible.

As in agriculture, so in industry and finance, there was conservatism as well as change. Great concentrations of merchant capital and elaborate credit and exchange mechanisms were a new feature of the 13th and 14th centuries. They arose when European industrial exports restored the balance of trade between Western Europe and the East.[18] The human agents of this development were those great merchants of whom the Italian bankers were the finest flower. Yet, in spite of their seeming power as international financiers, they adapted themselves like their ancestors of the 11th and 12th centuries to the existing social structure. The very diversity of their interests as bankers, money lenders, and traders, in any and every commodity, made them the more adaptable, both politically and socially, to the feudal ruling circles. For these rulers were their principal market for their luxury commodities, the recipients of private and government loans. Old methods and old relations of production must be emphasised. But there were none the less very great changes within medieval Europe between the 11th and 15th centuries. Without these changes, subsequent development would have been impossible. The point is that *in spite of* the expansion of production, of population and of trade in the 13th and early 14th centuries, the main features of the old social and political framework remained, not to disappear until the 17th and 18th centuries. Of course, forms of government and social relations did change greatly during the middle ages. But the states of Europe continued to be ruled by and for territorial aristocracies represented by feudal monarchies. They were not ruled by or for merchants or industrialists. That is why there had to be bourgeois revolutions before the full expansion of capitalism was possible. Our insistence on the persistence of the old structure in industry and agriculture has been to show the economic basis for the continued dominance of the old classes. This is one reason why an uncritical acceptance of the view that capitalism gradually expanded from the 13th century onwards may lead to a falsification of the real history of capitalism as well as of the preceding epoch. It follows from the line of criticism outlined above that a changed direction of research into capitalist origins is needed. This does not minimise the great value of work done by the various specialists in the history of commerce, banking and industry. The point is that a number of questions with which the contemporary historians have not dealt remain to be answered.[19] In order to promote the solution of the problems both of the chronology of capitalism and of its earliest characteristics, an approach might be made under two main heads. First a chronology of the *predominating* methods and relations of production should be established, and co-ordinated with the much better known chronology of the growth of commerce. Secondly, the inter-relationships of the economic, social and political aspects of society should be studied. In particular, the significance and consequences of the unevennesses in the development of these varied sides of human life require investigation.

We are likely to obtain the truest insight into the end of feudal and the beginning of capitalist society if we pay attention first to the techniques and relations of production. Naturally the commercial expansion of the Middle Ages must be examined in the closest association with the investigation of changes in the mode of production. But the history of trade alone will not tell us how and when the characteristic relations of feudalism gave place to those of capitalism, how peasant agriculture and artisan industry gave place to large concentrations of capital and of wage labourers, profit by rent to profit drawn from the value given to the finished product by the worker.

Political conditions need closer attention. The political structure and political movements ultimately arise out of the social relations based on production, but economic and political changes do not develop hand in hand. Though they develop unevenly, they are integrally connected. It is not possible to talk of a capitalist *society* when political power is still in the hands of a feudal aristocracy. It is unwise to speak of a capitalist system when the political and legal superstructure of society is still one shaped by pre-capitalist economic conditions. Political power, even in the hands of a ruling class whose economic basis is decaying can still retard the development of new economic and social forms. The history of England under the Tudors and Stuarts and of central and eastern Europe in the 19th century illustrates this point.

What kind of problems demand the attention of the research historian? The growth of capitalist production cannot be measured simply by estimating the level of commodity production. Developments in technique, the growth of the volume of total production, and the manner of application of labour to production also require study. These problems are common to both agriculture and industry; indeed it must not be imagined that in studying capitalist origins, attention should primarily be concentrated on industry. The history of England up to the revolution of 1640 would be but half told if it ignored the growth of capitalism in agriculture.

Questions of technique ought not to be considered simply as problems of technological evolution. What matters is their economic and social effects. One of the main obstacles to the accumulation and investment of capital was the small-scale of the units of production in agriculture and industry. Therefore one of the central problems for the student of capitalist origins is to find out about the number, size and methods of operation of the larger farms held in the late 14th and 15th centuries by the thriving elements in the country-side—the big peasants and the smaller gentry. All that we yet know about such farming units is that they were considerably larger than the traditional average peasant holding of the 13th century, being often more than 100 acres in arable area ; that they were heterogeneous in composition, including the farmer's ancestral holding, fragments of other peasants' lapsed holdings, and leased-out demesne ; and that they must have required hired labour for working them. We also need to know more about the chronology and scope of the turn-over to sheep farming for wool production. It is probable that in the middle of the 15th century England was producing less wool than at the beginning of the 14th century.[20] Yet there has been much loose writing about England being 'covered ... with sheep farms in place of corn fields.[21]

Problems of size of farms and type of farming immediately raise the question of the agrarian labour force of the later middle ages. Was there a proportionate decline or increase in the number of wage labourers in the country-side after the middle of the 14th century? In a recent article[22] Professor Postan has challenged the usual view that wage labour increased in importance during the period. From figures of rising real wages, he deduces a decline in the numbers of wage earners compared with other sections of the population. Landless labourers and small-holders were able, he believes, to move after the Black Death into the vacated holdings of victims of the plague. But who provided the labour on the enlarged holdings of the top stratum of the villeins, the yeomen and the lesser gentry? Whilst 14th and 15th century rentals and surveys confirm that the small-holding class had diminished relatively to other peasant groups, this type of evidence is naturally useless for estimating the number of totally landless. The best English evidence bearing on the subject is not entirely reliable. This is the Poll Tax return of 1381. Unlike earlier returns it gives the occupations of practically all of the taxed personnel. The lists are very incomplete, for there was a mass evasion of the assessors[23]

But those who hid and were not counted were more likely to be the landless than those whose houses and holdings could not be concealed. The returns are therefore likely to minimise rather than to exaggerate the proportion of wage workers. Such returns as have been examined show a surprisingly high proportion of wage workers, but much further investigation of the returns needs to be done before any firm conclusions can be reached.[24]

An estimate of the amount of wage labour in the late middle ages gives more than an indication of the growth of capitalist social relations. It is in addition indirect evidence for production for the market. As the peasants became landless, they not only became labourers. They became consumers with an income entirely in the form of wages (not all, but mostly money) who needed to buy in the market the goods which previously had not gone through the market[25] The quantitative significance of the home market in early times is so difficult to measure that international trade (for which there is much better evidence in the form of customs and toll figures) tends to dominate our ideas about production for the market to the exclusion of a sufficient consideration of internal demand.[26] Furthermore. in order to estimate the significance of the production of commodities for the home market in its relation to the productive system as a whole, it is advisable to attempt an estimate of the relative quantities of goods produced for direct use and for the market. A useful addition to what we already know about regional variations in English history would be a survey of how much of the total peasant product in different districts was consumed by the producer, how much went on to the market, and how much was left to spend when the rent was paid.

Some of these considerations apply also to industry. Here too the size and nature of the productive unit is of great importance. The continuing organisation of production on the basis of the artisan family unit prevented the development of capitalist relations of production. But simply to estimate the distance travelled on the road to capitalism from this factor alone would be insufficient. One of the most fruitful ways of tackling the problems of the earliest stages of capitalism in industry would be to compare the history of the cloth manufacture in medieval Flanders and Central Italy with that of England in the 16th and 17th centuries.[27] The concentration of capital and labour, the organisation of the supply of raw material, and of the sale of the finished product by capitalists in the Flemish and Italian towns at the end of the 13th and beginning of the 14th centuries was such that one could almost say that here were societies trembling on the brink of the capitalist mode of production. Yet modern capitalism derived its initial impetus from the English textile industry and does not descend directly from the principal medieval centres. Its foundations were laid in the rural domestic industry which had fled from the traditional urban centres. We know of course that gild restrictionism was one reason for the shift in the centre of gravity from town to country. But this is only one of many aspects of the problem.

One of the principal attractions in studying the failure of medieval Flanders or Italy to develop the capitalist mode of production is that it not only permits, but demands, the widest treatment. The problem is insoluble on the basis of a narrow concentration on technical and economic factors, for social and political developments were all important. How different were the Boinebrokes of Douai and the Bardi and the Acciaiuoli of Florence from the English entrepreneurs of the 17th century! These earlier capitalists had unspecialised commercial interests; they had close financial associations with the leading feudalists; they were disinclined to invest in industrial or agricultural production; they were so enmeshed in the political and social relationships of European feudalism that no break through to a new form of society was to be expected under their leadership. In Flanders at the beginning of the 14th century they lined up with the king of France and the feudal nobility against the urban craftsmen and the peasants. In 14th century Florence, the classic pattern of the bourgeois revolution in its least heroic aspects is anticipated like the spectre of the future—the bourgeoisie allying itself to its defeated feudal enemies out of fear of the workers and artisans, and in so doing destroying its own future as a class[28] To use Marx' phrase, the 'solidity and internal articulation' of feudal society was still sufficient, even during this period of economic and political crisis, to prevent the new mode of production from establishing itself. But exactly how and why is a matter for further investigation.

It is not enough to study capital, wage labour, and units of production in their economic aspects. Since men make their own history, the historian must know what part the political and social consciousness of the various classes played in advancing or retarding the tempo of capitalist development. Since that consciousness is by no means a direct reflection of the economic activity of these classes, the historian cannot but concern himself with law, politics, art and religion. Neither feudalism nor capitalism are understandable simply as phases in economic history. Society and its movement must be examined in their totality, for otherwise the significance of uneven developments, and of contradictions, between the economic foundation of society, and its ideas and institutions, cannot be appreciated. A failure to appreciate their significance is fatal not only to the understanding of the growth and final victory of the capitalist mode of production, but to an insight into the principle motive force of all human development.

23

Feudalism and the Origins of Capitalism

Maurice Dobb's *Studies in the Development of Capitalism* was published in 1946. Karl Polanyi, who reviewed it very critically in the *Journal of Economic History*, 1948, nevertheless described it in the following terms: 'a scholarly and original volume on the decline of feudalism, on mercantilism, the industrial revolution and the nineteenth century, the period between the two wars, in effect the whole history of western capitalism short of the Marshall Plan'. Polanyi thought that Dobb had retained from Marx what was bad (the labour theory of value) whilst discarding what he, Polanyi, thought was Marx's 'fundamental insight into the historically limited nature of market organisation'. Unfortunately, Polanyi's review was not long enough to develop this interesting criticism, but it indicated, on the reviewer's part, a serious attitude to the problems of a Marxist analysis of feudalism as a mode of production (which Marx himself had not systematically undertaken) and of the transition from feudalism to capitalism (about which Marx necessarily said more, though not enough).

R.H.Tawney's long review article of the book in the *Economic History Review*, in 1950, showed little interest in the theoretical problems of a Marxist approach. However, it was appropriate that a lengthy, appreciative, yet critical, review should be written by the one British historian of high calibre who had not only made the whole period of the 'transition' a lifetime's study based on original research, but had actually acknowledged the reality of capitalism as a distinct economic and social order—this at a time when economists, historians and politicians were trying to pretend that it had never existed. Many of Tawney's criticisms are of great practical interest to the historian of the 16th and 17th centuries and have to be taken seriously. However, although Tawney said in the review that 'the combination of history with theory is one of the merits of the book' he did not raise any of the general theoretical problems which Polanyi hinted at, and which have also exercized Marxist students of Dobb's work. All the same, Tawney, and presumably the editor of the *Economic History Review*, thought, with Polanyi, that a scholarly and original volume on a subject of such importance justified a sympathetic, even if sometimes severe, consideration.

Unfortunately this interest was not shared by the editors of some other historical journals nearer to the centre of what one might call the British 'historical establishment' than the *Economic History Review* was then. There was no review in the *English Historical Review*, supposed shrine of high scholarship, nor in *History,* through whose pages the message of that high scholarship is conveyed to history schoolteachers and others outside the circle of professional researchers. Nor were there reviews in the principal journals of economic theory, such as the *Economic Journal* and *Economica.*

The reasons for the general neglect of Dobb's book are fairly obvious. British academic historians do not like Marxism. In any case, the decade after the end of the war was hardly propitious for the unprejudiced discussion of a Marxist interpretation of capitalism. This is not the whole story, of course, which has to have added to it the suspicion, not only of theory and abstract concepts, but even of generalizing interpretations which may have relatively little theory about them, such as the Whig interpretation of history. What is preferred in the British academic tradition, at any rate since the end of the 19th century, is exact and detailed scholarship directed towards the amassing of verifiable data. The training of the historian does not lie in the discussion of hypotheses by which significant historical developments can be explained, still less in the attempt to penetrate to the essence or 'prime mover' of socio-political formations. It is in, supposedly, removing all elements of subjectivity from the study of a sequence of events over the short term, or in identifying the constitutive elements in the major (usually the ruling) institutions of society. This is done by recourse wherever possible to supposedly 'objective' administrative record sources, and by critical assessment of chronicles, narratives or letters, which are deemed liable to the risk of human bias.[1]

This type of historical scholarship is not, of course, exclusively British, but European. It was well exemplified by the French historical school which held sway before the establishment of the intellectual hegemony of the sociologizing Marc Bloch and his associates, whose expression is now found in the journal *Annales: économies, sociétés, civilisations.* Its achievements have been considerable and should in no way be under-estimated, particularly in the field of medieval research which especially interests us here. For, as readers of the debate will appreciate, it was not Dobb's treatment of the later history of capitalism which aroused the interest of the participants, but what he had to say about those forces which destroyed feudalism. For the most part the problems of the transition are tackled from the medieval, rather than from the modern end. Indeed it was largely on the basis of the work of the deservedly famous non-Marxist historian, Henri Pirenne, that Paul Sweezy launched his critique of Dobb. Pirenne's work is not, of course, to be classed with the narrower type of academic scholarship to which reference has been made, although he was as capable as anybody of a meticulous and critical treatment of source material. He was also, however, capable of wide-ranging generalization and it was no doubt the problem-orientated character of his research which inclined the Marxists to treat him very seriously. Giuliano Procacci, in his assessment of the initial debate, rightly drew attention to the formidable backing of non-Marxist scholarship which Sweezy was deploying against Dobb when he cited Pirenne. Perhaps Procacci rather overestimated the big guns on Sweezy's side. After all, whom does Sweezy quote apart from Pirenne? And as we now know well, Pirenne's interpretation of medieval European economic history has been severely criticized by many, other than Marxist, historians. His interpretation of the decline of the Mediterranean trade and of the de-urbanization of Western Europe, has suffered some hard knocks. His view that it was the revival of long-distance trade which re-vivified the European economy in the 11th century, is not generally accepted; nor is his opinion concerning the social origins of the urban merchants of the period of revival.[2] Nevertheless, Procacci's general point was entirely justified. The British Marxists may have had good ideas, but they needed to back up these ideas with research which would match that of the established schools of non-Marxist historiography which they were, in effect, challenging. Dobb's book, as he himself admits, and as his reviewers have reiterated, was the work of a Marxist economist who had made himself familiar with the then existing range of secondary works. His opponent in this controversy, Paul Sweezy, was in a similar situation, of being a Marxist analyst of contemporary capitalism who ventured into the field of medieval economic history on the basis of secondary work by non-Marxist historians. The same is true, though to a lesser degree, of the most formidable of the subsequent participants in the debate, for although Takahashi is an original worker in the field of Japanese feudalism and the problems of the transition to capitalism in the 19th century, his perceptions of the same problems in the history of the classic area of the formation of capitalism, western Europe, are again based on secondary works. The most recent of the longer contributions to the debate, that of John Merrington, is again not concerned with the research problems of the historian of the feudal economy. Thus, with the exception of Hill and Hilton, whose contributions to the original debate were relatively slight, the argument has been conducted by Marxists who have put their fingers on certain fundamental problems with regard to the feudal and capitalist modes of production but who, for lack of support from Marxist specialists (at any rate in the 1950s, when the debates began) were necessarily obliged to do much of their own spadework among non-Marxist secondary authorities.

Now it is evidently essential for anyone who takes the general concept of 'mode of production' seriously to establish the components of different modes. The practising historian, whose aims may not be the same as those of the sociologist or philosopher,[3] cannot rest at this point. There is a law of motion of feudal (as of other) societies, as well as particular sets of structural relationships. To define and elaborate the law of motion and the particular shifts which eventually generate the conditions for the transition from feudalism to capitalism requires an effort of research and not only of logic. It means the critique and the utilization of the achievements of bourgeois scholarship. It also means the application of critical method to contemporary sources. Such a critical method must be Marxist, based on an understanding of the concept of the mode of production. It must also take into account the critical methods developed by historians since at the latest the 17th century.

Marxist historians have significantly altered our understanding of the bourgeois revolution and of the development of capitalist society from the 17th century onwards. One need only mention the original researches of such leading English Marxist historians as Christopher Hill, Eric Hobsbawm and E.P.Thompson, not to speak of Albert Soboul in France, Giuliano Procacci in Italy and many others in the capitalist countries. B.F.Porchnev, A.D.Liublinskaya and J.V.Polisensky, well known in this country, are again only a few of the historians working on similar fields in the socialist countries. Marxist work on feudal society and on the medieval preconditions for the development of capitalism has been much more restricted, at any rate in the West, though E.A.Thompson's writings on early Germanic society deserve to be singled out. Otherwise the main focus of Marxist medieval research has been confined to the field of agrarian history. There are various reasons which could be suggested for this limited development. The young Marxist is likely to have a political commitment to socialist or communist politics, and therefore to be attracted to the study of the capitalist mode of production in all its political, social and cultural manifestations. This study, moreover, not only has the appeal of the direct influence of Marx's and Engels' own theory and practice, but the aid of a considerable company of Marxist practitioners who are engaged in constant theoretical and practical discussion of the problems of the Marxist historian of capitalist society and the transition from capitalism to socialism. The study of feudal society has few such advantages for most of the younger historians, who are therefore somewhat isolated, practically and theoretically. The republication of the transition debate will, it is hoped, help to encourage further consideration of the theoretical issues and further research on the unsolved problems posed in the earlier contributions and in this introduction.

It is now more than twenty years since the original debate in the pages of *Science and Society*. A considerable amount of research has been done by Marxist and non-Marxist historians which is relevant to the main topics which were discussed. It is not proposed in this introduction to produce a laborious historiographical memorandum of this research, but rather, as far as the author is capable, to re-examine some of the problems at issue in the original debate in the light of subsequent work—and subsequent thinking. These problems include: the definition of serfdom; the origin of towns; the role of handicrafts; merchants and the money economy; the unfettering of simple commodity production; the alternative paths for the emergence of capitalist production; the concept of the 'prime mover'.

Serfdom

The term 'serfdom' in Marxist discussion is often unnecessarily ambiguous, an ambiguity which seems to be derived from non-Marxist
historical research. Surely Takahashi is right to insist that serfdom is the
existence-form of labour in the feudal mode of production. Its essence
was the transference to the use of the lord of the labour of the peasant
family which was surplus to that needed for the family's subsistence and
economic reproduction. The surplus labour could be used directly on the
lord's demesne (home farm of the manor), or its product could be
transferred in the form of a rent in kind or in money, from the family
holding.

Given the effective possession of the subsistence-producing holding by
the peasant family, the transfer of the surplus must be forced, since the
peasant, as contrasted with the wage labourer, does not need to alienate
his labour power in order to live. Having accepted this broad definition
of serfdom as the enforced transfer, either of surplus labour or of the
product of surplus labour, many different juridical and institutional
forms of serfdom can exist which in many—perhaps most—cases are
not necessarily considered to be 'servile' in the eyes of the law. This has
given rise to much confusion among historians. For example, Marc
Bloch examined the enfranchisement charters of villages in ecclesiastical
estates in the north of France and observed that the peasants who
received those charters, constituting the majority of the inhabitants of the
villages, were thereby freed from a range of obligations, such as
formariage and *mainmorte,* which were generally regarded as servile. The
families which were designated as servile in those same villages in the
estate descriptions of the 9th century were much fewer in number than
those who had to be emancipated in the 13th. Bloch, therefore,
concluded that there had been a process of enserfment between the 9th
and the 13th centuries. However, the Belgian historian, L. Verriest,
showed that the proportion of families specifically designated as 'serfs'
(servi) had not changed in the intervening period. The majority of the
peasants enfranchized in the 13th century were juridically free *vileins*
who had been subjected to obligations which were analogous to those of
the 'true' serfs. As we shall see, although formally Verriest was right, it
was Bloch whose interpretation was nearer to the truth.[4]

During the early period of European serfdom, there was, during the
period in which the feudal landowning aristocracy was emerging in its
classical form, a great variety of forms of peasant subordination resulting
from different developments of the period. These included the establishment of demesne slaves on landed holdings, with or without manu-
mission of servile obligations; the subordination of free peasants to
powerful or threatening neighbours; the submission of free men to the
protection of a saint (i.e. to a monastic landowning community
supposedly devoted to the worship of the saint), and so on. The

nomenclature of the subordinated peasants varied from place to place according to the nature of the subordination, or even, as R. Boutruche suggested, according to the fantasy of the lords' clerical administrators. As Boutruche goes on to say, this led some historians into similar fantasies of erudition so that the characteristics of the peasantry as a social class were altogether forgotten.[5]

There was a real change in the nature of European, particularly Western European serfdom, between the 9th and 13th centuries. I propose to discuss this briefly because it illustrates an important element of confusion in some of the discussion about the character of the feudal mode of production. This confusion concerns the role of labour rent in the social relations of the period. Labour rent has often been regarded as the characteristic form of servile subordination of peasant to lord. Consequently, most of the English Marxists in the transition discussions have—even when acknowledging that labour rent is not the only form of feudal rent—regarded the commutation of labour services into money in England in the 14th century as being of special significance in the transition. This was, on their part, the consequence of a certain insularity of historical training, for the survival in 14th century England of large estates characterized by big demesnes using labour services from peasants on dependent tenures was exceptional, as Dobb had mentioned. But the general history of European feudalism shows quite clearly that labour rent was not an essential element in the feudal relations of production, although the coercive character of these relations perhaps appears most clearly in the organization of forced labour on the demesne.

We first become aware of the demesne-based form of estate organization in the estate descriptions (mostly ecclesiastical but also royal) of the 9th century. It may well be the accident of documentary survival that focuses our attention on Northern France and the Rhine valley, as well as on this particular period. The form of organization was certainly older than the 9th century, though whether there was direct continuity from the late Roman Empire is still disputed. It was also widespread, being found in central Italy as well as in England by the end of the 10th century, if not earlier. All the estate descriptions emphasize the importance of labour obligations from the holdings of both free and servile peasant holdings, so that although there were rents both in kind and in money, labour rent was apparently predominant. It is probable that at this period this was just as inefficient a form of the use of surplus labour as it was in Eastern Europe in the early modern period.[5a] At any rate it seems clear that the system was beginning to disintegrate at about the time when the descriptions were being drawn up. Various features of the European economy and society in the 10th and 11th centuries made it necessary to change this mode of appropriation of surplus labour. The capitularies and ordinances of the Frankish and Ottonian monarchies suggest that there was considerable peasant resistance to labour services as well as to legal enserfment. Although the severity of the Scandinavian and Magyar invasions must not be overestimated, they necessarily weakened the ramshackle structure of the Carolingian imperial hegemony. State power was not so much fragmented (or parcellized) as confined within practical limits, given the slow communications and effective radius of the exercise of military force. It is probable that there was a considerable increase in population, with a consequent subdivision of peasant holdings. The population increase may also have encouraged an increase in the number of families of the feudal warrior class which were enfeoffed on holdings. Although one must not exaggerate, it seems likely, too, that technical improvements increased agricultural yields.

There was, during this period, a noticeable change in the character of the feudal ruling class. Jurisdictional power, that is the right to try the subject population and to derive profit from the exactions implicit in jurisdiction, was devolved not only to the counts, but to castellans (lords of districts controlled from a castle), and even to simple lords of one or two villages. The big estates, especially the monastic, preserved to a certain extent their outward structure, but the demesnes tended to be broken up and taken over by estate officials or sub-let to peasant tenants. Within their judicial immunities, jurisdictional power was decentralized in the same way as it was in the counties. Labour services tended to disappear as the main form of feudal rent. Indeed, by the 12th century, peasant surplus was transferred to the landed aristocracy less in the form of a rent calculated on the size of the peasant holding, whether in labour, kind or money, than in seigneurial taxation (tallage) and in the profits of jurisdiction. These profits included not only court fines but the profit from various monopolies, such as the right to force the inhabitants, free or serf, of the area of jurisdiction, whether tenants or not, to grind corn at the lord's mill, bake in his oven or press grapes in his wine-press. In addition some extra labour services were demanded, but as from subjects rather than from tenants, being mainly for road and castle building, perhaps even to mow what remained of the demesne meadows or to cultivate the demesne vineyard. The sum total of these new aspects of feudal rent, it has been calculated, considerably exceeded the previous landlord income which had been based on the yield from the demesnes and the rents from the holdings. Yet, as the burdens increased, the term 'serf' was disappearing so that few peasants so called were left by the middle of the 12th century.[6] It was from these new forms of seigneurial exaction that the leading strata of many European peasant communities obtained some form of enfranchisement in the 12th and 13th centuries, usually at a heavy price in cash. Nor is this the end of the history of the complex evolution of feudal rent. However, I do not propose to pursue the subject further, for the purpose of this discussion of the change in the character of feudal rent between the 9th and 13th centuries has simply been to emphasize how varied were the forms in which the surplus was pumped out of the basic producers, and also how closely connected with these forms was the institutional superstructure.

The Origins of Towns

Of further importance in the history of feudal rent in this earlier period is the probable connection which it had with the growth of towns, small market towns as well as the bigger urban centres; for the urban revival of the 11th and 12th centuries coincided with the development of the new forms of serfdom. The enlargement of the surplus transferred from peasant production, more in the form of jurisdictional and monopoly profits than in the form of rent from landed holdings, meant that lords' incomes were in fact realized more and more in cash. The division of labour between town and country, the development of towns not simply as markets where rural produce was sold so as to raise cash for the satisfaction of lords' exactions, but as centres of craft production, can, no doubt, be *explained* in general terms, as the response to the more efficient concentration of surplus in the hands of a more differentiated (and from the point of view of its cultural demands more sophisticated) aristocracy.[7] The processes themselves must be *described* in more complex fashion. Some small towns undoubtedly were founded through seigneurial initiative simply to provide convenient market centres which could also yield profits from market tolls and stall rents. In other places, the nuclei around which developed urban crafts, and markets for local produce as well as for the luxury commodities of long distance trade, were pre-existing settlements of churchmen (cathedrals, collegiate churches, monasteries) or groups of warriors in the retinue of some great feudatory, such as a duke or a count. The necessary precondition in all cases was the increasing size and disposability of seigneurial incomes. At the same time it is likely that the increased population which provided the artisans, petty traders and providers of services in these new (or revived) towns was itself generated by the break-up of the old domanial system. For certain aspects of that break-up provided the conditions for population growth, namely the fragmentation of peasant holdings ; possibly greater scope for the operation of partible inheritance; and increased productivity of peasant agriculture resulting from the concentration of technical resources on the holding instead of their diversion to the demesne.

Max Weber[8] laid great stress on the political autonomy achieved by the urban communities of Western feudalism as compared with the cities of Asia. Non-Marxist historians (especially in France) described the same phenomenon when they referred to communes as 'collective lordships', inserted like other vassals in the feudal hierarchy.[9] Undoubtedly the independent urban commune has been an important component of the special features of European, as distinct from other feudalisms. It would, however, be as wrong to attribute to communal independence the development either of merchant capital, or of urban-based craft industry, as it would be to lay stress on the fragmentation of sovereignty (itself a concept of non-Marxist historiography). There was a very considerable range of urban autonomy from feudal control, and the towns which enjoyed the greatest political independence were not necessarily the most developed economically or socially; Paris, the biggest town in medieval Europe, being a case in point. Nor was the political autonomy of an independent commune the necessary condition for that type of urban or craft monopoly to which Marx referred, when he said that the towns exploited the countryside economically where the countryside (i.e. the feudal ruling class) exploited the towns politically. Many an English borough had its gild merchant in full control of the terms of trade on the market without, at the same time, enjoying the higher ranges of urban privilege. The problems of the divisions of labour between town and country are many, and however much we may learn from the labours of the best non-Marxist specialists in urban constitutional history, it would be unfortunate if it were thought that the problems of the urban element in feudal society were to be solved in these terms.

What is needed is detailed work on the degree of occupational specialization in towns of various sizes, various functions and at various stages of development. To give some examples, the presence of the feudal aristocracy in the Italian towns is a historical commonplace, while it is often asserted that the North European feudatories lived rather in the country; but these generalizations need testing, especially in England, where every sizable town had its ecclesiastical and feudal or royal-official enclaves. The agriculturally occupied element in urban populations is often referred to, but seldom measured and analysed. Lists of organized crafts within the urban jurisdiction are often available, but the total numbers of separate occupations, mainly unorganized, have not been systematically compared from town to town, so as to estimate the whys and hows of functional separation from the agricultural hinterland. Nor is the contrast between the gild dominated urban industry and the free industry of the countryside, the supposed theatre of development of capitalist Way I, as straightforward as it seems. Were the East Anglian industrial villages of the late 14th century town or country? Were not medieval Manchester and medieval Birmingham, often thought to typify the progress of rural industrialization, referred to at the time as boroughs or *villae mercatoriae*?[10]

Handicrafts

These questions are not posed in order to suggest that the contributors to our symposium are wrong in saying that the social differentiation developing within agricultural and industrial petty commodity production is the foundation for the subsequent development of capitalism. There is, however, a serious lacuna in our knowledge. English Marxists (and non-Marxists), fortunate in the documentary riches at their disposal, have investigated with some success, the history of the later medieval peasantry. This contrasts sharply with our ignorance of the artisans of town and country, whether organized in gilds (the best known) or not.

This ignorance, as so often, is not altogether the consequence of a shortage of evidence; it also results from an absence of theoretical analysis of the nature of this type of labour and its situation within the relations of production of feudal society, which are predominantly the relations between 'servile' peasants and ruling landowners.[11]

There was, of course, a primitive division of labour in prehistoric (in effect pre-class) society, whereby some members of the community specialized in weaving, iron work, making pottery and other necessary artefacts. This is well attested by the archaeological record, but the archaeological record is not able to reveal how these workers acquired their subsistence. Was there an exchange of manufactured goods and foodstuffs in the form of use values within the community, or did the artisans also work as agriculturalists, providing substantially, if not entirely, for their own subsistence? There seem to have been survivals in feudal class society of both these situations. On the one hand we find specialist artisans within the households or the demesne economies of lay and ecclesiastical magnates. On the other hand we find village craftsmen, especially smiths, who have landed holdings but whose surplus labour is appropriated as a rent in horseshoes, repair to plough shares, and so on.

Neither of these types of craft work implies simple commodity production, but when the craftsmen of large households of monasteries or feudal potentates began to produce not only for their lord, but for others who clustered around those centres of power, and for peasants bringing in their produce for sale as well as in the form of rent in kind, then we have the beginning of urban-based simple commodity production. Traces of feudal household provisioning by these urban artisans remain for a surprisingly long time; in Paris for instance where, in the 13th century, the king nominated feudal lords as official masters of the leading crafts, or in the much smaller cathedral town of Metz, where the bishop, who was also lord of the town, did much the same.

These were institutional relics throwing some light on previous relationships. But long before the 13th century, industrial craftsmen had become separated both from their rural and feudal household contexts and appeared as apparently autonomous industrial households within urban communities, producing for sale to anybody who had money. But what was the nature of these households? How are we to categorize the labour which produced shoes, knives, plough-parts, carts, cloth and other commodities (as we are entitled to designate these artefacts)? In view of the labour embodied in the craftsman's product, in view of the fact that there was evidently a considerable exchange of values between peasants and artisans, the craftsman's income cannot simply be regarded as part of the redistributed surplus from the peasant economy, mediated through the demands of the feudal aristocracy, as was the case with the profit on alienation which constituted merchant capital.

It is true that as monopolistic gilds developed, the exchange between peasant and artisan became unequal, but the relation between peasant and artisan was not exploitative in essence. In fact in the small market towns,[12] whose aggregate population probably constituted the greater part of the total urban population of Europe, the feudal exploitation of the artisan was parallel to the exploitation of the peasant, for the lords of those towns also skimmed off the product of the surplus labour of the artisans through house and stall rents, mill and oven monopolies, tolls and taxes. This exploitation was direct in the case of the unenfranchized towns, and was not entirely absent in the independent boroughs and communes which often had to pay a cash commutation for rents and tolls, as well as paying a high rate of taxation, whose weight fell more heavily on the artisans than on the ruling mercantile elites.

These tentative suggestions about the categorization of artisan labour within the feudal mode of production assume artisan households which are internally undifferentiated, as well as minimum differentiation between producing units. By the time we have adequate records, this state of affairs is mainly found in small market towns of about 500-1000 inhabitants, whose functional separation from the countryside was complete (in the sense that agriculturalists were an insignificant or non-existent element in the population). In the bigger centres we can no longer assume the equality of labour within the household, nor equality between artisan households. As the market for the artisans' commodities extended, we not only have the familiar process, well described in Dobb's *Studies,* by which the merchant interposes himself between the craftsman and the buyer. Inside the workshop the apprentice ceases to be simply a trainee (often the son of the master craftsman) and becomes an exploited labourer in receipt of his subsistence only.

In addition, journeymen are hired—not in great numbers, for the scale of production does not permit this—and represent another subordinated element within the workshop. To begin with, however, the journeyman was not simply a wage labourer, a direct source of surplus-value for the employer. In the 13th century Flemish textile towns there was still confusion concerning the payment made to the textile craftsman by the merchant putter-out. It was not quite a wage, and yet it was not simply a payment for a job done by an independent craftsman. Whatever it was, it is of interest for our present purposes that a municipal rate was fixed by the piece of cloth, so much to the master, so much to the journeyman—a smaller quantity for the latter of course, but a smaller difference than one would expect.[12] The same arrangement is found as late as the 15th century in some English towns. In other words, although the process of differentiation was beginning within the workshop, master and journeyman were still the common objects of exploitation by merchant capital.

Merchant Capital

Unlike the producer of manufactured goods, the medieval merchant capitalist has been the subject of many studies, based on the survival of a considerable amount of documentary evidence. Some of the most spectacular fortunes were accumulated by the merchants of the Italian towns, who illustrate in their activities the normally unspecialized character of the European merchant class as a whole—whether in Northern or in Mediterranean Europe, whether operating modestly in the regional markets or on a large scale in the international luxury trade. The Italian merchants, of whom the Florentines and the Venetians were the most successful, had as the basis of their profits the trade in high priced commodities, such as spices, jewellery, or silk textiles, from the Far and Middle East, high quality woollen textiles from Flanders and Central Italy, gold from West Africa. They also dealt in money, as bankers to the Papacy and other rulers (mainly war finance). Some of them, like the great merchants of the Flemish towns, organized the provision of the raw materials for the manufacture of cloth as well as the sale of the finished product without, in any way, altering the character of the productive process. Other products entered international trade, such as wine from the Île de France, from Gascony, Burgundy and the Rhineland; grain, timber and fur from the Baltic; salt from the Bay of Bourgneuf; alum from the Black Sea; woad from southern France, fish from Iceland, iron and steel from Sweden, not to speak of the standard commodities of regional trade, such as cereals or medium-priced textiles. The technical sophistication of the trading methods, the ability to concentrate funds to finance (at usurious rates of interest) governments and landed aristocrats, who were always short of easily realizable assets, the cultural patronage of these medieval merchant capitalists, has brought forth a chorus of admiration from their historians.[14] None, however, has been able to alter the estimate which Marx made of their historical role, that their capital remained always within the sphere of circulation, was never applied either to agricultural or industrial production in any innovative fashion. The so-called commercial revolution in no way altered the feudal mode of production.[15]

One might well ask, therefore, what reality can be attributed to the suggestion that 'the money economy' acted as a solvent of feudal relations. We have seen that feudal rent could be paid as well in money as in labour or kind, without affecting the relationship between lord and tenant. It has been suggested that other relationships, such as those between kings and barons, or between barons and their vassals, which had once been based on personal and specially military service, became transformed as a result of the replacement of the personal by the cash nexus. Examples of this include the granting of fiefs consisting of money incomes charged on state revenues instead of revenue-yielding landed property; the payment of cash scutage instead of military service in the royal host; the giving of loyalty by retainer to lord in exchange for a cash annuity; the mobilization of all military service on the basis of the payment of wages. Unfortunately for the advocates of the money-as-solvent theory, cash scutage is found as early as the beginning of the 12th century, and money fiefs not much later. Divided loyalties, treachery and self-seeking were just as prevalent when the feudal contract was based on the landed fief in the 11th and 12th centuries as in the days of so-called 'bastard feudalism', when it was based on money payments. Nor did big cash incomes transform the behaviour of the feudal ruling class, as any student of the English aristocracy between the 13th and 15th centuries can testify. If anything, it was the declining cash incomes of the feudal aristocracy which was the first symptom of the end of the feudal mode of production; for these incomes to the end represented peasant surplus, coercively extracted, and their diminution was the monetary sign of the failing grip of aristocratic domination of the old type.

The solvent qualities of money, as Marx has emphasized, only came into operation once the historic processes of the dissolution of the feudal modes of production were well under way. In the *Grundrisse* Marx pin-points as the essential aspect of this dissolution the separation of the labourer from the objective conditions of his existence—land, crafts-man's property, even (suggested Marx) subsistence as a lord's retainer.[16] In England, as in other areas of Western Europe, the failing grip of aristocratic domination was indeed a significant feature of the pre-liminary processes of dissolution to which Dobb and Takahashi, in the course of the Transition debate, have drawn particular attention. This was something which, before Marx, the pioneer English economic historian, James Thorold Rogers, had already documented.[17] Subsequent research has shown that the appearance for a short time of what seemed to Marx to be a predominance of free peasant property was the direct outcome of the class struggle between landowner and peasant. Marx was thinking particularly of developments in England, where the evidence is good. The disturbed situation in the middle of the 14th century, with the population collapse resulting from the bubonic plague and governmental financial shortage resulting from the Anglo-French wars, could very well have led to the strengthening of serfdom. The shortage of labour so strengthened the economic position of tenants and labourers *vis-à-vis* landowners and employers that one way in which the ruling class could have reacted would have been the tightening up of controls on the movement of unfree persons, increase in rents and jurisdictional fines, and a freeze on wages. For about two decades after 1350 this policy was tried, but with complete lack of success. The peasants already had considerable experience in resisting seigneurial encroachments. Village communities, though internally divided between rich and poor peasants, were very tough bodies to deal with, as many a local rebellion had demonstrated. Although major risings, such as the French Jacquerie of 1358 and the English revolt of 1381 were defeated, local resistance could not be overcome. The English situation is very instructive. Villein (or servile) land tenure, without changing its essential juridical character, was attenuated into copyhold. In the atmosphere of peasant self-assertiveness, copyhold became hardly distinguishable from free tenure, to such an extent that members of the landowning gentry were prepared to take portions of copyhold land to round off their estates.

Rents were sufficiently low and the ability of both landowners and the state to control the free movement of peasants and labourers so minimal in practice that, at the end of the 14th century, and for the greater part of the 15th century, the feudal restrictions on simple commodity product-ion virtually disappeared.[18] One must not expect to find, during this period, any dramatic developments in the direction of capitalist product-ion. The yeoman farmer employing wage labour certainly prospered; there was a free movement of craft production from the older gild-dominated towns to the village and the less restricted smaller towns, but no drastic social differentiation in the sense of a mass of wage labourers selling their labour power to agricultural and industrial employers. This was to be a long drawn out process, by no means completed even in the 17th century. The point is, however, that during the course of the relatively unfettered commodity production in the 15th century, the necessary pre-conditions were created for later capitalist development.

Feudal relations of production were by no means abolished during this period; the essential characteristics of a feudal ruling class and a feudal state (in the Marxist sense of the word) remained. The enormous incomes of the great aristocrats, such as the Dukes of Lancaster and York (founders of short-lived royal dynasties), the Earls of Warwick or Salisbury, were still largely based on rent, though they increasingly pillaged the resources of the monarchy in their efforts to keep effective patronage over their retainers and political supporters. The machinery of state, even after its re-shaping in the early 16th century, was essentially that of the medieval *regnum*. Moneyed wealth, which was not based on the possession of landed property, came from trade which was in the hands of monopoly companies of merchants like the Merchant Adventurers and the Merchants of the Staple. It did not come from industrial production, although the principal export from England was finished and unfinished cloth—the profit went to the sellers rather than to the producers. In other words, however important were the changes which gave free rein to the agricultural and industrial commodity producers, there was no transformation of the basic relationships constituting the feudal mode of production.

The Prime Mover

The contributors to the original debate, with the exception of Paul Sweezy (and whatever their own reservations about Maurice Dobb's formulations) all rejected the argument that the feudal mode of production was static and self-perpetuating, did not generate the preconditions for its own transformation and therefore needed an outside force to upset its equilibrium. Sweezy, following Pirenne, had found this outside force in the merchant capital accumulated in the Middle-Eastern-Mediterranean trading area, which was, as it were, injected into the stable feudal system through the agency of a set of traders of unknown social origin. Since feudalism was, according to Sweezy, a mode in which all production was for use, not for exchange, the future progress of feudal Western Europe, after the 11th century was due to factors external to it. Sweezy did not explain what was the nature of the social formation which generated this mass of merchant capital or indeed why it should be regarded as a separate social system from that of non-Mediterranean Europe. In response to criticism, however, Sweezy quite rightly asked what was the prime mover within the feudal mode which gave it an internal dynamic both for development and dissolution.

In my own short comment towards the end of the debate I suggested that the necessary if fluctuating pressure by the ruling class for the transfer to itself of peasant surplus labour or surplus product was the root cause of the technical progress and improved feudal organization which made for the enlargement of the disposable surplus. This was the basis for the growth of simple commodity production, seigneurial incomes in cash, international luxury trade and urbanization. This side of the story has been developed with great brilliance by Georges Duby in his recent book on the early development of the medieval economy. As I have explained elsewhere, I believe that his explanation is one-sided.[19] He stresses the pressure of the lord on the peasant. He does not pay the same attention to the efforts of the peasants to retain for themselves as much of the surplus to subsistence as was possible given the sociopolitical balance of forces. But this peasant resistance was of crucial importance in the development of the rural communes, the extension of free tenure and status, the freeing of peasant and artisan economies for the development of commodity production and eventually the emergence of the capitalist entrepreneur.

As has already been mentioned, the history of the English agrarian economy in the 14th and 15th centuries illustrates very well the consequences of successful peasant resistance to the lords' pressure for the transfer of surplus. In fact, this must be regarded as a critical turning point in the history of the 'prime mover'. The long period of the successful and multiform exploitation of peasant labour ended, at any rate in most Western European countries, between the middle and the end of the 14th century. Only with the successful reimposition of forms of legally enforceable serfdom could the landowners have continued their previous success. In the West this was politically and socially impossible. In Eastern Europe the story was different. In the West more and more of the disposable surplus was retained within the peasant economy. When the harsh yoke of landlordism was next felt by the rural population, it was something quite different in essence, if not always in form—the beginning of the emergence and long and uneven development of a new triad, landowner/capitalist farmer/farm labourer.

Meanwhile, since the original debate, other non-Marxist historians have made their own proposals about a prime mover in feudal society. The most persuasive of these are variants on demographic interpretations of medieval development. One of these, which might better be called an 'ecological' theory of history, has been cogently argued by M. M. Postan in various works.[20] It also emphasizes the agrarian, peasant base of the economy. It concentrates rather on the relationship of the cultivator to the environment, to the earth as his natural workshop as Marx would have put it, than on the relations between the cultivator and the exploiting landowner. Hence, the important events were the pressure of an increasing peasant population on scarce resources, the consequent fragmentation of holdings, exhaustion of the soil and impoverishment of smallholders. Nevertheless this expanding agrarian economy, before it choked itself, was dynamic and market-oriented, a dynamism to be seen especially in certain sections of the upper strata of society, such as the supposedly capitalistically inclined owners of manorial demesnes and the enterprising and innovating merchant capitalists of the great cities. When the equilibrium broke, however, at the turn of the 13th century and especially after the population collapse of the mid-14th century, the pressure on scarce landed resources relaxed and the peasant economy became more prosperous. But it also became more self-sufficient, less market-oriented. Regional and international trade contracted so that until the last quarter of the 15th century when population once again began to rise, the late medieval economy was stagnant.

There is another type of 'prime mover' interpretation, less wide-ranging than that briefly described above. This focusses on the internal composition of peasant families in their communities. Historians of this school examine family constitution, inheritance customs, problems of the absorption or rejection of younger sons and daughters by family and village communities and the associated question of non-agricultural by-occupations in the countryside. These topics are of great importance and must certainly enter into any serious research by Marxists into the detailed functioning of the feudal mode of production. This is all the more important in that this field of study can be made to bear conclusions of a very dubious character. Some of its devotees present the medieval family and community as though they were isolated and self-regulating social groups abstracted from the wider world, and in particular unaffected by the exploitative pressures of landowners, the church and the state. In so far as this outside world has to be acknowledged, the emphasis is on harmony rather than pressure. This leads to an interpretation of feudal society as part of a continuum of pre-industrial 'traditional' societies, whose main characteristic is stability, not to say stagnation. Medieval clerical estate theory, with its emphasis on the unchanging and organic relationship of the social orders, each fulfilling its proper function (ruling, fighting, praying, buying and selling, working) under God, is rehabilitated as the rational explanation of this type of social order. At the village level, the difference between rich and poor families is explained in terms of the ruling functions of the rich and the service functions of the poor. It is even suggested that this distinction is genetically determined.[21]

Some of the irrational excrescences of non-Marxist historical research into demographic aspects of the medieval economy should not lead to the rejection of the positive contributions made by certain historians of this school. Although kinship relations were not as important in feudal as in primitive societies they still played a vital role in the distribution of resources at all social levels. This must be acknowledged while at the same time the primacy of the exploitative relationship between lord and peasant in the feudal mode of production must be reasserted. The same applies to the inter-relationship of peasant populations and landed resources, the positive contribution of the Postan school to our understanding of the late medieval economy. Marxist scholarship cannot operate as a hermetically sealed system. Not only must it absorb the positive contributions of non-Marxist scholarship, but it can and should show that Marx's concept of the mode of production gives us the best tool for the analysis of the dynamic, not only of capitalism, but of feudalism.

NOTES

1. Kibworth Harcourt (pp. 1-17)

1 Albert Mathiez, quoted by Albert Soboul, in 'Sur quelques études locales', *La Pensée* No.17, 1948, p.59.

2 It should be borne in mind that the general survival of manorial demesne farming in the 13th century was peculiar to England.

3 The printed *Rotuli Hundredorum* of 1279 are in Vol. II of the Record Commission edition. Two useful articles on them are 'The Hundred Rolls of 1279-80' by E. A. Kosminsky, *Economic History Review*, 1931, and 'The Free Tenantry of the Hundred Rolls' by B. Dodwell, ibid., 1945.

4 The material for Cambs., Beds., Bucks., Hunts., and Oxon., is printed in The Record Commission volume. Unprinted are some rolls of London, Middlesex, and a transcript of some of the Warwickshire Rolls (see below n. 6). See M.S. Guiseppi, *Guide to the Public Records I*, pp. 341-2.

5 See R.H. Hilton, *Economic Development of some Leicestershire Estates*, p. 7, for a discussion of this document.

6 P.R.O., K.R. Exchequer Miscellaneous Books, Series I, Vol.15. An edition by the present writer is projected.

7 Bodleian Library, Rawlinson MSS. 350 f. 21. Nichols prints part of the transcript in Vol. I of his *History*, pp. cx-cxxi. He stops short at f. 17 of Burton's transcript, being apparently deceived into thinking that this was the complete document by another item which was inserted in the middle.

8 Wrong transcription by Burton; should be Ewelle.

9 Should be Faber.

10 In *Types of Manorial Structure in the Northern Danelaw.*

11 In his famous article, 'The Chronology of the Labour Services,' *Transactions of the Royal Historical Society*, IVth Series, XX, Professor Postan writes of the multiplicity of manors in single villages and quotes Cottenham, Cambs., where there were six.

12 G. Farnham. *Leicestershire Village Notes*, V, pp. 241-57. *Calender of Inquisitions Miscellaneous*, I, no. 295. *Merton College Manuscripts* No.2872. Richard de Harcourt, member of the major English branch of the Harcourt family, was grandson of Robert de Harcourt who in 1166 married the Camville heiress and brought Stanton Harcourt, Oxon., (subsequently the Harcourts main seat) into the family. Richard married Arabella, daughter of Saer de Quincey, and had two sons, William and Saer. See E.W. Harcourt, *The Harcourt Papers*, I, and W. Harcourt-Bath, *Harcuria; a History of the family of Harcourt*, (typescript) Pt. II, pp. 10-15. Richard de Harcourt's lands in 1258 according to his *inquisition post mortem*, lay in 10 villages in Leics., one in Oxfordshire and one in Staffordshire. *Calender of Inquisitions*, I, p. 111. Not much seems to be known

about Saer, apart from the fact that he was a knight of Simon de Montfort's entourage.

13 Farnham, loc.cit. and *Calender of Patent Rolls* 1266–72, p.150.

14 For details of the foundation of Merton College see G.C. Brodrick, *Memorials of Merton College*, Oxford Historical Society, 1885; P.S. Allen and H.W. Garrod, *Merton Muniments*, Oxf. Hist. Soc. 1928; F.M. Powicke and A.B. Emden, *Rashdall's Medieval Universities*, III, pp. 191 ff.

15 J.E. Thorold Rogers, *History of Agriculture and Prices*, Vols. I-VII, Oxford 1866-1902.

16 *The Administration of the Estates of Merton College in the Fourteenth Century with special reference to the Black Death and the problems of labour.* Bodleian MS. Oxford D.Phil. c.70.

17 *Merton College MSS*, Nos. 6196–6364, and 6376–6457.

18 ibid. Nos 6365–6375.

19 *Calender of Records*, (MS) Vol. X. I have to thank Major Millard of Merton College Bursary for his courteous assistance whilst I was working on these records.

20 *Merton MSS*. No. 2877. Cal. I shall add the reference 'Cal' to those MSS. for whose contents I have relied on the summary in the calender.

21 F.M. Powicke, *King Henry III and the Lord Edward*, II, p. 536.

22 No. 2873. Cal.

22a No. 2876. Cal.

23 No. 2884. Cal. The King in 1266 had revoked an acquittance of debt made by Cresse son of Geuth to Saer, when he (the King) had been in Simon's power, and when a general quittance of the debts owed to Jews had been made. *Calender of Patent Rolls*, 1258-66, p. 628. Cok and a Northampton Jew, Sampson, later got permission to sell Saer's debts to a King's clerk, Walter of Kent. *ibid.*, 1272-81, p. 156.

24 Allen and Garrod, *op.cit.* p. 9. The nephews provided for by a deed of 1262/4 were: John, William, and Roger de la Clithe (Clive), Robert and Philip de Ewelle, Thomas de Wortinge, Walter Ulvet, and Walter de Portesmue (Portsmouth).

25 No. 2871. Cal.

26 Farnham, loc. cit. Cal. Inqs., II, 247.

27 By the terms of the original grant, Saer was owed 20/- a year from Kibworth (Farnham, loc. cit.). In 1279 this was acquitted in the following proportions: one sixth each from Thomas of Worting, Master William of Ewelle (a son of Agnes), Alan of Portsmouth, and Edith of Tayllard, and two sixths from the scholars of Merton. No. 2886. Cal. For Hubert de Told see below. xxx

28 Nos. 2857, 2859, 2864, 2901, 2902, 2903, 2905, 2906, 2907, 2908.

29 Nos. 2867, 2895, Cal.

30 No. 6196.

31 Nos. 2907, 2908, Cal.

32 Recorded in a deed of that date, No. 2909, Cal.

33 Liveries by tally *ad opus Tayllard* amount to £4 18s. 8d. in the account. The MS. is torn and it is possible that an undecipherable entry would make the sum up to the amount of the rent charge. The charge appears later as 5 marks.

34 No. 2911 Cal.

35 Farnham, loc. cit., quoting a plea de Banco.

36 Agnes had claimed then, one third of a messuage, 8 virgates, a windmill, £5 rent, and the advowson of the church, Farnham, loc. cit. She may only have got the amount claimed by the Tayllards, and later renounced by William of Evesham.

37 No. 2944. Cal.

38 No. 6373.

39 E.g. the reeve's account of 33-34 Edward III, No. 6251.

40 No. 3094.

41 The name of Apetoft seems to be an anglicisation of Abbetot, or Abetot. Laurence of Apetoft is in one place called Abbetot (No. 2959. Cal.). I have not been able to connect the Apetofts with the Worcestershire Abbetot family. For similar corruptions of the name Abbetot cf. CCR. 1227-31, p. 207. *ibid* 1231-4, p. 288. *Cal Inqs.* II, 456.

42 Henry de Fodringeye, Fellow in 1284; Robert of Candever, Fellow in 1297. (Brodrick op. cit. pp. 175 and 176.)

43 No. 2868 Cal. A document dated 1323 (No.2959 Cal.) records a release by Thomas of Abbetot, son and heir of Laurence of Abbetot, to the College, of his right *in dominico et in dominio* in 10 virgates and six marks rent in Kibworth Harcourt. This, however, is no evidence for the actual date of transfer of the property. It is also unlikely that Thomas's father was the original Laurence of Apetoft, if this person *was* a contemporary of William de Harcourt.

44 *Cal. Close Rolls*, 1323-27, pp. 484-5; also Farnham, *loc. cit.*

45 This was John de Harcourt who did not meddle.

46 *Op. cit.* p. 62.

47 No. 6368.

48 The earliest being a deed of 1263, but most of them between 1270 and 1280.

49 Elsewhere (No. 6370) described as profits of the view of frankpledge— probably a sixth of the profits of one court.

50 No. 2928 Cal. The 8 acres were distributed in 13 blocks, varying in size from one rood to one acre, over ten named furlongs.

51 No. 6370.

52 No. 6251 (Reeve's account 33-4 Edward III).

53 Above p. 7. These are lighter services than those recorded for the majority of villein holdings, see below n. 71.

54 No. 6370.

55 In a bundle together with other rentals, No. 6368.

56 G. C. Homans, *English Villagers of the Thirteenth Century*, pp. 94-101, and *Annales d'Histoire sociale et économique*, 1936.

57 No 6367. This is the total after the payment of the Tayllard rent.

58 Nos. 6366, 6369, 6371 — No. 6369 is incomplete, only the list of free tenants having survived.

59 Since none of this group of rentals includes the Apetoft manor, and 1301 is the latest date of acquisition, assignable for that property.

60 1274 Statutes, especially cap. 28. Brodrick op. cit. p. 334.

61 Rogers is therefore incorrect in stating (*op. cit.* I, p. 24): 'The college never farmed on its own account its lands in Leicestershire.'

62 Lowry, op. cit., pp. 227-30.

63 N.S.B. Gras in his *Evolution of the English Corn Market* suggest that Leicestershire was in an economic backwater, p. 52.

64 Particularly Nos 6367 and 6371, of which the first is the later in date. The acquisition of the Apetoft manor brought an increase in the free and villein tenants, but not in demesne.

65 No. 6197.

66 Payments *super compotum* at the annual audit are discussed by N. Denholm-Young, *Seigneurial Administration in England*, p. 148, and for the Merton College estate by Mrs Lowry, op. cit., p. 22.

67 The increase in assize rent was in fact just £8 15s 4d.

68 Of which the profit of two views of frankpledge was £2 13s 1d. Strictly speaking the sum quoted is receipts, and the steward's expenses during the year of 14s. 8 1/4d. should be set against it.

69 This figure excludes 7s. 1.1/2d., included in the expenses total, which was the total for allowances for debts and amercements.

70 See W.Beveridge, 'On the Yield and Price of Corn in the Middle Ages', *Economic Journal, History Supplement I*.

71 The services in Kibworth Harcourt were fairly heavy by Leicestershire standards (see Hilton, op. cit., pp. 11-13), and the value of the labour services was about 30% of the total rent paid. The only full statement is in a defaced undated rental, probably drawn up soon after Walter of Merton's death (No. 6370). From a full virgate were owed: 2 days ploughing without food with own plough; 2 days harrowing and hoeing with food; 2 days mowing on lord's meadow with one man; gathering and carrying the hay in the lord's cart without food; reaping in autumn for 4 days without food with 2 men, on the 5th day with 4 men with food, on the 6th day with 4 men with food, and all other boon works with food; carrying the lord's corn to Leicester market on own horse, but no further unless within the county; (gathering) straw for one day with one man without food, and getting the straw together for roofing the buildings of the manor court whenever needed; (words illegible) ...or carrying coal on own cart within the county. It is the custom for the men of the village to mow the lord's meadow with 1/6 worth of beer whilst they do it. The virgate also owes heriot in the form of the second best beast to the lord and the best beast to the church as mortuary. A defaced portion of the MS. also appears to describe the merchet fines.

72 A few owed light labour services. In rentals Nos. 6370 and 6371 we find two virgates each owing a day's reaping at the *metebene* in addition to money rents of 14/- and 6/1 a year respectively. A half virgate paying a rent of a penny and 3 capons also owes 4 days' reaping besides the *metebene*, and another virgate owes 1/- rent and 2 days' reaping.

73 Manorial officials were conspicuous amongst these. For examples see M.Morgan, *English Lands of the Abbey of Bec*; R.A.L. Smith *Canterbury Cathedral Priory*. For the wealth of the yeomanry, see W.G. Hoskins, *The Leicestershire Farmer in the Sixteenth Century*, supra 1941-2.

74 The activities of the Polle family, some of whom at the beginning of the century were free, some villein, tenants, are described during the late 13th and

14th centuries in a document of Henry IV's reign (No. 6365). This consists mostly of extracts of court rolls, and the object of the compilation is to prove the villeinage of certain of them. They supplied many reeves of the manor and appear prominently in the Poll Tax lists and the 16th century subsidy rolls. Farnham, *loc. cit.*

75 The date suggested in the calender is 1320, but identifiable persons seem to flourish somewhat later, e.g. Roger Polle, villein at the date of the rental's compilation, appears in the document mentioned in the previous note between 1333 and 1351.

76 It would require a more detailed examination of other dated documents than I have as yet had the opportunity to make to establish the date of this new list.

77 Which must have been added at the same time as the final alteration to the tenants' list.

78 These virgates were once held by Hugh Harcourt and Robert Hokke who were tenants when the Apetoft manor was bought from William of Ingwardby in 1295.

79 So this virgate contained 21 acres of arable.

80 No. 6464, one of the documents drawn up to prove the villein condition of the Polles, establishes their pedigrees.

81 The demesne was leased, not to one farmer but to 21 tenants. It was divided up into the following parcels: 20 quarter virgates; 20 half virgates; one three quarter virgate; one full virgate; the manor garden and seven attached tofts; four cottages *extracta de manerio*; and a pasture for four beasts.

82 This impression could be confirmed by a study of the court rolls. I have not yet had the opportunity to extract more than a few samples from the series.

83 An early fifteenth century rental of the manor of Tanworth, Warwicks, deposited in Shakespeare's Birthplace, Stratford-on-Avon (uncatalogued), records a considerable number of 'lost' parcels of land.

84 No 6222. There were only three main items of receipts—arrears £5 19s. 2d.; rents, £40 8s. 3d.; pleas and perquisites of courts, £2 13s. 6d.

85 No. 6251. This total includes arrears.

86 No. 6252.

87 No. 6253. Most of this total seems to have been made up of unpaid rent, but probably also included unpaid amercements, etc.

2. Winchcombe Abbey and the Manor of Sherborne (pp. 18-35)

1 This article is a contribution to the work of the Birmingham University Cotswold Survey. The maps were very kindly prepared for me by Mr M.J. Wise.

2 Founded 789; refounded 959? *Landboc sive Registrum Monasterii de Winchel-cumba*, (ed. D. Royce, 1892-1903), II pp. xxiii-xv; cf. D. Knowles, *The Monastic Order in England*, p. 51.

3 According to *Valor Ecclesiasticus* of 1535, Winchcombe had a gross general

income of £812, and a net general income of £759. This put the abbey in the top 7% of English monasteries, among those houses with a net income of more than £700 a year. But for earlier poverty see Knowles, op. cit., p. 102.

4 *Register of Worcester Priory*, Camden Society, 1865 : *Hemming's Cartulary*, ed. Hearne : *Early Compotus Rolls of Worcester Priory*, Worcester Historical Society : *Historia et Cartularium Monasterii Gloucestriae ; Annales Monastici*, Vols. 1 and 4 : *Chronicon Abbatiae de Evesham* : all in the Rolls Series. The late R. A. L. Smith wrote an unpublished University of London thesis on Pershore Abbey.

5 Miss R. Graham has written a sketch of the abbey's history in the *Victoria History of the County of Gloucester*, II, and the Rev. Potto Hicks a popular summary entitled *The Story of Winchcombe Abbey*.

6 Although Winchcombe together with three adjoining hundreds paid £28 in 1086, in King Edward's time the farm of the borough alone was only £6. D.B., p. 162.

7 P.R.O. Lay Subsidies, 113/31. Cf. the fifteenth of 6 Ed. II, printed in *Landboc*, I p. xxvii.

8 For example the only textile workers were 7 weavers and 2 fullers.

9 *Cal. Close R. 1237-42*, p. 65.

10 The list of commodities available for a pavage of I Ed. III, in *Landboc*, p. xxxi, ranging from herring to teazles, from spices to alum, is suggestive, but in no way conclusive as to what commodities were of real significance in the town's trade.

11 *Cal. Close R. 1253-4*, p. 89 ; *1254-6*, p. 332.

12 *Landboc*, I pp. xxxvi and xli.

13 *Valor*, II p. 459.

14 Printed as an appendix to W. Cunningham, *Growth of English Industry and Commerce* I, 5th edition, and in Allan Evan's edition of Pegolotti's *Practica della Mercatura*, Medieval Academy of America, 1936, pp. 258-69. See his discussion of the list, ibid.,pp. xxviii-xxix.

15 N. Denholm-Young, *Seigneurial Administration in England*, p. 54.

16 See the article on Fourteenth-Century England by R.A. Pelham in *A Historical Geography of England*, ed. H.C. Darby. *The Taxatio Ecclesiastica* of 1291 (Record Comm.), pp. 228, 233, gives estimated figures of flocks for some monasteries, but only profits of stock for Winchcombe.

17 *Landboc*, I p. 11 ; II p. 309, 121 : *Cal. Pat. R. 1494-1509*, p. 599 : *L.and P. Henry VIII*, I p. 651.

18 *Landboc*, I p. 24.

19 *Landboc*, II p. 337.

20 I do not include post-Dissolution surveys of the abbey property in the records of the Augmentation Office.

21 Landboc, II p. lxii.

22 *Landboc*, I pp. 24-5, 89.

23 I have used a transcript made by Mrs. D. Styles, by permission of the late Lord Sherborne.

24 Cf. R.Graham, 'The Taxation of Pope Nicholas IV', in *English Ecclesiastical Studies*: W.E. Lunt, *Valuation of Norwich*, p. 147: Snape, *English Monastic Finance*, pp. 71-3.

25 Although Enstone *assart* rents are included in the of rents at the beginning,

neither assart nor assize rents from Enstone are included among the manorial rentals.

26 *Landboc*, II p. xxvi: *Cal. Pat. R. 1350-54*, p. 325.

27 *Cal. Pat. R. 1350-54*, p. 481.

28 This is shown by the phrase used, *et pro mess et falc' preter opera*.

29 A hint, though no more, of an earlier commutation of services is found in a payment of *Wikewerkesyler* on the manors of Honeybourne, Admington and Stanton. The payment was not heavy, being 11/9 from each village.

30 pp. 363-6.

31 *Landboc*, I p. 249; II pp. 203-12, 529-35. Cf. a letter patent giving the abbey the right to enclose 115 acres of land assarted in Wychwood Forest. *Cal. Pat. R. 1301-7*, p. 531.

32 *Calendar of the Muniments at Sherborne House*. Privately printed, 1900. The late Lord Sherborne kindly gave me permission to examine these documents.

33 Which the abbey held at farm at least as early as 1223. *Cal. Pat. R. 1216-25*, p. 415.

34 Not the only possible basis. A 13th century charter transferring 4 acres in the open fields refers to one as the *capitalem acram*, and to another as the *exteriorem acram*. Another charter transferring 12 acres (6 acres in each field) describes one of them as the *capitalis acra*, and the sixth acre in the same field as the *mediam acram*. *Landboc*, II pp. 233, 238; cf. also ibid., p. 244. The descriptions give the impression that the strips of a holding were counted in order from a known fixed strip.

35 I am much indebted to Miss M. Hand and Miss F. Redmond, Messrs. M. Bamfield, G.C. Summers and E.K. Vose, of Birmingham University, for help in investigating the Sherborne field system.

36 "The *ancient course* of the common fields of these hills was singular. Each township was divided into two fields; 'crop and fallow',—alternately: one year wheat and barley, the next a whole year's fallow: except a small part of each township, which was used as a kind of every year's land; for growing a few peas, oats or other subordinate crop." Marshall, *Rural Economy of Gloucestershire* (2nd ed., 1796), II p. 38 n. See *Landboc*, I pp. 208, 287; II pp. 233, 234, 235 ff, 282, 330, 335. The importance of the rotational scheme is shown by a charter of 1182 by which a piece of land in Farmington, immediately west of Sherborne, on transfer to the abbey, has to conform to the *consuetudo arandi* of Sherborne.—Ibid., I p. 197.

37 A reference in a charter of 1318 to an Eastfield as one of two fields would appear to be a slip of nomenclature rather than evidence of a third big field. A modern East Field however exists.

38 *Landboc*, II p. 249: Sherborne MS. 86, sub. tit. *vendicio feni*.

39 Sherborne MS. 84.

40 D.B., I p. 165: *Tax Eccl.*, p. 233: Rental, fols. 12-16: *Landboc*, I pp. 185, 196-7: II p. 273: Sherborne MS. 96.

41 I take the index 3.5 rather than 5 to derive population from landholders, as suggested by J.C. Russel in *British Medieval Population*, pp. 22-31. For landholding populations of Gloucestershire villages in pre-plague years, see ibid., pp. 86-7.

42 The Gloucestershire, and especially the Cotswold virgate, was large—'40 acres... to this day is the usuall content of a yardland in the ritcher soile of this

hundred (Berkeley); but in the wolds or hilly part thereof, a yardland is somewhat more.' Smythe, *Hundred of Berkeley*, p. 2. Cf. H.L. Gray, *English Field Systems*, p. 438, for a 48 acre virgate at Charlton Abbots. Virgates on the Cotswold manors of the Abbey of Gloucester varied from 32 to 48 acres. *Glouc. Cart.*, III pp. 35-213.

43 Sherborne MS. 65.

44 Gloucs. Cart.III, loc. cit.

45 Sherborne MS. 96.

46 There were holdings *ad opus* and *ad malam* in the 12th century on the estates of Burton Abbey. *Burton Abbey 12th Century Surveys*, Historical Coll for Staffs., 1916. Tenants' obligations on the manors of the Bishop of Worcester in the 13th century were calculated both *ad plenam operationem* and *ad firmam*. *Red Book of Worcester*, Worcs. Hist. Soc.

47 The charter is neither dated or witnessed. It is placed in the *Landboc* between two charters dated 1274 and 1276, I p. 122. John's charter granting the land is in II p. 240.

48 Ibid., II pp. 233-53.

49 Three virgates of meadow, i.e. the meadow appurtenant to 3 virgates, are referred to in the same deed as *3 acres* of meadow, indicating that here an acre was the normal amount of meadow appurtenant to a virgate. Ibid., II p. 250.

50 Ibid., II pp. 237, 252.

51 Sherborne manor and demesne were farmed at £20 and Cowham pasture at £10. Honeybourne demesne lands were farmed to the tenants at £8 and one pasture at £25. *Val.Ecc.*, II pp. 456, 457. Although Windrush is included with Sherborne in the *Valor* survey, the abbey only drew a few rents from there.

52 Op.cit., p. 11.

53 Pipe Roll, 8 Ed. III, no. 179, m 35d. This manor was farmed out by the Crown to the Bishop of Hereford. I owe this reference to Mrs D. Styles.

54 Marshall considered Cotswold soil particularly suitable for barley and implies that in his day Cotswold farmers had made the mistake of increasing the ratio of wheat to barley. Op.cit., p. 57.

55 See the *Regule compoti* of Beaulieu Abbey, printed as an appendix to N.Denholm-Young, op. cit., for a system of calculating money values for internal accounting.

56 But the sale of dairy produce in 1436 was in fact a simple transfer of produce to the sub-cellarer.

57 *Superplusagium* means here the accounting deficit between expenses and receipts.

58 The current local prices of grain are not available.

59 In 1426, 1436, 1446.

60 Stakes were made for two folds in 1453.

61 The Sherborne reeve writes that the issue of 12 sheep could be checked against the shepherd's account.

62 Accommodating 2,100 sheep in the summer months and 1,400 in the winter.

63 This account is printed in abstract in the *Calendar*, pp. 176-183. The author of the *Calendar* has made the mistake of supposing that a medieval account is convertible into a modern balance sheet.

64 Unless peasants' wool was added, as was likely. See below.

65 *Cely Papers*, p. 48. For an Italian buyer of wool from Winchcombe and elsewhere in 1443-4, see E.Power in *English Trade in the Fifteenth Century*, (ed. Power and Postan), p. 52.

66 More, if we take the wool sack to have contained 250 or even 300 fleeces, as was not unlikely.

67 The wool sale, quoted by Professor Power (loc. cit.), to an Italian in 1443 was only of 40 sacks all told from 4 religious houses of which Winchcombe was one.

3. Old Enclosure in the West Midlands (pp. 36-47)

1 Worcester County Record Office, Maps, 971 :2.

2 Published by the Dugdale Society, edited by the present author. See below chapter 5, pp. 63-101.

3 As we see from the description in the 1279 Hundred Rolls. Public Record Office, E/164/15.

4 Charter No. 79 in the collection of Stoneleigh Abbey Charters, Record Office, Shakespeare Centre, Stratford-upon Avon.

5 In the appendix to my *Social Structure of Rural Warwickshire in the Middle Ages*, Dugdale Society. 1950.

6 Cartulary of Coventry Cathedral, P.R.O. E/164/21.

7 P.R.O. E/164/21.f.54.

8 The Coventry city troubles are described by M. Dormer Harris, *Life in an old English Town* and in an article in the *English Historical Review*, vol. IX. Her main source is in the *Coventry Leet Book*, Early English Text Society, 1907-1913.

9 The Coventry Cathedral villages examined are Radford, Coundon, Keresley, Corley, Exhall, Foleshill and Henley-in-Foleshill.

10 This map, an eighteenth century copy, is reproduced by permission of the Trustees of the British Museum.

11 *Worcestershire Inquisitions Post Mortem*, Worcester Historical Society, 1894 and 1909.

12 *Red Book of Worcester*, ed. M. Hollings, Worcester Historical Society, 1934, 1937, 1939 and 1950.

13 British Museum Add Ch.49, 155.

14 T. Madox, *Formulare Anglicanum*, 1702. *Christopher Hatton's Book of Seals* ed. D Stenton, Northampton Record Society 1950.

15 *Libertas haiae* (Madox op. cit., pp. 2,276). Cf.'the law in Arden' quoted to the itinerant justices, 1221, *Rolls of the Justices in Eyre for Lincolnshire and Worcestershire*, Selden Society, vol. 53, p. 448.m.

16 Worcester County Record Office, Box 1188/12.

17 Cf. the Bederepe Court rolls in the Stoneleigh collection at Stratford-upon-Avon.

18 Cf. R.A.Pelham, 'Earliest Aulnage Accounts of Worcestershire', *Trans. Worcs. Archaeological Soc.*, XXIX.

4. The Ministers' Accounts of the Warwickshire Estates of the Duke of Clarence, 1479-80 (pp. 48-62)

Originally the Introduction to *Ministers' Accounts of the Warwickshire Estates of the Duke of Clarence, 1479-80*, (Dugdale Society Publications, XXI [1952]).

1 Public Record Office, Ministers' Accounts, DL. 29/642/10421. These accounts of 1480 (the first of a considerable series) are enrolled on membranes, 10¾ inches wide by between 28 and 29 inches long. The physical condition of the rolls is good, and the writing clear and elegant. There are few illegible portions, none of any great extent. Even the auditors' jottings in the left-hand margin of the membranes can in most cases be deciphered, although these are highly abbreviated, and in a hand which in some cases is little more than a scribble.

2 Earlier account material exists, for example the accounts of the guardians of the lands of the contrariant Guy Beauchamp (Min. Accts. 1123/4 and 5), but it is scrappy and incomplete.

3 P.R.O., Chancery Inquisitions Post Mortem, Edw. II, File 49.

4 See P.R.O. Lists 34, *Ministers' Accounts*, Pt. 2, pp. 160-1.

5 *Victoria County History of Warwick*, iii, p. 65; W. Dugdale, *Antiquities of Warwickshire* (1730), pp. 891-2, 494.

6 N. Denholm-Young, *Seignorial Administration in England*; E. Lamond (ed.), *Walter of Henley's Husbandry*; In Memory of J.P. Gilson, *Legal and Manorial Formularies*; D. Oschinsky, 'Medieval Treatises on Estate Accounting', *Economic History Review*, xvii, No. 1.

7 Cf. H.S. Bennett in *English Historical Review*, vol. 41.

8 *Constitutio quaedam* and *Scriptum quoddam* in *Historia et Cartularium Monasterii Gloucestriae, iii*.

9 P.R.O. Min. Accts., SC. 6/104/13.

10 The winnowing was accounted for seperately by the dairymaid, who must also have accounted for milk, cheese, and other dairy produce.

11 P.R.O Min. Accts., SC.6/1041/10. Now edited by Jean Birrell in *Miscellany I*, Dugdale Society, 1977.

12 According to the inquisition the Earl's demesne resources were as in the table on page 53.

13 A reference at the end of the Sutton Coldfield account (p. 43) shows the accountant respited from a certain sum due from rents of assize charged to him until such time as the rental which was the basis of the charge was renewed.

14 See the auditors' marginal note at a certain point on the list of the decayed rents at Warwick—*summa antiquorum decasuum*.

15 Birmingham Reference Library MSS. 168024, 167904, 168023.

16 Tanworth accounts at the record repository at the Shakespeare Birthplace, Stratford-upon-Avon, not yet catalogued

17 Birmingham Reference Library MSS. 47923, 347929, 347930, 347943.

18 An Erdington rental of 1463 (Birmingham Reference Library MSS. 347913) for lands whose ownership is not specified shows a rental total of £4. 7s. 7¼d. The 1461 assize rent total on the Warwick manor is £16. 18s. 9d. The total assize rent in 1480 is £22. 11s. 7½d., a figure near enough to the combined totals of the early sixties (£21. 6s. 4d.) to make the assumption of a combination

of the two manors reasonable. The figures are even closer if one takes the basic assize rent of 1480, without recent additions—£21. 12s. 3½d.

19 The Erdington accounts are not of course comparable.

20 It was stationary between 1460 and 1480.

21 *Domesday of Enclosures*, ed. I. Leadham, pp. 919,649, 652, 654.

22 The matter is discussed in the Appendix to the present writer's *Social Structure of Rural Warwickshire in the Middle Ages*, Dugdale Society Occasional Paper No. 9.

23 See the introduction to *Place Names of Warwickshire*, ed. Gower, Mawer, and Stenton.

24 P.R.O., Min. Accts., SC6/1123/5.

25 A process which was well advanced by the end of the thirteenth century. See Denholm-Young, op. cit., p. 6.

26 *Ordinances for the Royal Household*, Society of Antiquaries, 1790, pp. 89-105.

27 Op. cit., p. 566.

28 MS. in the possession of the Mayor and Corporation of Warwick, f.clxx.

29 See E.C. Lodge, *John of Gaunt's Register*, i, Camden Society, No. 56, Introduction.

30 The Warwick bailiff was sent by the constable of Warwick Castle to London to discuss repairs to the castle walls with the King and his councillors, p. xxx.

31 *Calendar of Patent Rolls* 1467-77, pp. 445 *et al.*, and 1476-85, pp. 220, 230.

32 *Letters and Papers Illustrative of the Reigns of Richard III and Henry VII*, ed. J.Gairdner, pp. 81-85. See also A.P. Newton, 'The King's Chamber under the Early Tudors', *English Historical Review*, vol. 32.

33 A.P. Newton, art. cit. T.F. Tout's *Chapters in Medieval Administrative History* deal exhaustively with earlier methods of by-passing the Exchequer in the interests of efficiency and of the financial independence of the King.

34 That is if they actually did the work. Some bailiffs appointed by the Crown were allowed to appoint deputies.

35 The bailiffs of Sutton Coldfield, Erdington, Brailes, and Lighthorne are allowed expenses for their journey to Warwick.

36 From the headings *Perquisita Curiarum* we find that the following courts were held in 1480.

Place	*View of Frankpledge*	*Court*
Warwick Castle Gate	2	..
Sutton Coldfield	2	2
Erdington	..	2
Tanworth	2	2
Berkswell	..	2
Morton	2	..
Brailes	..	2
Lighthorne	2	..

37 *Cal. Pat. R.* 1461-6, p. 105; 1467-77, p. 278; 1476-85, pp. 64, 110-11, 119, 220, 230, 495-5.

38 *Cal. Pat. R.* 1452-61, p. 416; 1461-7, pp. 24, 152, 13, 529; 1476-85, pp. 54, 177, 341.

39 Essex appears as an Exchequer official from 1452 to 1480 in *Kalendars and Inventories of His Majesty's Exchequer*, vols. ii and iii. In 1461 he was granted the office of Remembrancer of the Exchequer for life, *Cal. Pat. R.* 1461-7, p.24.

40 *Cal. Pat. R.* 1476-85, pp. 28, 35, 68, 70, 88, 92, 96, 98, 173, 179, 192, 390.

41 *Ordinances for the Royal Household*, p. 27.

42 *Cal. Pat. R. 1476-85*, p. 109. There is an account of the family in Dugdale, op. cit., pp. 287-9, where documents no longer extant are cited.

43 *Cal. Pat. R. 1478-85*, p. 155.

5. The Leger Book of Stoneleigh Abbey (pp. 63-100)

* The Introduction to *The Stoneleigh Leger Book* (Dugdale Society Publications XXIV [1960]).

1 Although Dugdale always calls the book 'Registrum de Stoneley' in his marginal references, he speaks of it in the text as 'that excellent Leiger-book, being the transcript of their evidences, wherein are all things historically entred that concern this monastery ...', *Antiquities* (1656), p. 172. Vinogradoff, who saw the book when it was in the late Lord Leigh's keeping, also calls it a Register in his *Villeinage in England* (1892), p. 91, note. The Leger Book now forms part of the collection of family and estate papers from Stoneleigh deposited by Lord Leigh at Shakespeare's Birthplace, Stratford-upon-Avon.

2 He was the inspirer of the disastrous Second Crusade of 1147. It is interesting to note that Roger de Clinton, Bishop of Chester (1129-48), who was a benefactor of Stoneleigh, died on this crusade. Roger is cited by the author of *Gesta Stephani* as one of the warlike and unspiritual bishops of the anarchy (ed. K. Potter, p. 104).

3 This first complaint only appears in the *Acta Abbatum*.

4 Cf. Z.N. and C.N.L. Brooke, *English Historical Review* i. 84-86.

5 Z.N. and C.N.L. Brooke, art. cit. The full transcript of the earliest charters to Radmore by Henry as Duke of Acquitaine and Count of Anjou in the text confirms the suggestion as to the date of the charters made by the authors of this article, who were relying only on the shortened versions in Dugdale's *Monasticon*.

6 Not in 1141, as in art. cit.

7 Dates determined by accession of Patrick to the Earldom of Salisbury (*Complete Peerage*, xi. 376), and Mathilda's probable last stay in England.

8 J.H. Round, *Geoffrey de Manderville*, pp. 83, 253.

9 *English Feudalism*, p. 243; B.M. Additional Charter, 1958. I owe the reference to this Reading Abbey charter to Professor H.A. Cronne, who suggests that as it was witnessed by Earl Eustace, the king's son, it is unlikely to be earlier than the beginning of 1147. Eustace was made earl at Christmas 1146 or early in 1147.

10 Harleian MS. 3650, fols. 5-7.

11 Osbert of Arden's Marston charter; Geoffrey de Clinton's Arlescote charter; and Ranulf, Earl of Chester's confirmation of Osbert of Arden's charter. A repeat of the Arlescote charter, but to Stoneleigh instead of to Radmore, is in *Sir Christopher Hatton's Book of Seals*, Northamptonshire Record Society, xv, p. 139.

12 This argument does not seem to be affected by the probability that Pype's year 1154 began on 25 March 1154 of our reckoning, ending on 24 March 1155.

13 *Staffordshire Historical Collections* (William Salt Society), ii. 241-2.

14 *Statuta Capitulorum Generalium Ordinis Cisterciensis*, vols. 1-8 ed. J.M. Canivez (1933-41); see his index.

15 Dugdale *Antiquities of Warwickshire* (1656), makes him the son of Richard Pipe. Dugdale's genealogical table is difficult to reconcile with John of Pype's appearance in the tax list, *Lay Subsidy Roll for Warwickshire* (1332) (Dugdale Society Publications,vi) pp. 21, 22, 68.

16 *Calender of Patent Rolls*, 1361-4, pp. 447; ibid., 1364-7, p. 29.

17 Cf. the taking over of Winchcombe Abbey, 1353 above, p. 23.

18 *Cal. Pat. Rolls*, 1361-4, pp. 460, 452, 527.

19 Sir John Pecche was a substantial Warwickshire landowner (lord of Wormleighton, Hampton-in-Arden, and other property); Simon Pakeman was a citizen of Coventry. The record is P.R.O., K.B., 27/413, mem. 14r.

20 The rental which comprises the second half of the Leger Book contains, as the reader will perceive, a considerable amount of evidence about tenants in the century or so before its compilation. Other evidence of persons who had dealings with the abbey is contained in the collection of charters.

21 Stated to be greater in number than the number of monks saying Mass.

22 'Item dicunt quod cum idem Abbas in curia domini Regis coram Rogero Illary et sociis suis justiciariis de Banco implacitasset Ricardum de la Cloude tenentem ipsius Abbatis manerii sui predicti de uno mesuagio uno carucata terre cum pertinentiis in Canley et Hurst et per quandam [*sic*] iuramentam inter predictum abbatem et Ricardum captam super quodam scripto raso et fabricato per predictum abbatem et fratrem Johhanem de Weston commonachum suum... recuperavit versus preditum Ricardum predicta tenamenta...'

23 A. 241.

24 *Cal. Close Rolls*, 1360-4, pp. 106, 400, 410, 438, 525, 529.

25 John of Holt was given by Abbot Pype a pension of forty shillings and a gown (or twenty shillings) for his counsel, in 1363. Another corrodian, Henry Dalamaigne, who, with his wife, from 1362 was to have maintainance for life in the Abbey, was supposedly sent there by the king. *Cal. Close Rolls*, 1360-4, pp. 404 and 555. But there is ground for suspicion here. Almayn is a family name in Stoneleigh manor and a Henry Almayn was joint lessee of Morhalle manor sometime before 1380 (S.L.B., 201, 204).

26 *Cal. Pat. Rolls*, 1364-7, pp. 145, 151; 1367-70, Leger Book now forms part of 136-259.

27 Idem., 1377-81, pp. 462, 509, 618; 1381-5, p. 311.

28 Parchment tabs making permanent bookmarkers are attached to fols. 27, 30, 50, 127, 128, 129, and 130 for ease of reference. They are probably pre-Reformation as are many of the marginal marks (such as pointing fingers) which emphasize matter of importance.

29 Deposited by Lord Leigh at Shakespeare's Birthplace, Stratford-upon-Avon.

30 Manors formerly of Winchcombe and Evesham Abbeys respectively.

31 Signatures by Rowland and William are on deeds in the Leigh Collection at Stratford, and William's signature is on a fly-leaf at the end of the original Leger Book.

32 It is copied into the original Leger Book at fol. 193b.

33 Dugdale, *Antiquities* (1656), p. 179.

34 He refers to his intention to consult the 'Leger Booke of Stonley' at Sir Thomas Leigh's house in a letter to Sir Simon Archer, dated 26 March 1637, printed in W. Hamper, *Life, Diary and Correspondence of Sir William Dugdale, Knt.*, 1827, p. 162. His transcripts are in the Bodleian Library, MS Dugdale, 12, pp.31-74.

35 *The Royal Demesne in English Constitutional History, 1066-1272* (1950); see also his article in *English Historical Review*, lxv, which became the final chapter of the book and is concerned most particularly with the matter under discussion.

36 He describes the book as 'certainly one of the most interesting surveys of a medieval manor extant, and gives a better insight into the condition of ancient demesne than any other document I know', op. cit., p. 426.

37 Not simply the royal demesne of 1066.

38 Cf. the interesting instruction by Edward I to his agents to inquire into alienations in Stoneleigh in which he refers to his wish to keep the property in good order in case it should one day return into Crown hands, pp. 44-45. Vinogradoff also noticed this, op.cit., p 207. Notice also that when Robert of Canley's usurpation of Canley hamlet was over-thrown, the king kept seisin of it for two weeks before handing it over to the abbey, pp. 69-70, 81-2.

39 Cf. cases quoted by E.A. Kosminsky in chapter vii of *Studies in English Agrarian History in the thirteenth century*.

40 Although Stoneleigh tenants owed heriot and merchet, they did no week work.

41 Vinogradoff's reference to this document is most vague. Had he examined it in more detail, it might have affected his ideas about the uniqueness of Stoneleigh. He was, of course, well acquainted with the printed *Rotuli Hundredorum* for Oxfordshire and the counties of the south-east midlands, but seems only to have glanced at the unprinted Warwickshire returns.

42 See R.H. Hilton, *Social Structure of Rural Warwickshire in the Middle Ages*, Dugdale Society, 1950; J.B. Harley, 'Population Trends and Agricultural Developments from the Warwickshire Hundred Rolls of 1280', *Economic History Review*, 1958. The above remarks must not be taken as being applicable outside this particular region. In many parts of the country the trend after 1086 was by no means in the direction of the extension of freedom of tenure.

43 Not to speak of a great quantity of post-Dissolution material at Stratford which would make possible a continuous of the property from medieval to modern times.

44 e.g. P.R.O. Ancient Deeds E326, B10089, 10091, 10092, and 10094 = Gregory Leger Book nos. 13,16,17, and 15.

45 Miss J. Lancaster in the *Bulletin of the Institute of Historical Research*, 27-28, p.113. This volume is at Shakespeare's Birthplace, Stratford-upon-Avon. The

Stoneleigh material is between pp. 193 and 256.

46 Charter of King John, Gregory Leger Book, p. 193 = Stoneleigh Leger Book, fol. 15; ditto, G.L.B., pp. 193-4 = S., fol. 15b; *inspeximus* of Henry III, G.L.B., pp. 194-5 = S., fol. 18b; ditto, G.L.B., pp. 195-6 = S., fol. 18b; Charter of Roger, Bishop of Chester, G.L.B., p. 196-7 = S., fol. 9b; Charter of Osbert of Arden, G.L.B., p. 207 = S., fol. 11b; Charter of Geoffrey, chamberlain of Clinton, G.L.B., p. 226 = S., fol. 12; Charter of William Croc, G.L.B., p. 226 = S., fol. 9; Charter of Roger, Bishop of Chester, G.L. B., p. 248 = S., fol. 9b; Charter of Richard, Bishop of Coventry, G.L.B., 249 = S., fol. 11b; Charter of Geoffrey of Clinton, G.L.B., p.255 = S., fol. 9b.

47 A few Radway and Ratley deeds and surveys are in a small (14 folios) sixteenth-century cartulary among the Early Deeds in the Leigh Collection, No. A.138.

48 Archbishop of Canterbury, and John, Bishop of Ely, are witnesses. The appropriation was by Alexander, Bishop of Coventry, in the eighth year of his pontificate (1232-3).

49 One version of the Ratley charter is in *Sir Christopher Hatton's Book of Seals*, pp. 96-97. A date early in Henry II's reign is suggested. Thomas, son of Henry of Arden, confirmed and extended the grant, which was in turn confirmed by Waleran, Earl of Warwick, who died in 1205.

50 Gregory Leger Book, pp. 227-8.

51 Ibid., pp. 221 and 224-5. For the connexion of the Arden family with Kingsbury see *V.C.H. Warwicks* iv. 104, W. Dugdale *Antiquities of Warwickshire* (1656), p. 760. (= 710).

52 e.g. the advowson of Radway in 1220-5; and charters of William, Earl of Warenne (d. 1240).

53 Cf. G.R.C. Davis, *Medieval Cartularies of Great Britain*, p.107.

54 It should be mentioned, too, that the collection deposited by Lord Leigh also contains deeds which can have had no connexion with the Stoneleigh Abbey estate.

55 It would also show how casual the use of seals could be. There are not a few cases where seals were used that belonged to none of the parties nor to any of the witnesses of the deeds.

56 Gregory Deeds, nos. 2 and 53.

57 e.g. a grant of three acres in Kingshill 'habendum et tenendum eidem Stephano et heredibus suis dare vendere vel assignare voluerit de dominis capitalibus feodi secundum consuetudinem manerii per servicia inde debita et consueta bene quiete et in pace in perpetuum'. The accidental omission of *cuicunque* before *voleurit* may be assumed. Gregory Deeds, no. 73 (late thirteenth or early fourteenth century).

58 Quitclaims by Alexander of Cryfield and Geoffrey his son of right in land in Hurst to William the son of Michael of Hurst. In one case 'quasquidem petii de predicto Willelmo Michel per breve de recto in curria domini abbatis de Stonle in Stonle', in the other 'quas petiuimus versus eundem Willelmum per breve domini Regis in curia Stanlega' Leigh Collection, Early Deeds, nos. A. 11 and A. 12. These men were probably living at the beginning of Edward I's reign.

59 Gregory Deeds, no. 26b.

60 See below, p. 81-2.

61 Leigh Collection, Early Deeds, nos. A.53, 164, 265, 51, 163, 167, 166, 233, 165, 289, 288, 161, 162, 231, 239, 247, 248, 242, 249, 230, and especially 50 and 204.

62 Below, p. 89-100.

63 e.g. A. 274, 66, 67, 74, 73, 68, 69, 70, 71. Berkswell free tenants had common rights in Westwood; xxx, where Pype notes that many Berkswell and Allesley men, as well as the Hospitallers' tenants in Fletchamstead, had released these common rights.

64 e.g. Leigh Collection, Early Deeds, A. 109, a lease of three fields in Stoneleigh parish for eighty years from Michaelmas 1422.

65 Gregory Deeds, 13-16.

66 They are contained in box no. 1 of the Leigh Collection, Court Rolls, at Stratford-upon-Avon. Box no.2 contains sixteenth to eighteenth century court rolls. There are also a few pre-Dissolution court rolls at the Public Records Office, Portf. 206/76, 77. They contain nothing of special interest.

67 Three separate views of frankpledge seem to have been held at Stoneleigh, Stareton and Bericote. Presentments to the Stoneleigh view were from Millburn, Cryfield, Hurst, Canley, Fletchamstead, Kingshill, Finham, and Stoneleigh; and to the Bericote view from Hill Wotton, Ashow, Bericote, and Cubbington.

68 The earliest and latest dates are July 28 (1484 and 1491) and 29 August (1481). The variation was caused, of course, by variations in the time of harvesting.

69 '...utrum messores ibidem abiles sunt ad messandum necnon utrum bene laborant vel non...' No.22, court on the Monday before St.Laurence, 3 Richard III.

70 Rentals as on p. 85. *Domesday of Enclosures*, ed. I. Leadam, pp. 405-6, 440-1; M.W. Beresford, '*The Deserted Villages of Warwickshire*', Trans. Birm. Arch. Soc. lxvi 96.

71 The sheep grazers at Cryfield Grange were the lessees of the grantee Robert Bosher; two graziers at Millburn were lessees of the James Cruse who had been granted the reversion of the estate by the Crown in 1538. Cf. *V.C.H Warwick*, vi. 234 ff.

72 *Rotuli Hundredorum*, ii, Record Commission, 1818. The most detailed account of these inquiries is in E.A. Kosminsky's *Studies in English Agrarian History in the Thirteenth Century*, 1956. The earlier inquiry of 1274-5 is described by H.M. Cam, in *Studies in the Hundred Rolls* (Oxford Studies in Social and Legal History, 1921) and in *The Hundred and the Hundred Rolls* (1931).

73 Public Record Office, Exchequer K.R. Misc. Bks., no. 15. There is also a copy of the return for Coventry in a manuscript book in the Leigh collection at Stratford.

74 J.C. Russel, *British Medieval Population*, 1948.

75 We may take it that these are real changes in rent income, not simply changes dependent on currency alterations.

76 This shown by a comparison of the figures taken from Domesday Book (1086) with those of the 1280 survey. See J.B. Harley, art. cit.

77 In fact in 1392 and later the abbey continued to lay claim to the boon

works which had always been the sole labour element in Stoneleigh tenants' rents.

78 The rent from the farmer for Bockyndene Grange at this time was only a rose (for sixteen years, to be raised to £4 for the rest of the seventy-year term).

79 On the other hand, where estate documents (especially manor court rolls) give an insight into peasant sub-letting, it is often found that poorer tenants are leasing their holdings in whole or part to the richer. This was the case in the fourteenth century on the nearby estate of Worcester Cathedral Priory, according to Mr E.K. Vose, who has analysed all the Cathedral manor court records.

80 Fragmentary survivals of the Poll Tax return of 2 Richard II are in the Public Record Office, E.179/192/3. This comparison between documents separated by a dozen years is, of course, uncertain. But an examination of the Leger Book will show that the names of tenants preceeding those of 1392, where succession was not by inheritance, are frequently given. Also surnames by this time seem generally to have been inherited.

81 This probably means they are quit of the licence fee paid to the lord for permission to sell stock.

82 e.g. fol. 15(v), after the list of Stoneleigh tenants: 'Isti dicti libere tenentes sicud Johannes filius Galfridi de Stanle' (the ancestor of the Robert le Eyr of the Leger Book) 'et Johannes de Monte debent sectam ad curiam abbatis de Stanle de tribus septimanis in tribus septimanis', etc.

83 The lesser tenants whom they supervised at the abbot's bederepe would, in many cases, be already accustomed to working for wages on the holdings of these wealthier tenants. There may be a causal relationship between the two patterns of subordination.

84 Stareton, with five villeins and seventeen cottars, does not, however, fit in with the scheme described. Aquired separately from the rest of the soke, the abbot had a separate view of frankpledge, and there is no mention of suit by Stareton tenants to the three-weekly court at Stoneleigh.

85 There is an interesting report of a case under the assize of fresh force in the Abbot of Bordesley's court of Tardebigge, known in the thirteenth century as the Hundred Court of Tardebigge (Tardebigge Court Rolls, Worcester County Record Office, court held on the Friday after the feast of SS. Simon and Jude, 19 Richard II). The assize was also employed in the nearby manors of Feckenham (Feckenham Court Rolls Worcester County Record Office) and Bromsgrove (Bromsgrove Court Rolls, ibid.). This method of procedure, also found in some boroughs, would appear to be particularly associated with the royal demesne. All four manors were *Terra Regis* in 1086.

86 Stoneleigh Court Rolls, Box 1, no. 2.

87 Domesday Book, i, fol. 238. H.C. Darby, *Domesday Geography of Midland England*, p. 291.

88 Boscus intrinsecus de Hasilwode incipit in Calloudon Lane et continet totum Stoke, multum de Harehal, partem de Whitemore et Henley, et boscum dominus [*sic*] Segrave in Hasilwode. *Coventry Leet Book*, ed. M. Dormer Harris (1907), p. 11.

89 Not to be confused with the more famous Arden family descended from Turchil of Warwick.

90 The earliest independent reference to Wood field which we have noticed is

in an indenture of 1284, Leigh Collection, Early Deeds, No. A. 278. According to estate maps belonging to Lord Leigh at Stoneleigh Abbey it kept this name as a common field in the eighteenth century.

91 A lease of Stoneleigh Grange in 20 Henry VIII for thirty years to Thomas Donton of Elmdon, husbandman, contains a description of the land appurtenant to the grange. Several of the place names cited by Pype appear on this deed. Leigh Collection Early Deeds, no. A. 308.

92 Reproduced from the map at Stoneleigh Abbey in *V.C.H. Warwick*, vi, p. 233. The element 'conynger' (rabbit warren) in what purports to be a mid-twelfth-century name makes one suspect this whole reconstruction of the earliest cultivated area of the Stoneleigh soke in view if the scarcity of the rabbit in inland areas before the thirteenth century. Cf. Elspeth M. Veale, 'The Rabbit in England', *Agricultural History Review*, v. ii.

93 Leigh Collection, Early Deeds, Nos A. 113, A. 50; Gregory Deeds.

94 In 1377 the abbey granted Bradelefeld with an attached close called Oxhey to the Hospitallers. This land was then bounded by the fields of Weston, Bradley Wood, the Cubbington to Coventry road, Waverley (Wethele) Heath, and Longhedge. It was given as pasture for their sheep. They were also given a droveway forty feet wide running via 'Wythegus', Cubbington Grove, and Home grange field. They were not to plough without licence. Leigh Collection, Early Deeds, No. A. 234.

95 Armeley does not seem to have survived in any modern place-name. It seems to have been on the north side of the road from Stoneleigh to Weston (or Wolsies) Bridge, between the Stockinglonds and the Finham brook. This land is called Little Heath in the eighteenth-century estate map. This position is consistent with references in the Leger Book and with a document among the Gregory Deeds (No.18) where it is described as Armeley Heath.

96 British Museum Map P. 12609. MI. 6b 1 (12).

97 Wood Field, Snite Hill Field, and Cloud Hill Field (Upper and Lower) seem in fact to have persisted as open fields until the eighteenth century.

98 Gregory Deeds, No. 101.

99 e.g.Culvecroft with Wodefeld; croft in Middle Stockynglond with Starhulle; croft in Lower Stockynglond with Stanydelf.

100 Cf. the still existing coppice called 'Hare's Parlour'.

6. A Rare Evesham Abbey Estate Document (pp. 101-107)

1. For a discussion of the estate documents of the West Midland counties, see my *A Medieval Society* (1983 reprint), pp. 65-74. The *Chronicon Abbatiae de Evesham*, ed. W.D. Macray, was published in the Rolls Series in 1863. Abbot Bromsgrove's register is in the British Museum, Cotton Titus C. IX. The two cartularies, also in the British Museum, are Cotton Vespasian B. XXIV and Harleian 3763.

2 The depredations are witnessed in the two Evesham cartularies and the chronicle. The chronicle tells of efforts at the reconstitution of the estate. The manorial histories in the Victoria County History illustrate the success of the

abbey in preventing the growth of freehold estates.

3 The manuscript in the Leigh Collection is not yet numbered. It is among the manorial manuscripts.

4 The chronicle is the chief source for the distribution of abbey property among the various obedientiaries. The impression is given that the cellarer drew on all of the estate which was not allotted to the lesser obedietiaries. *Chronicon...*pp. 205-221.

5 Vespasian B. XXIV, f.53. This shows a half yardland at Norton estimated at twelve acres. Six-acre holdings which might be quarter yardlands are not uncommon in these early surveys.

6 *Documents illustrating the Activities of the General and Provincial Chapters of the English Black Monks* (Camden Society, Third Series, LIV, 1937), ed. W.A. Pantin, p. 205.

7 Population increases are calculated by comparing Domesday Book figures with those from the manorial surveys in Vespasian B. XXIV. They are, of course, numbers of tenants. The figures for the bishop's estates are in the *Red Book of Worcester*, ed. Marjorie Hollings (Worcester Historical Society, 1934-50).

8 *Statutes of the Realm*, i (1810), p.307.

7. A 13th century Poem (pp. 108-113)

1 The case is reported by G. Farnham, in *Leicester Village Notes,* iv. 152 seqq. I have unfortunately been unable to check his abstract at the Public Record Office, as owing to the war these Coram Rege Rolls have been evacuated. However, Mr. Farnham's abstracts and transcriptions are usually reliable.

2 Farnham suggests that Philip and Robert were only attorneys: but himself admits that Robert appears later in the case as a villein. Philip does not appear later, not because he was an attorney, but because, as the poem tells us, he fled when the case failed.

3 Cf. Vinogradoff, *Villeinage*, p. 154, n. 2.

4 Cf. *ibid*. pp. 167 *seqq,*. on labour services as a definite factor in villeinage; and p. 170 for the use of the tag 'work with forks and flails'.

5 Knighton, *Chronicon, i.* 62-3, 147.

6 For a similar case see the dispute between seven tenants of the manor of Cottham (Notts) and Roger de Vaux; Stenton, *Danelaw Charters* p. lxxxvii.

7 They were probably Christiana de Bushby, who in actual fact was one of the four who acknowledged their villein ancestry in January, and either Mathilda the Panner or Mathilda Atpertre. Mathilda Apertre was one of the eleven who were the last to give in.

8 Vinogradoff, *op. cit.* p. 101.

9 Thus, according to an abstract of the 1279 inquisition into Guthlaxton and Gartree Hundreds (Nichols, *Hist. of Leicestershire, i,* appendix [incomplete transcription], and Burton's full transcript, from which Nichols copied, Bodleian Library, Rawlinson MSS.B 350) about 70 per cent. of demesnes were under 200 acres in arable area. Of lay manors, extents of whose demesne areas

are in the Inquisitions Post Mortem, 1272-1335, about 50 per cent were under 150 acres in area. Of sixteen demesnes in different villages worked by Leicester abbey at the beginning of the fourteenth century only two had more than 200 hundred acres. See B.M. Cotton MS. Galba E. iii, Liber de Terris Dominical-ibus, and Bodleian Library Laud MS. Misc. 625, *passim*.

10 I have examined all the I. P. Ms. 1272-1335 in which there are manorial extents. There are seventy-two of these full extents. Twenty-nine give definite information on either the absence of, or details of the existing villein services.

11 Connsuetudines Tenencium, in Charyte's Leicester Abbey Rental, Bodleian Library, Laud MS. Misc. 625, fol. 214. Most of this collection was probably compiled not later than the first part of the fourteenth century, but this particular copy was written in the fifteenth century.

12 Cf. Vinogradoff, *op. cit.* p. 156, where these disabilities are linked up with villein status.

13 The social attitude of the seigneurial class is expressed less in terms of the divine rightness of existing class divisions in a poem of the mid-thirteenth century satirizing the litigation of the villeins of Verson against the Abbey of Mont St. Michel. The villein services are set out in detail, and the more concrete danger of 'désériter lor seignor' is obviously in the poet's mind (L. Delisle, *Etudes sur la Condition de la Classe Agricole en Normandie*, Evreux, 1851, pp. 668-73). The poet Wace, describing more sympathetically the *armed* struggle of the Norman peasantry under Richard II, duke of Normandy, quotes the social attitude of the peasants: 'Nus sumes homes cum il sunt' (*ibid.* pp. 123).

14 Written *nimius* in the MS. The author of the poem presumably meant *nimis* (= magis).

15 Unusual contraction for *dominum* used here: d^m.

16 The meaning of this line is obscure. It might be a reference to Maud's poverty, or to her inability to appreciate values of goods (e.g. wool). Also in the manuscript, the first minim of *modo* (abbreviated mo) is attached to the *s* of *piperis*. This looks more like the mistake of an ignorant than of a hurried copyist.

17 The author would find this type of analysis of names in Isidore's *Etymologiae*, as well as the meanings of the two Greek words.

8. Medieval Peasants — Any Lessons? (pp. 114-121)

1 See below n.3.

2 See below Shanin, op. cit.

3 These movements are all dicussed in *Bond Men Made Free* [1973] in which references to works dealing with all the movements will be found. See in particular *Bloch* [1966]. An interesting recent book covering urban as well as rural revolt is *The Popular Revolutions of the Late Middle Ages* by Michel Mollat and Phillipe Wolff.

References

Bloch, Marc 1966, *French Rural History: its Original Characteristics*, London: Routledge.

Hilton, Rodney, 1973, *Bond Men Made Free*, London : Temple Smith.

Mendras, H., 1972 'An Analytical Framework for the Peasants of Western Europe', unpublished paper presented at the Peasant Seminar at the University of London, 1 December.

Mollat, Michel and Wolff, Phillipe, 1973, *The Popular Revolutions of the Late Middle Ages*, London : Allen and Unwin.

Shanin, Teodor, 1973, 'The Nature and Logic of the Peasant Economy 1 : A Generalisation', *Journal of Peasant Studies* 1 : 1 October.

Thompson. E.P., 1972 'Anthropology and the discipline of the historical context', *Midland History*, Spring.

Varagnac, A., 1948, *La Civilisation Traditionelle et Genres de vie*.

9. Peasant Movements Before 1381 (pp. 122–138)

1 A. Steel, *Richard II* (Cambridge, 1941), p. 187, n. 3.

2 Well summarised in E. E. Power's article in the *Cambridge Medieval History*, vol. VII. (1932), entitled 'Peasant Life and Rural Conditions'.

3 The description I give here of the lord–serf relationship as being one of exploitation must not be taken to imply a perjorative judgement of the historical role of the medieval landowning aristocracy, whose contributions in the cultural, economic and political fields, at any rate up to the thirteenth century, were immense.

4 *Cf.* Tacticus, *Germania* c 15 : 'mos est civitatibus ultro ac viritim conferre principibus vel armentorum vel frugum . . . ', also F. M. Stenton, *Anglo-Saxon England* (Oxford, 1943), p. 284.

5 M. M. Postan, 'The Chronology of Labour Services', in *Trans. Roy. His. Soc.* 4th ser., vol. xx (1937); M. E. Dobb, *Studies in the Development of Capitalism* (1946), p. 40 *et seq.*

6 Roxburgh Club, *Pembroke Surveys II*, App. A.

7 Selden Society, vol. 1, *Select Pleas in Manorial Courts*, passim.

8 P. R. O. Exchequer, K. R. Misc. Bks, 15, ff. lv^r, xii^v.

9 What follows is not intended to be an exhaustive list of the incidents of villeinage, but a reference to those restrictive of the movement of personnel and property.

10 Stubbs, *Select Charters*, 9th ed. (Oxford 1913), pp. 219, 221.

11 In *Cambridge Economic History* (1941), 1. 248. See his general discussion of serfdom, 'Comment finit l'esclavage antique ?' in *Annales*, Jan–March and April–June, 1947. The point is also illustrated in Selden Society, vol. 62, *Introduction to the Curia Regis Rolls* (1943), By C. T. Flower, pp. 228 and 234.

12 See P. Vinogradoff, *Villeinage in England* (1892), p. 60. Although one view was that bastards took their mothers' status, bastardy in the fourteenth century meant freedom. See *Calender of Patent Rolls, 1345-8*, pp. 7–8.

13 Glanvill in Stubbs, op. cit. p. 192. Also *Cal. Pat. Rolls, passim*.

14 W. O. Ault, *Court Rolls of the Abbey of Ramsey* (New Haven, 1928), p. 242.

15 See Denholm-Young, *Seigneurial Administration in England* (1937).

16 H. M. Stationary Office, *Curia Regis Rolls 1199-1220*; Selden Society, vols.

53, 56, 59, ed. D. M. Stenton: *Rolls of Justices in Eyre for Lincs (1218-19)*, and *Worcs (1221)*, (1934); do. for *Yorks (1218-19)* (1937); do. for *Gloucs, Warwicks and Staffs (1221-2)* 1940;vol, 30, ed. W. C. Bolland (1914), *Select Bills in Eyre (1292-1333)*; vol. 60 ed. Richardson and Sayles (1941), *Select Cases of Procedure without Writ*; vol. 57, ed. Sayles (1938), *Select Cases in the Court of King's Bench, II.*

17 Record Commission, 1811.

18 Bracton's Notebook, ed. F. W. Maitland (1887).

19 Selden Society, vol. 10, ed. Baildon (1896) *Select Cases in Chancery(1363-1471)*; vol. 35. ed. Leadam and Baldwin (1919), *Cases before the King's Council*; Record Commission, *Calender of Proceedings in Chancery*.

20 Postan, *loc. cit.*

21 The very full surveys of the manors of the Bishop of Worcester dated 1299, in the *Red Book of Worcester* (Worcester Historical Society) illustrate these points very clearly. Between 1182 (the date of the previous extant survey) and 1299 there may have been as much as a doubling of the population on some manors, especially of the smallholding population.

22 Cf. the well known case in *Bracton's Notebook*, 11, 70, discussed by Vinogradoff, op. cit. p. 78.

23 'Pedigrees of Villeins, and Freemen in the Thirteenth Century', in *Liberties and Communities in Medieval England* (Cambridge 1944); op. cit. and *Obligations of Society in the Twelfth and Thirteenth Centuries* (Oxford, 1946). There is of course the older and masterly discussion in Vinogradoff, op. cit.

24 *Notebook*, 111, 1005.

25 For a full discussion of the still obscure subject of ancient demesne, see Vinogradoff, *op. cit.* ch. 111.

26 Stats. 11, 2-3.

27 *Cal. Pat. Rolls, 1272-81*, p. 290. Other cases may be found in F. M. Stenton, *Documents Illustrative of the Social and Economic History of Danelaw* (1920), p. 87, n.; M. Morgan, *English Lands of the Abbey of Bec* (Oxford, 1946), p. 106; *Plac. Abb.* p. 303 (see also index); Bolland; *op. cit.* pp. 25-6; Richardson and Sayles,

op. cit. no. 74, 76 (both 1258); G. C. Homans, *English Villagers of the Thirteenth Century* (Harvard 1941), pp. 276-83.

28 *Op. cit.* p. 205, n. Vinogradoff does not describe or discuss the case, which is in *Plac. Abb.* p. 150

29 Above, pp, 108 *ff.*.

30 *Plac. Abb.* p. 303.

31 Additional, that is, to cases in the printed records listed (p. 78, n. 16), of which the above are but samples.

32 Mr. Homans, *op. cit.*, chooses mainly court-roll evidence, and Professor Levett is obliged, for lack of other types of evidence, to use Court Books to write the history of St. Albans Abbey. Mr Homan's chapter XXII should be read as an example of a conception of social peace in the medieval village, clearly opposed to the ideas expressed in this article.

33 *Studies in Manorial History* (Oxford 1938), p. 203.

34 *e. g.* Wystowe, 1279. Robert the son of Richard at the church is amerced 6d. *quia male messuit in autumpno.* Thirteen others were amerced for the same offence. Ault, *op. cit.* pp. 183-4.

35 Ault. *op. cit.* pp. 233, n., 243, 247. £36 For a petition from bondmen at Harewood, see Denholm-Young, *op. cit.* p. 154; J. S. Nichols, 'Early Four-teenth-Century Petition of the Tenants of Bocking to their Manorial Lord', *Econ. Hist. Rev. 11.*

37 The dicussions of Mr Denholm-Young ('Feudal Society in the Thirteenth Century: the Knights', in *Collected Papers in Medieval Subjects*) and Professor Treharne (*in the Bulletin of the Institute of Historical Research, XXI*) have shown what scarcity value knights had in thirteenth-century administration. Was there the same shortage of freemen for juries?

38 p. 81

39 *op. cit.* p. 281.

40 *Cal. Pat. Rolls, 1292-1301*, p. 461.

41 *Loc. cit.*

42 Lancashire and Cheshire Record Society, 1914, *Ledger Book of Vale Royal Abbey*, pp. 31-2, 37-42. The Darnhall custumal (pp. 117-20) reveals a harshness of exploitation unparalleled even on the old-established Benedictine house of the south.

43 *Cal. Pat. Rolls, 1338-40*, p. 65.

44 *Ibid. 1350-4*, p. 275.

45 *Cal. Pat. Rolls, 1338-40*, p. 67.

46 *Ibid. 1348-50*, p. 313.

47 *Ibid. 1348-50*, p. 453.

48 Recent works include R. A. L. Smith, *Canterbury Cathedral Priory* (Cambridge 1943); M. Morgan, *op. cit.*; R. H. Hilton, *Economic Development of some Leicestershire Estates* (Oxford, 1947). Older works illustrating the same theme include G. Poulett Scrope, *Manor and Barony of Castle Combe* (1852); F. G. Davenport, 'Decay of Villeinage in East Anglia', in *Trans. Roy. Hist. Soc.*., n. s. XIV (1900); R. H. Tawney, *The Agrarian Problem in the Sixteenth Century* (1912).

49 Above, n. 22. The free man who in this case took land in villeinage had to perform all villein obligations or lose the land.

50 Ault. *op. cit.* p. 226.

51 pp. 129-30.

52 *Op. cit.* Examples will be found on pp. 189, 198-9, 216, 221, 240, 243 (this is an example of a licensed exchange), 254, 259, 278.

53 Levett, *op. cit.* p. 149, n. 5.

54 Camden Society, *The Domesday of St. Paul's* (1858), p. 157. The farmer here must be understood as a Chapter official rather than as a mere lessee.

55 Nichols, *loc. cit.* p. 300, n.

56 Alienation by charter, or without charter when unlicensed, involved perpetual forfeiture at Stoneleigh, Warwickshire. Vinogradoff, *op. cit.* p. 198, n. 1, quoting the Stoneleigh Register.

57 *Cal. Pat. Rolls. 1338-40*, p. 326; 1364-7, p. 309; 1348-50, p. 234; 1358-61, p. 179.

58 Vinogradoff, *op. cit.* p. 172, n. 1, quoting a St. Albans Formulary.

59 St. Albans 1381 charters, of which that of Rickmansworth is a good example, will be found in *Gesta Abbatum III*, pp. 324-32.

60 *Cf.* Levett, *The Black Death on the Estates of the See of Winchester* (1916), p. 85.

61 *Cal. Pat. Rolls, 1348-50,* pp. 520, 521; 1350-54, pp. 447, 460; 1354-8, pp. 64, 335, 452; 1358-61, pp. 160, 284, 324; 1355-61, p. 581; 1361-4, pp. 283-4; 1364-7, pp. 361, 429, 1370-74, p. 98; 1374-7, p. 142.

62 'A Note on the Statute of Labourers', in *Econ. Hist. Rev.* IV.

63 Unless he took the manor on lease together with the tenants' services. Complete manorial leases are rare at this period, piecemeal leasing being the rule, and in any case only rarely was the farmer given control over the tenants.

64 *Cal. Pat. Rolls, 1354-8,* pp. 16-17, and *1358-61,* p. 35. see also B. Putnam, *Enforcement of the Statute of Labourers* (New York, 1908), p. 93. The Carthusian Priory of Hinton had similar problems and obtained a similar remedy. Their problem was additionally complicated by the fact that many of their tenants were clothworkers, whose services they lost because outsiders accused the Priory of paying them improperly high wages. *Cal. Pat. Rolls. 1354-8, p. 282.*

65 Putnam, *op. cit.* p. 218.

66 Rolls Series, *Chronica Monasterii de Melsa III,* pp. 131-2: *Ipse abbas. . . quosdam servos suos ad officium carucarum conductos a servitio ipsorum Johannis et Willhelmi vi cepisset et detinuisset, ad damnum uniuscujusque eorum centum solidorum, in contemptum regis et hominum suorum, ac contra formam statuti et ordinationis de operariis, artificibus et servitoribus, editorum, in comitatu Eboracensi observandorum.*

67 Putnam, *op. cit.* pp. 93-4; cf. *Cal. Pat. Rolls, 1350-54,* p. 158; 1358-61, p. 151. E. E. H.—G

68 E. Powell, *Rising in East Anglia* (Cambridge, 1896), Appendix 11, pp. 143-5.

69 *Worcestershire Inquisitions Post Mortem,* 1, p. 48 (Worcester Hist. Soc.).

70 For the fourteenth-century sermon background to these opinions, see G. W. Owst, *Preaching in Medieval England* (Cambridge 1926) and *Literature and Pulpit in Medieval England.* (Cambridge, 1933).

10. Inequality among Medieval Peasants (pp. 139-151)

1 *Selected Works,* I. I found this work immensely stimulating when I did my research into Leicestershire agrarian history, although under its influence I exaggerated the amount of wage labour in the post-Black Death period [*Hilton 1947*].

2 Domesday statistics in various works, e.g. Maitland [*1897*] and Finn [*1963*].

3 The ambiguity may even have misled Marc Bloch whose writings on early serfdom are still the best guide to the subject [*1963*]. He was attacked for confusing *vileinss* with *serfs* by Verriest [*1946*].

4 It is clearly expressed in the description of the duties of tenants on Anglo-Saxon estates [*Douglas, 1953*]. For plough and spade cultivation see Duby [*1966: Ch.1*].

5 Kula [*1976: 49: 1972*]. Apart from Duby [*1966*] Boutruche [*1959*], see much earlier works as Halphen [*1921*] and Perrin [*1935*].

6 See below, p. 150 for *communautés taisibles, etc.*

7 This phrase describes the lord's right of private jurisdiction over the inhabitants of the lordship. It was additional to the power which he held in his capacity as landowner over his tenants.

8 Génicot [*1962-3*]. He also gives comparative figures from other regions; Titow [*1969 : 79*].

9 See below.

10 Herlihy [*1965*]. The evidence for the fall of rents is summarised by Neveux [*1979*]. See also Verhulst [*1963*] and Bois [*1976 : Ch.8.*].

11 Kosminsky [*1956 : 226*]; Genet [*1972*]. These figures are only illustrative of the general situation in the Midlands. They are not derived from the same manors at the two dates.

12 A central theme of Duby [*1973*].

13 Hilton [*1975 : 41*]. Faith also comments on 'The rise of a peasant aristocracy which came to nothing', although in some Berkshire villages she also found that the middle peasantry tended to disappear [*1962*].

14 Harvey [*1969*]. Miss Harvey wishes to minimise the number of peasant lessees, but her own figures show their importance. Du Boulay [*1965*].

References

Bloch, Marc, 1947, 'Comment et pourquoi finit l'esclavage antique?', *Annales, ESC.*

Bloch, Marc, 1963, *Mélanges Historique*, I, Pt. IV.

Bloch, Marc, 1966, 'The Rise of Dependent Cultivation and Seigneurial Institutions', *Cambridge Economic History of Europe*, I.

Boutruche, R., 1935, 'Les courants de peuplement dans l'Entre Deux Mers', *Annales d'Histoire Economique et Sociale.*

Boutruche, R., 1959, *Seigneurie et Féodalité*, I.

Bois, G., 1976, *La Crise du Féodalisme.*

Charles-Edwards, T., 1972, 'Kingship, Status and the Origins of the Hide', *Past and Present*, No. 56.

Coleman, E., 1972, 'Note on Medieval Peasant Demography', *Historical Methods Newsletter.*

Douglas D.C., ed., 1953, 'Rectitudes Singularum Personerum', *English Historical Documents*, II.

Du Boulay, F.R.H., 1965, 'Who were farming the English demesnes in the later middle ages?' *Economic History Review.*

Duby, G., 1966, *The Rural Economy and Country Life in the Medieval West*, Bk. I.

Duby, G., 1973, *Guerriers et paysans.*

Faith, R., 1962, 'The Peasant Land Market in Berkshire', unpublished Ph.D. thesis, Leicester University.

Finn, R. Weldon, 1963, *Introduction to the Domesday Book.*

Fossier, R., 1968, *La Terre et les Hommes et Picardie*, I.

Fournier, G., 1962, *Le Peuplement Rurale en Basse Auvergne durant la Haut Moyen-Age.*

Fourquin, G., 1964, *Les Campagnes de la région parisienne à la fin du Moyen-Age.*

Ganshof, F.L., 1949, 'Manorial organisation in the Low Countries in the 7th, 8th and 9th centuries', *Transactions of the Royal Historical Society.*

Genet, J.P., 1972, 'Economie et Société rurale en Angleterre au XVe siècle, *Annales ESC.*

Génicot, L., 1962-3, 'L'étendue des exploitations agricoles dans le Comté de Namur à la Fin du XIIIe siècle', *Etudes Rurales.*

Génicot, L., 1965, 'On the Evidence of Growth Population in the West' in S.L. Thrupp, ed.,*Change in Medieval Society..*

Halphen, L., 1921, *Etudes critiques sur l'historie de Charlemagne* ('L'agriculture et la propriété rurale').

Harvey, B., 1969, 'The Leasing of the Abbot of Westminster's demesne in the later middle ages', *Economic History Review.*

Harvey, P.D.A., 1965, *A Medieval Oxfordshire Village, Cuxham.*

Herlihy, D., 1965, 'Population, Plague and Social Change in Rural Pistoia 1201-1430', *Economic History Review.*

Hilton, Rodney., 1947, *Economic Development of Some Leicestershire Estates.*

Hilton, Rodney, 1975, *The English Peasantry in the Later Middle Ages.*

Jones, A.H.M.,1958, 'The Roman Colonate', *Past and Present*, No.13.

King, E., 1973, *Peterborough Abbey.*

Kosminsky, E.A., 1956, *Studies in the Agrarian History of England in the 13th Century.*

Kula. W., 1972, 'La famille paysanne en Pologne au XVIIIe siècle', *Annales ESC.*

Kula, W., 1976, *An Economic Theory of the Feudal System.*

Le Roy, Ladurie, E., 1966, *Les Paysans du Languedoc.*

Lorcin, Th-M., 1974, *Les Campagnes de la Région Lyonnaise xive-xve siècles.*

Maitland,F.W., 1897, *Domesday Book and Beyond.*

Neveux, H., 1975, in G. Duby and A. Wallon, *Histoire de la France Rurale*, II.

Perrin, C.E., 1935, *Recherches sur la seigneurie rurale en Lorraine.*

Perrin, C.E., 1940, *Les Classes Paysannes et le Régime seigneurial en France.*

Perrin, C.E., 1945, 'Le Manse',*Annales d'Histoire Sociale.*

Phelps-Brown, E.H., and S.V. Hopkins, 1965, 'Seven Centuries of the Price of Consumables compared with Builders 'wage-rates', *Economica.*

Postan, M.M., and J.Z. Titow, 1959, 'Heriots and Prices on Winchester Manors', *Economic HistoryReview.*

Razi, Z., 1980, 'Birth, Marriage and Death in a Medieval Parish' Unpublished Ph.D. thesis Birmingham University.

Sabean, D., 1972, 'Tenure et parenté en Alemagne à la fin du Moyen-Age', *Annales ESC.*

Sahlins, Marshall, 1974, *Stone Age Economics.*

Sawyer, P.H., 1965, 'The Wealth of England in the 11th Century', *Transactions of the Royal Historical Society.*

Thirsk, J., ed., 1967, *The Agrarian History of England.*

Thrupp, S.L., 1965, 'The Problem of Replacement Rates in Late Medieval English Populations', *Economic History Review.*

Titow, J.Z., 1969, *English Rural Society 1200-1350.*

Toubert, P., 1973, *Les Structures du Latium médiéval*, I.

Verhulst, A., 1963, 'L'économie rurale de la Flandre et la dépression économique du bas moyenage', *Etudes Rurales.*

Verhulst, A., 1966, 'Genèse du régime domanial en France', *Agricoltura e mondo rurale in occidente nell'alto medio ero*, Settimane di Studio, Spoleto, XIII.

Verlinden, Charles. 1955, *L'esclavage dans l'Europe mediévale.*

Verriest, L., 1946, *Institutions Mediévales.*

Williamson, J., 1984, 'Peasant Holdings in Medieval Norfolk', Unpublished Ph.D.thesis, Reading University.

11. Popular Movements in England at the End of the
Fourteenth Century (pp. 152-164)

1 See E.B. Fryde's revised edition (1969) of C.Oman, *The Great Revolt of 1381*; R.B. Dobson's collection of documents, *The Peasants Revolt of 1381*, London 1970; and the present writer's *Bondmen Made Free*, London 1973.

2 The classic definition of bastard feudalism is by K.B. MacFarlane, *Bulletin of the Institute of Historical Research*, 1945. See also his *The Nobility of Later Medieval England*, Oxford 1973.

3 R.H. Hilton, A Crisis of Feudalism, *Past and Present*, 1978.

4 Marsilius of Padua's definition (in *Defensor Pacis* XII, 4) is the only one referred to in W. Ullman's, *Principles of Government and Politics in the Middle Ages*, London 1961, a work which is concerned precisely with the place of the people in theories of government. Although he briefly considers popular elements in rural and urban local government, he says of 'the ascending conception of government and law according to which law-creating power may be ascribed to the community of *populus*' that 'the composition of the latter (the populus), who does, and who does not belong to it, is of no concern in this context' (ibid., p. 20.).

5 See G. Duby, *Les trois ordres ou l'imaginaire du féodalisme*, Paris 1978

6 Some chroniclers called the rebels of 1381, 'the commons', but as W. Stubbs pointed out many years ago concerning the House of Commons, 'The commons are the *communitates* or *universitates* ...' and 'the estates of the commons is the *communitas comunitatum...*' (*Constitutional History of England*, II. Fourth Edition, Oxford 1896, pp. 174-75.)

7 See the discussion by P. Anderson in *Lineages of the Absolute State*, Oxford 1974.

8 See S.L. Thrupp, *The Merchant Class of Medieval London*, Ann Arbor 1962; the political analysis by R. Bird in *The Turbulent London of Richard II*, London 1949 has not been superseded.

9 Medieval Norwich lacks a good up-to-date history. Meanwhile, the introductions by W. Hudson and J.C. Tingay to *The Records of the City of Norwich* 2 vols., Norwich 1906-1910, must suffice.

10 The class analysis of London's medieval economy by G. Unwin, *The Guilds and Companies of London*, London 1908 is, in spite of recent corrections, of fundamental importance.

11 The *Calendars of the Plea and Memoranda Rolls of the City of London*, 6 vols. ed. A.H. Thomas and others, London 1926 seq., are full of cases illustrating illegal organisation, especially in the period between the plague of 1349 and the revolt of 1381. For illegal journeymens' organisations in Coventry, see M.D. Harris, *Life in an Old English Town*, London 1898, p. 97. The author of this neglected book was the editor of the major source for late medieval Coventry, *The Coventry Leet Book*, 4 vols., Oxford 1907-1913.

12 Rent movements are documented in a number of studies of individual estates, too many to enumerate here. The main general source for prices and wages is still J.E.T. Rogers, *History of agriculture and prices*, vols. I-IV. London 1866-1892. But see also W. Beveridge et al., *Prices and Wages in England from the twelfth to the nineteenth Century*, I, 1939. An important attempt to calculate real wages is by E.H. Phelps-Brown and S. Hopkins, 'Seven Centuries of the prices

of consumables, compared with builders wage rates', in *Essays in Economic History*, II, London 1972, ed. E. Carus-Wilson. But see also M.M.Postan, 'Some agrarian evidence of declining population in the late middle ages', *Economic History Review*, 1950. Cloth exports are calculated in *England's Export Trade 1275-1547*, eds.E. Carus-Wilson and O. Coleman, Oxford 1963.

13 R.H. Hilton, *The Decline of Serfdom in Medieval England*, London, 1969.

14 J.A. Tuck, 'The Cambridge Parliament of 1388', *English Historical Review*, 1969.

15 B. Wilkinson, 'The Peasants' Revolt of 1381', *Speculum*, 1940.

16 A ranking order of provincial towns is given in W.G. Hoskins, *Local History in England*, London 1959, Appendix.

17 M.D. Lobel, *The Commune of Bury St.Edmunds*, Oxford 1935; for St. Albans, see R.H. Hilton, *Bond Men Free*, pp. 198-203.

18 *Medieval York*, by E. Miller, in *Victoria County History of Yorkshire: the City of York*, ed. P.M. Tillot (1961); C.T. Flower, 'The Beverley Town Riots, 1381-2', *Transactions of the Royal Historical Society*, 1905. The fines were: York 1000 marks (= £666. 13s. 4d.); Beverley, 1100 marks; Bury 2000 marks.

19 *Les marginaux parisiens au XIVe et XVe siècles*, Paris 1976.

20 G. Williams, *Medieval London: from commune to capital*, London 1963, p. 317.

21 Unpublished paper by A.F. Butcher of the University of Kent.

22 R. Bird, *op.cit.*

23 *Calendar of Letter Books of the City of London, Letter Book G*, ed. R.R. Sharp, London 1905, pp. 179-81.

24 Calendar of the Plea and Memoranda Rolls of the City of London *(1364-81)*, London 1929, introduction by A.H. Thomas, p. lxxii.

25 *Ibid.* (1364-81), pp. 264 and 291-4; A.E. Bland, P.A. Brown and R.H. Tawney, *English Economic History: Select Documents*, London 1914, p.138.

26 *Calendar of Plea and Memoranda Rolls (1364-81), passim*; and C.M. Barron, 'The Quarrel of Richard II with London', in The reign of Richard II, 1971, ed.F.R.H. Du Boulay and C.M. Barron.

27 *Rotuli Parliamentorum*, III, London 1783, pp. 112-13; *Plea and Memoranda Rolls (1364-81)*, pp. 288-91; G. Unwin, *op.cit.*, Appendix A, II.

28 'Lollardy and Sedition', *Past and Present*, 1960.

12. Some Problems of Urban Real Property (pp. 165-174)

1 A. E. Sayous in his introduction to Sombart's *L'Apogée du Capitalisme* (1932) expresses the criticisms of a follower of Pirenne. The most recent support for Pirenne's general line will be found in H. van Werweke's edition of Pirenne's *Histoire Economique et Sociale du Moyen Age* (1963). A. Sapori's *Studi di Storia economica medioevale* (1946) contains the best of his generalizing articles, but on Sombart see especially his *Le Marchand Italien au Moyen Age* (1952).

2 See J. Lestocquoy *Les Villes de Flandre et d'Italie sous le Gouvernement des Patriciens* (1952) for a general reconsideration of the Pirenne position. Supporting evidence from studies of individual towns is too numerous to quote, but it

should be mentioned that E. Fiumi has strongly reaffirmed the purely mercantile origin of the Florentine patriciate, in 'Fioritura e decadenza dell' economia fiorentina: Nobilita feudale e borghesia mercantile', *Archivio Storico Italiano*, 1957.

3 A.J. Robertson, *Anglo-Saxon Charters*, (1939), No. XIX

4 J.W.F. Hill, *Medieval Lincoln* (1948), p. 35.

5 M. Bateson, 'The Laws of Breteuil', *English Historical Review*, Vols. XV and XVI.

6 William Dugdale, *Antiquities of Warwickshire* (1656), p. 514

7 *Original Charters relating to the City of Worcester* (Worcester Historical Society), ed. by J. Harvey Bloom (1909), Nos. 1073, 1074, 1100.

8 The bay was normally about twelve to fifteen feet long.

9 Domesday information for Worcester and Warwick in *Victoria County History, Worcestershire*, I, p. 294, and *ditto, Warwickshire*, I, p. 299. Information for Gloucester, 1096-1101, printed in *Rental of Houses in Gloucester, 1455*, ed. W.H. Stevenson, (1890), p. XIX.

10 D. Harris, *Life in an Old English Town* (1898), p. 32.

11 H. Stevenson, *op. cit.* passim.

12 M. de W. Hemmeon, *Burgage Tenure in Medieval England* (1914) ; *Red Book of Worcester* (Worcester Historical Society), IV, ed. M. Hollings (1950), p. 481ff.

13 In manuscript in the Leigh Collection at the Record Office, Shakespeare's Birthplace, Stratford-on-Avon. This is a copy of part of the great survey of which most has been printed as the *Rotuli Hundredorum*.

14 Four other burgages were held by the Burtons of the Prior for 1s., 2s., 1s. 4d. and 6d.

15 In another manuscript version of the 1280 survey, Public Record Office, E. 164, Vol. 15.

16 The records of the Stratford-on-Avon Holy Cross Gild are in the Shakespeare's Birthplace Record Office, and are calendared by F. C. Wellstood (in MS). See T. H. Lloyd, *Some Aspects of the Building Industry in Medieval Stratford-on-Avon* (Dugdale Society, 1961), and *The Medieval Gilds of Stratford-on-Avon and the Timber-framed Building Industry* (Birmingham University M.A. thesis, 1961.)

17 Public Record Office, E. 164, Vol. 22. I am grateful to Mrs Dorothy Styles for lending me her transcript of this document.

18 Public Record Office, DL43/9/21.

19 The Coventry Cathedral Priory cellarer's and pittancer's and rentals are in the priory's register, Public Record Office, E. 164, Vol. 21.

20 *Records of the Gild of the Holy Trinity, St. Mary, St. John the Baptist, and St. Catherine of Coventry*, ed. G. Templeman, (Dugdale Society) 1944.

21 A rare example of the terms of tenure of such a sub-tenant is as follows. The Hospitallers held a tenement in fee of the pittancer in Little Park Street and this was sub-let by the Hospital to John Preston for a term of years.

22 'English Provincial Towns in the Early Sixteenth Century', *Transactions of the Royal Historical Society*, 5th series, Vol. 6.

23 This fact may be attributed partly to the fact that Warwickshire was not a county dominated by big church land-owners, as were Worcestershire and Gloucestershire, and also to the late development of Coventry as a town.

24 *Minister' Accounts of the Warwickshire Estates of Duke of Clarence*, ed. R.H. Hilton (Dugdale Society. 1952), p. XXIX, see above pp. 60, 62.

13. Towns in English Feudal Society (pp. 175-186)

1 There is a considerable amount of information of a highly selective character about small towns in the volumes of the *Victoria History of the Counties of England* but usually no historical analysis or significant generalization. The same positive and negative remarks could be made about small town histories by local antiquarians, of which there are many.

2 Its manorial and borough records are deposited by the Stafford family in the Stafford County Record Office.

3 For Warwick, see above p. 49, 56.

References

Philip Abrams, 'Towns and Economic Growth: Theories and Problems', in P. Abrams and E.A. Wrigley, eds., *Towns in Societies* (London and New York: Cambridge University Press, 1978), 9-33.

M. Bateson, ed., *Records of the Borough of Leicester*, I and II (London 1899).

M.W. Beresford, *New Towns of the Middle Ages* (London: Lutterworth, 1967).

M.W. Beresford , H.P.R. Finberg, *Medieval English Boroughs: A Handlist* (London: David , Charles, 1973).

F.B. Bickley, ed., *Little Red Book of Bristol* (Bristol: W.C. Hemmons, 1900).

M. Biddle, ed., *Winchester in the Early Middle Ages* (Oxford: Oxford University Press, 1976).

H.M. Cam, 'Northhampton Borough', in *Victoria History of the County of Northampton* (London 1930), III, 1-67.

P. Coss, 'Coventry before Incorporation', *Midland History*, II, 3, Spring 1974, 137-51.

H.A. Cronne, *The Borough of Warwick in the Middle Ages*, Dugdale Society (Oxford: C. Batey, 1951).

L.E.O. Fulbrook-Legatt, *Anglo-Saxon and Medieval Gloucester* (Gloucester: J. Jennings, 1952).

Mary Dormer Harris, *Life in an Old English Town* (London 1898).

Mary Dormer Harris, 'Social and Economic History', in *Victoria History of the County of Warwick* (London: Constable, 1908), II, 137-82.

J.F.W. Hill, *Medieval Lincoln* (Cambridge: Cambridge Univ. Press, 1948).

Rodney Hilton, *English Peasantry in the Later Middle Ages* (Oxford: Oxford Univ. Press, 1975).

Rodney Hilton, 'A Crisis of Feudalism', *Past and Present*, No. 80, August 1978, 3-19.

W. Hudson , J.C. Tingey, eds., *The Records of the City of Norwich* I and II (Norwich, 1906-10).

J. Leland, *Intinerary*, Vol. V, ed., by L. Toulmin Smith (London, 1964).

M.D. Lobel, *The Commune of Bury St, Edmunds* (Oxford 1935).

M.D. Lobel, ed., *Historic Towns: Maps and Plans of Towns and Cities in the British Isles from Earliest Times to 1800*, I and II (London and Oxford: Lovell Johns, 1969, 1975).

A. Luchaire, *Les communes Françaises a l'époque des Capétiens* (Paris 1911).

F.W. Maitland, *Domesday Book and Beyond* (Cambridge 1897).

F.W. Maitland, *Township and Borough* (Cambridge 1898).

Lewis Mumford, *City in History* (New York: Harcourt, Brace and World, 1961).

C. Petit-Dutaillis, *Les communes françaises, caractères et evolution,* (Paris: Lib. A. Michel, 1947).

H. Pirenne, *Medieval Cities* (Princeton, 1925).

Colin Platt, *The English Medieval Town* (London: Secker, Warburg, 1976).

M.M. Postan, *Medieval Economy and Society* (London: Weidenfeld, Nicholson, 1972).

N.J.G. Pounds, *An Historical Geography of Europe, 450 B.C.-A.D. 1330*, (Cambridge: Cambridge Univ.Press, 1973).

Susan Reynolds, *Introduction to the Study of Medieval English Towns* (Oxford: Oxford Univ.Press 1977).

S. Seyer, *Memoirs Historical and Topographical, of Bristol* (Bristol, 1823).

Paul Sweezey, 'A Critique', in R. Hilton, ed., *The Transition fron Feudalism to Capitalism* (London: New Left Books, 1976), 33-56.

James Tait, *The Medieval English Borough* (Manchester, 1936).

P.M. Tillott, ed., *A History of Yorkshire: The City of York* London: Oxford Univ. Press, 1961).

W. Urry, *Canterbury under the Angevin Kings* (London: Athlone, 1967).

Max Weber, *The City* (New York: Free Press, 1958).

14 Small Towns and Urbanisation—Evesham (pp. 187-193)

1 Some seigneurial boroughs grew substantially, as for instance the cloth manufacturing town of Bury St Edmunds. One or two (like Warwick) had an ambiguous position as county towns, while regarded as fiefs of great lords. Leicester was the earl of Leicester's (later the earl/duke of Lancaster) town just as Warwick was completely dominated by the earls of Warwick.

2 *The English Peasantry in the Later Middle Ages* (Oxford, 1975), 77-84.

3 *Chronicon Abbatiae de Evesham*, ed. W.D. Macray (Rolls series, 1863), 75.

4 R.H.C. Davis, *The Early History of Coventry* (Dugdale Society Occasional Papers, no. 24, 1976), 17.

5 B.L. Harleian MS. 3763, fos. 61v and 71. The illegality lay in alienation without the consent of the monastic chapter.

6 *Ibid.*

7 B.L., Cotton Vespasian BXXIV.

8 *Ibid.*, f. 46.

9 *Victoria County History of Worcestershire* (hereafter *V.C.H.*), II, 372.

10 e.g. P. R. O., J1/1028 (3 Edward I), m .21.

11 *V.C.H.* I, 299, 304, 305, 306.

12 B.L. Vesp. BXXIV, f. 34. The rentals in the constitution of 1206 indicate that the prior of the abbey ran a home-farm in Bengeworth.

13 M. Bateson,'The Laws of Breteuil', *English Historical Review* XV (1900), 73-8, 302-18, 496-523, 754-7 ; XVI(1901), 92-110, 332-45.

14 *Chronicon Abbatiae...*, 208-17.

15 *Lay Subsidy ... circa 1280*, ed. J.W.W. Bund and J. Amphlett; *Lay Subsidy ... 1332-3*, ed. J. Amphlett (Worcester Historical Society, 1893 and 1899).

16 B.L., Vesp. BXXIV, f.41v ; and Titus CIX, f. 1v.

17 See note 10 above.

18 Stratford-on-Avon, Shakespeare's Birthplace Trust, Leigh MSS.

19 P. R. O., SC11/248.

20 See note 10 above.

21 R. A. Pelham, 'Earliest aulnage accounts for Worcstershire', *Transactions of Worcestershire Archaeological Society* XXIX (1952), 50-2.

22 16th century evidence suggests that there was a three weekly court and two courts leet a year; G. May, *The History of Evesham* (Evesham 1834), 167-70.

23 P. R. O., E179/200/130.

24 Hilton, *English Peasantry...*, 93.

25 *V.C.H.*, II, 373.

26 B.L., Cotton Titus CIX, fos. 10-11 ; *Chronicon Abbatiae ..., 304*.

15. Lords, Burgessesand Hucksters (pp. 194-204)

[A lecture given to the Denys Hay (Antiquary Whiskey) seminar in the University of Edinburgh, 1982.]

1 The most useful edition is *Piers Plowman by William Langland: An edition of the C-Text* ed. Derek Pearsall (York Medieval Texts, 2nd ser., London 1978). Of numerous commentaries on Langland, see D. Aers, *Chaucer, Langland and the Creative Imagination* (London 1980).

2 For François Villons's life in Paris, see B. Geremek, *Les marginaux parisiens aux XIVe et XVe siècles,* trans. D. Beauvois (Paris, 1976).

3 Haukyn is nearest to this image in the B-Text, as Pearsall points out: *Piers Plowman by William Langland*, ed. Pearsall, p.255.

4 *Piers the Plowman*, trans. J.F. Goodridge (Harmondsworth, 1959), p.106.

5 This is one of Susan Reynolds's criteria to distinguish town from country: S. Reynolds, *An Introduction to the History of Medieval English Towns* (Oxford, 1977).

6 These population figures are based on guesswork applied to numbers of poll tax payers in 1377. The problem is, what should be the multiplier to account for the exempt and the tax evaders? 1.5 or 2? The latter now seems most generally accepted. Useful data for quick reference are in W.G. Hoskins, *Local History in England* (London, 1959), p. 176, and M.W. Beresford and H.P.R. Finberg,

English Medieval Boroughs: A Hand-List (Newton Abbot, 1973).

7 An updated map of these boroughs and markets has appeared in the new edition of R.H. Hilton, *A Medieval Society: The West Midlands at the End of the Thirteenth Century* (Past and Present Pubns., Cambridge, 1983). See also R.H. Britnell, 'The Proliferation of Markets in England, 1200-1349', *Econ. Hist. Rev.*, 2nd ser., xxxiv (1981), pp. 209-21.

8 See the evidence presented in N.J. Mayhew (ed), *Edwardian Monetary Affairs 1279-1344* (Brit. Archaeol. Repts., no.36, Oxford 1977).

9 For example, C.M.Fraser, 'The Pattern of Trade in the North-East of England, 1265-1350', *Northern Hist.*, iv (1969), pp. 44-66.

10 The leading baronial founders were Beauchamp, Clare and Berkeley.

11 Summarized by E. Lipson, *The Economic History of England*, i (London, 1937 edn.), pp. 232-5.

12 *The Maire of Bristowe is Kalendar*, by Robert Ricart, Town Clerk of Bristol, ed. Lucy Toulmin Smith (Camden Soc., new, ser., v, London, 1872), pp. 69, ff.; *English Gilds*, ed. Toulmin Smith and Lucy Toulmin Smith (Early Eng.Text Soc., orig. ser., xl, London, 1870; repr. 1963); *The Records of the Guild of the Holy Trinity, St. Mary, St. John the Baptist and St. Katherine of Coventry*, ii, ed. G. Templeman (Dugdale Soc., xix, Oxford, 1944), pp. 6-7.

13 *Leet Jurisdiction in the City of Norwich during the 13th and 14th Centuries*, ed. W. Hudson (Selden Soc., vi, London 1892).

14 T.H. Lloyd, *Some aspects of the Building Industry in Medieval Stratford-upon-Avon* (Dugdale Soc., Occasional Paper, no. 14, Oxford, 1961); E.K. Berry, 'The Borough of Droitwich and its Salt Industry, 1215-1700', *Univ.of Birmingham Hist. Jl.*, vi (1957-8), pp. 39-61; *The Cartulary of Cirencester Abbey, Gloucestershire*, ed. C. D. Ross and M. Devine, 3 vols.(London 1964-77), i; R.H. Hilton, *The English Peasantry in the Later Middle Ages* (Oxford 1975), pp. 90-1. Above chapter 14.

15 See the work of the Toronto School, evaluated by Z. Razi, 'The Toronto School's Reconstitution of Medieval Peasant Society: A Critical View', *Past and Present*, no. 85 (Nov. 1979), pp. 141-57; and Z. Razi, *Life Marriage and Death in a Medieval Parish: Economy, Society and Demography in Halesowen, 1270-14* (Past and Present Pubns., Cambridge, 1980).

16 I.H. Jeayes, *Descriptive Catalogue of the Charters and Muniments of the Lyttleton Family* (London 1893), pp. 9-10; the records of the borough court are in the Birmingham Reference Library, Hagley Hall MSS., no.346512 onwards. Specific references to individual courts will not be given as a fuller work on Halesowen, Thornbury and other small towns in the west midlands is in progress.

17 G.C. Homans, *English Villagers of the Thirteenth Century* (Cambridge, Mass., 1941), pp. 276-83.

18 H.P.R. Finberg *(ed)*, Gloucestershire Studies (Leicester, 1957), p. 66; *Calendar of Charter Rolls, 1327-41*, pp. 424-6; the court rolls of the borough of Thornbury are in the Staffordshire County Record Office, D.641/1/4E/2 onwards. The evidences for Thornbury, which Halesowen does not have, include inquisitions *post mortem* into the possessions of the lords and a contrariants' survey of 1322: Public Record Office, London, E.142/24.

19 *Piers Plowman by William Langland*, ed. Pearsall, p. 119. The speaker is her husband, Covetyse.

16 Women Traders in Medieval England (pp. 205-215)

1 Among other works, see Georges Duby, *La Femme, le Chevalier et le Prêtre*, (Paris; Hachette 1981).

2 Eileen Power, *Medieval Woman*, ed. M.M. Postan (Cambridge, Cambridge University Press, 1975); M.K. Dale, *Women in the Textile Industries and Trade of 15th century England*, (London University M.A. thesis, 1928); id. 'The London Silk Women of the 15th century'. *Economic History Review*, (iv 1933) 324-35; R.H. Hilton, *The English Peasantry in the Later Middle Ages*, (Oxford: Oxford University Press, 1975), chap.VI, Women in the Village'. Sylvia Thrupp, *The Merchant Class of Medieval London*, (Ann Arbor, University of Michigan Press 1948,) chap. IV, 3.

3 However, see R.H. Hilton, op. cit., p. 105 for women ale-tasters in the manor of Halesowen. There may have been a female reeve in 1407 (Birmingham Reference Library MSS. 346930). I owe this reference to Dr. Z. Razi. At Heacham (Norfolk) at the end of the 13th century, women could be elected 'by the whole soke' as rent collectors and as shepherdesses. In 1348, twelve reeves were chosen, of whom two were women. See Jacques Beauroy, 'Offices manoriaux et stratification sociale à Heacham (Norfolk), 1285-1324.' in *Les Communautés Villageoises en Europe Occidentale*, Centre Culturel de l'Abbaye de Flaran, Quatrièmes Journées d'Histoire, 1982 (Auch, 1984).

4 Z. Razi, *Birth, Marriage and Death in a Medieval Parish*, (Cambridge, Past and Present Publications 1980), p. 25. Note that these figures refer to the rural manor of Halesowen, not to the borough of the same name, to which further reference will be made.

5 See R.H. Hilton, *op. cit.*, pp. 28-30.

6 See for example, *Yorkshire Sessions of the Peace*, 1361-4, ed. B.H. Putnam (Yorkshire Archealogical Society Record Series, C, 1939), p. 52 and passim.

7 *The Little Red Book of Bristol*, ed. F.B. Bickley, (Bristol: Bristol Corporation 1900), II p. 127.

8 *York Memorandum Book, I and II*, ed. M. Sellars, (Surtees Society, 1912 and 1915), passim.

9 The fullest printed records of urban courts leet are in *Leet Jurisdiction in the City of Norwich during the 13th and 15th centuries*, ed. W. Hudson, (Seldon Society, 1982). These will be frequently cited below. Less full records are to be found in such town records as *The Book of the Borough of Nottingham, I. 1155-1399*, ed. W.H. Stevenson, Nottingham; Nottingham Corporation 1882). Volumes II and III cover the 15th and 16th centuries.

10 Complete figures are not yet known. I quote the estimate by Alan Everitt in 'County, Country and Town' in *Transactions of the Royal Historical Society*, (1979, 79-108).See also, R.H. Britnell, 'The Proliferation of Markets in Medieval England' *Economic History Review*, 2nd series XXXIV, 2, 1981, 209-221.

11 Alan Everitt has listed mid-16th century markets in *The Agrarian History of England, IV*, ed Joan Thirsk, (Cambridge: Cambridge University Press 1966), chap. VIII. I owe the early figures of Lincolnshire markets to Graham Platts. The West Midland lists will be found in a revised edition of R.H. Hilton, *A Medieval Society*, (Cambridge: Cambridge University Press 1983.)

12 See Thrupp, op. cit., p. 3. for London and above, Chapter 15 (for Halesowen).

13 Enshrined in the London inspired (and soon abandoned) Statute of 1363.

14 *Piers Plowman: the C. Text*, ed. Derek Pearsall, (London: Edward Arnold, 1978) pp. 118-119.

15 *Some Sessions of the Peace in Lincolnshire, 1381-1396*, ed. E. Kimball (Lincolnshire Record Society, 1955, 1962.) II, p.112. All future references to Lincolnshire peace sessions come from this edition.

16 'The Grocers of London' in *Studies in English Trade in the 15th Century*, ed. E. Power and M.M. Postan, (London: Routledge and Kegan Paul, 1933.)

17 *The City of Worcester in the 16th Century*, (Leicester: Leicester University Press) 1973.

18 C.M. Fraser, 'Medieval Trading Restrictions in the North East', *Archeologia Aeliana*, 4th series, XXXIX 1961.

19 Norwich figures from Hudson, op. cit; Oxford, from *Medieval Archives of the University of Oxford*, II, ed. H.E. Salter (Oxford Historical Society, 1921) York from H.C. Swanson, *Craftsmen and Industry in Late Medieval York* (York University Ph.D. thesis, 1980); Bridgwater, from *Bridgwater Borough Archives*, I and II, ed T.B. Dilkes (Somerset Record Society, 1933, 1938); Leicester, from *The Records from the Borough of Leicester*, I and II, ed. Mary Bateson, (Leicester: Leicester Corporation 1899-1905); of Nottingham from W.H. Stevenson, op. cit; Winchester, from J.S. Furley, *Town life in the 14th century as seen in the Court Rolls of Winhchester City*, (Winchester: Warren 1946): the Thornbury and Halesowen figures are based on the unpublished records of the two boroughs in the Birmingham Reference Library and the Stafford County Record Office, respectively.

20 Examples of cornmongers will be found in R.H. Hilton, *English Peasantry...*, p. 89. Woolmongers are better known through the works of E. Power, *The Wool Trade in English Medieval History*, (Oxford: Oxford University Press) 1941 and T.H. Lloyd, *The English Wool Trade in the Middle Ages*, (Cambridge: Cambridge University Press 1977.) But see also N.S.B. Gras, *The Evolution of the English Corn Market*, (Cambridge Mass: Harvard University Press 1915.)

21 e.g. 'We command that no fisher of town nor of country buy no manner of fish on Thursday overnight by way of regratory nor on Friday till it be nine of the clock' *Coventry Leet Book*, I, ed. M. Dormer Harris (Early English Text Society, 1907), p. 25 'Item, that no baker nor brewer nor none other manner victualler buy no corn in the market afore xii of the bell...' *Great Red Book of Bristol* (Text Pt. I), ed. E.W.W. Veale, (Bristol Record Society 1933), p. 140. These extracts are quoted from lists of ordinances strikingly similar to those in many other boroughs.

22 In *Oxford City Documents, Financial and Judicial, 1268-1665*, ed J.E. Thorold Rogers (Oxford Historical Society, 1891).

23 This statement is based on an examination of the 1380-1 poll tax returns for about a dozen small towns. These returns are remarkable in that normally all persons' occupational designations are given.

24 Swanson, op. cit., pp. 169-73; *Calendar of Plea and Memoranda Rolls, 1381-1412*, ed. A.H. Thomas, (London: London Corporation, 1932) pp. 78-9.

25 Although one might hope to find quantitative evidence about retailers in

the very detailed *Coventry Leet Book*, it is not, in fact a record of judicial proceedings. Coventry figures are from the *Rolls of the Warwickshire and Coventry Sessions of the Peace* ed. E. Kimball, (Dugdale Society, 1939). Those from Kings Lynn are from *The Making of Kings Lynn*, ed. Dorothy Owen, a forthcoming publication in the British Acadamy's *Records of Social and Economic History*.

26 These references to migrants occur in the borough court records mentioned above. The large number of single women in the late medieval population has so far mainly engaged the attention of historical demographers. R.M. Smith, 'Some Reflections on the Evidence for the Origins of the 'European Marriage Pattern' in England, in *The Family*, ed. C. Harris, (1979 Sociological Review Monograph, No. 28).

27 Above Chapter 15.

28 Particularly in the East Anglian Counties, where the extant 1380-1 poll tax returns reveal a high proportion of textile craftsmen in these growing villages, which are, in fact, becoming towns in all but name.

29 *Statutes of the Realm*, I, (London : Record Commission, 1810) p. 200.

30 *English Peasantry...* pp. 104-5.

31 Calculations made from the collections of documents referred to in references above.

32 Pearsall op. cit, pp. 125-6. Although it is dangerous to make assumptions about medieval circumstances from early modern parallels, the seventeenth century alehouses described by Peter Clark in 'The Alehouse and the Alternative Society in D. Pennington and K. Thomas (eds) *Puritans and Revolutionaries* (Oxford: Clarendon Press 1978) have some parallels with their medieval predecessors.

33 Since writing this article, my attention has been drawn to 'Paltry Pedlars or Essential Merchants? Women in the Distributive Trade in Early Modern Nuremberg', by Merry Wiesner Wood in *The Sixteenth Century Journal*, XII, 2, (1981). The parallels to the situation I have described above are remarkable.

17. Social Concepts in the Revolt of 1381 (pp. 216-226)

1 A. Réville and C. Petit-Dutaillis, *Le Soulèvement des Travailleurs en Angleterre en 1381*, 1898, p. 85.

2 Most recently by R.B. Dobson in his very useful collection of documents illustrating the rising, *The Peasants Revolt of 1381*, 1970.

3 A.E. Levett in *Studies in Manorial History* 1963, edition p. 191.

4 E. Carus-Wilson, 'The aulnage returns: a criticism', in *Medieval Merchant Venturers*, 1954.

5 E. Carus-Wilson and O. Coleman, *England's Export Trade 1275-1547*, 1963.

6 Some printed returns in E. Powell, *The Rising in East Anglia in 1381*, 1896 and C. Oman, *The Great Revolt of 1381*, 1906 and 1969.

7 B.Wilkinson, 'The Peasants Revolt of 1381' *Speculum*, 1940.

8 R. Bird *The Turbulent London of Richard II*, 1949; M.D. Lobel, *The Borough*

of Bury St. Edmunds, 1935; N. Trenholme, 'English Monastic Boroughs', University of Missouri Studies, II, iii, 1927; H.M.Cam in *Victoria History of the County of Cambridge*, III, 1959.

9 R.H. Hilton, *Bond Men Made Free*, 1973.

10 *ibid.*, p. 221.

11 Rose Graham, 'The History of the Alien Priory of Wenlock', *Journal of the British Archaeological Society*, III, ser. IV, 1939.

12 R.H.Hilton, 'Peasant Movements before 1381', *Economic History Review*, 1949; above, chapter 9, pp. 122-38.

13 R.H. Hilton, *The Decline of Serfdom in Medieval England*, 1969.

14 B. Putnam, *The Enforcement of the Statute of Labourers*, 1908.

15 V.H. Galbraith, 'Thoughts about the Peasants Revolt', in *The Reign of Richard II*, ed. F.R.H. Boulay and C.M. Barron.

16 John Bellamy, *Crime and Public Order in England in the Later Middle Ages*, 1973.

17 P.D.A. Harvey, 'The English Inflation 1180-1220', *Past and Present*, 1973

18 R.S. Hoyt, *The Royal Demesne in English Constitutional History*, 1950, chapter VI.

19 R.H. Hilton, 'Freedom and Villeinage in England', *Past and Present*, 1965.

20 E.A. Kosminsky, *Studies in the Agrarian History of England in the Thirteenth Century*, 1956; B. Dodwell, 'The Free Tenantry of the Hundred Rolls', *Economic History Review*, 1945.

21 *Year Books of Edward II*, vol. III, 1905 (Selden Society), ed. F.W. Maitland, pp. 93-5.

22 G. Kriehn's interpretation of this demand for 'no law but the law of Winchester', seems to me to be still the best interpretation. 'Studies in the Sources of the Social Revolt in 1381', *American Historical Review*, 1901-2.

23 *The Anonimalle Chronicle*, ed. V.H. Galbraith, 1927.

24 e.g. G. Dumézil, *Mythes et dieux des Germains*, 1939; G. Batany, 'Des trois fonctions aux trois états', *Annales E.S.C.*, 1963.

25 *Chronicon Angliae 1328-88*, ed. E.M. Thompson, 1874 p. 310.

26 The late K.B. McFarlane did not think much of Wycliffe as an original thinker, *John Wycliffe and the beginnings of English Nonconformity*, 1952. For Lollards and subversion, see M. Aston, 'Lollardy and Sedition', *Past and Present*, 1960.

27 *English Writings of John Wycliffe*, ed. F.D. Matthew, 1880, pp. 229, 230.

28 D. Wilkins, *Concillia Magnae Brittanniae et Hiberniae*, III, 1737, pp. 64-5; 172-3; *Calendar of Patent Rolls 1374-7* (H.M. Stationery Office), p. 415.

29 Dobson, *op.cit.*, pp. 369-78.

30 J.A.F. Thomson, *The Later Lollards*, 1965; J. le Goff, 'Ordres mendiants et urbanisation au moyenage', *Annales E.S.C.* 1970.

31 K. Thomas, *Religion and the Decline of Magic*, 1971.

32 Passus V, 1.402. See J.A.W. Bennett's edition of the text, 1972. For the Robin Hood ballads, see F.J. Child, *English and Scottish Popular Ballads 1882-98*.

33 This was the richest landholding abbey in Yorkshire.

34 On the subject in general, see J. Peter, *Complaint and Satire in Early English Literature*, 1956.

19. Was there a General Crisis of Feudalism? (pp. 239-245)

1 See chapters 1 and 3 of M.E. Dobb, *Studies in the Development of Capitalism*, (1946); M.M. Postan, 'The 15th century', 'The rise of a money economy' and 'Some agrarian evidence of declining population', *Economic History Review* (1939, 1941, 1950); E. Perroy, 'Les crises du XIVe siècle', *Annales*, (1949); P. Sweezy and M. Dobb, 'The transition from feudalism to capitalism' *Science and Society* (1950).

2 During the discussion of this communication at the Congress, M. Perroy stated that he had not intended to imply that the profits resulting from the 13th century expansion were necessarily re-invested.

3 *Men, Machines and History* (1948)

4 *L'expansion économique Belge au moyen âge* (1946).

20. Ideology and Social Order in Late Medieval England (pp. 246-252)

1 R. Brenner's article 'Agrarian class structure and economic development' in *Past and Present* No. 70 will be debated by historians of both trends in the near future.

2 F.R.H. Du Boulay, *An Age of Ambition*, 1970.

3 *Latin Works of John Gower* ed. G.C. Macauley, IV. 1902.

4 'Stages in the Social History of Capitalism' *American Historical Review* No. XIX.

5 Above all in William Langland's *Piers Plowman*, of which there is a modern English version published by Penguin Books.

6 *loc. cit.* Book I.

7 R.H. Robbins, *Historical Poems of the 14th and 15th Centuries*. 1959. No. 20. and 'I understand that these three things signify the great vengeance and revenge that fall on us for our sins' ... 'This was a warning of which we should be aware'.

8 See my *English Peasantry in the later Middle Ages*, 1975, pp. 66-7.

9 *Kent Records*, XVIII, ed. F.R.H. Du Boulay, pp. 245-64.

10 ed. J.T. Rogers 1881, p. 133.

11 ed. W.W. Skeat, *Early English Text Society*, (E.E.T.S.) 1867.

12 *Medieval Welsh Lyrics*, ed. J.P. Clancy, 1965.

13 Robbins, *op. cit..*, No.37 'The husbandmen makes the mirth of all this land with the ploughing of his plough'.

14 ed. W.W. Skeat, 'Chaucer and other Pieces', supplement to the *Works of Geoffrey Chaucer*, 1897.

15 *The Townely Plays*, ed. G. England and A.W. Pollard, *EETS*, 1897. 'Before it was out and stacked, I had many a weary back. Therefore ask me for no more, for I have given all that I want to give.'

16 ed. W.W. Skeat, *EETS* 1867.

17 'Lollardy and Sedition' *Past and Present*, No.17.

18 *Regement...* ed. F.J. Furnivall, *EETS*, 1897; *Minor Poems*, ed. Furnivall, *EETS*, 1892. 'The people's voice is God's voice, men say' 'make no arguments about our faith' 'A bailiff or reeve or craftsman will stupidly rave' 'Even some women, though their intelligence is slight, will argue about the holy scriptures.'

19 *Middle English Sermons.* ed. W.O. Ross, *EETS* 1938, No. 22.

20 ed. T. Wright in *Political Songs and Poems*, II, 1861. 'with deceit and cunning win over mens wives and make them into scholars of the new school' 'neither carpenters nor cobblers, cardmakers nor purse makers, drapers nor cutlers,girdlers, boxmakers nor shoemakers, nor any sort of artisan should discuss this sacrament'.

21 *The Book of Margery Kempe*, ed. S.B. Meech and H.E. Allen, *EETS* 1940. She was an intensely religious merchant's wife from Kings Lynn, active in the first few decades of the 15th century.

22 Ed. M. Day and R. Steele, *EETS*, 1936. 'Where serving men and house-holders are equal, wretched is the house and all that live in it.'

23 *Regement...* 'When the greater obeys the lesser' - 'No man is content in his estate'.

24 *Twenty six Political and other Poems*, I, ed. J. Kail, *EETS*, 1904. 'Each king is sworn to government, to govern God's people in right. Each king carries the sword of God's Vengeance, to fell God's foes in the fight. And so does every honest knight, who bears the order (of knighthood). The plough and the church are God's champions to keep the peace'

25 'For just as in thy body, Jake, thy hands have been ordained to work for thy head and thy feet and thine eyes, just so the common people and the lords have been disposed by God to work for holy church... the sun is holy church and lordship is the moon and the stars are the commons'. *loc.cit.*

21. Social and Economic Evidence in Tax Returns (pp. 253-267)

1 M. W. Beresford, *The Lost Villages of England*, 1954; R. S. Schofield, *The Geographical Distribution of Wealth in Enland, 1334-1649*, 'Economic History Review', 2nd Series, 18 (1965), 3; W. G. Hoskins, 'English Provincial Towns in the Early 16th Century', 'Trans', Royal Historical Society, 5th Series, 6 1956.

2 With the exception of the south-western portion of the Gloucestershire Cotswolds, for which Poll Tax returns do not survive.

3 The returns are as follows: Poll Tax of 4 Richard II — E/79/113/31, 31d, 35a; Subsidy of 14-15 Henry VIII — E/79/113/201/213.

4 Cf. C. Oman, *The Great Revolt of 1381, 1906*, Appendix; M. W. Beresford, *The Poll Taxes of 1377, 1379, and 1381*, The Amateur Historian 3 (1958) nr 7; W. G. Hoskins, loc. cit., for a discussion of the 1523-4 returns; 1327 Gloucestershire subsidy returns are printed by Sir T. Phillips at the Middle Hill Press (n.d.).

5 By 1381 there was no money forthcoming from Bidfield, Hilcot, Lassborough and Lowsmoor. 'Nihil quia non inhabitatur' was the phrase used. By 1524 the disappearance of other villages such as Frampton and Naunton (to

quote only a few) was complete or nearly so. Most of these sites can be identified by earthworks.

6 These are guesses, of course. The 1280 figure is based on calculations made from the recently discovered Rotuli Hundredorum for Coventry; the four-teenth century figures are based on the 1377 Poll Tax (reading back to the pre-1348-9 figure); and on the figures in the Coventry Leet Book calculated by the city authorities in the case of grain needs in a dearth.

7 I draw these conclusions from a study of the Stratford Corporation documents at the Shakespeare's Birthplace Library. See also T. H. Lloyd, *Some Aspects of the Building Industry in Medieval Stratford-upon-Avon*, 'Dugdale Society Occasional Paper', 14 (1961).

8 I omit Minty, a small outlier in Wiltshire.

9 See above, p. 254.

10 Being Stonebridge, Lower Lypiatt and Tunley and Througham.

11 For a detailed study of Stroud Valley industrialisation in the fifteenth century, see E. Carus-Wilson, 'Evidence of Industrial Growth on some Fifteenth Century Manors', *Essays in Economic History*, II, Ed. E. Carus-Wilson, 1962.

12 Some of the Winchcombe hamlets which were separately assessed in 1381 do not appear in the 1524 assessment. I have included these in the 1381 total, the most important of them being Postlip.

13 Landboc... de Winchelcombe, ed. D. Royce, I, 1892, pp. 63, 258.

14 See above p. 255.

15 As described by J. F. Willard in *Parliamentary Taxes on Personal Property 1290 to 1334*, 1934. Dr Roger Schofield, who has helped me with comments on this paper, doubts whether the returns are formalised. All the same, when we find that (for example) a third of the Sherborne tax payers were all assessed. at 4s 0d., one doubts whether the returns exactly reflect varations in movable wealth.

16 In some respects it would have been more satisfactory to make calculations only of proportions in those villages for which we also have returns from 1381. But this would have narrowed the field of enquiry so much that I have risked reducing strict comparability in favour of as wide a coverage as possible at each date. In favour of this it can be said with reasonable confidence that the figures come from an economically and socially homgeneous region. But since the 1381 returns for Kiftsgate, Holford and Gretstone Hundreds give inadequate occup-ation data, I have not used the 1524 data from these hundreds.

17 If the industrialised parish of Bisley is subtracted, the figures are 30% and 50%.

18 Unfortunately the 1381 returns for Cirencester, Tetbury and Painswick are damaged and are useless for this purpose.

19 P.R.O., E 179/200/27.

20 Nevertheless, textile craftsmen—about a dozen—have a modest promin-ence, and there are nearly as many horners.

21 E/79/240/308 [159]. Professor E. Carus-Wilson kindly drew my attention to this.

22 E/179/240/308/142. Part of the list consists of people in 'Baylylone'. Bailey Lane is a street in the middle of Coventry. Some of the surnames, especially those embodying place-names, also suggest Coventry, e.g. Pacwode, Allesbury,

Keresley, Stoneleye—all villages near the city.

23 As A. Dyer has shown in his *Economy of Tudor Worcester*, 'Birmingham University Historical Journal' 10 (1966), 2, esp. pp. 124-31.

22. Capitalism—What's in a Name?

1 *Economic History Review*, 4. A thorough discussion of the uses of the term will be found in M.H. Dobb, *Studies in the Development of Capiltalism*, Chapter I.

2 *Economic History of England*, passim, but cf. e.g. p.468.

3 *Belgian Democracy*, p.30.

4 L.Halphen, *Etudes critiques sur l'histoire de Charlemagne*, p. 265. J. Calmette, *Le Moyen Age*, p. 135.

5 'Il giusto prezzo nella dottrina di san Tomasso', in *Studi di Storia Economica Medioevale*, 1946, p. 191 ; cf. p. 698.

6 See 'The Tenth Century', by the Abbé Lestocquoy, *Economic History Review*, XVII, I.

7 *Money,Banking and Credit in Medieval Bruges*, p. 11.

8 *Medieval Cities ; Histoire de Belgique ; Social and Economic History of Medieval Europe ; Mahomet and Charlemagne*.

9 G. Espinas, *La Vie Urbaine de Douai au Moyen-Age ; Sire Jehan Boinebroke* (Les Origines du Capitalisme) ; *Histoire de la Draperie de la Flandre Française*. A. Doren, *Florentiner Wollentuchindustrie* ; R. Davidsohn, *Geschichte von Florenz* IV. A. Sapori, *op. cit.*.

10 Besides the works of Sapori and de Roover already quoted, see R. Doehaerd, *Les Relations Commerciales entre Gènes et l'Outremont*, I. and Y. Renouard, *Les Hommes d'Affaires Italiens ;* also his *Relations des Papes d'Avignon et des Compagnies Commerciales et Bancaires*.

11 e.g. L. Delisle, *Etudes sur la Condition de la Classe Agricole en Normandie au Moyen-age* ; H. Sée, *Les Classes Rurales et le Régime Seigneurial en France au Moyen-Age*.

12 The pioneer book of N.S.B. Gras, *The evolution of the English Corn Market* requires special mention, though it does no more than break the ground.

13 R.R. Betts, 'La Société dans l'Europe Centrale et dans l'Europe orientale, *Révue Histoire Comparée*, 1948.

14 XX, Historical Data concerning Merchant's capital ; XXXVI, Interest in the Middle Ages ; XLVII, The Genesis of Capitalist Ground Rent. The whole volume was compiled from Marx' notes after his death by F. Engels.

15 The wage-earner, in order to live, is compelled to work for the capitalist ; the compulsion on him is economic. The feudal peasant, having his own means of production, has to be compelled by the immediate or ultimate threat of force to hand over his rent to the landlord. This is the reason for the medieval peasants lack of personal freedom.

16 The nearest approach to an organised proletariat was the Florentine Ciompi. Their weakness was revealed in the revolt of 1378 when their short-lived achievement of political power collapsed as soon as they were cut off from

their allies among the artisans and petty tradesmen. Additionally it was a measure of their immaturity that the big bourgeoisie could so easily isolate them.

17 See H. Van Werweke, 'Currency Manipulations in the Middle Ages', in *Transactions of the Royal Historical Society, 4th series, XXXI.*

18 See Marc Bloch, 'Le problème de l'or au Moyen-Age', *Annales d'Histoire Economique et Sociale*, 1933; 'L'or Musulman du VIIe au XIe siecle...' *Annales*, 1947, No. 2 by M. Lombard; and Monnaies et Civilisations... *ibid.* 1946, No.I. by F. Braudel.

19 It is interesting to note what Mme Doehaerd, in the admirable work mentioned above, considers to be the phenomena 'qui constituent l'ossature de la vie économique internationale et locale de tous le temps'. They are : 'la question des produits qui font l'objet du commerce... celle de leurs centres de provenance ou de production, des places ou ils sont échangés, des centres d'exportation et d'importation, des voies et moyens de transport, des agents d'échange,et méthodes d'échange, des moyens monétaires et du crédit', p.142. It is remarkable that questions of production do not come into the problem of economic life.

20 Estimate of 15th century wool production in E. Power, *Medieval English Wool Trade*, p. 37.

21 E. Lipson, *History of the English Woollen and Worsted Industries*, (1921) p. 16.

22 'Some economic Evidence of Declining Population in the Later Middle Ages'—*Economic History Review*, 2nd series II, 3.

23 See C. Oman, *The Great Revolt of 1381.*

24 e.g.in two Leicestershire hundreds, 28% of the taxed population were wage workers, excluding market towns and artisans in the villages. A comparison with 19th century Russia is here useful. The rise in wages was due not only to the shortage of labour but to the increase in pure wage-labour as compared with the incidental wage labour of small-holders; since part of their wages consisted of their small-holding, money remuneration could therefore be kept down, while the pure wage labourers' could not.

25 See Marx, *Capital* I, XXIV, 5 ; Lenin, *Selected Works* I, 223-5.

26 Compare the remarks on 15th century Poland by M. Malowist, *IXe Congrès des Sciences Historiques, Rapports*, p. 314.

27 For both of which there are many good secondary works.

28 See the first two chapters of F. Antal's *Florentine Painting and Its Social Background* and N. Rodolico's *I Ciompi.*

23. Feudalism and the Origins of Capitalism (pp. 278-294)

1 Interesting assessments of the nature of the modern historical writing are to be found in *Ideology in the Social Sciences*, ed. Robin Blackburn, London, 1972. They are 'History: the poverty of empiricism', by Gareth Stedman Jones and 'Karl Marx's contribution to historiography' by E.H. Hobsbawm. Jones somewhat over-estimates the revolutionary character of the *Annales* school, which, however innovative, is by no means Marxist.

2 See the collection of essays edited by A.F. Havighurst, *The Pirenne Thesis*, Boston 1958, and A.B. Hibbert, 'The Origins of the Medieval Town Patriciate', *Past and Present*, No. 3.

3 As L. Althusser seems to admit, *Reading Capital*, London 1970, p. 14

4 M. Bloch, *French Rural History*, London 1966, and 'Liberté et Servitude Personnelles au Moyen-Age' in *Mélanges Historiques* I, Paris 1963; L. Verriest, *Institutions Médiévales*, Mons 1946.

5 R. Boutruche, *Seigneurie et Féodalité*, I, Paris 1959, pp. 128-9.

5a W. Kula's *Théorie Economique du Système Féodal*, Paris-The Hague, 1970, analyses the serf run estates of early modern Poland and contains many useful hints for students of similar estates in medieval western Europe.

6 The ideas in the preceding paragraphs are based on a number of monographs, but some of the evidence will be found in the work of R. Boutruche (n. 5.) and in G. Duby's *Rural Economy and Country Life in the Medieval West*, London 1962.

7 See H. van Werweke's article 'The Rise of the Towns', with bibliography in *Cambridge Economic History of Europe*, III, Cambridge 1963. The author is a follower of H. Pirenne.

8 *The City*, London 1958.

9 See C. Petit-Dutaillis, *Les Communes Françaises*, Paris 1947, Bk. I, iii.

10 In other words, the dividing line between town and country is not necessarily the same as that between the regulated and unregulated urban areas.

11 It is significant that George Unwin's works especially *Industrial Organisation in the 16th and 17th centuries*, London 1908, still provide us with one of the best theoretically oriented analyses in English of craft production. It will be remembered that Dobb relies heavily on Unwin in the *Studies*. But see also the work of the Polish historian, B. Geremek, *Le Salariat dans l'artisanat Parisien aux XIII-XVe Siècles*, Paris-The Hague, 1968.

12 *English Medieval Boroughs: a Handlist*, by M.W. Beresford and H.P.R. Finberg, Newton Abbot 1973, gives a good idea of the large number of these smaller centres.

13 G. Espinas, *La Draperie dans la Flandre Française au Moyen-Age*, Paris 1923, pp. 617-49; *Little Red Book of Bristol*, II, ed. F.B. Bickley, Bristol and London 1900, pp. 58-61.

14 Much detail and full bibliographies in volumes I and III of the Cambridge Economic History of Europe, 1952 and 1963. The title of recent text books by an expert on the subject, Robert S. Lopez, is significant— *The Commercial Revolution of the Middle Ages 950-1350*, Englewood 1971. There are up-to-date bibliographies in N.J.G. Pounds, *An Economic History of Medieval Europe*, London 1974, one of the better text-books to have been published recently.

15 It seems to me that Marx modified his views about the role of merchant capital in the middle ages between writing the *Grundrisse* and the chapters in Vol. III of *Capital*, in the sense of believing less in the positive role of merchant capital at the later date. See K.Marx, *Grundrisse*, London 1973, pp. 504-8.

16 It must be emphasized that, contrary to the suggestions of some critics, Marx presented by no means a simple picture of the actual historical process by which peasants in England lost their landed property and communal rights. See *Capital*, I, Bk. VIII, 30; *Grundisse*, p. 511.

17 See chapters VIII and IX of his *Six Centuries of Work and Wages*, based on the material already published in his *History of Agriculture and Prices*, Oxford 1866. Marx used this work in writing *Capital* and thought reasonably well of him, even though he was a liberal economist.

18 My *English Peasantry in the Later Middle Ages*, Oxford 1975, is an attempt to discuss this phase of relatively unfettered simple commodity production.

19 G. Duby, *The Early Growth of the European Economy : Warriors and Peasants*, London 1975. My review of the French edition was published in *New Left Review* No. 83, January-February 1974.

20 Summed up in *The Medieval Economy and Society*, Annales d'Histoire 1972.

21 Current work produced by the school of Father J.A. Raftis of the Pontifical Institute of Medieval Studies exemplifies this approach. See for example E.B. Dewindt, *Land and People in Holywell-cum-Needingworth*, Toronto 1972 and J.A. Raftis, *Warboys*, Toronto 1975.

INDEX